DATE			

Isaac Asimov's
Treasury of Humor

Isaac Asimov's
Treasury of Humor

A lifetime collection of favorite jokes, anecdotes,
and limericks with copious notes
on how to tell them
and why

HOUGHTON MIFFLIN COMPANY BOSTON

Fourth printing   w

Copyright © 1971 by Isaac Asimov
All rights reserved. No part of this work may be
reproduced or transmitted in any form by any means,
electronic or mechanical, including photocopying
and recording, or by any information storage or
retrieval system, without permission in writing
from the publisher.
ISBN: 0-395-12665-7
Library of Congress Catalog Card Number: 70-153957
Printed in the United States of America

To Muriel Hirt,

at whose infamous suggestion
this book was written

Contents

Introduction

FOR NEARLY ALL MY LIFE I have been swapping jokes. At almost every friendly gathering that I have attended, there have been two or three people present with a large repertoire of funny stories and the ability to tell them with finesse, and so joke-swapping was almost inevitable. Modesty compels me to refrain from saying that of all those present I generally had the largest repertoire of jokes and could tell them with the most finesse, but if I weren't modest I would say so.

This has led to my having been asked, on occasion, why someone like myself, with pretensions to intellect, should content himself with endless joke-telling while shunning the ardent discussions of politics, philosophy, and literature which might be proceeding in another corner of the room.

To this my answer is threefold, in order of increasing importance:

1) I spend most of my day being intellectual at my typewriter, and telling jokes on an evening now and then helps balance the situation.

2) Jokes of the proper kind, properly told, can do more to enlighten questions of politics, philosophy, and literature than any number of dull arguments.

3) I like to.

Then, too, as it happens, this whole business of joke-telling saved my life not too long ago —

In June 1969, my wife and I, along with another couple,

Howard and Muriel Hirt, were off on a motor trip that was to end in a vacation. As it happens, vacations send me into deep melancholy and I had been achingly apprehensive of this one for weeks. It was only to last for a weekend but it was to be at an elaborate hotel of a type that I detested beyond measure.

With doom hastening closer at every turn of the whirling wheels, I tried to fight off my gathering misery by telling jokes in feverish succession.

Muriel was kind enough to laugh quite a bit and then she said, "Listen, Isaac, why don't you write a jokebook?"

That made it my turn to laugh.

"Who would publish it?" I asked.

She said, "I thought you said you could get someone or other to publish anything you wrote."

I do say things like that when I am feeling more than ordinarily megalomaniac, but that was not what suddenly began to circle wildly through the tortuous meshes of my mind.

A new thought arose —

Suppose that while I was ostensibly vacationing, and while everyone around me was going through the horrifying ritual of lying in the sun and volleyballing and hiking and doing whatever other forms of refined torture are supposed to be fun, I was secretly writing down jokes and, in that way, working on a book.

I would then be having no vacation at all! (Oh, magic words!)

As soon as we had registered and unpacked, therefore, I approached the desk and said, "I would like to check out a typewriter for the weekend."

This hotel, you must understand, is marvelously equipped. I do not remember the exact figures, but the impression I have is that the hotel possesses three swimming pools, four golf links, seventeen tennis courts, twenty-eight miles of hiking trails, and seventy-five thousand reclining beach chairs in serried ranks and files, each one laden with a vacationer slowly frying in his

own juice. It also has an enormous nightclub, fourteen buildings, and sixty miles of corridors.

With a hotel that has everything, I had no hesitation in asking
for a typewriter.

I was quickly disabused. The desk clerk said, "You want to
check out a *what?*"

"A typewriter!" I said.

He looked blank, and I could see he was wondering if a
typewriter might be anything like a set of golf clubs.

I said, "Well, then, do you have writing paper?"

He handed me a sheet of writing paper in which the mono-
gram of the hotel took up half the area, leaving just enough
room to write a message to a friend that might go: "Here I am
at the X Hotel, dying."

I said, "Give me about fifty."

He handed them over and for the next two and a half days,
wherever we were — tramping the corridors, lying in the sun,
sitting in the shade, waiting for food at the table, enduring the
unbelievable decibelic mayhem at the nightclub — I quietly
scribbled jokes on paper, while carefully maintaining a fixed
smile on my face to indicate how much I was enjoying the vacation.

Occasionally, I would overhear someone at a neighboring
table say, "Watch out, Sadie, and be careful what you say.
That fellow there is writing down every word he hears."

It was undoubtedly all that kept me alive.

I finished the vacation with a sheaf of hand-written jokes,
which I converted into typescript and brought to Houghton
Mifflin as a sample.

And eventually the book was completed and published, and
here it is!

Isaac Asimov's
Treasury of Humor

IT SO HAPPENS that I have no intention of just telling jokes. There are thoughts I have about humor generally, and about certain jokes specifically, and I want to include the thoughts as well as the jokes.

In order to do this, I intend to speak freely (and sometimes at considerable length) before, after, and between the jokes, whenever this seems advisable to me.

It is certainly any reader's right to ignore my commentary and just proceed from joke to joke, leaping over the intervening material if he so wishes. I couldn't stop him, but he would be the loser in that case.

To begin with, I ought to present my own theory as to what constitutes humor and what it is that makes people laugh. I disclaim any deep understanding of psychology or any extensive background in what others have had to say on the subject. However, I have been a practitioner in the field for many years, and I claim the right to speak from experience.

It is my feeling, to put it as succinctly as possible, that the one necessary ingredient in every successful joke is a sudden alteration in point of view. For instance —

❅ 1

Jones was having his first date with Miss Smith and was utterly captivated by her. She was beautiful, and intelligent as well, and as
dinner proceeded, he was further impressed by her faultless taste.

As he hesitated over the after-dinner drink, she intervened to say,
"Oh, let's have sherry rather than brandy by all means. When I sip
sherry, it seems to me that I am transported from the everyday
scenes by which I may, at that moment, be surrounded. The flavor,
the aroma, bring to mind irresistibly — for what reason I know not
— a kind of faerie bit of nature: a hilly field bathed in soft sunshine,
a clump of trees in the middle distance, a small brook curving across
the scene, nearly at my feet. This, together with the fancied drowsy
sound of insects and distant lowing of cattle, brings to my mind a
kind of warmth, peace, and serenity, a sort of dovetailing of the
world into a beautiful entirety. Brandy, on the other hand, makes
me burp."

In this joke, the alteration in point of view concerning the
lady, from a picture of ultimate refinement to one of common
humanity, is particularly extreme, and I chose it for that reason.

The alteration in point of view produces an incongruity
which elicits a laugh and a feeling of pleasure. The sharper the
incongruity and the more suddenly it can be introduced, the
more certain the laugh and the louder and longer it will be.

It is for this reason that in any good joke, the change in point
of view should come, with as little warning as possible, in the
last sentence. And it is for this reason, therefore, that the last
sentence is so often referred to as the punch line, for what is
wanted is an effect as sudden and startling as a punch in the
jaw. (In Joke 1, the change in point of view comes with the
final syllable — all the better.)

Although the presence of an incongruity is necessary for
laughter, it is not sufficient. A joke is nothing in itself; it must
be *told*. A joke is a social phenomenon; an interaction among
people. Like a glass of wine, or like a common sorrow — but

with fewer side effects and with utter lightheartedness — it breaks down reserve, eases tension, establishes contact.

But to be told effectively, a joke must be told well, and talents in that respect vary. In general, even those who tell jokes well are quite apt to find that their talent is not universal. A jokester may be able to handle slang perfectly and yet not be able to do the mock-refined. Or vice versa, for that matter.

In the case of Joke 1, it is necessary to be able to manufacture flowery prose in an offhand, unstrained manner. The joke won't work otherwise. Nor will memorizing do any good. Delivering a memorized joke deprives it of spontaneity and gives it a mechanical tang that is somehow noticeable and sure to lessen the impact on the audience.

If, then, you can't handle the necessary prose spontaneously, don't tell the joke. There are always many that will suit your particular bent, whatever it is, and since nobody is all-talented you need not feel cheated or deprived. Here's a joke, for instance, that practically anyone can make a reasonable stab at.

❧ 2

"Oh, poor Mr. Jones," mourned Mrs. Smith. "Did you hear what happened to him? He tripped at the top of the stairs, fell down the whole flight, banged his head, and died."

"Died?" said Mrs. Robinson, shocked.

"Died!" repeated Mrs. Smith with emphasis. "Broke his glasses, too."

Here the change in point of view, from the deep tragedy of accidental and unlooked-for death, to a sudden consideration of the comparatively trivial misadventure that had happened to accompany it, can also be effective in raising a laugh. A small laugh perhaps, for the joke, being short, does not lead the listener along the false path for as long, nor bring him up short as sharply.

Still, Joke 2, being short and simple, presents no difficulties and can scarcely be mishandled. For the beginner, a simple joke with a sure but small laugh is preferable to an elaborate one which may elicit a large laugh — or none at all.

In both 1 and 2, the change in point of view is from something we can take seriously to something else we can take much less seriously. This somehow runs counter to the natural progression of thought designed to make a solemn impression.

In dealing with a series of phrases, we tend to list them in such a way as to move on to progressively more serious things, saying, for instance, "Not merely did he save the town, he saved the entire country," or "He sacrificed his money, his health, and finally his life to the great cause." In doing this, we achieve a climax.

To reverse this seems so unnatural as to produce an incongruity in itself. That is the humor in the satirical cry of "For God, for country, and for Yale." To go from the more to the less serious is to go from the sublime to the ridiculous, producing what is called bathos or anticlimax, and (what is more to the present purpose) laughter, if it is properly handled.

Here is another anticlimax:

* 3

For thirty years, Johnson had arrived at work at 9 A.M. on the dot. He had never missed a day and he was never late. Consequently, when on one particular day 9 A.M. passed without Johnson's arrival, it caused a sensation. All work ceased and the boss himself, looking at his watch and muttering, came out into the corridor.

Finally, precisely at ten, Johnson showed up, clothes dusty and torn, his face scratched and bruised, his glasses bent. He limped painfully to the time clock, punched in, and said, aware that all eyes were upon him, "I tripped and rolled down two flights of stairs in the subway. Nearly killed myself."

And the boss said, "And to roll down two flights of stairs took you a whole hour?"

This makes three anticlimaxes in a row and that is not accidental. The exact manner in which the jokes were to be presented in this book was a matter of anxious editorial discussion.

The system I favored to begin with was that of telling the jokes in no particular order, putting them down just as they occurred to me, in imitation of what would occur at a joke-telling session. This would surely give the book an air of spontaneity, which would be desirable, but it would also give the book an air of incoherence, which would be undesirable.

A possible alternative was to divide the jokes into a large number of very narrow categories such as Fences, Manhole Covers, Tents, and so on, with one or two jokes in each section and all the categories arranged in alphabetical order. This might make the book particularly useful for after-dinner speakers who were searching for a funny story on some specific topic, but it would make the book too formal and bind me into a straitjacket. I was vociferously against this.

We therefore hit upon a compromise. Let there be categories, but let them be few and broad, and let them deal with types of humor rather than with specific subject matter. Let them be arranged in the order that would appeal to me best and let the jokes within each category be arranged as they occurred to me. In that way, we would end up (if all went well) with both coherence *and* informality.

One of the most basic categories in humor is Anticlimax, and I have chosen to let that be the first.

❧ 4

A condemned spy was being led out at dawn to the wall against which he was to be shot at sunrise. It was raining with ferocious intensity. On either side of him was a line of soldiers and to one of them the condemned spy said bitterly, "What beasts you all are to march me out to be shot in a rain like this."

And the soldier replied with equal bitterness, "What are you complaining about? We've got to march back."

The incongruity present in jokes often serves to illuminate facets of life more truly (and surely more tersely) than many a long, closely reasoned psychological treatise. Life is often incongruous and the silliest juxtapositions can be dreadfully characteristic of even highly intelligent men.

If someone has worn glasses all his life and spent much of his emotional strength striving to keep them unbroken, the fact of shattered glasses may momentarily fill his mind and replace even the greater fact of death, as in Joke 2. As an example from real life, I remember the case of a friend who once told me of the time when a rather new car of his had been stolen. "The thing that griped me the most," he said, "was that I had just filled the gas tank."

Similarly, we must recognize the existence of the sad fact of insensitivity to the suffering of others when our own inconveniences are involved. In Joke 3, the employer found his own inconvenience at his employee's lateness of more importance than the latter's serious accident.

Yet we laugh!

Where an anticlimactic incongruity becomes sufficiently sharp, when, in particular, it is something as serious as death that is downgraded by another's mere inconvenience — we have an example of what is sometimes called black humor.

The very name indicates that we somehow feel the joke isn't "really funny" and that, perhaps, we are a little ashamed at ourselves for laughing.

We shouldn't be. It is precisely the fact that we laugh that demonstrates our humanity. We *recognize* the incongruity and it is the recognition that elicits the laughter.

If it happened that, for some reason, we really felt that our own inconvenience took precedence over another's much deeper tragedy, we would find no incongruity in a joke that took that position, and hence we would *not* laugh.

Black humor, by the way, must be distinguished from sick humor. The former deals with the tragic, the latter with the grotesque and/or disgusting. Fashions are unpredictable and there are times when numerous sick jokes make the rounds. The response to these by a humane audience is very often a grimace and not a laugh, and regardless of fashion, I rarely find them worth telling, out of consideration for the discomfort of both the audience and myself.

Naturally, there are no sharp boundaries, and sickness grades imperceptibly into blackness so that it is difficult to tell sometimes whether a joke is one or the other. For instance —

✻ 5

Smith met Jones in the clubhouse one day and said, "I understand you experienced a great tragedy last week."

Jones sipped his drink and nodded, his eyes growing dark with the memory. "I was playing a twosome with Brown," he said, "and the poor fellow dropped dead at the ninth hole."

Smith said, "I understand you carried him back to the clubhouse. That must have been difficult, considering that he weighed two hundred pounds."

Jones said, "Oh, it wasn't the carrying that was hard. It was putting him down at every stroke, and then picking him up again."

Is this one sick or black? Much depends on the audience, something I will stress more than once in this book. Many a joke is funny to one audience and not to another.

To an audience that knows little of golf, the joke is grotesque and very likely unpleasant. The laugh, if it comes at all, will be uncertain.

To another audience, which has had personal experience with the game and which knows, either at first hand or through the behavior of others on the links, how tight a grip the game can seize, the joke is purely black and they will laugh joyously.

But how does one predict the nature of the audience? In some cases, there are reasonable methods. If someone tells of a golfing experience and the others respond with sympathy, you can always wait for a pause and say, "Have you heard . . ."

If a joke-telling session is going on, you might try a small golf joke to test the reaction before investing in a more elaborate one. And if all else fails, you can rely on instinct. The more experience you garner, the more somehow you can sense what the reaction of a particular audience will be.

✻ 6

A pompous, well-dressed businessman was encountered in the street by a young urchin who said to him respectfully, "Sir, can you tell me the time?"

The portly man stopped, carefully unbuttoned his coat and jacket, removed a large watch from a vest pocket, regarded it gravely, and said, "It is a quarter to three, young man."

"Fine," said the boy, "and at exactly three o'clock, you may kiss my foot."

With that, the youngster dashed off, and uttering a cry of outrage, the businessman set off in angry pursuit. He had not been running long when an old acquaintance grasped his elbow and brought him to a halt.

"Why are you running this way at your age?" demanded the friend.

Gasping and almost incoherent with fury, the businessman said, "That little brat there asked the time and when I told him it was a quarter to three he told me that at exactly three, I should kiss his foot."

At which the other said, "So what's your hurry? You still have ten minutes."

A number of jokes in this book have been deliberately bowdlerized. Thus where a joke as ordinarily told would make use of a word not ordinarily heard in polite society, I try to use some equally effective word or phrase that is more acceptable.

The necessity for doing so has been diminishing drastically in recent years. There was a time not too many years ago when women generally felt it important to disapprove of dirty words. Whether this was hypocritical or sincere depended on the individual, but either way the stand had to be respected. To tell a dirty joke before an audience that feels compelled to be (or pretends to be) embarrassed and disapproving is not only bad manners, but bad joke-telling. There will be no real laugh.

Nowadays, the sexual revolution and the common use of dirty words in books, on the stage, and even in the movies, has broken down feminine reserve. I find myself very rarely in any gathering in which the women bother to pretend that they are offended by dirty words.

Even so, the question of bowdlerizing may arise. It is my feeling that there is nothing wrong with being fastidious, when this will not utterly ruin a joke. If a joke simply must have a dirty word and if the audience will not object, then the word should certainly be used. Otherwise, if a suitable polite synonym exists, why waste the dirty word when not needed, thus making it less effective through overuse when needed?

In this book, I deliberately bowdlerize too much rather than too little. For one thing, the readership will, I imagine, be a heterogeneous one and I do not wish to offend anyone needlessly. For another, by being careful when I can be, I hope I will be forgiven those few occasions when the joke really forces the use of an improper expression.

As an example of how damaging even mild bowdlerization can sometimes be, consider Joke 6. Does anyone really think the boy said "Kiss my foot!" to his dignified victim? Can there be any doubt that in the joke, as properly told, he said, "Kiss my ass!" How much weaker it is in the foot version!

Again, in Joke 1, the young lady who rejects the brandy would, under most joke-telling circumstances, have said, "Brandy, on the other hand, makes me fart." My own experience is that the laugh is much louder then.

So don't bowdlerize unless you must. If the audience is exclusively male, or if it is bisexual but all good friends, or if it is an audience which has had no experience with one another but has been softened up by several drinks apiece, or if several jokes, unbowdlerized, have already been told and enjoyed — then go ahead.

Otherwise, play it safe.

❦ 7

At Gladstone's home, guests were engaged in a discussion of the knotty Irish Home Rule problem while waiting for their eminent host to make his appearance. Voices rose and tempers flared to no avail, and finally one guest said in resigned despair, "Well, there is one above who alone understands."

"Yes," said Mrs. Gladstone, brightening, "and the Prime Minister will be right down."

This is an example of a particularly specialized joke, deliberately told here in an uncompromising fashion. The anticlimax is sufficiently absurd in itself for a laugh to arise even from those who have never heard of William Ewart Gladstone, or never knew that he was prime minister of Great Britain on four occasions in the late nineteenth century, or that in his old age he fought unsuccessfully for Irish Home Rule. Nor do they have to know of the endless political in-fighting, and the long-drawn-out and frustrating complications involved in that issue (something like the Vietnam issue in contemporary America).

Naturally for those history buffs who do know all this and who know moreover that Gladstone was a notoriously moral person who always somehow gave the attitude of having a private pipeline to God (rather like our own William Jennings Bryan), the joke is clearly going to be far more successful.

What do you do then? Do you wait for the proper audience, which may come rarely or never, or do you waste the joke on an ordinary one?

What you ought never to do is to try to educate an ordinary audience to be a proper one. If you begin the joke with a preface, telling everyone all about Gladstone, and *then* tell the joke, you will end with polite smiles from all at best. Nothing will turn off an audience faster than any indication that they don't know enough to appreciate a joke — all the more so if this happens to be true. Far better to leave them ignorant and garner the minor laugh that will come even so.

A compromise which sometimes works if done well is to incorporate a little bit of education into the joke, without making it overly obtrusive. Suppose you began the joke: "When William Gladstone was prime minister of England for the fourth time toward the end of the nineteenth century, guests at his house were engaged in a discussion of the knotty Irish Home Rule problem which was then convulsing all England. While waiting for their eminent host, . . ."

It sounds stilted and may not strike you as worth the effort (you are the judge), but it might increase the laugh among an audience educated in some field other than history.

❀ 8

Moskowitz was retiring from business, and it occurred to him that he ought to take up golf as a means of diversion. One morning, therefore, he was out at the club bright and early, with a new bag of clubs and a caddy.

"Caddy," he said, "I know nothing about the game. What am I supposed to do?"

The caddy, sighing softly, said, "You take this club; you hold it at this end; you hit the ball with the other."

"And where do I hit it?"

"To the green over there. Do you see the little flag? There's a small hole under it and you have to get the ball into the hole."

Moskowitz nodded. He stepped in front of the ball, took a mighty swing, and hoisted the ball high in the air. Straight and true it winged its way toward the green in a graceful parabola.

The caddy, eyes wide and face a mask of astonishment, hastened out to the green and there, nestling in the cup, was Moskowitz's indubitable ball. It was a hole in one.

Moskowitz came trudging up, picked up the ball, and said calmly, "What next?"

The caddy could only gasp. "You go on to the next hole."

Moskowitz did so. Another swing, another mighty heave. This time the ball hooked somewhat, hit a tree, rebounded sharply, and rolled onto the green in the direction of the hole.

Heart in mouth, the caddy ran to the green and there in the cup —
you guessed it: another hole in one.

Moskowitz, utterly unperturbed, scooped up the ball and advanced to the third hole. The caddy, much too far gone for words, accompanied him.

A third swing and once again the ball went flying. This time it fell a trifle short, but bounded briskly forward across the green, aiming straight at the hole. Slowly and more slowly it went and finally halted — at the very lip of the cup.

Moskowitz came up at last, looked at the ball, turned to the caddy, shrugged, and said, "Oh well, a beginner's a beginner."

Why Moskowitz?

Until now, I have used no names at all in the jokes, or have used names which, in English-speaking surroundings at least, are thoroughly bland — Smith, Jones, Robinson, and so on.

The matter of names is an important one. If the joke is short, you can profit by doing without names altogether. Attaching names to characters always means running the risk of stumbling over them, reducing the free flow and, therefore, the possible laugh. In longer jokes, however, this risk is outweighed by the trouble you would have in keeping the characters straight. If you are reduced to saying, "Then the other guy said — I mean the guy who was holding the horse, not the first guy —" you have lost. In that case, introduce Smith and Jones — and Robinson, too, if necessary — and try not to stumble.

But then why Moskowitz in this case?

In the world of jokedom, there are ethnic stereotypes. The Jew is not, traditionally, a sportsman; and while in real life, these days, the golf links are full of Jews, some of whom are even named Moskowitz, the stereotype lingers and has force. In a joke, you may carefully *say* that a man knows nothing about golf, or have *him* say it, yet neither alternative is as forceful as having the fact fixed in the listener's imagination by having him picture a short, stout man who has spent his life in the garment district. There is no better way of doing it than to call the man Moskowitz, or some other clearly Jewish name. In this way, the name itself helps clear the deck for the eventual laugh.

Naturally, any other Jewish name would do; or, for that matter, some name attached to some other nationality which, in your opinion, would be associated by the audience with non-golf.

The general rule is: Let stereotypes work for you.

And remember, stereotypes do not have to be accurate to be effective.

Jokes are primarily verbal phenomena and nowadays there is a great deal of humor to be found in visual phenomena such as the movies or television. This does not mean that the pictures are a dead loss. There are scenes that can be adapted to the ear, particularly if they involve pictorial clichés with which everyone is familiar, so that the need for description is minimized.

For instance, everyone (or so nearly everyone that the exceptions do not matter) knows the stylized bars shown in movie Westerns. There are the swinging doors, the poker games, the professional gamblers, the hairy miners, the dance-hall girls, the bar itself, the bartender, and the inevitable cold-eyed lanky hero walking in.

My most fondly remembered scene of this type was in a Bob Hope picture, with Bob playing an effete easterner trying to make out among the tough guys of the West. Since everyone (or so nearly everyone that once again the exceptions do not matter) has seen Bob Hope, he needs no description and the clear memory of him and his mincing walk will set anyone up for a laugh.

❊ 9

The scene in the bar was even more stereotypical than usual, with hard-as-nails westerners coming up to the bar, and giving orders like: "Let me have a shot of redeye," and "Give me a slug of rotgut."

In the midst of all this, Bob Hope entered rather daintily, advanced to the bar, and said in a mild voice, "I'll have a sarsaparilla, please."

A dead silence of stunned astonishment fell over the roughnecks in the bar. All eyes turned on Bob, who became aware of the unfavorable attention and quickly added in a throaty growl, "— but in a dirty glass."

Naturally, you must select such episodes with care. You *cannot* depend on visual effects and expect to get away with having to describe in detail a scene the listener has not seen. Most of all, the joke cannot depend for its laugh on a final "— and you should have seen the expression on Bob's face."

You, remembering it, will laugh, but the listeners, not having seen the expression, will look at you with emotions varying from distaste to hatred.

❋ 10

Moskowitz was having his teeth examined and the dentist shook his head sadly. He said, "I am terribly sorry, Mr. Moskowitz, but you need a complete mouth job from wisdom tooth to wisdom tooth, both top and bottom, and this will cost you $3500."

Moskowitz looked glum indeed. He said, "I'll be frank with you, doctor. I'm afraid that $3500 is more than I can possibly afford. Is there no way of making the price more reasonable?"

"Not with me, I'm afraid. I could not do it for less. However, I can recommend another dentist, a younger man, who might possibly be able to give you a better price."

Moskowitz went to the younger man, who, after the examination, said, "I'm afraid, sir, that you require a complete mouth job and that will cost you $1700."

Moskowitz, however, was cautious. Saving money was one thing, but the condition of his teeth was also important. With some hesitation, he said, "Doctor, I'll be frank. You're a young man and perhaps you have insufficient experience. My regular dentist asked for considerably more money, and while I don't object to saving money, I don't want to do so at the expense of my teeth."

The young dentist said, "That is a very sensible attitude on your part, sir. I am indeed young and I am trying to establish a practice. That is why I am offering lower prices. As to my competence, I did precisely this sort of job on a Mr. Cohen two years ago. I will give you his telephone number and you may ask him if he is satisfied. If he says he is, we can talk further."

"Thank you," said Moskowitz. And that evening, he called Cohen and presented his problem.

Cohen, having listened, began politely, "As it happens, Mr. Moskowitz, I have a hobby —"

Moskowitz interrupted at once. "Yes, Mr. Cohen, but we can talk about that later. Right now, I am inquiring about your teeth."

"I quite realize that," said Cohen coldly, "but if you don't mind I will answer your question in my own fashion. As I said, I have a hobby. It consists of swimming in the nude. Every morning, except when the weather is too cold or too stormy, I go down to an isolated part of Jones Beach at 6 A.M. when I know I will be completely undisturbed. Taking off all my clothes, I venture into the sea and have half an hour of delicious enjoyment."

Moskowitz interrupted again, "I am delighted you have so entertaining a hobby, Mr. Cohen, but really it is your teeth I am interested in."

"Do you *mind*," responded Cohen, even more coldly than before. "Now one morning last week, after having disported myself in the water as is my wont, I emerged to dry myself and dress when I noticed a young lady approaching me who apparently had the same hobby I had. She was beautiful and had no clothes on, not a stitch. Naturally, I was horribly embarrassed and didn't know what to do or where to turn. The young lady, however, seemed not the least put out. She smiled in most friendly fashion and came closer and closer till our bodies touched. And for the first time in two years, my teeth stopped hurting."

This is my idea of a nearly perfect joke. The tale is interesting in itself and, properly told, can mislead the listener entirely. To play fair with the audience, Mr. Moskowitz should interrupt twice to ask about teeth. But after the second interruption, Cohen's story must become sufficiently interesting to make

the listener forget about teeth altogether, so that when the final
punch line brings everything suddenly and unexpectedly back
to teeth, the change in point of view is sufficiently extreme to
create pandemonium.

This is a long joke, of course, and can be made considerably
longer. In fact, the version I have included here is substantially
shorter than the one I tell.

A long joke is the culmination of the jokester's art, but it
bears its corresponding risks. In telling a long joke, there must
not only be intrinsic interest but definite mild humor throughout. If it is only interesting, then the audience, following the
tale with absorption and gravity, may get out of the laughing
mood, and the punch line will then fall into a well of dreadful
silence. You want, as far as possible then, to keep the audience
on the verge of laughter throughout.

One way is to insert small subsidiary points of humor, here
and there. As an example, I often start the joke by having the
first dentist announce to Moskowitz, in as pretentious a manner
as I can manage, "My dear Mr. Moskowitz, my investigation
presents me with an interesting problem, for you require what
we in the dental profession call, in technical terminology, 'a
complete mouth job of all the teeth.'"

In my experience this small anticlimax never fails to get a
chuckle, and to set the mood for the rest of the joke.

As you yourself repeat the joke, you will almost automatically develop other points here and there, and with each such
development you may stretch the joke out longer. (This is
creative joke-telling. In time, any accomplished jokester, in
adopting a joke, is bound to make it his own in this fashion, and
tell it differently than any other would.)

But why Moskowitz and Cohen, by the way? Because when
I tell the joke I use a thick Jewish accent (the only one I can
handle well) and for such an accent, names such as Moskowitz
and Cohen are essential.

The accent is useful in a long story. Properly done, the humorous turns of phrase and the manglings of pronunciations can keep the audience giggling and allow laughter to remain on instant call. Still, the Jewish accent is not essential. The joke is funny in itself and you can tell it with a Swedish accent or none at all. In the version I give here, though I keep the names Moskowitz and Cohen, I use formal and correct language. This, in itself, can be made to add to the humor. If you make the characters with names like Armstrong and Favisham, and use language so correct as to be stilted, you will get the same effect.

Which brings up the question: When ought one to use an accent in telling a joke?

The basic answer is: Only when you can do it well.

Unfortunately, the number of people who think they can handle some particular accent is far greater than the number of people who actually can; a poor accent is embarrassing at best, and downright insulting at worst, to any member of the audience whose ethnic group the accent is supposed to represent.

Rather than risk a poor accent, then, tell the joke straight, shortening it if necessary or using other devices to inject humor. You will be better off.

There are cases, of course, in which not only is a foreign accent almost compulsory, but the foreign language too, and its absence can only be mourned —

❧ 11

A ship, cruising in northern waters, was in terrible trouble, and the captain called in one of the passengers.

"You are, I know," he said, " a professional magician and I need your help badly. The ship is at this moment heading for an iceberg and there is something wrong with the rudder so we cannot steer past it. There is no real cause for alarm, however, because several ships are steaming rapidly to the rescue and aircraft already have us in view. All that is necessary is to keep the passengers from destructive panic. Please put on a show for them and rescue will reach us before we strike, perhaps. If, however, there is danger of an actual strike, I shall signal you and you must instantly announce that for your next trick you will break the ship in two. By the time the passengers gather that this is not a clever illusion and begin to panic, we will be saved."

The magician followed instructions exactly and for nearly half an hour transfixed his audience with disappearing canes, multiplying eggs, lighted candles that appeared out of nowhere, and cards that seemed to do everything but make love. Then the magician noted the captain waving at him frantically.

So the magician said, "And for my final illusion, ladies and gentlemen, I shall make the ship crash into an iceberg."

And as his hands spread wide in an impressive gesture, there was an awful rending crash and in no time at all everyone found himself on an eerily tipped vessel, with lifeboats being launched. Fortunately other ships were butting through the choppy seas on rescue missions, and the passengers were too confused by what had happened to be frightened.

The magician himself clung to the railing, watching a lifeboat being lowered. One of the passengers in the lifeboat called to him, "Hey, aren't you the magician whose final trick was to make the ship crash into an iceberg?"

"Yes, sir," said the magician, teeth chattering in the cold, "I'm the one."

The passenger shook his head. "So what was so smart about that?"

The way I first heard the joke and the way I like to tell it, everyone on the ship is Jewish. The passenger who questions the magician at the end speaks with a thick Jewish accent and the final punch line is then delivered in Yiddish and goes, "*Noo, vuzhe dih khukhme?*" And this happens to be untranslatable.

The rough equivalent is what I have given here, "So what was so smart about that?" but it doesn't quite carry the connotation. Nothing in English does. The fecklessness of the Yiddish protest, its utter inadequacy to meet the situation, is not quite reproduced in any English translation I can think of, with the result that I can never get the roar of response in English that I can in Yiddish.

Well, tough! Better to tell it in English for the lesser laugh than not tell it at all (or worse, tell it in Yiddish and translate — which would be a sure nothing). Still, when the audience contains a number of middle-aged Jews, I am sure to ask eagerly, "How many people here understand Yiddish?" If the number is enough I can tell this joke and others as well.

Yiddish is the only language other than English that I am sufficiently familiar with to tell jokes in (and that requires considerable familiarity, I had better warn you), so it is only the loss of Yiddish punch lines that frustrates me. Nevertheless, I am sure that there are such untranslatable expressions in all languages (including English most particularly), so that every language has a number of private jokes ineffective to foreigners even in translation. This may account, by the way, for the tendency to think of foreigners as having not much of a sense of humor.

Any mention of a ship hitting an iceberg naturally recalls the *Titanic,* and this in turn brings up the point of the manufacture of superstitions. Can you imagine any ship ever again being launched with the name *Titanic?* If one were, do you imagine anyone would go on board as a passenger? Which reminds me of an anticlimax I suffered in real life.

❊ 12

During and after World War II, Pearl Harbor came to be synonymous with treachery and disaster.

Having heard Pearl Harbor used in this fashion about one hundred thousand times too often (and no cliché is so mercilessly overused as one that appeals to the politician), I finally said to a friend out of sheer cantankerousness, "You'd think the navy would have had better sense than to moor all those ships in a place with a bad-luck name like Pearl Harbor."

All I was searching for was a mild chuckle at my attempt at whimsy, but I was floored when my friend said in all seriousness, "You'd sure think so, wouldn't you?"

(Or could it be that he topped my straight-faced whimsy
with a straight-faced acceptance and neatly put me down? I've
often wondered.)

❊ 13

It was the end of a typically hot, dank, completely miserable New
York summer afternoon, and the two psychiatrists, coming down in
the elevator, their day's work done, were a study in contrasts.

The younger man was utterly wilted and worn out. His hair was
rumpled, his cheeks were drawn, his clothing was wrinkled. The
older man was natty and, apparently, completely at ease, from the
part in his hair, through the starch in his collar, to the shine on his
shoes.

The younger man said, "How do you manage it, for heaven's sake,
Rumpelmayer? On a hot day like this, how do you end up so cool?"

"With air-conditioning," began Rumpelmayer.

"I have air-conditioning, too," interrupted the younger psychiatrist, "but the patients seem to bring the sultry misery of the New
York weather in with them. As I listen to their problems, their eternal whining, their maladjustments, their neuroses, their unhappiness,
it is as though the summer blast unmans me and leaves me a wreck.
Doesn't it bother you when you listen to your patients?"

"Ah," said Rumpelmayer. "There's the secret. Who listens?"

❊ 14

The young couple was engaged in a most affectionate embrace when
there came the sound of a key in the front door.

The young lady broke away at once, eyes wide with alarm.

"Heavens," she cried, "it's my husband! Quick, jump out the
window."

The young man, equally alarmed, made a quick step toward the
window, then demurred. "I can't," he said, "we're on the thirteenth
floor."

"For heaven's sake," cried the young lady in exasperation, "is this a
time to be superstitious?"

Jokes, and ridicule generally, are sometimes considered the most effective ways of destroying evils and abuses. Would it were so, but I feel that there are many evils built so firmly into the human race that nothing will help.

Superstition is one subject, I fear, too powerful to be swept away even by laughter. I doubt that anyone is immune to it, even those most against it from the intellectual standpoint. I myself have a tendency to knock wood when I make a vainglorious statement or to add a "barring acts of God" when I find myself behaving as though the future were certain.

How many millions of stories are told, designed to reinforce some superstition or other; how few are told to counter it. I remember with gratitude a perfectly true story once told me by a fellow member of the Boston University faculty.

(Did you notice, by the way, that between Jokes 13 and 14 I had nothing to say in the way of commentary? After all, there is only so much to say about jokes, and as I go along in the book the commentary is sure to get briefer. To those of you who would rather read jokes than commentary, this should be heartening news.)

❊ 15

My wife and I [he said] were going to take an excursion trip by ship. We had the tickets and were on the gangplank, when a sudden qualm overcame me. I had the strongest presentiment of disaster.

When I hung back, my wife asked what the matter was. I told her and she at once admitted to having the same presentiment.

Without another word, we stepped out of line and went home.

The excursion ship took off without us, went and returned safely, and everyone on board had a wonderful time.

❊ 16

In the days when the sun never set on Britain's empire, a servant of the crown was stationed in Khartoum. The central square of the city

was graced with a dramatic equestrian statue of General Charles
George Gordon, who died heroically in 1885 when Khartoum fell to
the troops of the Mahdi after a ten-month siege. Converted into
stone, Gordon now forever would survey the city from the back of
his spirited horse.

The British civil servant, surcharged with the spirit of imperial
obligation, made it his business to impress his son with the importance of the statue.

"That is Gordon," he said to his boy, and bowed his own head in a
moment of reverence.

The boy loved the statue and few were the days when he did not
run to the square to take a look at Gordon. When the time came for
the civil servant to be transferred from Khartoum to Lahore, the
boy's last deed before leaving was to proceed to the square to take a
reverent farewell of Gordon. His father's eyes misted over at this
action of his boy, and his heart swelled at the thought that within the
lad's chest there beat the heart of a true Englishman.

On board the steamer to Lahore, the boy turned to his father
thoughtfully and said, "Father, I have a question I have always
wanted to ask."

"Yes, my son?"

"It concerns Gordon. There's one thing I don't understand."

"What is that, my son?"

"Tell me. Who is that silly man who sits on Gordon?"

Here is a joke where there are compelling reasons for an
accent. The anticlimax is infinitely strengthened if you can
really get across the pukka sahib quality of the Englishman; the
old keen-eyed empire-builder bit. The more you can do that,
the more unthinkable it is that any English boy can for one
moment mistake horse for man. The final line, then, comes as
all the sharper an alteration in point of view.

The necessary impression can be built up most economically
by having both father and son speak in beautiful upper-class
British accents. Without even knowing it, the audience will get
precisely the impression you want it to have.

If you can do this, then by all means increase the conversational content of the joke; have the characters speak more; have the father describe Gordon; tell of his desperate stand at Khartoum while wiping away a manly tear. And, of course, always remember to keep matters ambiguous as to whether it is a man or a horse that is being referred to.

Alas, I can't do it. I can't speak British any more than I can Hindi. So I don't. I tell the joke without an accent and cut down the dialog to an absolute minimum.

(Incidentally, every once in a while I meet someone who speaks with the beautiful cadences of an educated Englishman. It is then beyond my ability to resist looking at him speculatively and saying, "You're a foreigner, aren't you?" He usually replies, "I'm English." And I respond, "I thought so. You speak our language funny." So far I have avoided being choked to death on the spot, but I have on more than one occasion noticed a kind of spasmodic twitching of the gentleman's fingers.)

❈ 17

It was in early 1962, on the day when John Glenn became the first American to go into orbit and the nation went wild over his feat of remaining in outer space for three revolutions.

The next day, Sadie, bubbling with excitement, said to her friend, Becky, "And what do you think of John Glenn?"

Becky raised her eyebrows. "Who?"

Sadie, astonished at the other's lack of knowledge, said, "John Glenn! John Glenn! He just went around the world three times."

Becky shrugged. "Well, if you have the money, you can afford to travel."

This is another case of the tragedy of translation. The punch line in Yiddish (note that it is Sadie and Becky who are speaking) would be *"Oz men hut gelt, fohrt men!"* This means exactly what the punch line means as I've given it in English, but the Yiddish version has a sententiousness the English does not. The application of a very common cliché to a situation for which it seems appropriate but for which it is actually wildly inappropriate is natural laugh material, but the cliché quality is lost in English.

❋ 18

At a military social function, the commanding general of the base delivered a welcoming oration in orotund fashion. A young second lieutenant, listening with extreme disfavor, muttered to the woman at his side, "What a pompous and unbearable old windbag that slob is."

The woman turned to him at once and said, "Lieutenant, do you know who I am?"

"No, ma'am."

"I am the wife of that unbearable old windbag, as you call him."

"Indeed," said the young lieutenant, looking stern, "and do you know who I am?"

"No, I don't," said the general's wife.

"Thank God," said the lieutenant, and he melted into the crowd.

❋ 19

Professor White, a respected Shakespearian scholar, in the evening of his life had decided to accept a position with a small woman's college. The schedule was undemanding compared to his former position at Harvard and would allow him much more time to write his definitive book on the Bard and his works.

The faculty wives were surprised, however, and badgered Mrs. White with questions. One in particular wondered, hesitantly, if Mrs. White felt it was entirely wise to have her husband lecturing to classes of young college girls in these days of campus unrest and revolutionary attitudes toward morals.

Mrs. White flushed, and said icily, "If you are implying that my husband would be tempted to misbehave with young ladies in his classes, you don't know what you're talking about. The professor is too great a gentleman to make such behavior conceivable. He is too decent, too rational, too fine, too fastidious in his morality, and most of all, *most* of all, he is too old."

☆ 20

Moskowitz and Finkelstein met in the garment district one day, each obviously weighted down with gloom. Moskowitz spoke first. With a deep sigh of agony, he said:

"Finkelstein, my friend, I have just lived through a summer the like of which I never thought I would see. June was already a disaster. Never in my entire business career have I seen a June like that. Yet when July came I realized that June had been quite good, for with July I went down through the floor and into the subbasement. July was absolutely unbelievable and indescribable and when I tell you —"

But by now Finkelstein had broken in. "For heaven's sake, Moskowitz, why are you coming to me with these piddling matters? If you want a tale of *real* trouble, here it is. Yesterday my son, my only son, on whom I had been placing all my hopes, came to me and told me he was getting married to another boy. Do you hear me? My son has become an open homosexual. What can be worse than *that?*"

"I'll tell you," said Moskowitz. "August!"

Moskowitz again! As you go through the book, it will become increasingly clear to you that for jokes where I want (for any reason at all) a Jewish flavor, I use Moskowitz over and over.

This is not because I think Moskowitz is a particularly funny name, or a particularly Jewish one. I know lots of names that are funnier, more Jewish, or both. Nor do I choose it because I want to get even with someone bearing that name. The only Moskowitz I know personally is a very good friend of mine, a prince of a fellow, and a man with muscles of iron whom I very much do not wish to offend.

Actually, it's a matter of pure chance. It is important, as I said earlier in my commentary, not to stumble over the names of characters in jokes. They are, after all, evanescent characters who are only with you for minutes, sometimes seconds. Therefore it is wise not to extend yourself by inventing new names each time; you won't remember and you will be trapped into saying "At that point Arbuthnot reached up — I mean Armitage reached up —" and the joke is seriously deflated at once.

Stick to a name, then, and make it second nature. I happened once, years ago, to pick the name Moskowitz and it is too late to change now. If I need a second Jewish name in the same joke, I use Finkelstein, because it has the same rhythm but a distinctly different sound. What's more, I always use Moskowitz as the first speaker and Finkelstein as the second, so that it all comes naturally and I don't mix them up.

In the same way, I use Jake and Becky for a Jewish man and wife, Becky and Sadie for two Jewish women (or Mrs. Moskowitz and Mrs. Finkelstein). Well perhaps not always, at that; sometimes I change things merely because my own ears feel the need for variety. Not often though, for the risk of stumbling becomes too great, and the first law of the jokester is not variety, but "Get a laugh!"

Naturally, there is no mystic value in the particular names I happened to choose. Use those you wish; those which you feel most at home with.

For the jokester, the disappearance of radio comedy was a tragedy. Television comedy is fine except that so much of it is sight-gag material, difficult to adapt for the jokester's purpose.

Radio, on the other hand, by the very nature of the medium had to be entirely sound. Well do I remember, for instance, a program called "Can You Top This?" in which listeners sent in jokes, while a panel of jokesters (if I remember correctly they were Harry Hershfield, Senator Ford, and Joe Laurie, Jr.) competed to see who could tell the funniest joke on a given subject.

Sometimes, when I am more than usually euphoric, I try to play the game myself. When someone asks for a joke, I may say with a careless wave of the hand, "Name the category!" Often I come a cropper (as I deserve), but once I managed to pull it off against the odds.

I had just finished talking about a book on Shakespeare which I had recently completed, and so when the jokes began and I asked that a category be named, someone present said, "Tell a joke about Shakespeare." This is what I told:

❋ 21

Cabot Martingale, a Boston Brahmin of the staunchest sort had, as it happened, never seen, or even read, any play by Shakespeare. When this fact came out, his friends were appalled, and one of them brought him a Complete Works of the great man.

"You simply must read this," he said.

Weeks later, the two met again, and the friend said, "Well, Martingale, have you read any of Shakespeare?"

"Every word," said the Brahmin. "Every word."

"And what did you think of him?"

"Why, I thought the man extraordinary. His ability with the language was almost beyond belief. I don't think there are twenty men in Boston who could equal him."

Actually, this business of choosing a category and telling a joke to fit is by no means as impressive as it seems. Here is the Shakespeare joke, 21. Had I been asked to tell a joke about Homer, Dante, Milton, Cervantes, or Dickens, I would have told the same joke with appropriate slight modifications. Had I been asked to tell a joke about an artist such as Leonardo, or a musician such as Bach, or even a scientist such as Newton, the same joke would still have served.

Every joke can be modified to a certain extent by changing only a few words, and the skill of the game on "Can You Top This?" rested as much with the ingenuity of on-the-spot modification as with the brute force of memory.

❄ 22

Joe was sitting on the corner stool at the bar, sunk in misery. The
bartender said, "You look awful, friend. What's your problem?"

Joe stared into his whiskey and said, "I'm tired of being a social
outcast. I'm with the circus, you see, and clean up the animal cages.
The result is that I can't help smelling a little. Naturally, people
avoid me and I don't like it."

The bartender sniffed. "Yes, I see what you mean and I've got to
admit it's not the best fragrance in the world. But look here, there
are openings down at the factory. You could get yourself a job there
that will probably pay better than your circus position."

"What!" said Joe, outraged. "And leave show business?"

Yes, there are some professions that seem to have a built-in
glamour that compensates for all the hardships and failures they
may entail. But such glamour is very much a function of the
social milieu. It was not too long ago that show business was
the very opposite of glamorous, when actors were considered
vagabonds and actresses, prostitutes.

A profession with unlimited social glamour among the Jewish
immigrants to this nation is that of medicine. In the ghettos of
Europe to become a physician was one way (almost the only
way) of breaking away from the binding restrictions of social
and economic misery.

Proud indeed, then, was the first-generation Jewish couple
whose son had made it through medical school. It proved difficult for them to refer to their son without mentioning his profession as well, a failing satirized in the following:

❄ 23

Mrs. Moskowitz, distraught, ran along the beach toward the distant
lifeguard, pointing out to sea and screaming, "Help! Help! My son
the doctor is drowning!"

❄ 24

"You know," said Moskowitz, "being a doctor these days isn't so great. There are some kinds of scientists with much more prestige. I think lots of Jewish boys are going to become scientists instead of doctors."

"Never," said his friend Finkelstein.

"Why not?"

"Because," said Finkelstein, "it's too hard to say 'My son, the nuclear physicist.'"

Talking about difficulty reminds me —

❄ 25

At the meeting of the local Hadassah, Mrs. Moskowitz was making a report on the progress of the Americanization of the membership.

"In the last month," she said, pronouncing her English with meticulous care, "no less than five of our members have received their nat —— their nat-ur-al — their nat ——."

At which point, the lady president leaned forward impatiently and said in a hoarse whisper, "Mrs. Moskowitz, don't be fancy and say already, in plain Yiddish, 'tzitizenship papers.'"

The confusion in languages in a melting subculture sometimes has its tragicomic sides. When my father first arrived in the United States from Russia, he was overwhelmed at his new illiteracy. The world was suddenly full of signs he could not understand. The very letters were strange, for they were neither of the Hebrew nor of the Cyrillic alphabet.

And then he noticed a sign in Hebrew letters before a storefront. He hastened toward it in order to read it and restore the sensation of literacy, which naturally he valued. But when he got there he found himself in worse straits than ever. The sign was indeed in Hebrew letters and he could read it, but what he read (literally) was "*Vindehz gefikst*," and it left him in despair for he could not understand it. It was only long afterward, when he had begun to learn English, that he came to realize that he had stumbled on a place where they "fixed windows."

Something in reverse happened to me recently when I received a copy of one of my own books published in Israel in (naturally) a Hebrew translation. I can't understand Hebrew, but I know the Hebrew alphabet and can pronounce some of the words. I searched for my own name, therefore, eager to see the first name in its original Hebrew form, Itzchak. (Sorry, but it is unpronounceable in English.)

I found it all right, but to my annoyance the Hebrew publisher had carefully chosen the Hebrew letters in such a way that my first name was pronounced "Isaac," exactly as in English.

* 26

The indignant soldier, barely into his basic training, was writing a furious letter to his Congressman, detailing all the various indignities and evils to which he was being subjected. At one point, he waxed almost lyrical —

"And the food, sir, I can describe only as slop. I wouldn't feed it to pigs for fear they would get sick to their stomachs and die of it. It would be rejected by any decent garbage man. And to make matters still worse, they serve such small portions."

Yes, I went through it. Beginning in 1940, a stay in the army grew to be a common experience for young Americans, and I did not escape.

Nor did I particularly enjoy my own stay in the army. Even though no one treated me cruelly, and I was never in any real danger, I still found it difficult to bear. In fact, what grim pleasure I got out of it was in observing the irrationality of army life.

My introduction to that irrationality came quickly. On the very first morning on which I had to be wakened by reveille, a corporal came storming through the barracks yelling at the brand-new soldiers, "All right, rise and shine, up and at 'em, hubba-hubba," and all the other phrases that were soon to become so hateful.

I have never in my life risen later than sunrise and so I was awake when he came in.

"Corporal," I said, "what time is it?" It was sheer curiosity, for I am a time-bound individual.

"I don't know," he snarled at me.

That surprised me. "If you don't know," I reasoned, "how do you know it's time for reveille?"

And of course he stopped short and said, "Okay, soldier, what's your name?" and I found myself on report for insolence.

❋ 27

There are some cities which have a general reputation for being unexciting. Perhaps the largest city to suffer from this canard is Philadelphia.

At least there is the case of the television quiz show that announced a first prize in which the contestant would be awarded a one-week, all-expenses-paid vacation in Philadelphia. For second prize there would be a two-week, all-expenses-paid vacation in Philadelphia.

As it happens, I lived in Philadelphia for three years during World War II. The city *was* duller than New York, the job I held was duller than my work at Columbia University had been, and wartime conditions made everything grayer. I was homesick, naturally, and I gleefully listened to and retold any joke made at Philadelphia's expense. It helped me endure the city, and in all seriousness, that is one of the important functions of humor.

To my Philadelphia readers, I hasten to say that I have visited Philadelphia a number of times since the war, and its improvement is astonishing. I have always enjoyed my visits.

✻ 28

The great man-and-wife acting team of Alfred Lunt and Lynn Fontanne made just one motion picture, *The Guardsman*. On the day of
the première, Lunt was sick in bed and couldn't go. Miss Fontanne
went alone and returned, distraught.

She was already talking as she came in, and almost weeping with
despair.

"Alfred," she said, "it was a total disaster. I cannot imagine what
the photographer can have been thinking of, or the director. For
some reason I came out as an ugly witch, with my makeup all wrong,
my cheeks cadaverous, my hair a mess. The sound system managed
to make my voice sound half a squeak and half a groan. You at least
were fine in every respect, except for a tendency to have thin lips for
some reason, but I was impossible. The close-ups were invariably
taken at such an angle that all you could see of me were my nostrils,
or else my eyelashes cast such shadows that I looked as though I had
large bags under both eyes. I shall certainly never be able to hold up
my head again in public and I intend to go into retirement at once."

And, thoughtfully, Lunt said, "Thin lips, eh?"

This is a difficult joke to tell. Fontanne's speech must be
given in the rapid, nearly incoherent tones of an hysterical
woman, with the short comment about the thin lips carefully
buried in the precise middle.

If you *hear* a joke such as this, told by a proficient jokester,
you can be guided by what you have heard (always allowing
for the modifications of your own temperament). If, however,
you *read* a joke and wish to tell it, it might be well to think it
through first and observe the pitfalls.

Some punch lines, by the way, can be adopted for concise
communication and used to speak volumes in a few syllables
(another function of jokes). My wife found many occasions on
which she might use the punch line to Joke 28. Often, when I
was deeply concerned over something I considered important

to the exclusion of competing matters in which she was involved, she would say, "Thin lips, eh?"

Well, I suppose writers are as bad as show people in their capacity for self-absorption. David Frost says that what a writer means by constructive criticism is six thousand words of closely reasoned adulation, and if that is true (and I suspect it is) a little self-centeredness among them is to be expected.

❋ 29

The young lady whom Jones had just met seemed delightful. She had beauty, charm, and intelligence. She was highly educated and had a keen sense of humor. He praised her and she cheerfully agreed to all the virtues which he attributed to her. Nervously, Jones suggested they retire to her apartment and was ecstatic when she agreed.

She took him to a fancy apartment house in the best part of town and up they went to the penthouse. But when the door opened, there in the middle of the living room floor lay a dead horse.

The young lady, observing the shocked look of horror on Jones' face, said defensively, "Well, I never claimed to be neat."

Notice the similarity between this joke and Joke 1. Clearly, if you tell one, you will be reminded of the other. I would resist the temptation, however, to tell two closely similar jokes in rapid succession. The second is to a large extent wasted; save it for another time.

❋ 30

The sergeant was briefing the rookie paratroopers. "We're going to go over the target at three hundred feet and then jump."

One of the rookies raised his hand. "Isn't that a bit high, Sergeant? Two hundred feet might be safer."

"It would be *less* safe," said the sergeant impatiently. "You have to allow room for the parachutes to open."

"Oh," said the rookie, "*parachutes!*"

Ought a jokester make fun of paratroopers, the bravest of the brave? Well, why not? In the world of jokes, nothing is sacred, as we shall see in ample measure before the book is over. And as for making fun of big brave fellows by implying that they are stupid — perhaps there are special reasons.

The jokester is a member of a subculture of his own. He has to have a good memory; he has to be nimble witted; he has to have a sense of the ridiculous, a feeling for satire, a tendency to make fun. These qualities receive most exercise in the littler and weaker sorts who are forced to rely on them for lack of the more satisfying ability to beat up the enemy.

The chances are that in his younger days, before he has learned discretion, the budding jokester has offended other youngsters, who, not yet possessing the social restraints of adulthood or the physical disadvantages of the sharp-tongued gadfly, have beaten him up.

I think of the jokester, then (and there are individual exceptions, I'm sure, as to every generalization) as a person who in youth has sometimes pitted a quick tongue against a quick fist and gotten the worst of it — and has then spent his adult life getting even. At least jokes frequently equate largeness, muscularity, and physical bravery with stupidity.

When I think of jokes, I think of convivial sessions after dinner, with a drink in the hands of those who drink. All the jokes in this book, and many that are not, I have told on such occasions.

Nevertheless, jokes are also at home under much more formal conditions. It is a common practice, for instance, to begin a serious speech with some lighthearted banter designed to put the audience at ease. Very often this takes the form of a joke.

But not just any joke, I hope!

A large fraction of the more literate type of funny story can make a serious point after the laughter has died down — a point that will penetrate deeper for having been driven by laughter. Some of the jokes I have already presented are of that sort. Here is another —

⁂ 31

Jones, a wealthy financier, had on many an occasion in the good old days, when trains were flourishing and coaches were the last word in technological luxury, crossed the continent by Pullman. He was well known and well served and was accustomed to every convenience, particularly when dining. Imagine his exasperation, then, when it turned out that the chef did not have tutti-frutti ice cream.

"No tutti-frutti?" he shouted. "I *always* have tutti-frutti."

"I'm sorry, sir," said the waiter, soothingly. "We have chocolate, vanilla, strawberry, black walnut, cherry, mocha almond —"

"I want tutti-frutti," cried Jones, banging the table and turning red. "I have always had tutti-frutti and I won't have anything else."

For miles he muttered, scowled, growled, and snarled at everyone, so that every train employee on board had visions of angry reprisals. Finally, the train stopped at a station; a word to the conductor kept it there while the crew scoured the town for tutti-frutti ice cream.

Finally, a whole pint of the delicious concoction was obtained and all of it was presented to Jones, with huge gobs of cherry sauce on it, together with a sliced banana and a swirl of whipped cream.

"Here is your tutti-frutti ice cream, Mr. Jones," said an obsequious waiter.

Jones looked at it with a scowl, then with a sudden swipe of his arm hurled it to the floor, shouting, "I'd rather have my grievance."

And how many of the world's miseries are caused by people who won't be consoled because they would rather have their grievances. And how many speeches on the Middle Eastern situation of the sixties and seventies might profitably begin with a story like the one above.

⁂ 32

The young lieutenant was drilling his platoon under the eyes of a ferociously scowling colonel. The lieutenant's nerve was trickling away under his senior's fierce glance and his voice was beginning to break. Finally, having completed an intricate maneuver, the lieutenant found the entire platoon marching, eight abreast, toward the edge of a cliff.

He broke down completely at that and stared at the marching men, frozen and helpless.

And the colonel finally barked, "Good heavens, man, at least say good-bye to them."

There's something about being a private in the army (as I was) that creates hostility to officers. No officer ever mistreated me in the army; none was even unreasonable to me. Yet I had an aversion to them just the same.

Things changed after my discharge, however. On the very first day after, when I was in civilian clothes at last and on my way home, a major inadvertently stepped on my shoe at the subway station.

"Pardon me," he said, civilly.

And eyeing the oak leaf on his shoulder, I said loftily, "That's all right, kid."

Somehow that made it all even.

❋ 33

The young lieutenant was putting his company through its paces and was none too sure of himself. To his horror, he suddenly realized the men were marching stolidly toward a fence.

"Company-y-y halt!" he called out, voice cracking. Then, "At ease." Now came the hard part. How was he to order them across the fence in proper military fashion?

He studied the fence and then said, "Company-y-y, fall out!" The men promptly broke formation.

The lieutenant then said, "Company-y-y, fall in — on the other side of the fence."

❋ 34

The newly minted lieutenants were undergoing an oral examination from a hard-bitten colonel. Up and down the line he went, saying to each one in turn, "You are going to have to pitch a tent. What is your first order?"

Under the colonel's frosty eye, lieutenant after lieutenant shriveled and fell mute. One attempted to answer, "Break out tent equipment," but was cut off at once.

And then finally the colonel reached the class goof-off and low-scorer in all things military. "Well, lieutenant," said the colonel, "if you were going to pitch a tent, what would be your first order?"

The lieutenant snapped to rigid attention and barked, "Sir. My first order would be my only order. It would be 'Sergeant, pitch a tent.'"

How rapidly times change and headline favorites give way. There was a time in the nineteen forties when Vyacheslav Molotov was Soviet foreign minister. He was a shrewd man and a hard bargainer but of course it was the dictator, Joseph Stalin, who was boss.

❋ 35

A story (undoubtedly apocryphal) tells that Molotov was once overheard talking to Stalin by trans-Atlantic telephone during the course of some very intricate negotiations with the West. He said, "Yes, Comrade Stalin," in quiet tones, then again, "Yes, Comrade Stalin," and then, after a considerable wait, "Certainly, Comrade Stalin."

Suddenly he was galvanized into emotion. "No, Comrade Stalin," he barked. "No. That, no. Definitely, no."

After a while, he quieted and it was "Yes, Comrade Stalin," again.

The reporter who overheard this was probably never so excited in his life. Clearly, Molotov was daring to oppose the dictator on at least one point, and it would surely be important to the West to know what that point might be.

The reporter approached Molotov and said as calmly as possible, "Secretary Molotov, I could not help but hear you say at one point, 'No, Comrade Stalin.'"

Molotov turned his cold eyes on the reporter and said, "What of it?"

"May I ask," said the reporter, cautiously, "what the subject under discussion was at that time?"

"You may. Comrade Stalin asked me if there was anything which he had said with which I disagreed."

In a case like this, where Stalin has been dead for three decades and Molotov, while still alive, has been forgotten for as long, it might pay to transfer the tale (which isn't true anyway) to some later individual.

Unfortunately (or fortunately, I think) we have had nothing quite like Stalin since his death, and it would weaken the joke to transfer it even to the overbearing Lyndon Johnson or to the self-admiring Charles De Gaulle, though this is for each individual jokester to decide for himself.

To be sure, these latter governmental figures have not escaped the transfer of jokes that have probably poniarded strong rulers for generations, if not centuries. As examples —

❋ 36

It is reported that Madame De Gaulle, in bed one night, said, "My God, it's cold."

To which her husband, lying stiffly by her side, replied, "In bed, Madame, you may call me Charles."

❋ 37

It is also reported that De Gaulle once stated proudly to President Johnson, "My mission to save France came to me directly from God."

And Johnson answered quietly, "Strange! I don't recall ever giving you any such mission."

It is not only historical figures who are victimized by tales that can't possibly be true. Almost anyone who has achieved a certain notoriety can be made the central figure of a joke into which he is inserted for no other reason than that something associated with him helps make the joke funnier. Here's one about Conan Doyle, for instance, which shows without trouble why it is he who was chosen to grace the joke.

✳ 38

Sir Arthur Conan Doyle, author of the famous Sherlock Holmes stories, once hailed a cab in Paris. He threw his handbag inside and climbed in after it, but before he could say a word, the driver said, "Where to, Mr. Conan Doyle?"

"You recognize me?" said the author in surprise.

"Not really. I've never seen you or a picture of you."

"Then how do you know I am Conan Doyle?"

"Well," said the driver, "I had read in the newspapers that you were on vacation in the south of France; I noticed you getting off a train that came from Marseille; I see you have the kind of tan that bespeaks a week or more in the sun; from the inkspot on your right middle finger, I deduce you are a writer; you have the keen look of a medical man, and the cut of clothes of an Englishman. Putting it all together, I felt you must surely be Conan Doyle, the creator of the great detective, Sherlock Holmes."

Conan Doyle burst out, "But you are yourself the equal of Sherlock Holmes since you recognized me from all these small observations."

"There is," said the driver, "one additional fact."

"And that is?"

"Your name is lettered on your handbag."

As I said earlier, I suspect that jokesters as a class are on the sunny side of the IQ average. That may be a self-serving suspicion but that's what I think.

And yet jokes that make fun of the stupid are neither as numerous nor as good as those that make fun of the intelligent. Is it masochism on the jokester's part? Or is it that intelligence makes a much better target and that, to a jokester, the target's the thing?

Anyway, here is a tale of the triumph of stupidity over intelligence that I never tell more than once a year because the effort is so great. It is long and complicated (I tell it here in somewhat condensed form), requires a thoroughly warmed-up audience, and involves a set of gestures which are of the essence (and because of which something is lost on paper). But here goes —

✿ 39

Back in medieval times, a thoroughly apocryphal story tells us, the Roman Pope was persuaded by some of his more conservative advisers to endure no longer the presence of Jews in the very heart and core of world Christianity. The Jews of Rome were therefore ordered evicted from their homes by a certain date.

To the Jews of Rome this was a great tragedy, for they knew no refuge where they might not expect worse treatment than in Rome. They appealed to the Pope for reconsideration and the Pope, a fair-minded man, suggested a sporting proposition. If the Jews would appoint one of their own number to engage in a debate with him, in pantomime, and if the Jewish representative were to win the debate, the Jews might remain.

The Jewish leaders gathered in the synagog that night and considered the proposition. It seemed the only way out but none of their number wished to volunteer to debate. As the chief rabbi said, "It is impossible to win a debate in which the Pope will be both participant and judge. And how can I face the possibility that the eviction of the Jews will be the result of my specific failure?"

The synagog janitor, who had been quietly sweeping the floor through all this, suddenly spoke up. "I'll debate," he said.

They stared at him in astonishment. "You, a cheap janitor," said the chief rabbi, "debate with the Pope?"

"Someone has to," said the janitor, "and none of you will."

So in default of anyone else, the janitor was made the representative of the Jewish community and was appointed to debate with the Pope.

Then came the great day of the debate. In the square before St. Peter's was the Pope, surrounded by the College of Cardinals in full panoply, with crowds of bishops and other churchly functionaries. Approaching was the Jewish janitor, surrounded by a few of the leaders of the Jewish community in their somber black garb and their long gray beards.

Pope faced janitor, and the debate began.

Gravely, the Pope raised one finger and swept it across the heavens. Without hesitation the janitor pointed firmly toward the ground, and the Pope looked surprised.

Even more gravely, the Pope raised one finger again, keeping it firmly before the janitor's face. With the trace of a sneer, the janitor raised three fingers, holding the pose just as firmly, and a look of deep astonishment crossed the Pope's face.

Then, the Pope thrust his hand deep into his robes and produced an apple. The janitor thereupon opened a paper bag that was sticking out of his hip pocket and took out a flat piece of matzo.

At this, the Pope exclaimed in a loud voice, "The Jewish representative has won the debate. The Jews may remain in Rome."

The janitor backed off, the Jewish leaders surrounded him, and all walked hastily out of the square.

They were no sooner gone than the church leaders clustered about the Pope. "What happened, Your Holiness?" they demanded. "We did not follow the rapid give-and-take."

The Pope passed a shaking hand across his brow. "The man facing me," he said, "was a master at the art of debate. Consider! I began the debate by sweeping my hand across the sky to indicate that God ruled all the universe. Without pausing an instant, that old Jew pointed downward to indicate that nevertheless the Devil had been assigned a dominion of his own below.

"I then raised one finger to indicate there was but one God, assuming I would catch him in the error of his own theology. Yet he instantly raised three fingers to indicate that the one God had three manifestations, a clear acceptance of the doctrine of the Trinity.

"Abandoning theology, I produced an apple to indicate that certain blind upholders of so-called science were flying in the face of revealed truth by declaring the Earth was as round as an apple. Instantly, he produced a flat piece of unleavened bread to indicate that the Earth, in accord with revelation, was nevertheless flat. So I granted him victory."

By now, the Jews and the janitor had reached the ghetto. All surrounded the janitor, demanding, "What happened?"

The janitor said indignantly, "The whole thing was nonsense. Listen. First the Pope waves his hand like he's saying 'The Jews must get out of Rome.' So I point downward to say 'Oh yeah? The Jews

are going to stay right here.' So he points his finger at me as if to say
'Drop dead, but the Jews are leaving.' So I point three fingers at him
to say 'Drop dead three times, the Jews are staying.' So then I see
he's taking out his lunch, so I take out mine."

❋ 40

Three men were engaged in one of those profitless conversations
which involve all of us at one time or another. They were considering the problem of what each would do if the doctor told him he had
only six months to live.

Said Robinson, "If my doctor said I had only six months to live,
the first thing I would do would be to liquidate my business, with-
draw my savings, and have the biggest fling on the French Riviera
you ever saw. I'd play roulette, I'd eat like a king, and most of all,
I'd have girls, girls, and more girls."

Said Johnson, "If my doctor said I had only six months to live, the
first thing I would do would be to visit a travel agency and plot out
an itinerary. There are a thousand places on earth I haven't seen,
and I would like to see them before I die: the Grand Canyon, the
Taj Mahal, Angkor Wat, all of them."

Said Goldberg, "If my doctor said I had only six months to live,
the first thing I would do would be to consult another doctor."

This is, in its origins, a joke of the type that begins, "There
were once a Scotsman, an Irishman, and a Jew, who . . ." Invariably, it is designed to show the superior cleverness of one
over the other two.

It is only natural that, for reasons of dramatic climax, the last-
named be the clever one; and it is also only natural that, for
reasons of parochial pride, the last-named represent the jokester and the audience when possible. I myself, for instance, am
accustomed to have this sort of joke end with the Jew, who will
then demonstrate his superiority. Thus, in Joke 40, I used the
name Goldberg for the third character in this vestigial remnant
of this now old-fashioned (and essentially racist) type of joke.

It stands to reason that Gentile versions of this joke would *not* have the Jew at the end, and yet he is. I wonder if anyone has ever heard a joke that began, "There were once a Scotsman, a Jew, and an Irishman . . ." — even with an Irish jokester. Why? Because cleverness is not always admirable, and because it easily degenerates into a kind of shrewdness that is detestable. And in that case someone who doesn't particularly admire Jews will be sure to let Goldberg have the last word. Thus —

✲ 41

MacTavish, O'Rourke, and Goldberg were mourning the loss of a mutual friend.

MacTavish said, "As you well know, my friends, I am a thrifty soul, but there is a legend in my family that if one places a wee bit of money in the casket so that it may be buried with the body, it will ease the way into the next world. For the sake of our friend, I will place ten dollars in the casket with him."

And, with a flourish he released a ten dollar bill and let it flutter onto the dear departed's breast.

O'Rourke had no intention of being outdone. "Well," he said, "this strikes me as mere superstition, but I will not be behindhand. To go along with the family tradition of yours, MacTavish, I too will contribute that sum." And a second ten dollar bill joined the first on the dead man's breast.

Goldberg said at once, "Do you think I won't join in this kind deed?" And whipping out his checkbook, he quickly made out a check for thirty dollars, placed it on the dead man's breast, and took the two bills as change.

✲ 42

Old Mr. Moskowitz, long since retired, was having trouble sleeping. Night after night, he lay awake and stared at the ceiling. His health was suffering visibly.

His son, who loved his father dearly, was much concerned. He tried everything.

He took his father for invigorating walks; he fed him warm milk in the evening; he played soft music on the radio; he placed vibrators in the bed. Nothing helped. The old man remained sleepless and grew steadily weaker.

And then the son read of a hypnotist in Chicago who specialized in cases of insomnia. He could hypnotize people into a natural sleep and plant a posthypnotic suggestion that would keep them sleeping every night. His fee was enormous but money was no object.

In no time, the son had the hypnotist flown in by a chartered plane and he did indeed make an impressive appearance. He was dark, long faced, delicate featured, with a thin mustache and a Van Dyke. Most of all, his eyes were both somber and brilliant.

The hypnotist was introduced to the old man. Bringing out a shiny pendant, the hypnotist stared fixedly at Mr. Moskowitz and said in a soft and mellifluous voice, "Watch the pendant, Mr. Moskowitz. Watch it — don't take your eyes off it — watch it swing — back and forth — back and forth —" His voice became a liquid croon. "You are getting sleepy, Mr. Moskowitz — warm and sleepy — gently tired and sleepy — you are getting so sleepy — so sleepy — your eyelids are so heavy — you can't keep them open — you want to close them — sleepy — sleepy —sleepy—your eyelids are closing —"

On and on he went, the son silent in the background, almost falling asleep himself. And as the hypnotist spoke, old Mr. Moskowitz's eyes did indeed slowly close, and his breathing grew deep and regular.

The hypnotist's voice sank lower and lower and finally, in a whisper, he said, "You will wake eight hours from now, completely rested, completely rested. And every night, you will fall asleep at midnight and wake at eight in the morning, completely rested, completely rested."

His task done, the hypnotist pocketed the enormous fee he had been promised and left. The son could scarcely believe his good fortune. Overwhelmed with happiness, he tiptoed in softly so that he could gaze at the dear sleeping face of his father. And as he stood there, smiling with pleasure, one of the old man's eyes popped open and a thin, quavering voice said, "Well, has he left yet, that lunatic?"

✹ 43

In Victorian times, two matrons of insuperable respectability were watching a production of Shakespeare's *Antony and Cleopatra*. In the play, there is one scene where Cleopatra receives the news of Antony's marriage to a Roman woman. She explodes in rage and anger in a piece of most effective theater.

The matrons watched Queen Cleopatra's passion and violence, her screaming threats against the cowering messenger, and finally one of them, leaning over toward the other, whispered in deep shock, "How different from the homelife of our own dear queen!"

Excess is relative, and inveterate liars often find it hard to understand why others object to a bit of embroidery. And in this view I sympathize a little, for what jokester would refuse to stretch a point here, fill a gap there, round a corner in the other place, if that were needed to make a true story better? I am myself, in most things, as honest as I can conveniently be, and when I tell you a true story as I have already and will do frequently in the remainder of the book, I will do my level best to tell it as accurately as I can. But where a bit of polish . . . Well, it comes with the territory.

Still, enough is enough, and outrageous lying is worth an occasional shaft.

✹ 44

Joe Anderson was addicted to the most ferocious exaggerations, and this had made him the laughingstock of the entire community, and the despair of his brother Jim.

Jim often lectured his wayward brother, and many were the promises of reform he obtained. "Listen, Joe," said Jim earnestly, "if you've got to tell stories, okay, but if I'm around and I catch your eyes and shake my head, it means you're going too far and you just back down, will you?"

Tearfully, Joe promised and, for a while, he was pretty good about it, but then on one occasion when all were sitting over a convivial drink in the bar, Joe forgot.

"Talking about hotels," he said, "I once owned one that was the biggest on the East coast. It had five bars in it, each one bigger than this one. It had two indoor swimming pools, three bowling alleys, and a large gymnasium. It had two thousand rooms, each with color television. It was a hundred and thirty-five stories high, with the top of the television mast sixteen hundred and seventy feet above the sidewalk; it was a full block wide," and here he finally caught sight of his brother signaling him desperately, so he concluded, "and one foot deep."

There are some tragedies which by their very nature are ridiculous and which invite the kind of laughter for which the person laughing must gasp out apologies between howls. I have a good friend, for instance,* for whom I have the profoundest affection, who said to me recently:

"Half a year ago, I had a beautiful suit made to order when I was visiting England. It was a perfect fit and looked great, and I hated to wear it for anything but a really important occasion. Finally, the occasion arrived and I put on the suit and it looked terrific. And as I stepped out of my door, a pigeon flew over and shit on my shoulder."

Well naturally I doubled up, and managed to choke out an apology while my friend just shook his head and said, "Gee, I thought I'd get sympathy."

But of course he expected no such thing. The tragedy of a bird making you a target would force a saint to laugh.

So, to conclude the section on anticlimax, let's multiply the sadness and the ridiculousness of it all and see just how immense a tragedy can be and still get nothing but laughter.

---

* As a matter of fact, he's an editor, Lawrence P. Ashmead of Doubleday. It's amazing how many editors are wonderful people. From what other writers have told me, I expected the reverse — but never found it so.

❅ 45

Cecil B. De Mille was well known for his spectacular motion pictures in which the lavish use of special effects sometimes utterly drowned out their more prosaic virtues. He had filmed everything, from enormous pagan orgies to the parting of the Red Sea, but (one thoroughly apocryphal story goes) he planned, shortly before his death, the most magnificent of all his magnificent spectacles.

He was going to film the six days of creation — the coming of light, the forming of the Earth, the separation of the sea from the land, the appearance of sun, moon, and stars, and the coming of life.

The whole spectacle was to cost uncounted millions of dollars, and for this purpose a huge valley in Spain was rigged up with incredible engineering devices. The process could be carried through only once. To try it twice would have meant undoing all the first attempt had brought about and multiplying the cost tenfold.

To guard against all eventualities, therefore, C. B. De Mille set up four separate camera crews on four separate peaks overlooking the valley, each under instructions to film everything.

The creation was then carried through and everything worked perfectly. De Mille himself was reduced to awed and speechless tears at its magnificence, and when it was all over he hastened to check on the camera crews.

He put in a call to Camera Crew 1 on the specially installed telephone lines. "How did it go?" he asked.

"Gee, Mr. De Mille," came back a shocked voice. "I don't know how to tell you, but when the creation started, we were all so fascinated by it that we actually never thought to roll the cameras."

Quietly, C. B. De Mille uttered a few imprecations, but after all he had expected trouble. That was why he had four camera crews. He put in a call to Crew 2.

"Gee, Mr. De Mille," came back a terrified voice. "I can't explain it. We were all set, but it turned out we just didn't have any film. Somehow no one had ever thought to bring any. Mr. De Mille, I could just die."

"Do that," ground out De Mille, and he rang up the third.

"Gee, Mr. De Mille," came back a panicky voice, "we were ready, we were running, we were loaded, we took everything, but Mr. De Mille — I don't know how it happened but we just somehow never took the cap off the lens."

Now C. B. De Mille was really in a state of shock. He had only one camera crew left and it was with a trembling hand that he dialed the final number.

For once a robust, cheerful voice answered, "Hello, Mr. De Mille."

De Mille said, "Is everything all right?"

"Couldn't be better," said the cameraman cheerfully.

Wild hope sprang up within De Mille's heart. "You have film?"

"Of course."

"The right film?"

"Of course."

"The cap is off the lens?"

"Of course."

"There is nothing wrong?"

"Not a thing."

"Thank God."

"Relax," said the fourth cameraman. "We're in perfect shape, so get started. We're ready whenever you are, C.B."

PART II *Shaggy Dog*

THERE COMES A POINT where anticlimax can be so outrageous that it provokes not laughter but annoyance. One tells a joke with apparently mounting suspense, dragging it out for as long as one dares, and then ends it with an absolutely flat thud. Nothing!

Why is that done? The only possible explanation is that the jokester is tempted to have fun at the expense of the audience.

This can delight only the jokester, but obviously it is expensive delight. An audience that is made fun of is not an audience to remain responsive, and what has the jokester then gained? Certainly less than nothing.

If you must tell such a story out of a sheer desire to practice your virtuosity — to see to how high a pitch you can carry an audience and how suddenly you can let it drop — I suppose I can't stop you. But do it as infrequently as you can, for your own sake.

Often this kind of beyond-the-limits-of-anticlimax story is called a shaggy-dog story. One might wonder why, and the only satisfactory explanation I ever heard (from Frederik Pohl, a science fiction editor and a friend of long standing) was to the effect that a prototype joke of this genre involved a shaggy dog.

Here are the bare bones of the joke in question:

✤ 46

A hobo, noting an advertisement in the paper for a large shaggy dog of a certain description, simultaneously noted a large shaggy dog of the same description sniffing at his shoes. Since the advertisement offered a generous reward, the hobo at once seized the dog and began to make his way to the address given in the ad.

When he finally reached his destination he rang the bell. A butler answered, and the hobo said, "Here is the lost dog you advertised for."

To which the butler replied with indignation, "Not at all. When we said shaggy, we didn't mean *that* shaggy."

Did you laugh? It's possible you did, because the way I have written the joke here removed much of its shaggy-dog character. The punch line conceivably might be strong enough to support a short, snappily told joke and elicit a smile. It is the essence of this type of shaggy-dog story, however, that the joke is deliberately made long and that to it all kind of superfluous detail is added (in the case of 46, all the invented adventures of the hobo and the dog on the way to the destination) until the listener is convinced the punch line will have the jolt of an elephant gun. And then there is the pop of a cap pistol, and it is over.

Here is another example which I remember because when it was told, many in the audience laughed while I felt outraged. (Why do I include jokes that outraged me? Because I am not the final authority and *you* may find it funny. And further, because a joke that isn't funny may be every bit as instructive to the would-be jokester as one that is.) Anyway, here it is, in condensed form:

✤ 47

A traveler checked in at a hotel that advertised itself widely as offering everything a client might desire. The traveler at once called room service.

"I want to have brought to my room," he said, "a young virgin between the ages of eighteen and nineteen, who must have blond hair and blue eyes. I also want sent up four pieces of strong rope, each exactly four feet in length, and a cat-o'-nine-tails. Finally, I want a Hungarian coachman, thirty years of age, with a dark complexion. And hurry, because I'm tired and need to unwind."

It was a full hour before room service called back and with a deeply apologetic tone said, "Sir, we have the rope and the cat-o'-nine-tails. It was more difficult to find the virgin you required, for in this area of the country, few girls reach the age of eighteen with virginity intact. We have one of the rare ones, however, and she is fairly blond. We are devastated to have to report, though, that we could find no Hungarian coachman of the kind you requested. We do have a Rumanian coachman. Would he do?"

"I am afraid not," said the traveler sadly. "So in that case, just send up a piece of Danish pastry and some hot tea."

I must judge only by my own reaction, of course, but I find that anticlimax too outrageous to support any joke less condensed than the one I gave here, and the versions I have heard were stretched out abominably.

An even more unbearable example, which I can't bear to tell formally in even a shortened version involves a person who wakes up one morning and finds that there seems to be the head of a screw in his navel. He attempts to remove it, fails, and wanders from hospital to priest to mystic, always failing to get it removed. Finally he finds himself on a Himalayan mountain peak where a Hindu wise man advises him to go through some rigmarole as the first rays of the morning sun strike the navel. He does so, the screw slowly twists and emerges, and "as it came out, his ass fell off."

I once sat through fifteen minutes of tedium waiting for that punch line.

Naturally, no classification is perfect. When does an anticlimax produce legitimate laughter and when a groan of outrage? The boundary is at different places for different audiences, and even at different places for the same audience at different times.

Still, you can bet I will make no attempt to include a section of jokes so bad that they can only outrage right-thinking individuals (in my opinion). In fact, I am through with shaggy-dog stories of this type right now.

However, the name has been applied to another kind of joke that is much more tolerable, at least to me.

Perhaps because the original shaggy-dog story involved an animal, the term came to be used for animal stories generally that were by no means long and tedious and that *were* funny. They had to be a special kind of animal story, however, one that involved an impossibility (usually the attribution of human intelligence to an animal). From that, the classification spread over to a joke that involved an impossibility even in the absence of animals. In short, the shaggy-dog story became roughly equivalent to what we might consider humorous fantasy.

Often, the anticlimax of such a fantasy consists of the calm acceptance of the impossibility, with attention called, instead, to a minor aspect of the situation. Thus —

✲ 48

A man entered a tavern which he found empty except for the bartender, who was playing chess with a dog. The dog, watching the board intently, made his moves by grasping the particular chessman in his teeth. He wagged his tail wildly when he made a good move and, on occasion, would bark sharply to indicate "Check!"

The customer, finally recovering from his stupefaction, gasped out, "Hey, that's a smart dog you've got there."

And the bartender answered, "Not so smart! I've beat him three times out of five so far."

As it happens, many shaggy-dog stories have bars as their background. If you have noticed this, do not jump to the hasty conclusion that this is essential. It isn't. Shaggy-dog stories can take place outside the bar; they can involve animals other than dogs; they can involve no animals at all. What they do need is fantasy, and perhaps it is because the genial camaraderie of a bar and its general alcoholic haze makes the fantastic a little less fantastic that so many shaggy dogs find a happy home there.

❋ 49

Jones, seated in a movie house, could not help being aware that the man immediately in front of him had his arm around the neck of a large dog which occupied the seat next to him.

The dog was clearly observing the picture with understanding, for he snarled softly when the villain spoke, yelped joyously at the funny remarks, and so on.

Jones leaned forward and tapped the man in front of him on the shoulder. He said, "Pardon me, sir, but I can't get over your dog's behavior."

The man turned around and said, "Frankly, it surprises me, too. He hated the book."

❋ 50

Jones watched in astonishment as the man standing next to him at the bar ordered a dry martini, poured its contents into the sink, then nibbled away at the bowl of the glass. He did not stop till only the stem was left. He placed that carefully before him and ordered another dry martini.

This continued until five stems were standing before him and then the man left.

The bartender, noting Jones' astonishment, said with a smile, "You seem surprised, sir."

"I'll say I am," said Jones. "The darn fool left the best part."

❋ 51

Jones was in the barroom one evening when the gentleman at his left put down his empty glass, walked over to the wall, and without the slightest sign of discomfiture, walked up its surface and onto the ceiling. He crossed the ceiling, upside down, till he reached the wall in which the door was located. He walked down the wall to the top of the door, somersaulted to the floor, landed on his feet, and left.

Jones, recovering with an effort, said to the bartender, "That's certainly an odd way of leaving."

The bartender shrugged. "You get used to it. He always leaves without saying good-bye."

✳ 52

The man at the bar had been following a steady pattern. He would order a dry martini, pour a little of the contents into his upper left vest pocket, and then drink the rest.

He did this for five martinis in a row and then, a little the worse for his alcoholic elevation, he issued the classic challenge, "I can lick any bum in this place."

Whereupon from his upper left vest pocket there emerged a little mouse, who cried out in a shrill treble, "And that goes for any rotten cat in the place, too."

When is the element of fantasy strong enough to classify a joke as shaggy-dog? Who knows? All classifications are man-made and it doesn't matter what a joke is really. There is no such thing as "really" in such a matter. I choose to consider the next joke a shaggy dog, and who is to say me nay?

✳ 53

Jones, preparing for a safari into deepest Africa, was going over the list of supplies he had ordered, and his friend Smith, who was present, clucked disapprovingly over it.

"No good," he said. "You've left out the most vital item."

"What's that?" demanded Jones.

"Vermouth. You've got to have vermouth in case you get lost."

"What good would vermouth do in that case?"

Smith shook his head at the other's ignorance. He said, "Listen, suppose you're a thousand miles from any outpost of civilization. Your bearers have all deserted and you're alone, surrounded by trackless jungle. So you sit down and start making a dry martini for yourself while you collect your wits — and that's where the vermouth comes in. It saves you. You just add a good shot of vermouth and from all over the jungle people will spring out at you shouting, 'That's no way to make a dry martini.' And you're rescued."

I must confess to one bad habit that has set up barriers on my road to jokesterism. I don't drink!

This is not because of any superior morality on my part. It is simply because I have no capacity for the stuff. One cocktail (only one, and I know because on occasions I try) is enough to make me distinctly high and to cause me to break out in funny-looking blotches accompanied by shortness of breath and a feeling of sharp internal discomfort.

This means I must run a larger than normal risk in telling jokes with a bar atmosphere, and there are vast numbers of these. Oh, I pick up the necessary knowledge intellectually. For instance, I gather that to connoisseurs the contribution made to a dry martini by the vermouth is minimal and that to add more than a minimal amount is a felony.

Still there is a distinct disadvantage in not having that knowledge ingrained as second nature. No amount of purely intellectual understanding can make me tell Joke 53 with real comfort. Nor can I get across the proper feel for the matter of mixing a dry martini, no matter what I do. I strongly suspect that a successful social drinker, telling this joke with perhaps less flair than I might, would nevertheless get a bigger laugh.

By this, I do not mean that you must have a thorough knowledge of whatever subject a joke deals with. Not at all. I merely say that having a thorough knowledge, all else being equal, will allow you to squeeze the greatest possible potential out of a joke; and that in telling a long and complex joke, it might pay you to learn something about the subject under discussion. The jokester's art, like any other, is surely worth some investment of time and effort.

And ignorance can be dense enough to ruin everything. I have heard people tell jokes in which their lack of understanding concerning the subject of the joke was so embarrassingly obvious that the funniest punch line in the world couldn't have raised more than a snicker.

The element of fantasy that is the hallmark of the shaggy dog raises the possibility of socially acceptable jokes about madmen.

There was a time, you see, and not so very long ago either, when madmen were considered objects of legitimate fun; when they were treated with the utmost cruelty; when they were penned up in madhouses that were really zoos — except that no real zoo would be so inhumane. Crowds of the "sane" would arrive at the madhouses as sightseers and would be hugely entertained by the howling antics of the inmates.

Under such circumstances, jokes at the expense of the mad would be legion, but those circumstances are gone. Nowadays, the mentally ill are no more a subject for fun and humor, in themselves, than cancer patients would be, and the jokester, if he is a humane person, must keep that in mind.

Does that mean that jokes about madmen are ruled out of court altogether? Not at all! One must merely be careful in aiming the fun. A proper target is the oddly distorted logic of a man who is irrational, and if that target is struck without mistreating the man himself, then the joke remains admissible and becomes really nothing more than the type of illogic at which such old-time radio comediennes as Gracie Allen and Jane Ace were so expert.

And if the illogic has a sufficiently mad quality about it, sufficient fantasy enters to make it shaggy-dog in my opinion. For instance —

❋ 54

The governor was inspecting the new state-supported psychiatric hospital and on being taken through the isolation wards was struck by the fact that in one cell there was sitting a man of distinguished appearance who was reading a copy of the *Wall Street Journal* and who was wearing nothing but a glossy silk top hat.

The inmate looked up, and saw the governor and his surrounding cluster of doctors and other functionaries.

The inmate thereupon rose, bowed politely, and said in cultured tones, "Sir, I perceive you are a man of importance and it strikes me that you must be curious as to why I sit here in the nude."

"Well, yes," said the governor cautiously. "The thought had indeed struck me."

"It is not at all mysterious," said the inmate. "The cell is air-conditioned as you will note and is maintained at most comfortable temperature, and I am, moreover, quite private. Since clothing is not necessary either for warmth, modesty, or adornment, why bother with it at all?"

"True," muttered the governor, rather taken aback at the other's obvious rationality. "But tell me," he said, "in that case, why the top hat?"

The inmate shrugged. "Oh, well, someone *might* come."

❋ 55

Mr. Jones badly needed to know the time, but his wristwatch, alas, turned out to have stopped hours before. The streets were deserted and the only living soul in sight was a man sunning himself in a deck chair on the large, fenced-off lawn of the local mental hospital.

A little dubious, but observing that the man really looked quite harmless and reflecting that in any case he had no choice, Mr. Jones called out, "Sir, do you by any chance have the time?"

"The time? One moment." The man on the lawn was galvanized into action. Leaping out of his deck chair, he withdrew a small stick from one pocket and a small hammer from another. He tapped the stick into the ground, adjusted it carefully until he was satisfied it was vertical, then whipped out a measuring tape. He measured the length of the stick above the ground and the length of its shadow. Throwing himself prone on the ground, he sighted the top of the stick against some point on the building, made a mark on the ground, and then made a few new measurements.

Out from his back pocket came a slide rule. Back and forth he manipulated it and finally, perspiring slightly, he said, "It is exactly 3:22.5 P.M., provided this is June 30, as I think it is."

Mr. Jones, who had watched all this with astonishment, could not help but be convinced, and adjusted his watch carefully. He then said, "This has been a most impressive use of the solar position to tell time, but what do you do at night, or on a cloudy day, when there are no shadows to measure?"

"Oh, then," said the inmate, holding up his left arm, "I just look at my wristwatch."

This is another example of a joke told in almost painfully correct written English. There is a purpose to it, since by the precision of the prose I help keep the reader from anticipating the enormous imprecision of the final bit of illogic.

I might as well warn you, though, of something that you may well know for yourself — that there is a distinctly noticeable difference between good written English and good spoken English. If Joke 55 were memorized and told word for word as I have given it here, the phrasing would sound unnatural to the ear and the laugh would be weakened. Remember, good spoken English is far less tolerant of long sentences and complicated subordinate clauses than good written English is, and far more tolerant of incomplete sentences and grammatical imprecision. Where written English must depend on careful punctuation, spoken English must depend on intonation, facial expression, and even gesticulation.

In telling a joke, then, never feel bound by the devices I must use in writing one, but make full use of the greater freedom and versatility of speech, and enjoy it.

❦ 56

A stranger came into a bar in which there were only the bartender, a dog, and a cat.

As the stranger ordered his drink, the dog rose, yawned, and said, "Well, so long, Joe," then walked out.

The stranger's jaw dropped. He said to the bartender, "Did you hear that? The dog talked."

"Don't be a jackass," said the bartender. "A dog can't talk."

"But I *heard* him."

"You just *think* you heard him. I tell you dogs can't talk. It's just that wise-guy cat over there. He's a ventriloquist."

❦ 57

An earthworm, curving past a stalk of grass, came upon another earthworm of surpassing beauty and fell in love at once.

"Marry me," he cried passionately, "and make me happy."

Whereupon the object of his affection said querulously, "Oh, shut up, you old fool. I'm your other end."

Sometimes particular types of jokes come in clusters. A fad starts and millions of people labor to construct humor according to a set formula. The percentage of good material that arises in this fashion is distressingly low, for spontaneity is lacking and the limitations of the formula quickly require people to scrape the barrel.

One fad which ran rampant in the early nineteen-sixties was the so-called elephant joke. This was a type of shaggy-dog microjoke, in which ridiculous questions were asked concerning elephants, with answers which had to be even more ridiculous. For instance:

❦ 58

Question: Why does an elephant wear green sneakers?
Answer: Because his yellow ones are at the cleaners.

✳ 59

Question: What is large, gray, and buzzes?
Answer: An electric elephant.

Transform the latter question to "What is yellow, grows on trees, and buzzes?" and the answer becomes "An electric banana."

The humor is primitive, for it does not truly involve a sharp alteration of point of view from rational to irrational, for instance, but instead the much spongier alteration involved in going from the somewhat less irrational to the somewhat more irrational. It is not surprising, then, that elephant jokes are favorites of youngsters and of unsophisticated adults.

But before I get entirely too lofty in my superiority, I want to say that I did hear an elephant joke some years ago that met all reasonable qualifications for sophisticated humor, for it went from the irrational to something that seemed more irrational but carried a quick overtone of chill rationality.

The moral is that one must be tolerant even of those who approach you and say, "Hey, have you heard the latest elephant joke?"

Don't say hastily, "I don't want to hear it." If you want to be a jokester, *listen!* It is almost sure to be painful; it will almost certainly be difficult to force the necessary polite smile; but on the other hand, there is that small chance that you may hear something worthwhile, and it is the jokester's trade to play for that small chance.

The elephant joke I'm thinking of came in late 1963, after the United States had gone through the nightmare of President Kennedy's assassination, followed by the incredible events in Dallas where the alleged assassin, Lee Harvey Oswald, was shot down by Jack Ruby, who had calmly brought a gun with him into the jailhouse under the eyes of half the Dallas police force. The following made the rounds and the laughs were bitter indeed:

✻ 60

Question: What did the Dallas chief of police say when the elephant walked into the police station?
Answer: Nothing! He didn't notice.

✻ 61

Robinson was an inveterate gambler, and time and again, he labored to make his fortune at Las Vegas. Many were the systems he had tried, from complicated mathematical formulas to pure guesswork — but nothing had worked.

One evening, as he was in the process of once again parting with his bankroll, he was holding his last chip irresolutely when a small voice in his ear said, "Put it on twenty-seven."

Robinson started and looked about. There was no one near him. The small voice said, "Put it on twenty-seven."

So he did and twenty-seven won.

The small voice said, "Put it all on twelve."

He did and twelve won.

The small voice said, "Put it all on fifteen."

He did and fifteen won. By now the pile before him had grown large, and other players had stopped and begun to watch. Robinson allowed a confident smile to cross his face. The small voice said, "Put it all on five." Without hesitation he did and five won.

Now he had a fortune before him and the small voice said, "One last time. Put it all on seventeen."

He did and the wheel spun. Round and round, and the little ball hovered, hovered, hovered, began to drop into seventeen, and in a final twist, hopped out again.

And the little voice said, "Oh, heck!"

I just want to point out, in case you haven't noticed it, that Joke 61 combines both classes of shaggy dog: fantasy and way-down anticlimax.

❊ 62

Two mice met in the early nineteen-sixties, when manned flights in orbit were as yet in the planning stage. After the usual exchange of pleasantries, one said, "But you look worn out, Michael. What's the matter?"

Michael shrugged his little shoulders and said, "Life isn't easy for us scientists, you know. I'm in space research, and those experimental flights in rockets, with the weightlessness and the acceleration and the uncertainty of safe return — Well, it's hard on one's nerves."

"In that case," said his friend, "why don't you quit and take a job in some other line of work?"

"That's easy to say," said Michael, "but stop and think — Is a job in cancer research any better?"

❊ 63

A man walked into a bakery and said, "I want a birthday cake baked for me in the shape of the letter S."

The baker nodded. "I'll have it ready for you by two this afternoon. But it will cost money."

"Money is no object," said the customer.

At two o'clock the customer was back. The cake was proudly presented in all its serpentine glory, and the man flew into a passion. "Not an ordinary capital S, you idiot," he shouted. "I want a beautiful flowing S in script."

The baker said, "But you didn't say so. If you can come back at eight in the evening, I'll have it for you."

The customer was back at eight. Another cake was presented. He looked at it critically and said, "I don't like the frosting. Could you make it with a pinker cast? I'll pay for the extra trouble."

"I can fix that in no time, if you'll wait," said the baker. By eight-thirty he was back, and the cake was perfect. With a sigh of relief, the baker pulled a box down and prepared to package the cake.

"Hold it," said the customer. "I'm eating it here."

A jokester's accent must be on telling a joke well. Still, even with the best will in the world, success depends on a certain minimal cooperation from the audience. There are certain literal-minded people who have trouble grasping whimsy. (In whimsy, there are deliberate, logical gaps, and even people with senses of humor sometimes fail to negotiate those gaps.)

I once told Joke 63 and had someone say to me argumentatively, "But if he was going to eat it there, what did it matter how it was shaped?"

There is in such a case no point in explaining, because for that particular listener the joke is lost forever. An attempt to explain will merely create hard feelings on both sides, so I simply shrugged and said, "He was eccentric," and let someone else tell the next joke so that I had time to recover.

❊ 64

Jones, sitting over a few drinks at the club with Anderson, said thoughtfully, "I bought a parakeet some time ago, but it was a bad investment. It doesn't say a word, and I expected it to talk."

"It should," said Anderson forcefully. "I have several that talk. What have you bought for it?"

"A cage. What else?"

"Plenty else. A parakeet isn't a canary. It has to be kept occupied. You have to buy it a little ladder on which it can hop up and down. It needs a little swing to swing on, little cakes of candied seeds to peck on, and a little mirror for company. *Then* it will talk."

Jones thought, nodded, and said, "I didn't know. Thanks for the information."

Two weeks later, they met at the club again and Jones said savagely, "You and your advice! I bought a ladder, a swing, a cake of candied seeds, and a mirror, and that parakeet never talked. In fact, this morning I found it dead at the bottom of the cage and my entire investment is lost."

Anderson was astonished. "I can't understand it. You mean it never said a single word?"

Jones said thoughtfully, "Well, come to think of it, it *might* have said something. Just before I found it dead, I heard a small voice say, 'Who moved the ladder?' "

※ 65

Two sparrows had agreed to meet at a particular tree in Central Park in order to visit the bridle path and enjoy themselves.

One of them, whose regular beat was far uptown in Washington Heights, flew down at the appointed time and landed in the appointed tree in plenty of time. He settled down to twitter and wait for his friend, who generally patrolled the area far downtown in the Battery. It was a beautiful late spring day, with all nature in bloom.

But first the minutes and then the hours passed and the other sparrow didn't show up. Could a cat have gotten him? Could a horse have stepped on him? Our friend grew more and more distraught, but just as the sun was sinking toward its rest, the downtown sparrow appeared.

The uptown sparrow hastened to him with a whirr of wings. "Good Lord," he said pettishly, "where were you? I've been worried sick."

And the one from the Battery said with a gay chirrup, "Sorry I'm late. But you know, it's such a beautiful day that I thought, what the heck, why not walk?"

Every once in a while someone begins to tell a joke which you recognize after the first paragraph. If you are one of a group listening to the joke, you must not say anything. It is the height of ill manners to interfere with the possible enjoyment of those in the group who may not have heard the joke. It is even rather gauche to nod your head wisely (or wearily) and ostentatiously detach your attention, as though to demonstrate the superiority of *your* sophistication and the excellence of *your* repertoire. After all, you may be telling a joke next and you wouldn't want someone to do it to you. (Question: Have I myself ever fallen prey to this kind of petty behavior when listening to a familiar joke? Answer: Yes, indeed. There is probably no form of pettiness of which I am not guilty at one time or another; but don't do as I do, do as I say.)

Even if the joke is being told privately and you alone make up the audience, try not to stop the jokester even if you recognize the joke, especially if he's good. In the first place, he may use an angle you haven't thought of or introduce a little jiggle that strikes your funny bone and which you can adopt the next time *you* tell the story. And sometimes, the joke you recognize suddenly deviates from the form you know in the last paragraph and becomes a joke you haven't heard before after all. Not often, I admit — but you can never tell.

Anyway, the two-sparrows joke (65) can continue word for word as given until the downtown sparrow arrives, and then it goes on as follows:

✿ 66

. . . the downtown sparrow appeared, woozy and shaken, with every feather awry.

The uptown sparrow hastened to him with a whirr of wings. "Good Lord," he said in concern, "what's happened to you? You look awful."

"Well," said the downtown sparrow, "I was flying up here minding my own business when I noticed a crowd at the downtown end of the park. Just out of curiosity, I flew down to see what it was all about, and suddenly I found myself involved in the darndest badminton game."

Dividing jokes into categories has its peculiar difficulties. For instance, later in the book I will have a section on Jewish Jokes. Yet I have one right now which is a perfect Jewish joke. The only trouble is that it is also a perfect shaggy dog, and I have to decide in which category to put it. Believe me, you go through the complete bit, walking up and down, chewing the lower lip, and so on.

But finally, I thought that I had more Jewish jokes than shaggy dogs; so I not only put it in the shaggy-dog category but I put it last as climax of the section.

❉ 67

Moskowitz had bought a parrot and one morning found the bird at the eastern side of the cage, with a small prayer shawl over its head, rocking to and fro, and mumbling. Bending low to listen, Moskowitz was thunderstruck to discover the parrot was intoning prayers in the finest Hebrew.

"You're Jewish?" asked Moskowitz.

"Not only Jewish," said the parrot, "but Orthodox. So will you take me to the synagog on Rosh Hashonah?"

Rosh Hashonah, the Jewish New Year, was indeed only two days off, and it would as always usher in the high-holiday season which would end with Yom Kippur, the Day of Atonement, ten days later.

Moskowitz said, "Of course, I'll take you, but can I tell my friends about you? It isn't a secret, I hope?"

"No secret at all. Tell anyone you want to." And the parrot returned to his praying.

Moskowitz went to all his friends, full of the story of his Jewish parrot. Of course no one believed him, and in no time at all Moskowitz was taking bets. By Rosh Hashonah, he had a hundred dollars, all told, riding on the parrot.

Grinning, Moskowitz brought the parrot to the synagog in its cage. He put him in a prominent place and everyone turned to watch even as they mumbled their prayers. Even the rabbi watched, for he had seven dollars that said the parrot could not pray.

Moskowitz waited. Everyone waited. And the parrot did nothing. Moskowitz carefully arranged the prayer shawl over the bird's head, but the parrot ducked and the shawl fell off.

After the services, Moskowitz's friends, with much mockery, collected their money. Even the rabbi snickered as he took his profit of seven dollars.

Utterly humiliated, Moskowitz returned home, turned viciously on the parrot and said, "Prepare to die, you little monster, for I'm going to wring your neck. If you can pray, now's the time."

Whereupon the parrot's voice rang out clearly: "Hold it, you dumb jerk. In ten days it's Yom Kippur, when all Jews will sing the tragic, haunting Kol Nidre. Well, bet everybody that I can sing the Kol Nidre."

"Why? You didn't do anything today."

"Exactly! So for Yom Kippur, just think of the odds you'll get!"

PART III *Paradox*

SOMETIMES THE ALTERATION in point of view is a flicker, rather than a curve or angle. That is, there is a moment when the punch line seems to make sense and then suddenly does not. If it makes sense, there is no alteration in point of view and no joke, but if it doesn't . . .

It is the quick flip from sense to no-sense that is itself the change in point of view and that brings the laugh (all the stronger for the feeling of self-admiration at catching the shift). The greater the subtlety of the sense/no-sense shift and the greater the ease with which it is caught, the better the laugh.

My personal taste runs strongly in favor of this Paradox joke (a more straightforward title would be Double-Meaning, but that has taken on the special significance of clean/dirty). However, I must admit that while its returns are great when the point is caught, the risks are great, too. The listener must cooperate to a greater extent than usual because more is demanded of him. He must make that shift and every once in a while even a quick-witted person may miss.

On rare occasions, if you wait a moment or two, the listener will finally negotiate that shift and there will then be a delayed laugh — though never as unforced and delighted as an instant laugh would have been. The delay, you see, always embarrasses the listener, and the greater his usual ability to see the point, the greater his embarrassment when he doesn't, so that it is precisely the person you value as a good audience who will fade off most quickly when he misses. (I have missed many a point in my time and can testify to the discomfort of the embarrassment.)

If the delay continues for more than perhaps ten seconds, there is no laugh at all, for by that time the listener, even if he finally makes the shift, is sufficiently embarrassed to find refuge in annoyance with you for having tried something too subtle on him (except that he is likely to think of it as too stupid), and laugh is one thing he won't do. For heaven's sake, don't try to explain. Shift the conversation to the weather.

Here, for instance, is a joke I almost never get a laugh out of, and I tell it only for the glum misery of convincing myself that people are hopeless:

❄ 68

Jones was having difficulty with the telephone. "Ottiwell," he was saying. "I want to speak to Reginald Ottiwell."

And the operator said predictably, "Would you spell the last name?"

Jones sighed and began, "*O* as in Oscar; *T* as in Thomas; *T* as in Thomas again; *I* as in Ida; *W* as in Wallace —"

Whereupon the operator interrupted, "*W* as in what?"

In my younger and stronger days, when this was greeted with dead silence, I would say with some heat, "Don't you see? What's the difference what the *W* stands for as long as she heard the *W*? If she heard the *W* . . ."

But by that time I have to fade out under the stony glances of hostile individuals, and it would have been better to have faded out to begin with.

A much more straightforward paradox, and one which is much more likely to get a laugh, is:

❄ 69

On the commuter train, Robinson looked up from his newspaper and couldn't help but be surprised at the actions of the man across the aisle. The man was dipping his fingers into his hat, then waving them in this direction and that. To all appearances, however, the hat was empty and the man was accomplishing nothing.

Finally, Robinson said, "Pardon me, but what are you doing, sir?"

The man, thus accosted, smiled and replied courteously, "I have a supply of antitiger dust here. By scattering it over the train I am keeping tigers away."

Robinson was astonished. "But," he protested, "there are no tigers within thousands of miles from here."

And the other said, "See how effective my dust is?"

❊ 70

Cordell Hull, the American secretary of state from 1933 to 1944, was reputed to be an extremely cautious man, ungiven to advancing an inch past the evidence, as perhaps befits a secretary of state.

Once, on a train trip, Hull and a companion watched while the locomotive dragged its load of cars slowly past a large flock of sheep.

Making conversation, Hull's companion said, "Those sheep have been recently sheared."

Hull stared thoughtfully at the animals, then said, "Appears so. At least on the side facing us."

Can you get rid of Cordell Hull in 70? After all, isn't the joke funny as it stands no matter who says the final punch line? In a way, yes, but Hull helps immeasurably. Suppose you began Joke 70 by saying, "Two fellows were on a train ride once, and one of them was a very cautious guy who never took anything for granted . . ." In that case, I'm sure the laugh would be much more subdued. The kind of caution the joke requires is not the sort of universal trait with which a listener can quickly identify.

By attributing the story to Cordell Hull, you allow the audience to picture the very epitome of a careful government functionary, a man who for many years had to deal with difficult diplomatic problems. They will know the kind of personality Hull had, either from memory or from having read about it, or just from a general estimate of the kind of caution required of

an American secretary of state these days. This in itself puts
the audience into the mood of the tale and heightens the delight at the final extension of caution into no-sense.

A story like that can be told with equal effect at the expense
of anyone roughly equivalent to Hull. At the expense, for instance, of Vermont-born Calvin Coolidge, thirtieth President of
the United States and a model of Yankee caution and tacitur-
nity —

❊ 71

At a government function in the nineteen-twenties, a young lady
took the privilege of her sex and, approaching President Coolidge,
said gushingly, "Oh, Mr. President, I have made a wager with a
friend of mine that I could persuade you to say more than two words
to me. Could you?"

And Coolidge, without expression, said, "You lose!"

And did Hull and Coolidge really say these things? I don't
know. The humorous anecdotes that fill history (and of which
I have included a number in this book) may all be inventions.

I rather suspect they must be, at least to some extent, for who
would spoil a funny story by inquiring too closely into its factu-
ality? Or who would refrain from polishing and improving it
for fear it would then become less authentic?

In fact, I have myself reached that pitch of minor fame
where anecdotes are told about me, believe it or not, and I can
judge the matter from a personal standpoint. One such anecdote was published in the daily Boston *Globe* a couple of years
ago, and its point rests on the fact that, as it happens, I publish
seven or eight books a year. It went roughly as follows (and I
quote from memory):

❊ 72

At a *Globe* cocktail party, Isaac Asimov said to one of the novelists
attending, "And when will you be publishing your next book, Miss
Coolidge?"

To which the novelist at once replied, "And when will you *not* be publishing your next book, Mr. Asimov?"

Funny? I don't know. I didn't laugh when I read it in the *Globe* because my immediate reaction was to mutter with some indignation, "I don't remember that!" (Perhaps I have blocked the incident out of my memory because of the chagrin I feel at having served as a straight man.*)

But then who cares whether an anecdote really happened or not? If the purpose is to give pleasure, to pass time gaily, to bring forth laughter — why worry too much about authenticity? I'm sure that many historical characters remembered chiefly for clever things they never really said would be the last to object if they could be made aware of what was happening.

❊ 73

A newcomer to a certain summer resort was surprised to find a group of men gathered on the lawn one evening shouting numbers at each other.

"Sixteen," one would yell, and all would laugh.

"One hundred and thirty-five," another would say, and all would laugh.

"Twenty-seven," a third would say, nearly choking with glee, and all would laugh.

"Two hundred and three," shouted someone, and this time everyone fell off his chair howling. The laughter continued till some turned blue in the face and had to be pounded to keep them from suffocating.

Numbers continued to be called thereafter, and laughter, now more subdued, also continued.

Finally the newcomer spoke to one of the men on the fringes and said, "Pardon me, but tell me what's going on."

---

* A "straight man" is one who delivers the "straight line," which carries the original point of view and makes it possible for someone else to deliver the punch line, with a sharply altered point of view. To the jokester, the role of straight man in real life is an embarrassing one, for it delivers the glory to another.

"Well," said the other, "this group meets every year at this resort, and night after night we swap stories. Naturally, we all know the stories, so we gave them numbers and save time by calling the numbers."

The newcomer nodded. "I see. But tell me this. When someone shouted, 'Two hundred and three,' everyone laughed particularly loudly. Why was that?"

His informant chuckled. "Oh! Well, you see, *that* one we had never heard before."

Here is another case (as in the tale of the two sparrows in Jokes 66 and 67) where there is an alternate ending with merit of its own.

✳ 74

The newcomer at the summer resort, listening to the men on the lawn shouting numbers and laughing, asked for an explanation. When he was told that the numbers all stood for well-known jokes, the newcomer said, "But I noticed that when one of the men shouted, 'Twenty-two,' nobody laughed. Why was that?"

"Oh," said his informant. "That was Lefkowitz. That fool can never get it through his head that he can't handle Swedish dialect."

When you have twin jokes like that, it doesn't pay to tell both. The second mines the same territory as the first and there is simply less laugh to be gotten. But then, which one do you tell? Sometimes you can judge by the audience, which may have identified itself by its response to previous jokes as particularly sophisticated or unsophisticated.

Keeping that in mind, you might further decide that Joke 74 is less subtle than 73. To see that giving the number of a joke does not require skill at dialect is easy. To see that giving the number of an unknown joke gives no information at all is perhaps not so easy. If you decide that, then tell 73 to the sophisticated audience, which will laugh harder at it than at 74, and tell the latter to the rather uncomplicated one which may not laugh at all at 73.

I must admit, though, that sometimes you can't be certain about the audience or about the relative qualities of the two sister jokes. In which case, what can I say? Follow instinct!

✻ 75

Nathan Rothschild, who lived in London in the early decades of the nineteenth century, was the most famous rich financier of his time. Once, getting out of a hackney cab, he included with the fee an exceedingly modest tip.

The driver touched his hat and said, "You know, Mr. Rothschild, your daughter Julie gives me a much larger tip than that."

And Nathan growled, "That's all right for her. *She's* got a rich father."

Sometimes a paradox only sounds like one, but on deeper thought turns out to lack a no-sense aspect altogether. Do you suppose that Nathan Rothschild didn't realize that he himself was the rich father? Of course he did. Was he just being paradoxical? Perhaps not. Perhaps he realized that *being* a rich father and *having* a rich father are two entirely different things in actual sober fact.

I am myself moderately well-off now, but that fact still has the virtue of novelty to me, and when my children want something which seems exorbitantly priced, I am apt to say gruffly, "Too much money."

And then they chorus, "Don't be cheap!"

"Cheap!" I will say, outraged. "Listen. When I was a kid, do you know how long it took me to save up even half a dollar to —"

And they say with distaste, "Oh, Daddy, that was *olden* times."

All that saves me from a serious case of choking is the memory that my own father made those same speeches to me when I was young and I reacted with the same impatience.

✻ 76

Mrs. Jones, deeply troubled, was consulting a psychiatrist.

"My husband," she said, "is convinced he's a chicken. He goes around squawking constantly and sleeps on a large bar of wood he has fixed up as a perch."

"I see," said the psychiatrist thoughtfully. "And how long has your husband been suffering from this fixation?"

"For nearly two years now."

The psychiatrist frowned slightly and said, "But why have you waited till now to seek help?"

Mrs. Jones blushed and said, "Oh, well — it was so nice having a steady supply of eggs."

✻ 77

Mr. Smith sat moodily over his drink, and his friend said, "You look pretty down in the mouth, Smith. What's the matter?"

Mr. Smith said, "My psychiatrist says I'm in love with my umbrella and that that's the source of my troubles."

"In love with your *umbrella!*"

"Yes. Isn't that ridiculous? Oh, I like and respect my umbrella and enjoy its company, but *love?*"

In many circles today, the profession of psychiatry has come to seem almost a secular priesthood. Psychiatrists seem to have answers that unlock the riddles of the personality, and the ability to control mystic forces by means that pass ordinary understanding. Such views are all wrong, of course, but they're there.

Any group that seems to have powerful secret knowledge is bound to gain respect, but there is always a strong element of fear in that respect, and where there is fear there is bound to be hatred. One might argue that it is one function of a joke to express hatred in a more or less harmless fashion. If, then, the psychiatrist figures in a more than fair share of today's sophisticated jokes (as in 76 and 77), this may well serve to evaporate some of the hostility he arouses and leave him in a stronger position to help humanity.

(I mention this as merely one example of how jokes can contribute to social sanity — just in case anyone is thinking at this moment that jokes are pure frivolity and that anyone compiling a jokebook is merely wasting his time.)

❋ 78

It is said that Groucho Marx, the comedian, was once bored by an overenthusiastic friend who was growing lyrical over the beauties of a piece of shore-front property. Finally, the friend stopped long enough to ask Groucho's opinion.

Groucho said, "Don't think much of it. Take away the ocean and what have you got?"

❋ 79

Said the sweet young lady, "Oh, I see how astronomers figure out the distance of the stars and their sizes and temperatures and all that. What really gets me is how they find out what their names are."

Notice that it is a sweet young lady who is making the naive remark in Joke 79. Very often, when something really naive must be uttered, it will prove funnier if you put it in a woman's mouth. I have done this in some earlier jokes in this book (you can find them easily enough if you look), and I will do it in some jokes later on.

This is done because people somehow assume that women, on the whole, are sillier than men, and will accept the naiveté with greater tolerance and less reluctance (hence with a bigger laugh) if it is blamed on the lady in the case.

In reality, of course, there is every bit as much silliness in the masculine makeup as in the feminine. If you feel that your personal observations have given you cause to doubt this, remember that in our own culture at least, women are actually encouraged to be silly and men are not. A silly woman is often characterized as cute and treated with fond affection, while a silly man is irritating or worse, and generally avoided.

Nor is silliness the worst characteristic of the feminine stereotype as it shows up in jokes. Both joke-telling and joke-listening are generally masculine activities and male chauvinism therefore has free play. Intellectually I disapprove of this, for I am a great believer in the equality of the sexes; but in a practical sense, I feel helpless. If I were to refuse to tell any jokes in which women were unfairly treated, I would scarcely be able to tell a single joke that involved women at all, and I simply cannot carry my idealism that far.

I'll have more to say on this subject later in the book.

✱ 80

An American scientist once visited the offices of the great Nobel-prize-winning physicist, Niels Bohr, in Copenhagen, and was amazed to find that over his desk was a horseshoe, securely nailed to the wall, with the open end up in the approved manner (so it would catch the good luck and not let it spill out).

The American said with a nervous laugh, "Surely you don't believe the horseshoe will bring you good luck, do you, Professor Bohr? After all, as a levelheaded scientist —"

Bohr chuckled. "I believe no such thing, my good friend. Not at all. I am scarcely likely to believe in such foolish nonsense. However, I am told that a horseshoe will bring you good luck whether you believe in it or not."

Scientists are as eagerly joked about as psychiatrists are, and for the same reason. The trouble is, though, that jokes involving real individuals are most successful when the person involved is known to the audience. In the case of scientists, this limits matters drastically.

To a general audience, even one that is highly educated in the humanities, Bohr must be defined — and yet he was one of the greatest physicists of all time and died no longer ago than 1962. But defining Bohr isn't that easy; if it isn't done carefully,

it will sound condescending, and even the suspicion of conde-
scension will cool the laugh drastically.

If you despair of getting the joke across by using Bohr, use
Einstein. Everyone has heard of Einstein and anything can be
attributed to him. Nevertheless, if you think you can get away
with using Bohr, then by all means do so, for all things being
equal, the joke will then sound more literate and more authentic. Unlike Einstein, Bohr hasn't been overused.

❊ 81

A large firm was once offered a chance at a pension plan with remarkable advantages, but there were conditions. Every employee
without exception had to join, and it had to be all done within the
month. There was great enthusiasm for this among the personnel,
and huge lines were formed to sign up. Within a week, everyone
had signed up except Joe Green in the shipping department.

He was adamant. "It's too complicated," he said, "and I don't
understand it."

Everyone in the plant argued with him: his fellow workers, the
union representative, his immediate superiors. He wouldn't budge.

The deadline was approaching, and Joe Green was ushered into
the plush office of the president of the firm. A copy of the pension
plan was on the desk; so was a pen filled with ink.

The president said, "Mr. Green, I have the approval of your union
in what I am about to say. We are now on the seventh floor. If you
do not sign this paper by the time I have counted ten, I will have you
thrown out the window."

Without waiting for the president to start counting, without a
word, without the slightest sign of displeasure — Joe immediately
placed his name on the paper. The president glanced at it, folded it
neatly, and said, "Now, why on earth couldn't you have signed the
pension plan before?"

And Joe said, "Because you're the first person who explained it
clearly."

It is just possible that there may be someone who, after a joke
like 81, may ask: "But why did everyone have to sign?" or

"Why was there the tight deadline?" or "Why didn't they fire the guy with union approval if they had union approval to throw him out the window?" (And did they have a court order granting them the right?)

This can be very frustrating, but the chance of people asking such questions afterward is small. The real danger is that they may be troubled inwardly by these things during the telling of a joke and in this way weaken or entirely destroy their ability to laugh.

It is important to remember that a joke doesn't always make sense even when it is not a fantasy and is supposed to be realistic. A joke is very often like a chess puzzle. In a chess puzzle you almost always have an arrangement of pieces which couldn't possibly have been arrived at in the course of a legitimate game. The only purposes of the arrangement in the chess puzzle are to obscure the necessary move that leads to checkmate and make sure that only one such move is possible.

In the same way, the situation in a joke may be far removed from reality out of an effort to make possible the necessarily quick alteration in point of view.

Usually experienced listeners understand this and cooperate in the necessary suspension of disbelief. It is your job, however, to keep the strain from being too great. Do that, however, lightly. In telling a joke, purportedly realistic but with a flimsy situation, make up for that by telling it earnestly, seriously, and rather briskly — skating over the thin ice. Don't ever try to shore up the flimsiness by elaborate explanations, however. Even if you improve its plausibility, you are likely to do so only at the cost of making a tedious shaggy dog out of it.

❋ 82

The university president sighed as he went over the proposed budget offered him by the head of the department of physics.

"Why is it," he said, mournfully, "that you physicists always require so much expensive equipment? Now the department of mathematics requires nothing of me but money for paper, pencils, and erasers." He thought a while longer and added, "And the department of philosophy is better still. It doesn't even ask for erasers."

I hate to say this, for I like to think of jokes as fun, but quite a good proportion of intelligent jokes can give rise to all kinds of provocative questions that will turn the evening into heavy weather indeed. For instance, the immediate laugh after Joke 82 may arise from the thought that philosophers never admit mistakes.

But think again, is there any system for detecting mistakes in philosophy? Can philosophers weigh the value of what they say? And do they want to?

It is only with certain audiences that there is a danger of so radical a conversion from lightheartedness to dense ratiocination, but unless you want it to happen, you had better be prepared to abort it — perhaps with another joke of less dangerous content.

❊ 83

Mr. Anderson had worked his way upward in business and although totally illiterate, had come to be worth a small fortune. Though he signed his checks with a pair of crosses, they were cashed without trouble.

And then one day, one of his checks bounced. He went to the bank, filled with ire, and demanded the reason.

The bank official protested, "But, Mr. Anderson, you have three crosses here, and your signature *always* consists of two crosses. Naturally, we assumed something was wrong."

Anderson reddened. "Oh, that," he said. "Well, that's my wife's fault. She said that since we were now getting up in the world, I ought to have a little class and adopt a middle name."

I imagine that it is easy to conclude that the paradoxical punch line is the property of the simple, the naive, the uneducated, the unsophisticated. Not so. The ability to come up with a bit of no-sense does not entirely neglect the mental aristocracy. If I may use myself as an example (and whatever my faults, my IQ stands at a respectable figure), I have committed some beauties, and the following is my favorite example, and word-for-word true.

❦ 84

My wife and I were once listening to Peter Ustinov on a television talk show. The interviewer remarked that Ustinov was one of the few Englishmen who could speak American convincingly.

At once Ustinov demonstrated by ceasing to talk with an English accent and speaking exactly as any carefully educated American might.

At this, I turned to my wife in utter and honest (I swear it) astonishment and said, "But if he can talk regular, why does he bother with an accent?"

And sometimes, perfectly intelligent men and women are trapped into paradox by their emotions, which for example will lure them into a double standard: a feeling that it is right to have one set of rules for one's self or one's group, and another for everyone else.

Here, for instance, are two true stories:

❦ 85

At a gathering at which I was present, a Jewish woman argued, with considerable feeling, that she could never feel real confidence in the good will of any Gentile, because as a group they had stood aside and allowed Nazi Germany to torture and kill Jews by the millions.

So I let a few minutes pass, then asked her quietly, "What are you doing about Negro civil rights?"

And she answered sharply, "Let's tend to our own problems before we take on those of other people."

✽ 86

A woman I know was once telling me of the many conquests of her son, a handsome fellow who had no trouble doing well with the girls.

"Of course," she said, "I can't say that I approve of the girls. They seem willing to get into bed with him on slight acquaintance. I can only conclude that they must be disgustingly promiscuous."

"But," I protested, "it seems to me that your son has as slight an acquaintance with the girls as they have with him. Isn't he equally promiscuous?"

At which she turned on me fiercely and said, "He's *entitled!*"

In neither case was I able to convince the woman concerned that she was inconsistent.

And I might say, in connection with Joke 86, that women have very little chance of obtaining equal status with men, sexually or in any other way, as long as so many women are themselves so fiercely intent on applying the double standard in favor of their sons and against their own sex.

✽ 87

The inveterate horseplayer paused before taking his place at the betting windows, and offered up a fervent prayer to his Maker.

"Blessed Lord," he murmured with mountain-moving sincerity, "I know You don't approve of my gambling, but just this once, Lord, just this *once*, please let me break even. I need the money so badly."

I don't have many gambling jokes in my repertoire because I don't move in gambling circles. In fact, I gambled for money only once in my life, just once. Here's the story, and absolutely true:

✽ 88

Shortly after I had married, my wife left town to visit her folks. I was at loose ends and I was lured into a poker game with the boys.

When it was all over, my conscience smote me, for I had been brought up by a puritanical father to eschew gambling in all its forms (and I had never rebelled). All I could do was confess.

On my next trip home, I said with all the casualness I could manage, "I played a game of poker with the boys, Papa. For money."

My father stared at me in astonishment and said, "How did you make out?"

I said, "I lost fifteen cents."

And he said, "Thank God. You might have *won* fifteen cents."

He was probably right. Winning first time out might have hooked me. As it was, I never played again.

✳ 89

Over a glass of tea, Moskowitz was sometimes prone to grow philosophical. He said to his companion, "Tell me, Finkelstein, if you were marooned on a desert island for a month, what would you consider the best thing to have with you?"

"A whole delicatessen," said Finkelstein promptly. "And you, Moskowitz?"

"Me?" said Moskowitz dreamily. "I would like to have Sophia Loren with me."

At which Finkelstein brought his fist down on the table with resounding anger, and said, "Stick to the terms of the question. You said the best thing, not the *very* best thing."

✳ 90

Moskowitz, having spent considerable time tramping the corridors of the museum, paused for a refreshing cigar.

He had not been smoking long when a museum guard approached him angrily and said, "Do you see that?" He was pointing to a sign on the wall which said in glaring red letters NO SMOKING.

Moskowitz regarded it for a moment, then said to the guard, "It doesn't say 'positively.'"

❋ 91

Mrs. Moskowitz and Mrs. Finkelstein met for the first time after a long separation, and inquiries as to status and health at once arose.

"Tell me, Mrs. Finkelstein," said Mrs. Moskowitz, "how is your sister Sadie?"

"Oh Sadie, poor Sadie," mourned Mrs. Finkelstein. "She has cancer."

Whereupon Mrs. Moskowitz said consolingly, "Listen. Cancer, shmancer — as long as you're healthy."

Some punch lines enter the language. For years I've heard ineffectual attempts at consolation countered with a "Yes, I know, cancer-shmancer—" And, of course, the punch line serves for any sardonic commiseration between friends along the lines of "Fired-shmired, as long as you have a job," "Bankrupt-shmankrupt, as long as you're making money," and so on. You can't do it very often, of course.

❋ 92

It was a rough ocean crossing and Mr. Jones was suffering the tortures of the damned. During one of the more unsettled periods, he was leaning over the rail, retching miserably, when a kindly steward patted him on the shoulder.

"I know, sir," said the steward, "that it seems awful. But remember, no man ever died of seasickness."

Mr. Jones lifted his green countenance to the steward's concerned face and said, "For heaven's sake, man, don't say that. It's only the wonderful hope of dying that's keeping me alive."

❋ 93

Two seedy individuals stopped on the street to watch a funeral procession pass. It was done in elaborate style, from the long, gleaming hearse, through the cars packed with flowers, to the impressive line of automobiles following.

Said one of the individuals, "It's a rich guy. I've watched funerals like that before. There's a solid mahogany casket, polished so you can see your face in it, with satin lining and gold carved handles. They put it in a big mausoleum, with stone doors, statues, flowers, praying and singing."

"Wow," said the other, eyes shining. "Now that's what I call living."

✳ 94

Mr. Anderson, a suspicious man at the best of times, deliberately came home from a business trip early and went through the house in a fury, throwing open closet doors while his distracted wife followed him about wringing her hands and crying.

At last in one of the bedrooms, an opened closet door revealed a young man wearing considerably less than the normal quantity of clothing.

"Aha," shouted Anderson. "And what are you doing here?"

The young man spread his hands. "Well, everybody's got to be *somewhere*, buddy."

Joke 94 is one of those which I suppose could well be described as a chestnut. This means it is considered an old joke that has long outlived its usefulness and could no longer be used to raise a laugh.

Why a chestnut?

Well, there is a tale that some centuries ago a certain English gentleman was wont to tell a captive audience in boring detail a long, unfunny story, which everyone in the audience had heard many times but at which he was still compelled to laugh. He was beginning the tale once again, to the suppressed groans of everyone within earshot, and opened it by saying, "At one time, under a certain old oak tree that had been planted in my great-grandfather's time —"

A guest promptly interrupted. "It was an old chestnut tree."

The old gentleman frowned. "No, an old oak tree."

Whereupon the guest said decisively, "I have heard your story a hundred times and it has always been an old chestnut."

But now that that's understood, the question arises: When is a joke an old chestnut? Answer: When you have heard it before.

And when is an old chestnut a funny joke? Answer: When you have not heard it before.

Any joke that someone has never heard before is a new joke to him, even though it might be as old as half a lifetime to someone else.

To a jokester, then, the rule is: Don't let the fact that a joke is old stop you. If you are dealing with a new audience, it may be that the joke is new to them. If the joke is old to all or most of them, they may — if they are in a genial mood — tolerate it, and even perhaps enjoy your method of telling it.

If you are listening to jokes as part of a group, it would be bad manners to interrupt any joke with a sneer to the effect that it is an old chestnut. Maybe it is to you, but perhaps not to the others.

And by the way, Joke 94, chestnut or not, has the advantage of raising an interesting mathematical point —

Imagine a circle three feet across, toward which you throw a sharp-tipped dart. The dart strikes inside the circle and the point at the very center of the dart tip strikes a particular point inside the circle. The question is: Which point?

There are an infinite number of points within the circle so that the chance of the dart point striking a particular point is one divided by infinity, or zero. The chance of the dart point striking *any* particular point chosen in advance is zero.

Yet the fact that a dart point, landing inside the circle, will strike *some* point is certain; that probability is one. In other words, when you add up a lot of zeroes, you get one. In ordinary affairs that seems ridiculous, but in dealing with infinite quantities, it makes sense, and that sort of thing can lead to deep mathematical discoveries.

The question of points and probability is not likely to attract the average nonmathematician when placed in this bald fashion. But faced with the incongruity of a man who thinks that because everyone must be somewhere, he himself might well be in another man's closet, one laughs. Yet that is precisely the same situation, and to understand the joke completely is to grasp the mathematical point as well — and vice versa.

Incidentally, the sneer that a joke is an old chestnut comes most easily from those who can't tell jokes. To a true jokester, the oldest of chestnuts is merely a challange to ring in a new variation on it that will wring out a new laugh.

For instance, what is the very epitome of the hoary joke that is long since dead of extreme old age? Here it is:

❋ 95

Jim said, "Who was that lady I saw you with last night?"
And Joe answered, "That was no lady; that was my wife."

Did you ever hear anyone laugh at this (a joke which may be classified Paradox, by the way)?

Of course not; but part of the reason for that, if you really want to know, is that the joke is funny only in English, and not in American. In England, a lady is a woman of good birth, whereas in America, a lady is any woman.

To get the English effect, substitute "beautiful woman" or "sweet young thing" for "lady" and try the punch line, and see if you don't get at least a smile out of someone who hasn't already had it pounded into him that he mustn't laugh at such a joke.

Another joke used as an archetype for all old chestnuts is the following:

❃ 96

> Question: Why did the chicken cross the road?
> Answer: To get to the other side.

The humor here lies in expecting a witty retort that will offer
a sharp alteration in point of view and getting a straightforward answer that does not. The absence of alteration is itself an
alteration from the expected and you should laugh — except
that everyone is carefully trained not to.

So it becomes a challenge to think up a variation, and here's
one that made *me* laugh — and heartily, too:

❃ 97

> Question: Why did the chicken cross the highway?
> Answer: To lay it on the line.

But it's time to change the subject —

❃ 98

King George II of Great Britain had a most capable wife, Caroline
of Anspach, but eighteenth-century monarchs had mistresses also, as
a matter of course.

Caroline was the brains of the family and George was just about
intelligent enough to know that. Even when, in 1737, Caroline was
on her deathbed, she tried, with her last breath, to advise George on
the best possible choices, from the standpoint of international politics, for his second wife.

But poor George, in tears over the imminent loss of his wife, kept
shaking his head. "No," he said, "Never. No more wives. From now
on, only mistresses."

❋ 99

Maurice Chevalier, the famous French singer, was asked how he felt about having reached the age of seventy.

"To tell you the truth," he said, "I am not pleased with having done so, but I prefer it to the alternative."

❋ 100

Young Sammy came prancing into the room and said, "Papa, may I have another apple?"

His father raised his eyes from his newspaper to glance sternly at the boy.

"Again an apple?" he demanded. "Listen, where do you think all those apples come from? You think they grow on trees?"

That last joke rings a little hollowly to a city dweller such as myself. When I was young the thought of apples growing on trees was strange indeed; I thought they grew in boxes at the fruit store. I was brought up in city slums, after all, and never recovered. My suspicion of green fields and country noises is still extreme, and the following is a true story:

❋ 101

Friends of ours, having moved into the suburbs, invited us to visit their new house. We went, and I was taken on a tour of the grounds.

The host was particularly anxious to show us the garden they had inherited and which they were improving. He reached down, wrenched loose a giant cucumber from its moorings, and handed it to me, saying, "Here. Try this!"

And I jumped backward in horror, saying, "From the *dirt?*"

I passed it off as a humorous remark when I had recovered, but strictly between ourselves, I think I was serious.

✤ 102

Mr. Jones, who was pushing sixty, and who was feeling generally under the weather, went to a doctor for a physical checkup. The doctor was not at all pleased with the results.

Leaning back in his chair, he said, "Mr. Jones, I will be frank with you. You are getting on, and if you want to live out your life in reasonable health, you're going to have to slow down. That you don't smoke or drink is good, but you will have to go further. How about giving up, say, half your sex life?"

Mr. Jones considered this, then nodded gravely. "All right, doctor, as you say! But which half do you suggest I give up — the thinking, or the talking?"

✤ 103

The doctor looked benignly at the woman who had come to him for an examination.

"Mrs. Brown," he said, "I have good news for you."

The woman said, ' I'm glad of that, doctor, but I'm *Miss* Brown."

"Miss Brown," said the doctor without changing expression, "I have bad news for you."

✤ 104

Mrs. Johnson had just met her old friend, Mrs. Green, and surveying her narrowly, said, "But, dear, whatever have you done to your hair? It looks exactly like a wig."

"To tell you the truth," said Mrs. Green with some embarrassment, "it is a wig."

"Really? Well, you certainly can't tell."

While I'm in the section on paradox, I might point out that the funny story all too easily can become the last bastion of free speech and criticism, the last weapon of the weak and peaceful against the strong and tyrannous.

It is my opinion that a tyrant, by his very profession, must lack the ability to understand a joke. (After all, to laugh at a joke is to be tolerant of, and even to enjoy, the unexpected and abnormal; and how can one do that and be a tyrant, too?) If a grim and unsmiling establishment is unaware of the shafts let fly by humor, it may well be stung without knowing it and therefore take no action in reprisal; it may be pilloried to others less blinkered, and the thoughts of its misdeeds will be kept alive.

In particular, oppressors might be expected to fail to make the shift from sense to no-sense (or sometimes vice versa) that the paradox requires.

✻ 105

An old man was sitting on a park bench enjoying the late spring sunshine when another old man sat down at the other end of the bench. They viewed each other cautiously and finally one of them heaved a tremendous, heartfelt sigh.

The other rose at once and said, "If you're going to talk politics, I'm leaving."

We in the United States don't have the task of finding subtle ways of expressing hostility in the guise of innocent humor. We can, as yet, make fun of the Establishment (if we wish to do so) openly. Not so in other places and other times.

Under the Nazi regime of Adolf Hitler, the lot of the humorist must have been difficult indeed. Without a true appreciation of the humorous (what humor could be expected in a man who would make use of his own name in an everyday phrase, Heil Hitler, in greeting and farewell, and then even use the greeting himself?), and with a paranoid sense of suspicion, anything that even sounded suspicious must have been mowed down.

Yet I did read of one daring humorist in the early days of the Nazi regime who had a small routine that went as follows:

* 106

He would goose-step on stage, bring his arm up with a snap in a perfect Naxi salute, saying, "Heil —" and then pausing. He would try again, giving the salute even more stiffly if possible, saying, "Heil —" and pausing once more.

He would then fall into a posture of relaxation, scratch his head, and say, "Now what *is* that fellow's name?"

You could not ask for anything that seemed more harmless than that, but it attacked Hitler at a particularly vulnerable point, since the unsmiling grotesqueness of his demand was to be treated with adoration. Undoubtedly, it was the laughing of the audience that gave the situation's absurdity away to the crude Nazi mind, and the humorist was stopped.

The politically inspired cartoon for centuries now has been using humor, in quite a modern sense, to get across a point with more sardonic effectiveness than many serious pages might.

* 107

During the days before World War II, a cartoon showed a rowboat, with figures representing Great Britain, France, and the United States at one end, and others representing Austria, Czechoslovakia, and Poland at the other. A jet of water labeled Nazi Aggression is shooting upward among the small nations, and Great Britain is saying, "That's a nasty leak! Lucky it's not at our end."

* 108

"In view of the present world situation," said the parlor philosopher, "the best thing that can happen to a man is not to be born at all in the first place. But I doubt that even one man in a hundred thousand is that lucky."

Sometimes a nonparadox becomes a paradox because words change their meaning while the phrases containing those words remain intact. For instance, how many times have you heard the phrase "The exception proves the rule" used to argue that a rule is all the stronger and more meaningful when you can point out times when it may be broken?

The phrase, however, uses the word "prove" in its older meaning of "test." You would come closer to the real meaning of the phrase by using a sister word and saying, "The exception probes (i.e., investigates the validity and finds it wanting) the rule."

To illustrate another example, let me first tell the following:

✻ 109

In the pages of Herodotus, we hear that the Athenian lawgiver, Solon, told a tale of two pious Greek youths whose mother prayed that they be granted the greatest gift the gods could bestow — and both youths promptly died, quietly and peacefully.

It is tales such as these that illustrate the common statement "The good die young." This is used almost invariably these days with the connotation that there is a kind of spiteful rule of the universe that punishes the deserving and rewards the undeserving.

Yet it seems obvious to me that the statement is no paradox at all, but has become one only through misunderstanding. To me, the statement arises out of hope and piety. The kindly gods do not allow their favorites to be tortured too long by life, but take them to their bosoms as soon as possible, while the evil live on and on in the purgatory that men make of this world.

✻ 110

Little Johnnie, aged five, was bending over a sheet of paper, guiding his pencil with most meticulous thoroughness.

His mother, smiling at him fondly, said, "What are you drawing, Johnnie?"

"A picture of God," said Johnnie, without looking up.

"But, Johnnie, nobody knows what God looks like," said his mother.

And Johnnie said, "They will, once I'm finished."

A jokester with a philosophic bent of mind might pause after the laugh this joke is very likely to get, to point out that there have been many grownups in the history of the world who, like Johnnie, have had their private vision of God and have insisted that this was what He was like in every detail, and who were perfectly willing to torture and kill all those who denied it might be so.

If you are tempted to do so, however, don't. It will be much more effective if the others see it for themselves. And they may — even long after the joke has been told and apparently forgotten. The good joke is insidious, and though its effect can be delayed, it becomes no weaker for that.

The mindlessness of secular fanaticism can be great too.

❊ 111

Anderson lived only for the day when the social system could be overturned by violence and remolded closer to his heart's desire.

"Come the revolution," he said fervently to his friend Johnson, "you won't have to live on bread and potatoes. You will eat strawberries and cream."

"Actually," said Johnson, "I don't like strawberries and cream."

"Come the revolution," said Anderson violently, "you will eat strawberries and cream and you will *like* it."

❊ 112

A couple of centuries ago, when illiteracy was more common than it now is, young Smith acted quickly when the job of sexton at the local church fell vacant. He was first in line with his application. The minister was sorry to refuse him, for he was a hardworking young man and a capable one — but the fact remained he could neither read nor write.

The minister explained that there were numerous occasions in church functions when illiteracy would prove a serious drawback, and Smith withdrew in embarrassment.

He found another job, worked hard, saved diligently, invested wisely, and by the time he reached middle age, was the richest and most respected man in all the region.

It invariably came as a shock to others to discover that solid, prosperous Smith could neither read nor write. One person said to him, "It is amazing, Mr. Smith, that you have come so far without being able to read and write. Can you imagine what you would be today if you could?"

"Certainly," said Smith dryly, "I would be a church sexton."

❧ 113

At an ecumenical conference for clergymen of various faiths, three of the delegates were relaxing one evening after the arduous duties of the day. To put not too fine a point on it, Father O'Connell, Reverend Wilson, and Rabbi Cohen were indulging in a friendly game of poker.

Unfortunately, in their excitement they grew a little noisy and the hotel detective, in a burst of overzealousness, entered the room, confiscated the chips and cards, and held them for arrest under the strict antigambling statutes of the town in which the conference was being held.

The magistrate before whom they appeared was acutely embarrassed.

"Gentlemen," he said, "I would rather this had not happened, but there seems to be evidence of a misdemeanor, and since you have been arrested, I cannot dismiss the case without some investigation. Nevertheless, in view of your profession, I feel I can trust you to tell the truth. I will ask for no evidence other than your bare words. If each of you can tell me that you were not gambling, that would be sufficient for me and I will release you. Father O'Connell —"

The worthy priest said at once, "Your Honor, surely it is important to be certain that we define what we mean by gambling. In a narrow, but entirely valid sense, what we describe as gambling is only truly so if there is a desire to win money, rather than merely to enjoy the suspense of the fall of cards. In addition we might confine gambling to situations where the loss of money would be harmful, as otherwise such loss might merely be viewed as a variable admission fee —"

"I understand," interrupted the magistrate. "I will take it, then, that you, Father O'Connell, were not gambling by your definition of the word. And you, Reverend Wilson?"

The good minister straightened his tie and said, "I entirely agree with my learned colleague, Your Honor. Further, I might point out that gambling is gambling only if there are stakes involved. Admittedly, there was money on the table, but it remains to be determined whether this money would eventually have found its way into the possession of an individual not its owner at the start of the game, or if, in fact, it was merely being used as a convenient marker that would indicate the progress and direction of successive —"

"Yes, yes," interrupted the magistrate again. "I will accept that as satisfactory indication that you were not gambling, Reverend Wilson. And now you, Rabbi Cohen. Were you gambling?"

The pious rabbi's eyebrows shot upward. "With whom, Your Honor?"

Joke 113 offers an excellent object lesson in how a jokester can make a joke his own even if he has not invented it. I heard this joke twice; once at a party where the jokester had the priest and the minister each tell a flat lie, both saying no when asked if they were gambling, but preceding it with a prayer under their breaths, asking for forgiveness because the lying was for the sake of the good name of the church. This I found offensive and, worse still, unimaginative.

I heard it a second time when Myron Cohen told it on television. In his version, the priest and the minister didn't lie. Instead they made incoherent sounds when asked the question and the magistrate chose to accept that as a protestation of innocence in each case. But then Myron Cohen, with his wonderfully expressive face, can get away with such a device.

I needed something else, so I added the scholastic reasoning with which priest and minister attempt to evade the flat truth.

Before the proper audience, this greatly increases the effect of the joke in my opinion. The priestly and ministerial reasoning is in itself amusing to the sophisticated audience. They will, moreover, automatically expect a bit of Talmudic jargon from the rabbi, so that the final "With whom?" involves an unexpectedly large and sudden shift in viewpoint evoking all the heartier laughter.

❋ 114

Frederick II, the eighteenth-century king of Prussia, fancied himself an enlightened monarch, and in some respects he was. On one occasion he is supposed to have interested himself in conditions in the Berlin prison and was escorted through it so that he might speak to the prisoners. One after the other, the prisoners fell to their knees before him, bewailing their lot and, predictably, protesting their utter innocence of all charges that had been brought against them.

Only one prisoner remained silent, and finally Frederick's curiosity was aroused.

"You," he called. "You there."

The prisoner looked up. "Yes, Your Majesty?"

"Why are you here?"

"Armed robbery, Your Majesty."

"And are you guilty?"

"Entirely guilty, Your Majesty. I richly deserve my punishment."

At this Frederick rapped his cane sharply on the ground and said, "Warden, release this guilty wretch at once. I will not have him here in jail where by example he will corrupt all the splendid innocent people who occupy it."

❋ 115

The man at the bar slammed his fist down hard and said, "There are two things I just can't stand, race prejudice and Negroes."

✲ 116

Bella was terribly upset. Her fiancé, Marvin, had been to a clinical psychologist, and the results had not been entirely consoling.

She said to her mother, "I'm not sure the marriage would be happy, Ma. The psychologist says Marvin tests out to have a pronounced Oedipus complex."

Her mother shrugged and said, "Don't listen to that fancy talk. I've watched Marvin and I tell you he's all right. Look how he loves his mother."

The day is approaching when I may become a grandfather. Some of my friends no older than myself are already grandfathers.

I don't relish the thought, however. On separate occasions, two women knowing me only slightly, asked after my grandchildren, assuming that I must have some. I reacted badly and have not forgiven either one. It is not surprising then that I find the following joke less funny each day.

✲ 117

Jones' oldest daughter had just given birth to a beautiful baby boy and Jones was being congratulated. He looked downcast, however, and a friend said, "What's the matter, Jones? Don't you like the idea of being a grandfather?"

Jones heaved an enormous sigh. "No," he said, "I don't. But that doesn't bother me so much. It's just that it's so humiliating to have to go to bed with a grandmother."

✲ 118

Mr. Schmidt, having come into a great deal of money, was in a position to pamper his whims, and he had a really giant one. All his life he had wanted to lead an orchestra in selections from Wagner. That he knew nothing about music didn't stop him. He hired a symphony orchestra, brought it into his home, got up in front of it, and led it tirelessly.

The musicians of the orchestra understood at once they must totally disregard what Schmidt was doing with his baton, but that was difficult in itself. Without proper guidance, they produced enough cacophony to tear at their ears dreadfully.

Finally, the cymbalist, unable to endure another moment of it, brought up his cymbals during a soft and delicate passage and, with one mighty swipe, delivered the loudest and most resonant cymbal clash the musical world had ever heard.

The entire orchestra came to a stop in the trembling of that resounding cymbal clap, and Mr. Schmidt himself felt his head vibrating as though it would never stop.

Finally, after long minutes, the last echoes of that volcanic vibration died away, and Mr. Schmidt, face contorted in fury, said, "All right, which one of you wise guys did that?"

Now it may be that I have somehow given the impression here and there in this book that I am a marvelous person with an unfailing intelligence and a preternatural wit. If so I must place on record my utter failure when I first heard this joke.

I looked puzzled and said, "Why is that funny?" (Politeness would have required me to laugh gently even if I didn't find it funny, but as a jokester I must understand these things.)

The gentleman who told the joke looked astonished. He said, "Can you imagine how ignorant of music someone must be to fail to realize that a cymbal clash can come only from the fellow holding the cymbals?"

Well, that's how ignorant I was.

Stuttering is not really a legitimate target for fun, any more than any physical handicap is. Yet, historically, it has been almost as sure-fire a subject for humor as insanity. I have made any number of good resolutions not to tell stuttering jokes, but I find myself occasionally impelled to tell this one, even though it is particularly cruel, simply because of the paradoxical unfitness of the punch line.

❋ 119

Robinson, who stuttered badly, said with impassioned earnestness, "I t-t-tell you, n-n-nations must ab-b-bandon all s-s-selfish cons-s-sideration and c-c-c-come togeth-gether in w-w-w-w —— in w-w-w-world union if cha-cha-chaos is to b-b-b-be prev-v-vented."

Williams, listening skeptically, said, "Sure, that's easy enough for you to say."

❋ 120

The chess game had begun, and White moved his king's pawn to K-4 in the standard opening. Black studied the board with painful concentration for fifteen minutes, then whispered in a tone of husky emotion, "*Got* you! Mate in fifty-four moves!"

Chess jokes such as 120 are usually lost causes for anyone who doesn't play chess, but I have to include it out of self-respect. After all, I play chess. To be sure (I think because some fairy godmother placed a curse on me when I was born) I always lose, but I play chess.

That reminds me of a chess story that doesn't involve the game itself and that happened to me.

❋ 121

Once while I was in the army, I read "The Royal Game," surely the best chess story ever written. It filled me with a wild desire to play chess and I began approaching various soldiers who seemed the chess type. No luck! To each one I came with a wistful "Would you like to play a game of chess?" and from each one came a cold "No."

Finally, I had the idea that I should have had to start with. I came to a soldier and said, "Would you like to read a terrific story?" and handed him "The Royal Game."

I waited. An hour passed. And then he came to me and said, "Would you like to play a game of chess?"

*

But what's the use? He beat me.

Still, I myself have earned a footnote in the history of chess, believe it or not. You see, I don't like the vague way chess games are almost invariably treated in fiction, even in "The Royal Game." So when I wrote my first novel, *Pebble in the Sky,* and had a chance to use a chess game as a means of developing the plot, I did it *right.* I found an actual chess game and used it. In the course of the conversation between the two chess players I actually described the game, move by move.

One of my readers, a chess enthusiast, reading the book late at night, came across the passage involving the chess game and was astonished to find that the moves looked legitimate. He got out of bed, went to his chessboard, and played the game. The next thing I knew, a copy of a chess journal reached me through the mails, and there on page three was a column headed "Asimov's Game," describing it and the circumstances under which it had been discovered. (Naturally, I wrote a letter at once disclaiming any personal credit.)

What amused me most was that the writer of the column had described the game as "rather interesting." I had needed, for purposes of the plot, a particular kind of chess game and I had carefully picked one that had won a first prize for brilliance. Rather interesting indeed!

Humor is where you find it, and the jokester should always be alert in all his reading to encounter material that could be turned into a good joke. You can even get it out of *Aesop's Fables.* I'll include one here, more or less as Aesop tells it, and I will leave it to you to see how easily it can be adapted in a number of ways.

❊ 122

A lion, a donkey, and a fox were hunting, and the kill had been good. With evening upon them, the weary three paused to rest and the lion said, "Friend donkey, divide the kill into three parts, one for each of us."

The donkey did so, producing three piles of almost miraculously equal size. The lion promptly slew the donkey, threw his body onto the rest of the kill, and said, "Friend fox, divide the kill into two parts, one for each of us."

The fox promptly shoved all of it together except for the corpse of one crow, which he put to one side. He said, "Do you, friend lion, have this heap for your half, and the dead crow will be my half."

The lion smiled broadly and said, "Well done, friend fox, but who taught you to divide so cleverly into equal halves?"

"The dead donkey," said the fox.

It is this fable, by the way, that gives rise to the term "lion's share" for a quantity that is well over half the total.

If you don't see how Aesop can be adapted to suit a modern occasion, by omitting the animal-tale aspects and even giving the tale an appearance of spontaneous wit — consider the following, which is quite true:

❊ 123

Driving from Boston to New York once, I finally reached sight of my destination, whereupon I announced in weary tones, "Well, we're halfway there."

"*Half!*" said my wife. "Why, there's the building we're heading for."

"The other half," I said, "is finding a parking place."

❊ 124

An aging professor said to some of his colleagues at the luncheon table, "One time recently, I dreamed I was lecturing to my class. I woke up with a start, and by heaven, I *was*."

A confirmed jokester (Joke 124 reminds me) is very apt to be a successful lecturer, if the occasion arises. The talents needed are the same in either case. Even when the lectures have to be given in a classroom to a weary audience, and when they require such distracting items as chalk and a blackboard, years of jokestering can be helpful.

My own professorship is in biochemistry, and for years I was compelled to turn my back to the audience in order to scribble diagrams and equations on the board.

The silence is deadly. Even if you manage to get the students (instinctively hostile to begin with) interested, that fragile spark is likely to be extinguished as you stand there for minutes at a time working away at the blackboard.

If I happened to be in top form, I tried to counter this by talking as I wrote. Naturally, I couldn't say anything that would require note-taking since the students were transferring the blackboard scribble to their notebooks and were busy enough with that. Nor could I say anything really profound since I was working with only half my mind, the rest concentrating on my scribbling. So I would try to be amusing.

Once I got particularly good results. It went something like this:

"I suppose many of you [I said as I wrote] are already beginning to wonder what specialties you will be engaging in. You might consider neurology since neurologists ask enormous fees — and naturally so, since neurologists might be expected to have a lot of nerve. [Groans; a few chuckles.]

"On the other hand, consider dermatology. That has its conveniences since people with skin troubles never die, but never get better, either. [A few more chuckles.]

"Still you must remember that dermatology is, of all specialties, the one most difficult to prepare for and the one that most requires all the branches of medicine at the fingertips. [I could almost feel their astonishment at this remark with my very back.]

"After all, gentlemen, as dermatologists, you will be studying the skin — and that covers everything."

I timed it to have the last phrase cover the last scribble and turned, solemn faced, and waited for the laughter to die down before I continued.

Now not all professors agree that this business of jollying along a class is good. Professors who approach their lectures as though they were showmen are sometimes looked down on by their good, gray, dull colleagues as mere popularity-seekers whose students laugh but don't learn.

This, however, is in my opinion mere sour-grapes consolation. It seems to me self-evident that a student who keeps alert so as to miss nothing, and who every once in a while is jolted by something unexpected, is going to be more alert, more attentive, and readier to learn, than one who is kept in a state of half-waking boredom.

✳ 125

Anderson and Johnson sat silently over their beers, each sunk in misery.

Finally, Anderson heaved a sigh and said, "I wish I were dead."

Johnson sighed in his turn and said, "If only *I* felt that good."

✳ 126

In the fifth century B.C., the Athenians had a unique system for avoiding dictatorship. Every once in a while, they got together to determine whether any statesman had better (for Athens' sake) be sent into a ten-year honorable exile. The citizens voted on pieces of pottery (*ostrakon*), and anyone getting sufficient votes was exiled (ostracized).

In 482 B.C., the dispute between Themistocles and Aristides on how best to meet the Persian menace had grown dangerously bitter. Themistocles was brilliant but shifty, while Aristides was so renowned for his honesty that he was called Aristides the Just, though at the same time he was stodgy and conservative. The only way out was to have a vote on ostracism.

In the course of the vote, one illiterate Athenian called on a passerby to help him. The passerby, who happened to be Aristides, asked which name to put down.

The voter said, "Aristides!"

Obediently, Aristides scratched his own name on the scrap of pottery, then said, "But tell me, why do you vote for the ostracism of Aristides? Has he done something of which you disapprove?"

"Not at all," said the voter. "It's just that I'm so infernally tired of hearing him referred to as the Just."

* 127

Mrs. Moskowitz was not entirely at home in the new world of American culture, but she did understand that her daughter's new boy friend might be very desirable indeed, for he had been introduced to her as Dr. Levy.

Nevertheless, there were possible misunderstandings, and a mother couldn't be too careful.

"Pardon me, Dr. Levy," she said with a gentle smile, "are you a dentist-doctor or a doctor-doctor?"

Do you think that that is a question that can only be asked in the world of jokes? Hah!

I myself belong to the subculture that worships the status of physician, and when I was young, it was assumed by my parents that I would someday become one of those divine beings. I assumed it myself, since I took it for granted that my parents knew best.

However, the older I grew, the less I liked the notion, since it became ever clearer to me that the mere thought of blood and disease doubled me up with queasy nausea. So I switched to chemistry and gained a Ph.D. Then, just in case that in itself might not be enough in a physician-centered subculture, I went further and joined the faculty of a medical school. Surely, I might now feel safe, but —

✳ 128

On my first day of laboratory supervision at the medical school, a young student approached me. I gazed at him benignly from my empyrean height, and then he said to me, "Dr. Asimov, are you a Ph.D. or a real doctor?"

I might have said that, from a consideration of history, it was the Ph.D. who was the real doctor and the practicing physician was merely a tradesman, but what was the use? I never really recovered. For years I kept saying that Ph.D. stands for Phony Doctor.

✳ 129

Old Mrs. Finkelstein sidled up to a guest at one of her daughter's social evenings. She had heard him addressed as doctor and now she said diffidently, "Doctor, may I ask a question?"
     "Certainly," he said.
     "Lately," said Mrs. Finkelstein, "I have been having a funny pain right here under the heart —"
     The guest interrupted uncomfortably and said, "I'm terribly sorry, Mrs. Finkelstein, but the truth is, I'm a doctor of philosophy."
     "Oh," said Mrs. Finkelstein, "I'm sorry!" She turned away, but then overcome with curiosity, she turned back. "Just one more question, doctor. Tell me, what kind of disease is philosophy?"

Jokes that take up the subject of alcohol are almost always prodrinking. Perhaps that is because joke sessions flow most freely when helped along by a current of liquor. Perhaps nondrinkers are too serious by nature or too nonlubricated to tell jokes. Perhaps — but perhaps not, for as I have said earlier in the book I am a teetotaler.
     I have no moral objections to drinking, however (in moderation), and I am perfectly willing to stand on the side of the social drinker in the world of jokes.

❅ 130

The temperance speaker had drawn a lurid picture of the misery to which alcohol would lead its devotees. No extreme had been unplumbed, and finally the speaker lifted both hands to heaven and cried out, "So I ask you, ladies and gentlemen, what under the sun is so unbearable as drink? What on earth can make you as miserable as drink?"

And from the rear of the crowd came the loud retort, "Thirst!"

The temperance speaker, I suspect, has largely passed from the American scene, but he is still to be found in jokes which are, and always have been, very slow in changing with the times.

But then, who isn't? In these days of plane travel, I resolutely refuse to travel by air. Almost everyone I meet is flabbergasted at my reactionary attitude in this respect and labors to overcome it (so far without success). Anyway, my bruised spirit always reacts with joy at any antiplane joke.

❅ 131

Jones had, for years, refused to take planes, and all arguments urging him to do so were made in vain. Finally one friend said in exasperation, "Listen, Jones, why don't you take a philosophic approach? Tell yourself that if your number isn't up, then it isn't up, and take the plane."

"Ah," said Jones, "and what difference would it make if my number wasn't up, if the *pilot's* number is up?"

Sometimes I explain my own reluctance to take planes by citing religious reasons. "I'm a devout coward," I say.

❅ 132

Clancy had sworn off drink over his vacation and had clung to his decision stubbornly for weeks. He knew, nevertheless, that the real crunch would come when he went back to work, for on his way home he would have to pass not one, not two, but five bars in rapid succession.

On his first day at work, he spent the whole day working up his will power. Finally, with perspiration bespangling his brow, he set off on that journey home.

He passed the first two bars with a grim set to his jaw and without a sideward glance. At the third bar, he looked at the windows longingly, but never slowed his step. At the fourth, he faltered, then forced himself on with an effort.

Finally, he was at the fifth, Joe's Bar, a favorite of his over many years. Inside were his friends. Inside was warmth, song, joy, camaraderie — all that gave life its special flavor. For long minutes, he stood there on the sidewalk, gazing at the doorway and filled with yearning.

But then he gave himself a shake and remembered his resolution. With a supreme effort, he forced his muscles to his will and walked away.

He had gone half a block before it really sank in that he had beaten temptation: he had actually passed five bars in a row — he had even passed Joe's Bar!

And in sheer ecstasy, he went back to Joe's Bar for a drink to celebrate the victory.

✷ 133

When my daughter was eleven, her mother took her shopping and, among other things, bought her a nightgown. My daughter was in great excitement over it, and although it was well past her bedtime when they arrived home, nothing would do but that she model it for me at once.

She put it on, rushed into the living room, and pirouetted for me. I nodded my approval. "Very sexy, Robyn," I said. "Very sexy."

She stared at me with great annoyance. "Very *sexy?*" she said. "What good is it to look very sexy when you're going to bed?"

❊ 134

A shy young man, desperately tongue-tied in the presence of girls, sought for advice from an older and wiser head.

"My boy," said the man of experience, "all you have to do is get started with one remark. Let me give you three topics that never fail: relatives, food, and philosophy. Make one comment on any one of these fields, and the girl is sure to start talking. From her talk you will derive another comment, and so on. It never fails."

On the very next occasion when the young man found himself in the company of a girl, the usual appalling silence fell, and they sat there on the sofa like frozen statues. Finally, the agonized man remembered the advice he had received and forced himself to make a remark on the subject of relatives.

He said, "Do you have a brother?"

And the young lady replied briefly, "No!"

The young man retreated into his shell at once. Had she only said yes, he might have inquired about his age, the color of his hair, the place he went to school. There could have been infinite room for discussion.

Well, what about food, then? After several false starts, the young man managed to say, "Do you like noodles?"

And the young lady replied, just as briefly as before, "No!"

Again, he was stymied. Had she said yes, he could easily have gone on to ask if she liked them in soup or with meatballs, and from there to a discussion of Italian cooking.

The moments passed and the haggard young man fell back on the final topic, philosophy.

Tensely he said, "Tell me, *if* you had had a brother, would *he* have liked noodles?"

❊ 135

Old Mr. Rosenberg said to his physicist son, "Tell me something. Everyone says Albert Einstein was one of the greatest minds in the world. But what did he do?"

"Among other things, Papa," said his son, "he worked out the theory of relativity."

"And what is that?"

Rosenberg's son hesitated, then said, "Well, Papa, without going into detail, it's a way of working out a theory of the universe by beginning with the assumption that some matters we have always considered to be absolute are really relative."

"I don't understand. What's absolute? What's relative?"

"It's hard to explain, but let me give you an example. Time is time, isn't it? An hour of time is an hour of time, no matter what. Right?"

"Right!"

"Yet under certain conditions, that's not so. To use an example that will give you an idea of what I mean, you will agree that if you spend an hour playing pinochle with your friends, it seems like a minute, but if you sit on a cake of ice for a minute, it seems like an hour."

Old Rosenberg stared at his son and muttered softly, "An hour playing pinochle is like a minute; a minute on a cake of ice is like an hour." Then he said, "One more thing — is it from nonsense like this that Einstein made a living?"

I've seen Joke 135 in print a number of times and heard it told a number of times, and every single time, without exception, it was the product of someone who knew nothing about relativity. Since usually the listeners are equally innocent of knowledge of the subject, the jokester's ignorance doesn't matter, and the punch line will stand by itself and raise a laugh, even if a physicist winces at what goes before. Nevertheless, just for the record, I am glad to seize the opportunity to tell the joke properly.

Of course, part of the effectiveness of the joke rests on the fact that it makes fun of Einstein, and nonscientists are always ready to laugh at scientists.

❈ 136

The late, great Professor Norbert Wiener of M.I.T. was the type of absent-minded genius concerning whom stories are told that have been told of every other absent-minded genius from Archimedes on.

A friend, so it was said, stopped Wiener in the street one day and engaged him in conversation. After a few minutes, they were about to separate when Wiener said, with a puzzled look on his face, "Pardon me, Smith, but when we stopped to talk, in which direction was I walking?"

"Why, that way," said Smith, "toward Massachusetts Avenue."

"Oh, good," said Wiener. "In that case, I've already had lunch."

❈ 137

"I have brought a frog," said Professor Krumpelmayer, beaming at his class in elementary zoology, "fresh from the pond, in order that we might study its outer appearance and later dissect it."

He carefully unwrapped the package he carried and inside was a neatly prepared ham sandwich.

The good professor looked at it with astonishment. "Odd," he said, "I distinctly remember having eaten my lunch."

❈ 138

The gigantic computer took up the whole of a monstrous wall, completely dwarfing the two tiny mathematicians standing before it. A sliver of paper had emerged from the vitals of the computer, and one mathematician, after studying it gravely, turned to the other and said, "Do you realize that it would take four hundred ordinary mathematicians two hundred and fifty years to make a mistake this big?"

In telling a series of jokes, it is well to avoid too long a string on a particular subject. The same would hold in writing a book of them, but of course the rule is a little harder to follow when one is writing in categories. Still, I try to do my best; if a series on scientists begins to reel out, I'd interrupt with one involving an artist —

＊ 139

In 1878, the American-born artist James McNeill Whistler sued the art critic John Ruskin for damages over the latter's harsh attacks on the former's paintings — attacks which Whistler considered had passed the bounds of legitimate criticism and invaded those of libel.

Naturally, Ruskin's lawyer had to do his best to denigrate Whistler's paintings. He took one which was rather abstract and not at all calculated to win the hearts of a nonartistic Victorian jury, and said, "Now, Mr. Whistler, how long did it take you to paint this one?"

"Most of a day," said Whistler calmly.

"And do you ask this jury to believe that you are justified in asking five hundred pounds for the labor of less than a day?"

"Not at all," said Whistler icily, "I am charging for the experience of a lifetime."

Whistler won his case but was awarded exactly one farthing in damages. But then, how does one estimate the value of creativity even in callings less lofty than that of art? As, for instance:

＊ 140

The gigantic generator had stopped working, and the entire vast industrial plant which depended on it ground to a halt. Distraught engineers did their best to start it again, but without success, and every minute of idleness that passed cost the firm thousands of dollars.

Finally, an expert on generating machinery was brought in from outside. Coolly, he walked the length of the generator, studied its dials, and pondered.

At last he said, "May I have a small hammer?"

One was handed him, and walking up to a certain pipe, he felt it delicately, located a particular point, and tapped that point sharply with the hammer. Instantly, the generator sprang into action.

"Your fee?" asked the gratified head of the firm.

"Five hundred-five dollars," said the expert.

The other's eyes opened wide. "Five hundred-five dollars for just hitting the pipe with a hammer?"

"For that," said the expert, "five dollars. For knowing where to hit, five hundred dollars."

✻ 141

Mrs. Smythe dashed into the small but high-priced shop of her favorite clothing designer.

"Pierre," she said, "I must have a new hat of startling design that is absolutely original and I must have it now. What can you do for me?"

"Let me see," said Pierre. Pulling out a length of ribbon of a warm and glowing mottled orange, he cut it deftly and then began to fold it. Skillfully, he wove it into shape and in a few minutes, without pinning or clipping it in any way, he had a hat for Mrs. Smythe.

Mrs. Smythe looked at herself in the mirror with awe. "That's marvelous, Pierre," she said. "How much?"

"Two hundred dollars, madame," said Pierre.

Mrs. Smythe said, "Two hundred? Isn't that rather high for a length of ribbon?"

Pierre smiled. He removed the hat and, as skillfully as he had wound it, he now unwound it. He handed the unwound length to the lady and said, "The ribbon itself, dear madame, is yours for nothing."

Most jokes that are more than trivial carry some kind of moral, but it isn't always safe to suppose that the opinions of the joke are necessarily those of the jokester. There is at least one story I like to tell which makes a point with which I violently disagree —

✻ 142

In the fourth century B.C., the great Athenian philosopher Plato established a school (the Academy) at which mathematics was a key portion of the curriculum. It was taught with the utmost rigor of which the times were capable, and it dealt with idealized shapes on which idealized operations were performed.

One student, who was put to stern mental exercise over the Platonic conception of mathematics, kept searching in vain for some application to the various forms of artisanry for which he knew mathematical concepts were useful.

Finally he said to Plato, "But, master, to what practical use can these theorems be put? What can be gained from them?"

The old philosopher glared at the inquiring student, turned to a slave, and said, "Give this young man a penny that he might feel he has gained something from my teachings and then expel him."

The moral is, of course, that art is for art's sake alone — that the pure creation of the mind is somehow sullied by contact with the real world, and that the more divorced from use knowledge is, the more noble it is.

This Platonic concept has long swayed both artists and scientists and has helped make learning at once austere and unreal. In the case of science, it has produced the paradox of minds that create dangers deadly to humanity, yet deny all responsibility.

Since the coming of the atomic bomb, however, more and more scientists have come down from the ivory tower; more and more feel they cannot, after all, evade the responsibility for the applications others make of their own refined, above-the-world researches.

That represents the growth of humility, without which science can make no progress, for without humility there is the tendency to assume too great a certainty and therefore too small a need to learn more.* For that reason there is another story of the period which I tell less often, but with greater pleasure —

* The reader may at this point feel it necessary to point out my own apparent lack of this great quality, as demonstrated here and there. Okay, consider it pointed out.

✻ 143

In the late fifth century B.C., the Delphic oracle was asked to name the wisest man in Greece and Socrates received the nod.

The Athenian philosopher, on being told this, said, "Since the god proclaims me the wisest, I must believe it; but if that is so, then it must be because I alone of all the Greeks know that I know nothing."

✻ 144

Science has a language of its own which sometimes puzzles laymen. The word "obvious" is a case in point.

Thus a professor of physics, deriving some profound point of theory for the class, scribbled an equation on the board and said, "From this, it is obvious that we can proceed to write the following relationship —" and he scribbled a second equation on the board.

Then he paused. He stared hard at the two equations and said, "Wait a while. I may be wrong —"

He sat down, seized a pad and started to write furiously. He paused for thought, crossed out what he had written, and began over. In this fashion, half an hour passed while the class held its breath and sat in absolute silence.

Finally, the professor rose with an air of satisfaction and said, "Yes, I was right in the first place. It *is* obvious that the second equation follows from the first."

It may be that Joke 144 was inspired by the true life story of Pierre Simon Laplace, the great French mathematician of the Napoleonic era. He was impatient with petty computation, and in his massive five-volume book *Celestial Mechanics,* which completed Newtonian theory, he would often write an equation and then say, "From this it is easy to see . . ." and would then write another equation.

In each case this was the signal for despair among his readers, for what was easy for Laplace to see required hours of hard work for those ordinary souls who tried to follow him.

Mathematicians are the intellectuals par excellence, perhaps. No professor is so absent-minded, in the jokester's folklore, as a mathematician. A possibly true story that raises absent-mindedness to horrifying heights is told about Karl Friedrich Gauss, who may have been the most gifted and remarkable mathematician of all time.

✻ 145

Gauss was keeping vigil while his wife lay ill upstairs, and as time passed, he found himself beginning to ponder a deep problem in mathematics. He drew pen and paper to himself and began to draw diagrams.

A servant approached and said deferentially, "Herr Gauss, your wife is dying."

And Gauss, never looking up, said, "Yes, yes, but tell her to wait till I'm through."

✻ 146

A deputation from the class waited upon the professor and most politely explained their situation.

"Professor," they said, "we have difficulty following your lectures. You go too rapidly and it is impossible to take notes when you do that."

"Ah," said the professor, "I am sorry. Have you any suggestions as to how I might correct this?"

"Yes," he was told. "If you would be so kind as to write your equations on the board when you come to them, we will be able to copy them down."

"I see," said the professor. "Writing them on the board will slow me up. Now why didn't I think of that?"

The next day he began to lecture, and caught up in the excitement of doing so, he forgot the complaint of the students and worked his way quickly from equation to equation, and said at last, "And so you see the whole thing is as clear and obvious as the fact that two and two is four."

The words clear and obvious reminded him, finally, of his students' complaints, so conscientiously he wrote on the board, $2 + 2 = 4$.

Sometimes it is the students who earn the shaft. Consider the slide rule, for instance. It is a mechanical device which enables one to make rapid calculations that are good to three, or sometimes four, decimal places. Properly used it is a tremendous help, but —

✻ 147

In the course of a test, an earnest young student was observed to make use of his slide rule while muttering under his breath, "Let's see . . . three times two is five point nine nine ni —— Oh nuts, call it six."

✻ 148

Mark Twain used to say that it was possible to learn too much from experience. A cat, he said, that had squatted once on a hot stove lid would never sit down on a hot stove lid again. The trouble was that it would never sit down on a cold one either.

✻ 149

Miss Smith had read through *Hamlet* for the first time and was asked her opinion of it.

"Really," she said, "I don't know why people rave about it. It's nothing but a bunch of quotations strung together."

By substituting (and with considerable justice, really) the Gettysburg Address for *Hamlet*, Joke 149 becomes suitable to tell in the course of Lincoln's Birthday celebrations.

❊ 150

Mrs. Anderson, the leading socialite in her small town, was berating
the local handyman. "Really, John, you drink too much. It can't be
good for either your health or your family."

"But I am not that much of a drinker, ma'am."

"How can you say that when you were in Tony's Bar all last
night?"

"But I wasn't."

"But you were. I saw your wheelbarrow outside the bar yesterday
afternoon and it was still there this morning."

The handyman said not another word. That afternoon, before going home, he carefully placed his wheelbarrow outside Mrs. Anderson's home and left it there for the night.

❊ 151

Moskowitz met his business rival, Levinson, at the airport and asked
him, with an elaborate pretense of casualness, "And where do you
happen to be going, Levinson?"

Levinson, just as casual, responded, "Chicago."

"Aha," said Moskowitz, shaking his finger triumphantly. "Now
I've caught you in a flat-footed lie. You tell me Chicago because you
want me to think you're going to St. Louis, but I talked to your
partner only this morning and I happen to know you *are* going to
Chicago, you liar!"

❊ 152

Frederick William I, who ruled Prussia in the early eighteenth century, was a fat, choleric eccentric who stood on no ceremony at all.
He walked the streets of Berlin unattended, and when anyone displeased him (and he was easily displeased) he did not hesitate to
use his stout walking stick as a cudgel.

Small wonder, then, that when the Berliners saw him at a distance, they quietly left the vicinity.

One time, as Frederick William was pounding down one of the

streets, a citizen spied him, but too late, and his attempt to slide quietly into a doorway proved a failure.

"You," called out Frederick William, "where are you going?"

"Into the house, Your Majesty," said the citizen, trembling violently.

"Is it your house?"

"No, Your Majesty."

"A friend's house?"

"No, Your Majesty."

"Why are you entering it, then?"

And the poor citizen, fearing he might be accused of burglary and at his wit's end, finally decided on the truth, and said, "In order to avoid you, Your Majesty."

Frederick William frowned. "To *avoid* me? Why?"

"Because I fear you, Your Majesty."

Frederick William promptly turned purple and, lifting his cudgel, pounded the other's shoulders, crying, "You are not supposed to fear me. You're supposed to love me. *Love* me, scum, *love* me!"

❋ 153

Henry VIII, a bluff and hearty, but pathologically tyrannical king (especially in his later years) appointed an ambassador to France at a time when relations between the kingdoms were poor indeed.

The ambassador was a reluctant one, particularly because of the truculent nature of the message he was to carry. "Your Majesty," he said diffidently, "King Francis will be perfectly capable of removing my head on receipt of a message so phrased."

"Fear not," said Henry. "Francis well knows that if he were to behead my ambassador, the head of every Frenchman in my dominions would be removed within twenty-four hours."

"I am sure of that, sire," murmured the ambassador, "but consider that among all those French heads, not one will be found to fit my shoulders."

❋ 154

There have been few times in military history when the situation was so confused and uncontrollable as in the first month of World War I, when generals were handling unprecedentedly large armies under unprecedented circumstances. On the western front that month, the German advance ended in the Battle of the Marne, which stabilized the front and saved France from certain defeat.

Controlling the French armies that first month was Marshal Joseph Joffre, a stolid unimaginative warrior, who could not conceivably be viewed as brilliant. Many military commentators in later years analyzed the Battle of the Marne and tried to pin down the actual details in order to discover to whom the credit for the victory really belonged. Surely some general had made some crucial move at the correct moment.

Experts disagreed; opinions varied; and finally the question was put to Joffre himself. He smoked for a while and considered. Then he said, "You know, I really don't know who ought to get the credit for the victory at the Marne. I know only one thing. If we had been defeated, everyone would have agreed at once that the fault was mine."

❊ 155

In 1756, during the Seven Years' War, the French won one of their rare naval victories over the British and took the island of Minorca. The British, unused to naval defeat, were enraged, and the defeated admiral, John Byng, found himself under court-martial.

He had fought his best, actually, but someone had to pay, so in 1757, he was convicted of dereliction of duty and was shot accordingly.

It was a clear miscarriage of justice, but it undoubtedly spurred other officers on to greater efforts. Or, as Voltaire sardonically put it, "His execution will serve to encourage the others."

❊ 156

Finkelstein had made a huge killing at the races and Moskowitz, quite understandably, was envious.

"How did you do it, Finkelstein?" he demanded.

"Easy," said Finkelstein. "It was a dream."

"A dream?"

"Yes. I had figured out a three-horse parlay, but I wasn't sure about the third horse. Then the night before, I dreamed an angel was standing over the head of my bed and kept saying, 'Blessings on you, Finkelstein. Seven times seven blessings on you.' When I woke up, I realized that seven times seven is forty-eight and that horse number forty-eight was Heavenly Dream. I made Heavenly Dream the third horse in my parlay and I just cleaned up; I simply cleaned up."

Moskowitz said, "But, Finkelstein, seven times seven is forty-nine."

And Finkelstein said, "So *you* be the mathematician."

✾ 157

It was spring, the weather was delightful, and a man on a park bench breathed deeply and listened to the melodious chirping of numerous birds. Turning to the stranger who happened to be sharing the bench with him, he said, "Isn't the music of the birds delightful?"

The other man scowled and said, "How the devil can I hear what you're saying over the damned noise of those stupid birds?"

✾ 158

Once when I was a teen-ager, I was walking with my mother on a winter day. It was quite cold but (knock wood) low temperatures don't bother me much, and as is my custom, I had left my overcoat unbuttoned.

My mother, obviously uncomfortable, finally said sharply, "Button your coat, Isaac; I'm freezing."

As you might guess, I was unable to convince my mother she had said anything funny.

✾ 159

The grizzled fireman was being badgered by a young lady who insisted on knowing of any particularly unusual rescues he had carried through.

"Well," said the fireman, "there was one time when we had someone on the eighth floor window in a narrow alley. We couldn't get the hook and ladder in place; we had no ordinary ladder that would reach; there was no landing net available; and the progress of the fire left him no escape by going back through any window."

"My goodness," said the excited young lady. "What did you do?"

"I went up the side of the building like a human fly, carrying a rope with me. He took one end of the rope and tied it firmly around his own waist. Then we dropped the other end to the firemen waiting on the ground, and they pulled us both down."

✻ 160

There is a tale (not to be found in the pages of Conan Doyle, you may be sure) concerning Sherlock Holmes and John Watson on board a train. They passed a herd of sheep and Watson said, "A sizable herd, Holmes, eh?"

"Exactly seven hundred-eighty-four in number, my dear Watson," said Holmes sleepily.

"Good heavens, Holmes," said Watson, "surely you can't have counted them."

"Not directly," said Holmes. "I made use of a simple trick any school child knows. I merely counted the legs and divided by four."

I imagine that just as any comedian longs to play Hamlet, and any pianist yearns to play in Carnegie Hall, so any nonprofessional jokester has the secret dream of telling a joke on television.

That finally happened to me in January 1970. I was on a talk show, along with a *professional* jokester, and the moon flights were mentioned. The professional asked if I had heard the joke about the Israeli space venture and I said yes. (This was a slip of jokester's etiquette. I ought to have said no and asked him to tell it.)

Naturally, he asked *me* to tell it. With belated humility, I tried to back out, but he wouldn't let me. He insisted I tell it. Trembling a little with stage fright, I told the joke and (thank heaven) got an entirely satisfactory laugh — from the live audience, anyway.

This has placed this one joke in a quite special class for me, and so I shall use it to close and climax the section on Paradox.

✻ 161

On the glorious day of July 20, 1969, when the first human being stepped onto the surface of the moon, an Israeli said to an American friend, "That is a great achievement, but we Israelis will do much better. We are planning a manned expedition to the sun."

"To the sun?" exclaimed the astonished American. "But the heat? The light? The radiation?"

The Israeli chuckled. "Do you think we Israelis are fools? We will send the expedition at night."

AN ABRUPT CHANGE in point of view can hurl itself like a spear at some more or less innocent party. Where sympathy is the natural expectation, for instance, sudden further insult is added instead. Human nature being what it is, this is delightful to the person making the retort and to innocent bystanders who listen to the retort — to everyone, in fact, but the person at the receiving end.

That gives us the class of jokes that we might term the Putdown. For instance —

✳ 162

A poet of very limited ability once complained to Oscar Wilde that critics were ignoring his latest volume.

"I'm being made the victim of a conspiracy of silence, Oscar," he said. "What shall I do?"

"Join it!" said Wilde.

This joke is an example of the simple put-down, and it has its disadvantages, for Oscar Wilde seems needlessly cruel. The poet may be of very limited ability but that is not his deliberate doing, and Wilde, in saying what he did, seems to be utilizing his rapier wit on an ill-armed adversary. If it were a physical battle, he would be displaying the characteristics of a bully, and there is something a little uncomfortable about this to a humane person whether he tells the joke or listens to it.

To demonstrate this in more extreme form, here is a joke that was told well (by someone else, not me) and was laughed at. I didn't laugh, however, and it seemed to me that some of the laughs that did come were forced. Here it is:

❋ 163

A cowboy loping along the trail (or whatever it is that cowboys on horses do) heard feeble cries for help coming from a farmhouse nearby. He rode over, tied his horse to a stake, and entered.

There on the bed was a nude female, each limb tied to a different bedpost. She said faintly, "Help me, please. Two men came here not long ago, knocked my husband unconscious, then tied me to the bed. Each one raped me in turn; then they left me here and carried off my husband. Please help me."

The cowboy thought a moment, then began taking his clothes off. "Ma'am," he said, "I guess this ain't your lucky day."

For a humane person, the put-down is most satisfactory and most easily greeted with pleasurable laughter when the person being put down has done something to invite it — in other words, if he has made the first move and has attacked.

Then it is lunge-and-riposte, and at the riposte we can laugh with a clear conscience. Let me tell you an exchange, for instance, that I really heard in those long-distant days when I was serving in the army.

❋ 164

Said one soldier to another angrily during an altercation, "Kiss my ass!"

Said the other quietly, "All right, but mark the place you want kissed, because you look all ass to me."

Sometimes, it seems to me that the gentler the put-down, the more effective it is. Here are three examples in what appears to

me in order of increasing gentleness. You can judge for yourself.

✳ 165

A man, far gone in drunkenness and in dreadful disarray, staggered
down the street and bumped against a stout woman of appalling
respectability. She glowered at him and said, "You horrible creature.
You are the drunkest man I have ever seen."

The drunk paused in his uneven progress, turned slowly, and said,
"Lady, you're the ugliest woman I have ever seen, and that's worse.
Because when I wake up tomorrow morning, I'm going to be sober."

And you will still be ugly!

✳ 166

The late entertainer Al Jolson is reputed to have been a hard man
to handle. A young director once tried to get him to alter a piece of
business, and found himself in trouble at once.

Jolson halted the proceedings, stared at the young man scornfully,
and said, "Listen, kid, I've got a million dollars. What do you have?"

And the director said quietly, "Friends!"

✳ 167

A portly, scowling gentleman walked into one of those English trains
where people ride in separate compartments. He pulled out a large
cigar and was about to light it when he noticed that the only other
passenger in the compartment, a thin, rabbity fellow, was looking at
him with what was clearly apprehension.

The man with the cigar said gruffly, "I hope you don't mind my
smoking this cigar."

"Not at all," said the other, "provided you don't mind my throwing
up."

The idea has somehow arisen that it is wrong for a jokester to
laugh at his own jokes. Why on earth should it be?

I generally laugh at the jokes I tell (in moderation), and especially at these lunge-and-riposte jokes which I find particularly enjoyable.

And why not? Telling a joke well is a pleasurable experience. Watching people laugh because of your skill in telling it is delightful. And laughter is contagious. So why not laugh?

What *is* wrong is having a jokester laugh *while* he is telling a joke. This not only impedes the joke, but it invariably irritates the listener, who is bound to find the punch line anticlimactic after all that laughter, making the whole thing fall flat.

In the days before movies became as permissive as they now are, there were occasional attempts to have a character tell a dirty joke without falling foul of the censor. (This was done, for instance, in the enormously overrated movie *Faces.*) The joke is usually not particularly dirty, but in an effort to mask what bawdiness it may seem to contain, the device is used of having the person telling it laugh continuously as he talks, thus obscuring the words. No jokester can watch this without a feeling of nauseated contempt.

So there's one more rule for you. If a joke strikes you as so funny that you can't help laughing while you are trying to tell it — then don't try. Write it out and let someone else tell it.

Sometimes it is possible to get the put-down into a very few words, as for instance:

*** 168**

A guest, leaving a party, shook his host's hand and said, "I've had a wonderful time, but this isn't it."

*** 169**

A guest, leaving a party, shook his host's hand warmly and said, "Don't think this hasn't been a wonderful party, but it hasn't."

✳ 170

A young boy, leaving a party, said to his hostess, "I must say I've had a wonderful time — because my mother will wallop me if I don't."

On the whole, though, the put-down must be a simple one in the short joke, and it is only in the longer one that the more valuable lunge-and-riposte can be used.

I have a tendency to repeat successful ripostes when made by myself and plan to do so shortly. Lest anyone think I mean to imply that I go through life with wit flashing, demolishing all and sundry, let me tell you of one occasion on which I myself was neatly poniarded to the immense enjoyment of a rather sizable crowd.

✳ 171

I was interviewed on the "David Frost Show" one time, and at a social gathering some few days later, one of the people present mentioned having seen me.

A young man about half my age was part of the group, and he said with genial cynicism, "And what did you do, Dr. Asimov? Read commercials?"

With a haughty determination to squelch the young cockerel at once by a thrust too outrageous to parry, I said, "Not at all! I was demonstrating sexual techniques."

"Oh," he murmured sweetly, "You remembered?"

This is an example of lunge-and-riposte-and-counterriposte. The more flashes back and forth, the better the final result of course, but successive "toppers" are hard to manage in numbers. One topper is usually sufficient.

I must use Joke 171 to make an important point, by the way —

A jokester must guard against his own unpopularity — if only because unpopularity will diminish his effectiveness. The mere fact that a person knows many jokes, can tell them well, and enjoys dominating the conversation may sometimes weary those he insists on dominating.

The weariness becomes active dislike if the jokester has a touch of cruelty about himself. It is very likely that an accomplished jokester will have a sharp wit, reinforced by the memory of many punch lines which, by practice, he can instantly modify. It follows that he can easily demolish someone else's feeble attack, and sometimes cannot resist the impulse to do so. Jackie Leonard and Don Rickles are examples of professionals who have converted this ability into a fine art of insult, and people laugh; but I don't think you would want them around if they were like that in real life (which I'm sure they aren't).

One way of countering the perennial danger of unpopularity is to accept, at least occasionally and with good grace, the role of victim. The damage to one's dignity is minute compared to the increased pleasure with which the audience will listen to one's next fifty jokes. (Jack Benny has built one of the most durable records of continued success in comedy and has remained one of the most loved comics, through having carefully poked almost all his fun at himself and invariably handing the riposte to someone else.)

Heaven knows it's difficult to suppress a riposte, or to laugh at the lunge you can't (or won't) counter, and I must admit I'm not very good at it; but I do try.

Consequently, when Joke 171 took place (and it is an absolutely true story that happened word for word as I have described it), and when everyone was laughing uproariously at my expense, I managed to laugh too, and heartily.

Actually, I can think back on that monumental squash of myself with far greater satisfaction than I can think of two monumental squashes of others which I delivered a number of years ago. (I was far pricklier in my early youth than I am today, far readier to take offense, and *far* more apt to hand back instant overkill.) The momentary satisfaction those ripostes gave me certainly did not compensate for the sneaking shame I later felt. My only defense is that in the two cases I intend to describe, I was not the aggressor and the attack on myself was, in each case, utterly without provocation. Here they are —

✻ 172

When I was twenty-three and working at the Philadelphia navy yard, I decided to grow a mustache (a project I did not adhere to for long). My burgeoning adornment was not met with universal favor.

In fact, one of the secretaries, a rather swarthy brunette, lifted her nose in the air and said, "Are *you* trying to grow a mustache?" in accents that seemed to me to be a direct reflection on my virility.

"Why not?" said I, staring at her upper lip. "*You've* managed."

✻ 173

On another occasion, I was standing in the chemistry laboratory and was carefully decanting a solution from an Erlenmeyer flask into a test tube, holding both up to eye level. I'm afraid I have always had something of a prominent abdomen, and in the stance I then had assumed, it was particularly noticeable.

One of the lab technicians, a very thin girl, found this amusing. Lifting a long glass rod she aimed it at my abdomen, spear-fashion, and said, "I'm going to let all the air out of you, so you'll look more like a man."

And I said, "Fine, and use that air to pump up your chest, so you'll look more like a woman."

In both cases, the girls involved were furious beyond description, and I was forced to leave the room hastily and stay away for the rest of the day. In fact, the second young lady threw a chair at me as I departed; a chair that seemed, at the time, to be considerably larger than herself. (She missed, thank goodness.) If either of them happens to read the book and recognize the incident, I hereby apologize. And I want to assure them that I never do such things anymore. Well, hardly ever.

As long as I'm telling stories about myself, let me introduce my mother. She is no jokester, but she laughs easily. Indeed, when I was a youngster, she laughed at every joke I told her, however feeble it might have been. This may merely have been her maternal duty as she saw it, but it was very encouraging and I am grateful to her.

I am also grateful to her because she had the capacity of saying funny things without knowing it, thus making them twice as funny. For instance —

✻ 174

My parents had a candy store at various locations in Brooklyn for many years. When the years had crept on sufficiently, they sold out one last time and retired. Soon, however, they found that unaccustomed leisure time hung heavy on their hands. My father got a job, and my mother decided to go to night school to improve her knowledge of English, in which subject she was entirely self-taught.

In particular, she wanted to learn to write English. She worked hard at school, and in a surprisingly short time she was able to write in perfectly legible fashion.

Then one day a teacher said to her, "Pardon me, Mrs. Asimov, but I am curious. Are you a relative of Isaac Asimov?"

My mother said, with poorly suppressed maternal pride, "Yes, indeed. He is my son."

Whereupon the teacher said, "Oh! No wonder you're so good at writing."

And my mother drew herself up to her full four-feet-ten and said freezingly, "I *beg* your pardon. No wonder *he's* so good at writing."

✻ 175

My mother was sometimes easily hurt. I was quite used to her loyal laughter when I made jokes at her expense, so I was quite surprised when, on her fiftieth birthday, she reacted differently to my joshing comments about her age.

She said in an aggrieved tone, "All right, but I'll laugh at you good and hard when *you* become fifty."

Finally, her chance came. Like the loyal son I am, I phoned her long-distance and said, "Okay, mama. I'm fifty today. Go ahead and laugh."

"What's the good?" she said indignantly. "You arranged so that when you became fifty, I should be seventy-four."

My father, on the other hand, though he had many virtues, was precisely the wrong kind of father for a budding jokester. The sad truth is that he had no sense of humor.

There are a variety of reasons why a person might lack a sense of humor. He might be hopelessly short of intelligence or imagination and be unable to catch the sudden alteration of point of view, or fail to appreciate it if he did. My father certainly didn't fall into those classifications.

With him, rather, it was a matter of dignity. There are some people who, for whatever reason, equate laughter with folly. They see the joke but school themselves not to laugh, and in the end they come to see no reason to laugh at all.

And that was my father. He was dignified and, but for the fact that he was clean-shaven, had the bearing of an Old Testament patriarch. Laugh? At foolishness? Never!

My most utter fiasco was the following, which I told my father because I was sure that even he would laugh.

❉ 176

Miss Jones, the proprietress of a well-populated boarding house, woke one morning at about 4 A.M., hearing the most terrible noises outside her room. She threw open the door and outside she could see Mr. Smith, one of her boarders, much the worse for drink and forcing a horse up the stairs.

"Mr. Smith," she shrieked. "What are you doing?"

He said, "I am pushing this horse into the bathroom."

"But why?"

"Because the other boarders are wise guys, that's why. In the morning, one by one, the boarders will go to the bathroom; and one by one, they will come out shrieking, 'There's a *horse* in the bathroom.' Then it will be *my* turn to be the wise guy, for each time I will be able to say, in a calm and superior way, 'Yes, I know.' "

I doubled up when I got the last line out, but my father, having listened disapprovingly all through said, "You're making a fool out of yourself. You're a city boy and you have no idea how much a horse weighs. You can't push it into a bathroom if it doesn't want to go."

Of course, when I heard my father's comment I burst into new peals of laughter, and said between gasps, "Oh, Papa, that's funnier than the joke."

But he never knew why.

❄ 177

Mr. Johnson had weighed himself on one of those old-fashioned penny machines that delivered a card with a fortune printed on it.

The formidable Mrs. Johnson plucked it from her husband's fingers and said, "Let me see that! Ah, it says: 'You are firm and resolute, have a decisive personality, are a leader of men, and are attractive to women.' "

Then she turned the card over, studied it a moment, and said, "And they've got the weight wrong as well."

❄ 178

Benjamin Disraeli, who in his lifetime was twice prime minister of Great Britain, and who was the great political rival of William E. Gladstone (himself fated to be four times prime minister), once meticulously corrected himself in debate, withdrawing the expression "calamity" and substituting "misfortune."

He was questioned afterward as to his reasons therefor and was asked if there were indeed so tremendous a difference between the two words.

"Definitely," he responded, "and I will explain by an example. If my honorable friend Gladstone were accidentally to fall into the Thames River, that would be a misfortune; but if anyone were then to pull him out again, that would be a calamity."

✻ 179

John Wilkes, an English politician noted for his firm opposition to George III, was a man of courageous liberal principles, but one who led a personal life of great dissipation.

At one time, an opponent of Wilkes, shaking with rage at some quip the latter had made, said to him through clenched teeth, "Sir, I predict you will die either on the gallows or of some loathsome disease."

To which Wilkes serenely replied, "Which it will be, my dear sir, will depend entirely on whether I embrace your principles or your mistress."

✻ 180

Aristippus of Cyrene and Diogenes of Sinope were contemporary philosophers of fourth-century-B.C. Greece. Aristippus preached pleasure as the greatest good and had a prominent position in the court of Dionysius, powerful ruler of Syracuse in Sicily. Diogenes, on the other hand, held that all possessions were corrupting and favored a life of rigid virtue, which could be achieved only in poverty.

Aristippus once met Diogenes when the latter was engaged in washing lentils prior to making himself the soup that was the main article of his diet.

Aristippus said, "Oh, Diogenes, if you could but learn to do a small thing such as flattering Dionysius, you would not have the sad fate of living on lentils."

And Diogenes answered, "Oh, Aristippus, if you could but learn to do a small thing such as living on lentils, you would not have the sad fate of having to flatter Dionysius."

It is not necessary to go to long-past history to find some good put-downs. One was delivered with remarkably gentle grace by our all too shortlived President, John F. Kennedy —

❄ 181

In 1961, the American government encouraged refugee Cubans to invade Cuba. There was, however, egregiously poor intelligence on our part, and when the Cubans landed in the Bay of Pigs they were killed or captured to a man.

After the fiasco, there was a great deal of scrambling among government personalities, who attempted to implicate others in the misjudgment while clearing themselves. President Kennedy (who had found the matter already in progress when he became President) rose to magnificent heights of manliness in stoically accepting the blame, though he could not withhold a sardonic comment: "It has often been said that victory has a thousand fathers, but defeat is an orphan."

Well, it may have "often been said," but no one has ever been able to trace that saying. We have to leave it as Kennedy's.

Having introduced my mother and my father, may I now present my teen-aged daughter? She is beautiful (really!), blond and blue-eyed, and has a tongue that has been whittled to a fine point. She can put me down with ease even at her tender age, and what will happen when she reaches full maturity, I dread to think. (Well, perhaps she will develop some filial respect, though there seem no signs of it so far.)

In any case, she often reflects the modern mood of rebellion, affecting an utter libertarianism for herself, and scorning all old-fashioned conventions — except on behalf of me. As far as *I* am concerned, she comes over all Victorian.

If I as much as bestow a paternal smile on some delectable young female, she is at my side at once, glaring suspiciously at the object of my fatherly solicitude and surreptitiously kicking me in the shins. Worse still, she exerts a tyrannical and utterly conservative influence over my style of dress. Witness the following:

* 182

I like to wear clip-on bow ties because they are easy to put on and take off, but my daughter frowns on them as utterly gauche and demands four-in-hands. Furthermore, I like a dash of color here and there, while Robyn prefers a more funereal style of dress — for me, not for herself.

One time, taking my courage in both hands, I prepared for an outing by putting on a large bow tie covered with bright orange stripes. I walked into the living room defiantly and said, "How do I look?"

Robyn looked at me calmly and replied, "You look great, Dad. Now all you have to do is paint your cheeks white and your nose red."

So I changed back to a four-in-hand and have never worn that particular bow tie again. Oh, how sharper than a serpent's tooth it is . . .

* 183

Lady Nancy Astor, who entered the House of Commons in 1919 as its first woman member, had few betters in the art of vicious repartee. But she did have some, and Winston Churchill was one of them.

After one hot and heavy Parliamentary set-to, Lady Astor is reported to have said to Churchill, "Winston, if you were my husband, I would poison your coffee."

"If you were my wife, Nancy," replied Churchill suavely, "I would drink it."

* 184

John Randolph, a vitriolic legislator from Virginia in the early decades of our nation, had a high squeaking voice and was well known to be impotent. Few were the men, however, who dared cross him, and the House held its breath when a member, in the heat of debate, made some slanting reference to Randolph's sexual neutrality.

Randolph rose to his feet and said coldly, "Sir, you pride yourself on an ability in which any barbarian is your equal and any jackass immeasurably your superior."

❀ 185

Alexander H. Stephens, Congressman from Georgia, and later vice president of the Confederacy, was a small man. He weighed not much more than ninety pounds and was no bigger than a child, but his intelligence was anything but small, and he knew it.

A large Congressman once said to him in anger, "Why, you pip-squeak, I could *eat* you without trouble."

And Stephens replied, "In which case you would end with more brains in your belly than in your head."

❀ 186

Johnson had rented a room in a boarding house and offered to pay a substantially higher than usual rent on condition that the landlady prepare a lunch each morning for him to take to work.

The first morning she prepared a generous roast-beef sandwich as the main item, and when Johnson returned, she asked how he had found lunch. Sourly, Johnson retorted, "Pretty good — what there was of it."

She made two large sandwiches the next day, but on his return, Johnson said once more, in response to her query, "Pretty good — what there was of it."

More than a little angered, the landlady took a whole loaf of rye bread, sliced it lengthwise, and stuffed the entire thing with a variety of cold cuts.

This time, when Johnson returned, he did not wait to be questioned. He fixed a cold eye on the landlady and said, "Back to one sandwich again, eh?"

As another example of the ease with which jokes can be modified to suit the occasion, here is how Joke 186 once came in handy for me:

✻ 187

I once ordered Lobster Diavolo in an Italian restaurant and my wife did the same. The chef prepared a double helping with a generous hand, and it was brought out on a gigantic platter which the waiter presented to me with a flourish.

I couldn't for the life of me resist spoiling the entire effect by saying calmly, "And my wife's?"

How did that come in handy? Well, I laughed and my wife laughed and the waiter laughed, everyone else at the table grinned, and the general tone of the entire dinner was made just a little merrier. All for three words. Oh, and before I forget —

✻ 188

As he was leaving, the diffident guest murmured to the hostess, "The meal was delicious, what there was of it."

Noting the hurt expression on his hostess's face, the guest blushed and hastened to say, "Oh, oh, and there was *plenty* of food, such as it was."

✻ 189

The barber had talked his way through three haircutting jobs, and now a fourth customer, who had been waiting patiently, was in the chair.

"And how would you like your hair cut?" asked the barber.

The customer replied curtly, "In silence."

✻ 190

Miss Beatrice Lillie, the well-known English comedienne, married Sir Robert Peel in 1920, but was always known by her stage name.

Once she was being waited on in a fur salon while the wife of a prominent and wealthy meat-packer was awaiting her turn most impatiently. The rich woman finally allowed herself to say, in a perfectly audible tone, "I wonder when that actress-person will be through?"

Beatrice Lillie gave no sign of having heard, and did not hurry herself for a moment. When she finally left, she sailed out haughtily, saying in perfectly enunciated and clearly audible words to the woman who had waited on her, "Now that Lady Peel has made her purchase, you may see what the butcher's wife wants."

My favorite Beatrice Lillie story, though, is —

❋ 191

One evening, Beatrice Lillie was part of a dinner party that included a fabulously beautiful showgirl who sat at the table, rarely speaking, but presenting a perfect profile for the breathless admiration of every man in the place.

At another table was a friend of Miss Lillie's. Hastily, he scribbled a note and sent it to her by way of the waiter. Miss Lillie opened the note which read: "My God, Bea, who is that incredibly gorgeous creature at your table?"

Beatrice Lillie scrawled an answer; the waiter carried it back to the questioner. He opened it hastily and found written there, "*Me!!!*"

❋ 192

The man at the bar, deep in private thoughts of his own, turned to a woman just passing and said, "Pardon me, miss, do you happen to have the time?"

In a strident voice she responded, "*How dare you make such a proposition to me?*"

The man snapped to attention in surprise and was uncomfortably aware that every pair of eyes in the place had turned in their direction. He mumbled, "I just asked the time, miss."

In a voice even louder, the woman shrieked, "*I will call the police if you say another word!*"

Grabbing his drink, and embarrassed very nearly to death, the man hastened to the far end of the room and huddled at a table, holding his breath and wondering how soon he could sneak out the door.

Not more than half a minute had passed when the woman joined him. In a quiet voice, she said, "I am terribly sorry, sir, to have embarrassed you, but I am a psychology student at the university and I am writing a thesis on the reaction of human beings to sudden shocking statements."

The man stared at her for three seconds, then he leaned back and bellowed, "*You'll do all that for me all night for just two dollars?*"

Joke 192 reminds me that until quite recently I had made my way, on occasion, through some of the swingingest sections of several big cities without ever having been accosted by a young lady intent on sex for pay.

For public consumption, I attributed this to the look of modest virtue that shone resplendent on my face. In private, however, I was increasingly obsessed with the fear that perhaps I was too ugly, or looked too married or too impotent, or in other ways seemed, on the very face of it, to be an unworthwhile prospect.

At 4 P.M. on a bright, shiny, sunny day in May 1968, on my way to my motel I passed a film house in midtown Manhattan that showed dirty movies. I paused to bestow a scientific look on a few of the stills and was just walking away again when a young lady, possibly no older than eighteen, rushed up to me and said, "Hello, there."

Thinking for a moment that this was someone I had met at a science fiction convention or in a publisher's office, I tried desperately to place the face while killing time by saying with a huge smile, "Hello yourself. How's everything? What are you doing down here?"

Accepting my cheerful good nature for what it seemed, the young lady promptly grabbed my wrist and began to drag a very astonished me into the neighboring doorway, saying, "Come, I will show you something nice."

I must say that I gave no evidence of the quick wit which I insist (at every opportunity) that I have. It took me fully half a minute to realize who and what she was.

At this point I would give a twenty-dollar bill to tell you how suavely I handled the situation — to be able to say that I had detached myself firmly and walked away with respectable virtue; or that with great efficiency I had led her to my motel room (half a block away) which had a pair of remarkably clean double beds in it.

But truth is mighty and will prevail, and the fact is — I wasn't suave. No sooner had I become aware that I was talking to a young and rather attractive prostitute, than I fell into a ridiculous stammer. Hanging back with what must have been a look of absolute terror on my face, I went "Ab-ab-ab-ab-ab —" for what seemed to my own ears to be five minutes.

The poor thing had no choice but to let me go, with a distinct expression of pity on her face; and I *ran*.

And that, I am afraid, is the sum and total of my life's experience with that subspecies of femininity.

The New York taxi driver is supposed to be a great talker, and a profound philosopher as well. I can only say I have not found it so. Still, sometimes things aren't too bad, and I routinely double my planned tip for any taxi driver who happens to make me laugh.

Once, for instance, I noticed that my taxi driver had the name Joseph P. O'Brien on his identification card, and because I had nothing better to do, I said, as we drove along, "I'll bet your middle name is Patrick."

"Yes," he said, and added thoughtfully, "a great deal of creative originality went into my name."

Another case was sharper and didn't involve me —

❊ 193

My taxi driver made a very tricky U-turn in Manhattan midtown traffic (*not* at my request), and another taxi driver, moving past, called out disapprovingly, "I got a ticket once, doing that."

And mine called back cheerfully, "Sooner you than me, buster."

❊ 194

The Spartans, at their height in the fifth century B.C., were admired by all the Greek world for their rigorous discipline, their absolute bravery, their readiness to die rather than be conquered. To maintain that discipline, they lived a harsh, communistic life. All ate at a common table at which the famous "Spartan porridge" was served — nourishing but simple.

An Athenian, a member of the most cultured and refined city in the Greek world, asked permission to join the communal life of Sparta for one day.

Permission was granted, and at the close of the day, the Athenian turned to a Spartan and said, "Now at last I understand why you Spartans are so fearless in battle and so scornful of death."

"You do?" said the Spartan.

"Of course. With food like yours to return to, I too would prefer death."

Except for physical courage (a relatively common virtue, really) there is little to admire in the Spartan subculture. Still, the stand at Thermopylae compels admiration even from those who disapprove of Sparta in general. In 480 B.C., when a large Persian army was in northern Greece, advancing southward, a much smaller army of Greek allies held them back for a lengthy period in the narrow pass at Thermopylae.

Finally, the Persians outflanked the pass, but three hundred Spartans (plus a number of other Greeks) refused to take part in the forced withdrawal of the defending army. They prepared to fight to the death in accordance with the Spartan ethic which forbade retreat. One tale is told of the moments immediately before the final battle, in which all the Greeks died —

✤ 195

Persian envoys came to demand surrender of Leonidas, the Spartan king who led the death stand at Thermopylae. "You are fools to resist," they said. "The Persian archers alone are so numerous that their arrows will darken the sun."

"So much the better," said Leonidas, unmoved, "we will then fight in the shade."

✤ 196

The Spartans practiced the art of being laconic — that is, of laboring to put their thoughts into the fewest possible words. The very word laconic comes from the fact that the district of which Sparta was the central city was Laconia.

The most condensed laconism in history was produced in the fourth century B.C. when Philip of Macedon was reducing all the Greek cities to obedience. The last holdout was Sparta, which, now past its time of power, nevertheless remained in stubborn isolation.

Philip didn't really need it for his future plans, but it annoyed him that there should be a patch of obstinacy on the map. He therefore sent the Spartans a message that went: "You had better submit without delay, for if I march my army into your land, I will ravage your farms, kill your men, and destroy your city."

And the Spartan leaders turned Philip's anger to admiration (so that he decided to leave them alone after all) by sending back a one-word answer: "If!"

✤ 197

The Spartans maintained their sullen noncompliance even during the reign of Philip's still more victorious son, Alexander the Great, refusing to send a contingent to join him in his invasion of the giant Persian Empire.

Alexander, however, won without the Spartans and became an

oriental monarch over immense territories. In accordance with Eastern custom (which he had to obey if he were to solidify his rule), he allowed himself to be worshipped as a god.

The Greek cities were expected to join in this worship by setting up altars in their temples, and they did so. It cost them very little, it meant nothing, and there was no point in offending Alexander.

Only Sparta resisted. When envoys arrived, telling them that Alexander had to be accepted as a god, the Spartan elders replied, "If Alexander wishes to be a god, let him be one." And that was all.

It is possible for a put-down to backfire. The most remarkable example I know of the highest praise evolving out of a universal put-down comes from Greek history.

☀ 198

Before the key battle of Salamis in 480 B.C., when the ships of the small collection of Greek city-states faced the navy of mighty Persia in a do-or-die moment, Themistocles, the Athenian leader, argued mightily and persistently for forcing a battle, since only by victory could Greece remain safe. The Spartan leader (in titular control of the fleet) was in favor of strategic withdrawal — for the Spartans were by no means as brave at sea as upon land — and grew impatient at Themistocles' flood of words. He raised his staff of command as though to strike the Athenian.

Themistocles said at once, "Well, then, strike — but *listen!*"

The Spartan lowered the staff and listened. The battle was joined and the Greeks won. The Persian fleet was shattered and the Persian menace permanently lifted.

The exultant commanders of the Greek fleet now met again and voted to see which one among them should be awarded the honor of having contributed most to the victory.

It was a multi-tie vote, for each commander voted for himself in first place. And every single one of them voted for Themistocles in second place.

The Greek fashion of history was different from ours. It was far more anecdotal for, in the absence of the modern system of documentation, it was far more difficult to get at the details. There was therefore far more temptation to make up what might have happened and invent incidents that would turn history into dramatic excitement or a moral lesson.

But I don't care. I like the anecdotes with which Greek history is riddled. For instance —

❈ 199

The ancient Greek world was divided into a thousand independent city-states of which Athens was the most remarkable and famous. When Themistocles of Athens was the most renowned leader in all Greece, a politican from the small provincial town of Larissa said to him: "A great deal of your fame, Themistocles, arises from the accident of your birth in Athens. Had you been born in Larissa, you would not have grown great."

To which Themistocles replied with a scornful smile, "Nor you, had you been born in Athens."

It was also Themistocles who said that his infant son ruled all Greece. When asked how that could be, he replied: "Athens dominates all Greece; I dominate Athens; my wife dominates me; and my infant son dominates her."

But enough of the Greeks for a while.

❈ 200

The jovial lawyer, rising to address a gathering after dinner, noticed that in the audience was another gentleman who was well known as one of the foremost after-dinner speakers in the nation.

The lawyer, striking an informal pose, with his jacket open and his hands in his pockets, said, "How odd to see my good friend George in the audience, demonstrating that a speaker can listen to someone else's words on occasion."

And from the audience, George cried out, "And how odd to see my good friend Henry on the podium, demonstrating that a lawyer can have his hands in his own pockets on occasion."

✻ 201

Mr. Chauncey Depew, lawyer, Senator, and one of the great wits of the nineteenth century, capped it all by attaining the age of ninety-four. But he didn't always win.

Once, very late in life, he was at a dinner sitting next to a young lady who was wearing an off-the-shoulder dress of extreme cut. Depew couldn't help but eye the effect in astonishment. Finally, he leaned toward the young lady and said, "My dear girl, what is keeping your dress on you?"

And the girl said demurely, "Only your age, Mr. Depew."

✻ 202

The two ladies were sitting in the living room, waiting for their hostess, who was slightly delayed. The daughter of the family was with them, on the theory that she would keep the visitors occupied during the wait.

The child was perhaps six years old, snub nosed, freckled, buck toothed and bespectacled. She maintained a deep silence and the two ladies peered doubtfully at her.

Finally, one of them muttered to the other, "Not very p-r-e-t-t-y, I fear," carefully spelling the key word.

Whereupon the child piped up, "But awful s-m-a-r-t!"

Dwellers of large cities usually find an endless source of fun in the small towns that rim them. Small towns are even surer sources of fun (for some reason) if their names include the letter K. All you have to do is say such names as Keokuk, Kankakee, Kalamazoo, Podunk, Shamokin, and even Brooklyn, and you're a long way toward your laugh.

The habit is dying, though. It originated with the feeling that small towns were not as sophisticated and advanced as the big city, but in these days of mass education, mass communication, and mass transportation, it just isn't true any longer. Furthermore, with television reaching everywhere, too much fun with individual towns induces angry responses from their citizens.

And yet —

❊ 203

A New Yorker had met a charming lady at a party but as time wore on, she began to make her excuses. "I have to make my way out to Hoboken."

"To Hoboken!" said the New Yorker. "Why would you want to do that?"

"I live there," she explained.

And he said, "But that's no excuse."

And once again, just to point up the difficulty of making categories, here's another combination — a shaggy-dog put-down.

❊ 204

Two hens met after a long absence and one said, "How are you Mrs. Leghorn? I trust your eggs are doing well."

"Quite well, thank you, Mrs. Rhode Island Red. They are selling for sixty-five cents a dozen."

"Indeed?" said Mrs. Red, with more than a little complacency. "Mine sell at seventy cents a dozen."

"Is that so? Why is that, I wonder."

"I presume it is because mine are larger."

Mrs. Leghorn shrugged with elaborate unconcern. "Good luck to you, then. As for me, I have no intention of tearing up my gut for a lousy five cents extra a dozen."

❊ 205

Professor Henry Augustus Rowland was a well-known American physicist of the nineteenth century, renowned for the sweetness of his disposition and his shy modesty.

At one time he was testifying as an expert witness at a trial, and the lawyer in his cross-examination said sharply, "Now, Professor Rowland, what are your qualifications as an expert witness in this case?"

Rowland answered with quiet calm, "In the subject under discussion, I am the greatest living expert."

After the trial, a friend said to him, "Henry, you amazed me. It was completely out of character for you to praise yourself so."

Rowland frowned. "What did you expect me to do? I was under oath."

✤ 206

The gentlemen of past centuries were perhaps a little more free and easy with respect to personal hygiene than most moderns are.

At least it is reported that Charles Lamb, the English essayist of the early nineteenth century, watching a game of cards, finally said to one the players, "George, if dirt were trumps, what a hand you'd have."

✤ 207

Gilbert Keith Chesterton, the author best known for his Father Brown detective stories, swung his ample girth up the steps of his club and met George Bernard Shaw emerging.

Chesterton looked at Shaw's beanpole figure with amusement and said, "Shaw, to look at you, anyone would think that famine had struck England."

And Shaw replied, "And to look at you, Chesterton, anyone would think that you had caused it."

✤ 208

Shaw was one of those clever and witty men who had a complete (and sometimes irritating) appreciation of his own cleverness and wit.

Once, on the opening night of one of his plays, he stepped forward with obvious complacence at its conclusion to accept the rousing plaudits of the crowd. There was one dissenter, however, who seized the occasion of a lull in the applause to call out in stentorian tones, "Shaw, your play stinks!"

There was a momentary horrified silence, but Shaw, unperturbed, exclaimed from the stage, "My friend, I agree with you completely, but what are we two," — here he waved his hand over the audience — "against the great majority?" And applause returned more loudly than ever.

❊ 209

James McNeill Whistler (whose most famous painting is popularly known as "Whistler's Mother") had delivered himself of one of those mordant witticisms for which he was so well known.

Oscar Wilde, no mean wit himself, heard it with chagrin and said, "I wish I had said that, James."

And Whistler answered, "Don't worry, Oscar, you will, you will."

Oscar Wilde was involved in a famous trial in 1895. He had been accused of homosexuality and had the poor judgment to launch a suit for libel when, as it happened, the accusation was true. He lost and was eventually sent to jail and treated so savagely that he was broken in body and spirit and didn't live long thereafter. Nevertheless, there were good moments.

❊ 210

To one question put him by the cross-examining attorney, Wilde made some irrelevant remark concerning his physician.

"Never mind your physician," said the lawyer angrily.

And Wilde answered loftily, "I never do."

I suppose nearly everyone has dreams of being a witness at a trial, facing a hostile lawyer, and poniarding him with bland wit to the delight of the audience, the jury, and even the judge. I'm told, however, that one should never do this; that nothing so irritates and angers a jury as a wise-guy witness. His wit certainly did nothing to help Wilde.

This makes life difficult for a jokester, for I seriously suspect that once on the stand (and so far, knock wood, I never have been), I won't for the life of me be able to resist the obvious riposte — which I'm sure the opposing lawyer will cheerfully elicit — and ruin my side.

I suppose my favorite of all writers is Mark Twain (or Samuel Langhorne Clemens, to use his real name). It isn't that I like his books better than anyone else's; it's rather that I love his way with words. I believe he once said, "The difference between the right word and the nearly right word is the difference between the lightning and the lightning bug." I have hugged that thought to myself all my life, and though there must be millions of times when I did not choose the right word, it has always seemed to me that Mark did.

He was a master of the epigram, too — remarks that in a few words could say a great deal, usually in the fashion of paradox. Witness his paradoxical put-down of pride:

❊ 211

Don't be proud. Secondhand diamonds are better than none.

He was one of the most uxorious men who ever lived. (That's the right word; look it up.) In one respect, though, he and his wife clashed. Mark Twain was earthy, and without any effort could and did drop into the ripest kind of language. His wife, on the other hand, disapproved of such matters and is supposed to have acted as an in-house censor of his writings.

❊ 212

There is a story that Mark Twain reached for a fresh shirt one morning and after putting it on, found crucial buttons missing. Ripping out a sulfurous expletive, he removed the shirt, took another, and found buttons missing there, too.

He expressed himself at considerably greater length, and put on a third shirt. When he found that one also had buttons missing, he lifted his face to heaven and relieved his soul of a good deal of pent-up emotion.

With the air about him still flickering blue, he turned and found his wife standing in the doorway, looking at him sorrowfully. To teach him a lesson, she now proceeded to repeat all that he had said, as meticulously as she could, pronouncing each filthy word with great care while the thunderstruck Mark listened.

When she was finally done, Mark heaved a great sigh and said, "My dear, you have the words, but you don't have the music."

Mark Twain, it is pleasant for me to note, had the last word even with other renowned wits.

✻ 213

James McNeill Whistler is reported to have displayed a just completed painting to Mark Twain.

Mark looked at the painting judiciously from a variety of angles and distances while Whistler waited impatiently for the verdict.

Finally, Mark leaned forward and, making an erasing gesture with his hand, said, "I'd eradicate that cloud if I were you."

Whistler cried out in agony, "Careful! The paint is still wet."

"That's all right," said Mark coolly. "I'm wearing gloves."

✻ 214

Around the turn of the century, the United States was still a parvenu among nations, much patronized by the sophisticated society of Europe. Some well-placed Frenchman remarked, for instance, that any time an American had nothing to do he could amuse himself endlessly by trying to find out who his grandfather was.

Naturally, Americans did not in the least like this hint that they were a mongrel people of no descent, and there was loud jubilation (and very nearly an international incident) when it was reported that Mark Twain had countered by saying, "And whenever a Frenchman has nothing to do, he can amuse himself endlessly by trying to find out who his father was."

☀ 215

Charles de Talleyrand-Périgord was a French politician, remarkably capable but utterly unprincipled, who survived innumerable changes in the government by adroitly betraying his associates in time. A republican during the French Revolution, he served as Napoleon's foreign minister, intrigued with Napoleon's enemies in time to survive the emperor's fall, and then managed to survive the falls of the restored kings as well.

Finally in 1838, having reached the age of 84, it was time for him to die, and King Louis Philippe was at his bedside.

"Oh," muttered Talleyrand, who was in great pain, "I suffer the tortures of hell."

And Louis Philippe, unmoved, said politely, "Already?"

☀ 216

Madame de Staël, a French writer of the Napoleonic period, was renowned for her cutting tongue. She strongly disliked Talleyrand, who, however, could easily take care of himself.

"Prince," she said to him once. "There is a new book out in which the author has represented each of us in thin disguise. He can scarcely value your masculinity, however, for he saw fit to portray each of us as an attractive woman."

"Indeed?" said Talleyrand, with an unperturbed bow. "And wrong in each case."

A contemporary of Talleyrand, and perhaps even more successfully cold-blooded, was Joseph Fouché, chief of Napoleon's secret police. He was probably one of the most subtle intriguers in history, survived all changes in government, and died in peace. His opinions have a certain grisly value, therefore.

☀ 217

Napoleon was irked at attempts to assassinate him. In order to put an end to plots against his life on the part of the exiled royalists of France, he determined to execute one of them as an object lesson.

Therefore, against the advice of Fouché, he had his agents seize the Duc d'Enghien, a young member of the royal family, who was completely innocent of any wrongdoing. In seizing him, moreover, Napoleon's agents had to cross the border and violate the neutrality of the small German state of Baden. The duke was given a farcical trial and was shot on the spot.

The plan worked in a way. Attempts to assassinate Napoleon ceased. However, a thrill of horror swept through Europe. The death of the poor duke was considered an unforgivable crime, and because of it, Napoleon suffered a propaganda disadvantage he never managed to overcome.

And Fouché, weighing the consequences, said cold-bloodedly, "It was worse than a crime; it was a blunder."

❋ 218

Simon Cameron of Pennsylvania served as secretary of war in the first year of Lincoln's administration, and there was some question as to his integrity. Indeed, Thaddeus Stevens, a Pennsylvania Congressman, was reported to have given it as his opinion that Cameron would steal anything but a red-hot stove.

That came to Cameron's ears and, in great dudgeon, he complained to President Lincoln. There was nothing much that Lincoln could do except suggest to Stevens that he might care to say he had been misquoted.

Stevens, a harsh curmudgeon of a man, promptly stated that to keep the peace within the party, he would be glad to state that he had been misquoted. What he had really said, Stevens explained, was that Cameron would steal anything, *including* a red-hot stove.

I once adapted Joke 218 for my own fell purposes. Willy Ley, the great science writer who died in 1969, for many years had been writing a science column for each issue of the science fiction magazine *Galaxy*. For many years, I myself have been writing a science column for each issue of the science fiction magazine *Fantasy and Science Fiction*. Willy and I were the best of friends and the most amicable of competitors. Nevertheless —

❀ 219

At a science fiction convention which I was toastmastering, I introduced Willy as "the second-best science writer in science fiction."

There was a snicker, of course, and a broad smile from Willy, who rose to say some words. When he was through, and before introducing the next speaker, I said, "Willy, I introduced you as the second-best science writer in science fiction, and on thinking that over, it seems to me that this was a conceited thing for me to do. I wish to apologize publicly. Willy, I'm *sorry* you're the second-best science writer in science fiction."

❀ 220

There is the tale of a downy-cheeked young lieutenant, freshly minted and assigned to his first company. He lined up his men for inspection and stood before them, trying to look martial. A voice from the rear suddenly sounded forth the Biblical quotation, "And a little child shall lead them!"

The lieutenant flushed, but made a painful pretense of not having heard.

The next morning, on the duty roster, was the printed announcement that the entire company was going to take a twenty-mile hike with full field equipment. And under that was a handwritten message reading, "And a little child shall lead them — on a damned big horse."

❀ 221

In the early decades of Washington, D.C., our capital was a small town of wooden houses and muddy streets. Two Congressmen, John Randolph of Virginia and Henry Clay of Kentucky, met face to face on a narrow plank. One was going to have to step out into the mud.

Randolph, who was easily offended and never forgiving, had no love for Clay and stood his ground. "I never turn out for scoundrels," he said.

Clay, a man of polished manners, merely bowed politely and said, "I always do." And he stepped into the mud.

✿ 222

According to one story, Dorothy Parker (to whom a tremendous number of epigrams have been attributed) was once trapped at a social gathering with some unconscionable bore who tortured her with long, tedious tales concerning other bores.

Finally he said, with lofty self-righteousness, "What it amounts to is that I simply can't bear fools."

And Dorothy Parker said, "Odd. Your mother apparently could."

✿ 223

Charles II of Great Britain was easy-going and hedonistic. Though highly intelligent, he was lazy and inclined to let things slide. His private life was notoriously immoral but he was nevertheless popular with his subjects.

His amours were sometimes fruitful, but of legitimate children he had none, and his heir was his younger brother James, Duke of York — serious, hardworking, narrow-minded, bigoted, and exceedingly unpopular.

Charles, with his usual careless ways, would have been the despair of the Secret Service if he had had any watching him, and his brother James expostulated with him, urging him to show himself less freely in public. After all, there was always the danger of assassination.

"Nonsense," said Charles good-humoredly, as he patted his brother on the shoulder. "There isn't a person in my kingdom who would dream of killing me in order to make you king."

✿ 224

Jascha Heifetz was a child prodigy and still a young boy when he made his triumphant musical debut on the violin. In the audience, seated side by side, were Mischa Elman, who had already established his own reputation as a violinist, and Artur Rubinstein, the pianist.

As the recital continued, and as Jascha played the violin like an angel, Mischa Elman writhed in increasing discomfort. Finally he leaned over to Rubinstein and said, "Isn't it terribly hot here?" Calmly, Rubinstein replied, "Not for pianists."

❈ **225**

A young man is reported to have approached the renowned composer Wolfgang Amadeus Mozart (one of the great musical prodigies of all time), and asked, "Herr Mozart, I have the ambition to write symphonies and perhaps you can advise me how to get started."

Mozart said, "The best advice I can give you is to wait until you are older and more experienced, and try your hand at less ambitious pieces to begin with."

The young man looked astonished. "But, Herr Mozart, you yourself wrote symphonies when you were considerably younger than I."

"Ah," said Mozart, "but I did so without asking advice."

I think of Joke 225 with a sigh. I get numerous letters from people who want advice on how to get started writing. I try to be helpful in my answers, and encouraging too, but when I feel unusually pressed for time and overharried by deadlines, I wish I had the courage to give them some version of Mozart's final remark.

In the early nineteen-sixties, for a couple of years I was a member of Mensa, an organization of high-IQ individuals who, by test, are supposed to be in the uppermost two percent of the population. It didn't work out for me, alas. I was entirely too self-conscious, and so was everybody else. You see, most of the members were young, in college, and eager to demonstrate their Mensa-level intelligence.

It seemed easy and convenient for them to do this by choosing me to cross swords with. In no time I felt like an old gunfighter being challenged by a succession of young aspirants, and I didn't like the role. So I quietly dropped out and let the youngsters labor to get the drop on each other.

Still, I may have felt a little wounded by the experience, for when I was invited to speak at a Mensa convention in New York, this is how I began —

* 226

It is with some trepidation [I said] that I address an audience of people, all of whom are smarter than I am. All of whom *put together*, that is.

I swear to you that I had no intention of beginning so; it just came out as I stared at them. Fortunately, though, they were good-humored about it and laughed. If they had taken it amiss, I might have been embarrassed indeed because *The New Yorker* discussed that convention in "The Talk of the Town" in their next issue, and they saw fit to repeat my remark.

The difficulty with my talks, you see, is that they are extemporaneous and represent a kind of interaction between the audience and myself. When the audience is receptive and warm, I am lured into following instinct and taking chances. Sometimes I break into a cold sweat thinking about it afterward, but the only real measure of whether I did the right thing is whether I got the proper reaction — and usually the reaction I want is a laugh.

For instance —

* 227

I addressed a gathering of college students once, and having made a point that seemed to show a certain pessimism concerning the future, I went on. "I know that all of you are saying to yourselves, 'This is a strange attitude to find in someone who is the very best science fiction writer in the world.'"

At this, there was (predictably) a kind of uneasy stir at this casual display of ego, at which I looked surprised and said, "Don't get me wrong. I'm not saying I'm the best. *You* are!"

And that got the laugh.

Still, no matter what I do and what I write, the matter of ego comes up, and I suspect nowhere more than in this book. Well, I'm not going to apologize. I see no virtue in pretending to a modesty one doesn't feel. I would rather be me as I am, ego and all, than be Uriah Heep (assuming you've read *David Copperfield*).

And even if you haven't read *David Copperfield*, let me tell you one last joke for this section:

❊ 228

I was having lunch with a Catholic priest, and I couldn't resist telling him the story of what happened once when I was giving a talk at a Catholic college.

A priest was showing me and a group of other people around the campus, and at one point he ushered us all into the elevator. All entered but myself, and I politely gestured the priest to precede me. For a moment, we kept everyone waiting while each of us tried to maneuver the other into the elevator. Finally, the priest gave in and got on, and I followed him with a somewhat smug smile.

Chuckling a little, he said, "Well, I lose in humility that time."

The Catholic priest to whom I told the story said, "It made you feel good to win in humility, didn't it?"

"Yes," I said, "it did, rather."

And he said, "We're acquainted with that feeling in our profession. We call it the I'm-the-humblest-man-here-and-proud-of-it syndrome."

PART V *Word Play*

SOMETIMES THE SUDDEN ALTERATION in point of view depends
on the ambiguity of the language.

I suspect that no language is utterly clear and straightforward; I suspect that no language can be. As a language ages
and develops, there are bound to be accretions. A word or
phrase will gain a new meaning without abandoning the old;
words of distinctly different meaning and appearance, like to
and two, will gradually grow alike in sound; or if similar in appearance and meaning to begin with, will gradually grow gro-
tesquely different, like queen and quean.

What's more, I strongly suspect that of all languages English
lends itself the most easily to all these ambiguities of word and
phrase. It has the largest vocabulary of any language, and a
vocabulary, moreover, drawn from the most various sources. It
is, of all the major languages, the most disorderly in spelling
and the least inhibited in grammar. It is most widespread over
the world, most spoken by those whose first language is something else, most dialected, most distorted, most mangled — and
it has survived it all.

The result is that more games can be played with it than with
any other language, and to anyone who loves English — who
truly loves it — who loves the intricacies of its countless words
and phrases and all its ridiculous and unruly idioms, those
games represent the purest fun one can have with nonmusical
sounds.

I will admit that I am intoxicated with English and that not everyone is. I will admit that I am pleased by any ingenious double meaning, and that I will go to inordinate lengths to invent one and drag it into the conversation — and that to many this is annoying.

But what can I do? This is *my* book; and though I desperately want to please my audience, I must please myself first — so love me, love my puns.

For instance —

* 229

Some years ago, New York's Third Avenue elevated railway was taken down. Visiting the city some time later to lunch with an editor, I was amazed to note the unaccustomed nakedness of the vista when I faced east.

Thoughtfully, I said to my lunch companion, "Third Avenue reminds me of Christmas."

Surprised, he said, "Why?"

"No el," I said.

Where the point of a joke rests on a play on words, a sudden and sharp ending is particularly essential. Ideally, the listener should take the final word or phrase at face value and then see the secondary meaning an instant later. That produces the necessary change in point of view. (It is customary in our culture, to be sure, to groan at a pun rather than laugh, but in this case the groan is the equivalent of the laugh, so don't let it bother you.)

Not only did my companion groan melodiously when I made the "No el" comment, but he then actually published the pun in an editorial* carefully attributing it to me, and accompanied it with denigrating phrases that were the written equivalent of a groan.

* The gentleman in question was Robert P. Mills, who was then editor of *Venture Science Fiction.*

Please note that a pun is more effective when one makes the victim a party to his own immolation; and it is worth considerable trouble to work out a plan designed to do just that. If I simply had said, "Third Avenue reminds me of Christmas because there is no el," nothing would have happened. By suspending my first comment about Third Avenue and Christmas, and making the obviously incongruous remark with an absolutely straight face and casual tone, I virtually forced the "Why?" in the anticipation of some sober, sensible answer. By making the victim an accomplice to his own downfall, you insure a most stentorian groan which is (or should be) music to the punster's ear.

So effective is this particular pun, in fact, that I once elaborated it. During a Christmas season about fifteen years ago, I invented a song in the shower. It was to the tune of "The First Noel," which begins: "The first Noel, the angels did say, was to certain poor shepherds in fields as they lay . . ." I'm sure you know it.

My parody, which I will leave for you to fit to the tune by distorting syllables where necessary, is:

> When they tore down the el, our mayor did say
> That soon in its place there would be a subway.
>   'Twould be new, 'twould be clean,
>   'Twould be painted white and green,
> So give three cheers for our bright new subway.
>   No el,   No el,
>   No el,   No el,
> So give three cheers for our bright new subway.

I never got past that first "No el" before the groans and laughter stopped me. Now, year after year for fifteen years I have been singing this at the Christmas season to audiences composed (I like to think) of quick-witted individuals who are thoroughly acquainted with the Christmas carol I am parodying. Yet never, not once, not *once*, has anyone anticipated the pun.

Very few people think punnily, and that's all there is to it; but if *you* do, then bless you, because, despite the groans, punny is funny.

Word play, I hasten to emphasize, does not by any means refer to puns only. Consider the ambiguity in the following, which involves no pun, no word distortion at all —

❊ 230

Ernestine Schumann-Heink was an operatic contralto in the early part of this century when it was still permissible for great singers to carry the bulk deemed necessary to give their lungs the necessary power.

One day she sat down with the greatest possible satisfaction before a platter on which reposed a huge steak, sizzling and flavorful. Enrico Caruso, passing by, gazed at it with surprise and said, "Surely you don't intend to eat that steak all alone?"

"Of course not," said Madame Schumann-Heink with scorn. "1 intend to eat it with potatoes."

❊ 231

Jimmy Durante, who in his later years had developed excellent comedy routines with the operatic contralto Helen Traubel, is reported to have blundered into her dressing room once when she was not expecting visitors.

Emerging again hastily, he is reported to have said, "Nobody knows the Traubel I've seen."

Word play, more than any other form of humor, places the jokester at the mercy of the audience. It is necessary for it to see the double meaning, and this sometimes requires an understanding of a particular literary allusion.

Jimmy Durante's alleged remark involves nothing extremely

arcane, but the audience must know that there is a famous spiritual "Nobody Knows the Trouble I've Seen," or the aptness of the punch line is lost. The audience then remains blank or, dimly aware that you were intending a word play of some sort, groans tentatively. If you try to explain, you succeed only in offending an audience which naturally will be reluctant to enjoy its own ignorance and which, in any case, will find nothing funny in a slow and gradual alteration in point of view.

Punsters, and others adept at word play, must therefore cultivate a thick skin and a philosophic attitude.

Recently, for instance, I was in a group where someone spoke scornfully of a prominent law-and-order politician who had called for a reordering of American goals. The speaker said, "What does that jerk know about goals? His specialty is jails, not goals."

No one in the audience had the slightest notion that a word play was being attempted, and it was only later that it occurred to me that the speaker was English and that what he meant was "gaols, not goals." He must have been terribly disappointed at not having earned one smile, yet he continued bravely.

There is another lesson here. Word plays are meant for the ear, not the eye. Words or phrases which are similar in appearance but different in sound lose in the telling, however clever they may seem on the printed page.

✸ 232

The chieftain of an African tribe had died, and his heavy and elaborate throne was hoisted to the top of his lofty grass-thatched royal hut in order to keep it out of the way until his heir should reach the age when he might properly sit upon it in full adult regalia.

Unfortunately, the young heir was playing under the place where the throne had been stowed for safekeeping at just the moment when the rope broke. The falling throne killed the boy.

Moral: People who live in grass houses shouldn't stow thrones.

Joke 232 is an example of a class of jokes which have grown popular in recent years (and in most cases, undeservingly). The punch line consists of a twist on a well-known saying (in this case, of course, "People who live in glass houses shouldn't throw stones"), often by a reversal of initial sounds. Such a reversal is called a spoonerism after Reverend William A. Spooner of Oxford, a cleric of the turn of the century who apparently made such reversals involuntarily.

Such jokes are easily invented but the joy of invention is usually greater than the joy of hearing. I myself love to construct them. Many years ago I remember saying to someone on an occasion when it seemed to follow naturally:

✷ 233

"You know," I said, "that Sherlock Holmes was remarkable for his great dignity."

"He was?" said my victim, undoubtedly searching his memory of the stories.

"Oh, yes," I said gravely, "I'm sure you have often heard of the stately Holmes of England."

This led me on to invent a game called They Wrote a Song About It. I will give you just one example. Someone had spoken approvingly of Denmark and its people, and I said, "I know. I know. They've written a song about it." My friend was astonished and said, "They have?" "Sure," I said. "You've heard it, haven't you? 'There is nothing like a Dane, nothing in the world.'" And if you have any voice at all you sing the well-known song from *South Pacific* for as long as you remain un-lynched.

The game never caught on, nor did its sister games, They Wrote a Play About It and They Made a Movie About It. I can only attribute this failure to envy in high places.

But, going back to spoonerisms, my most successful one ever is the following:

✲ 234

Mortimer H. Stein, having absconded with $100,000, stepped into a time machine, went seven years into the future, and stepped out again, feeling that the statute of limitations now protected him from trial.

He was arrested anyway, and the prosecution claimed that in order to avoid trial, the criminal ought to have lived through seven years in constant apprehension of arrest — that being considered the adequate punishment that made sense out of a statute of limitations.

The defense contended that the law said nothing about living through seven years. It only said that seven years had to pass. The defendant had hidden in time, so to speak, and that was no different from hiding in space, unless the law was amended to make it so.

The judge finally handed down his decision in favor of the defendant. It was in six words only, for he said, "A niche in time saves Stein."

What makes it my most successful spoonerism? Why, a very practical consideration: In a slightly expanded form, I sold it to a science fiction magazine for fifty dollars and have had it reprinted twice since, each time for an additional sum of money. (Who says making up jokes is an idle occupation?)

Actually, though, I've made up an even better one that involves an even smaller variation from the original; but it isn't as successful in the sense that I haven't gone commercial with it. It goes like this:

✲ 235

Joe Brown had long bored every one of his acquaintances with long tales of his surfing prowess. It was decided at last to call his bluff.

When all were at a beach, with the waves curling in perfectly, a surfboard was suddenly thrust into his hand, and he was told, "Show us, Joe. Show us what you can do with a surfboard."

Joe did not hesitate. He took the board, marched toward the

water line, but then stopped ten feet short of the highest reach of the waves. Holding his surfboard vertically beside him, he stood as though graven in stone.

His companions finally lost patience. "Come on, Joe," they yelled, "get into the water."

"I don't have to," he yelled back.

"Why not?"

And Joe shouted, "Because they also surf who only stand and wait."

I don't always get a laugh out of this. Some listeners haven't read the great sonnet "On His Blindness" by John Milton, which ends with the immortal line "They also serve who only stand and wait."

This, incidentally, ought to be used as an argument in favor of culture. By broadening the base of our knowledge of man and the universe, we also broaden our base for the construction and understanding of jokes of all kinds (not merely word play) and increase the store of fun and laughter in the world.

The trouble with word play is that once you get started, you begin to reach farther and farther and take greater and greater liberties. You can be sure that the more tortured the change, the greater the indignation. So inevitable is this progression from tolerable to bad to worse, that I would urge everyone to tell no more than one such joke in any one session. To tell two will start a series and the evening may be ruined.

Of course, my tolerance is greater than that of most others. As an example, I find the following amusing but have detected outright virtuous indignation on the part of others when I tell it.

✲ 236

Smith came into the house, dripping wet and looking incredibly bedraggled. Outside the window, the pelting rain was all too visible.

His sympathetic wife said, "Oh dear, it's raining cats and dogs outside."

"You're telling me," said Smith. "I just stepped in a poodle."

Cross-purposes are an unfailing source of humor, but they are hard to set up in a brief tale. A well-known example is:

❋ 237

Two gentlemen, both hard of hearing and strangers to each other, were about to ride the London Underground. One of them, peering at the station they were entering, said, "Pardon me, sir, but is this Wembley?"

"No," said the other, "Thursday."

"No, thank you," said the first, "I've already had my little drink."

Or there can be humor in attempting to take an idiomatic expression literally —

❋ 238

Miss Jones was fascinated by the nature lecture. She came up afterward to ask questions. She said, "You mean the female fish just lays its eggs in a depression, and the male fish then swims over the eggs and fertilizes them after they have been laid?"

"That's right, miss."

"You mean that fish don't — uh —"

"No, they don't, miss."

Miss Jones thought about that a moment, then her face brightened. "Oh," she said, "so *that's* why people say, 'Poor fish!'"

❋ 239

A young swain, on an automobile drive in the country with his loved one, left the car long enough to venture into a field where he might pick a bouquet of wild flowers for his lady fair. He had barely plucked the blossoms, when he became aware of a bull present in the same field.

The bull, a large specimen, was facing him with head lowered. It made distinct snorting sounds and one leg scraped the ground.

Far away, on the other side of a fence, stood a farmer who was taking in the situation with a serene eye. The young man yelled out to him, "Hey, is that bull safe?"

The farmer shouted back, "Safe as anything." He considered a moment more and shouted, "Can't say the same about you, though."

Again I must avoid giving the impression that I am deadly keen on word play and that I am so infernally quick-witted that it is impossible to catch me. Would that that were so, but it isn't. My garage man, a worthy soul with a painfully raucous idea of what constitutes humor, is responsible for the following —

✳ 240

He said to me, "Listen, doc, a deaf and dumb man went into a hardware store in order to buy some nails. He banged his fist on the counter and the salesman brought him a hammer. The deaf and dumb man shook his head, put two fingers together as though he were holding a nail and hammered at that. The salesman brought him nails; he showed the right size and how many, made his purchase, and left.

"And then a blind man entered in order to buy a pair of scissors. Now how do you suppose he showed the salesman what he wanted?"

Completely mystified as to what my garage man was getting at, I patiently raised my left hand, pointed the first and middle fingers, and made scissoring gestures.

And my garage man looked contemptuous and said, "No, he didn't, you dumb jerk. He used his voice and asked for it."

He told me afterward, when I questioned him with considerable interest, that he had caught every one of his customers with the story. He also said that he was particularly sure he would catch me specifically, because anyone with all my education couldn't be very smart.

I didn't try to argue that last point. He may be right.

I suspect that by the time you readers will have reached this far in this section, most of you will have muttered under your breath: "A man who will make a pun will pick a pocket," or "A pun is the lowest form of wit."

Well, they are both misquotations. It was John Dennis, a dramatist and literary critic, who was reported to have left the room in fury in 1693 when someone punned, saying, "A man who could make so vile a pun would not scruple to pick a pocket." But that refers to *vile* puns, not good ones. Besides, Dennis's plays were all failures, so I'm not sure that he was such a great judge of wit.

Then, too, it was Noah Webster who said, "Punning is a low species of wit." To make that into "the lowest form of wit" changes it utterly. Besides, Webster was a pedant who couldn't bear to see words misused, and punning sometimes involves that which, to a straight-laced grammarian, would be misuse.

Thus, there is a tale about Noah Webster (possibly apocryphal) which goes —

❋ **241**

Mrs. Noah Webster, entering a room, caught her husband deeply involved in kissing the maid.

Mrs. Webster said in awful tones, "Mr. Webster! I am surprised!"

Mr. Webster, coming up for air, said, "*I* am surprised, my dear. You are merely astonished."

The point of this joke has, alas, grown feeble with the years. Nowadays, the proper meaning of surprised (caught unprepared) has become secondary, with Mrs. Webster's improper meaning (astonished) in universal use.

In any case, one might offer counterquotes. Edgar Allan Poe, whom I consider a better judge of things literary than both Dennis and Webster, put together and multiplied several times over, said, "Of puns it has been said that those most dislike who are least able to utter them."

The most perfect pun I know involves three separate words.

✲ 242

Three brothers went out West to establish a cattle ranch, but couldn't think of an appropriate name for it. So they wrote to their father back East, and he replied, "Call it Focus, for that's where the sun's rays meet."

The pun is so perfect that it may well raise no laugh. There is no distortion of sound to warn the ear and the listener may hear only one of the possibilities: "sun's rays meet" or "sons raise meat," but not both, and wonder what the joke is.

To introduce a small imperfection is thus good; to do it on the spur still better; and to build it on a previous pun is best of all.

Who, for instance, could possibly find anything but delight in the following exchange among the panelists on "Information Please," the hit radio show of the late thirties and early forties. Who said what, I don't remember, but it went as follows:

✲ 243

"One man's Mede is another man's Persian."
"Are you Shah?"
"Sultanly."

Well, perhaps it wouldn't be funny to those who don't know the connection between Medes and Persians; or between Persians, Shahs, and Sultans; or never heard that "one man's meat is another man's poison." But then, that only proves that puns, far from being a low form of wit, appeal of necessity only to the most cultured.

The most specialized piece of simple word play I know follows (after a fashion):

❧ 244

One of the basic equations of theoretical physics is $e = h\nu$, where ν is the Greek letter nu (pronounced new). By simple algebraic manipulation, this is equivalent to $\nu = e/h$.

Consequently, if one physicist were to ask another, "What's new?" it would not be surprising if the other were to answer, "e/h."

Put that way, it is hard to imagine the joke getting a laugh. The explanation is wearisome (even though I have made it as short as possible), and it manages to telegraph the punch line.

Suppose, however, I were to say, "One physicist, meeting another, said, 'What's new?' The other answered, 'e/h.' "

That two-liner would be absolutely meaningless to anyone without at least college physics in his background. A physicist with a sense of humor, however, who had not heard this before, would be liable to laugh (or groan) loudly and long.

I offer this free of charge, by the way, as the gimmick in a murder mystery. At the crucial moment, the detective tells the joke and the person who is trapped into smiling reveals his till-then-hidden knowledge of physics. (If you use it, though, do give this book a mention.)

Word play is of particular delight to grade school children. They have, after all, just discovered it; it is a fresh game to them; and they have not yet been taught by mentally cramped elders that they aren't supposed to laugh at such things.

As a result, generation after generation of subteen-agers brings them home to their parents with all the zeal (and the effect) of a cat bringing home a dead mouse.

✻ 245

I steeled myself once when my daughter (still quite young) said to me, "Pronounce *t-o*, Daddy."

"To," I said obediently.

"And *t-o-o*."

"To," I said again.

"And *t-w-o*."

"To," I said again.

"And the second day of the week."

"Tyoosday," I said carefully, pretending the trap lay in forgetting the proper (but nearly universally neglected) pronunciation, in favor of the lower-class "Toosday."

Whereupon my daughter said, "Funny, *I* always pronounce the second day of the week, 'Monday.' "

She burst into loud laughter at having trapped me. Had I let her see I knew the joke, I would have cruelly disappointed her. Here is one more (only one more, and I plead for your tolerance), which goes through the fourth grade each year:

✻ 246

Questioner: With which hand do you stir your coffee?
Victim: With my right hand.
Questioner: Funny, I use a spoon.

As in everything else, however, it never pays to underestimate even what seems most underestimable. My daughter came home with a mimeographed sheet once and asked me if I would play a game that had amused her class that day. It consisted of correctly following all the directions listed on the sheet, directions which she warned me were "pretty tricky."

Well, directions that sixth-graders (which she was at the time) find "very tricky" don't bother good old *me*, so I thought I'd oblige. The first direction told me to read the entire page before proceeding further, which of course I ignored. The second direction told me to make a dot in the center of a blank piece of paper. The third direction told me to make a square around the dot, and so on and so on. I made all kinds of figures; I punched holes in the corner of the sheet with the pencil; I announced briskly, "I am a good boy and follow orders" — all in accordance with the instructions.

Finally, with the page festooned with marks of all kinds, I reached the last direction, which said, "Follow only the first direction and ignore all others."

Almost every kid in the class had been caught that day, and I suppose almost every parent was caught that evening.

It reminds me of the classic way of inducing a nervous breakdown. You send a telegram to some good friend in a distant city, saying, "Ignore previous telegram. All may yet be well."

✻ 247

Computers have been developed which can translate one language into another. Ideally, if the translated passage were then translated by computer back into the first language, the original words ought to be regained. This, however, does not allow for the ambiguity of languages.

Thus, there is the story of the computer that was ordered to translate a common English phrase into Russian and then translate the Russian translation back into English.

What went in was "Out of sight, out of mind."

What came out was "Invisible insanity."

✻ 248

There was once a newspaper headline that read SOCIALITE WEDS MIT GRADUATE, with the initials omitted from M.I.T. to save space. *The New Yorker* quoted the headline, and its comment was "Dod'z nize."

There are erudite puns, of course, and even bilingual puns where to be appreciated the ambiguity requires the knowledge of two languages. The best example I know is a laconism that served as the dispatch of a (who else?) general. Naturally, it was a British general.

✻ 249

In 1843, Sir Charles Napier won smashing victories in Sind, a region along the lower reaches of the Indus River in what is now Pakistan. With security in mind and with the realization that British public officials were routinely expected to know Latin, he sent the one-word message, "Peccavi." It is Latin for "I have sinned," and that was all anyone needed to know.

✻ 250

The sweet young thing was being shown around the large aircraft carrier. She spied an officer who was in a particularly resplendent uniform and said, "Who's that?"

"That," she was informed, "is the naval surgeon."

Her eyes grew round. "Heavens," she said, "how medical men specialize!"

Naturally, with puns expected to be "bad" by folklore and social custom, there sometimes arises an active competition for the deliberate invention of bad puns. Of course, "bad" is subjective. No pun is so bad, that *someone* won't think it good, but there are bound to be many puns which most would agree lack all cleverness and possess only irritants. I won't plague you with many examples, but may I present my own personally invented candidate for worst pun in the world? (Why say "May I?" I'm going to include it here and you can't stop me.)

✻ 251

Did you ever hear of the accountant who added up his columns of figures so queerly that he always ended with "$79.25 plus a cat," or "$1568.13 plus a cat," and so on?

It seems he had an "add-a-puss complex."

Some of the fads in joking involved word play of one sort or another. There was once a whole rash of "Little Moron" jokes that plagued the world, and I only heard one that as much as induced a smile:

❊ 252

Did you ever hear about the little moron who walked through a screen door and strained himself?

Then there were the "Knock, Knock" jokes, and out of the myriads I can only remember one offhand:

❊ 253

> Knock, knock!
> Who's there?
> Ammonia!
> Ammonia who?
> Ammonia bird in a gilded cage.

Oh well, it appeals to the chemist in me.

❊ 254

The young lad was struggling out of the small lake, fully clothed and dripping. A kindly passerby stopped to give him a hand, and then said, "But how did you come to fall in, my boy?"

The boy allowed an expression of contempt to cross his face and said, "I didn't come to fall in! I came to fish."

A dream of glory that I'm sure dwells in the mind of everyone capable of giving a quick retort (a few) or imagining himself capable of giving a quick retort (many) is that of rising from the audience and neatly topping some witticism of the speaker's. The best example I can think of (and one I'll bet never

really happened) is the following, which involved a pun topping another pun.

✵ 255

The speaker had droned on and on in his discussion of the local
electric generating plant, talking of all the manifold blessings that
electricity had brought mankind, not the least of them being the
abolition of darkness once and for all with the substitution of blessed
light.

"In fact," said he, reaching his peroration, "let me borrow from the
poet Tennyson, and cry out with him, 'Honor the Light Brigade!' "

And a man in the audience rose at once and yelled out, "Oh, what
a charge they made."

Actually, the correct quote from Tennyson's "The Charge of
the Light Brigade" is "O the wild charge they made!" but that
would not be as funny, in my opinion, and pedantry must never
be allowed to interfere with a joke.

✵ 256

Mrs. Goldfarb, rather advanced in years, had finally been persuaded
to consult a psychiatrist for the first time.

The psychiatrist, viewing her ruefully, said, "Mrs. Goldfarb, with
your permission I will try an experiment with you. It may serve to
advance us more rapidly. I am going to have you lie here on the
couch for half an hour, and during that period of time I want you to
think of nothing but sex. Do you understand me? Just think of sex.
When I come back I will ask you what you have thought and we
can proceed from there."

In half an hour, he was back. "Well, Mrs. Goldfarb, have you
been thinking of sex?"

"Yes, doctor," she said.

"And what have you been thinking?"

"I've been thinking," she said, "that by me, Sex Fifth Avenue is not
as good as Macy's."

☆ 257

The Latin professor arrived home in a state of utter confusion, and much the worse for wear. His jacket was torn, his trousers muddy, his hat a battered ruin, his eyeglasses bent askew.

His wife ran to him, startled. "Septimus," she cried, "whatever has happened to you?"

"Why, my dear," said the professor, seating himself carefully, "I scarcely know. I was passing the corner of Second and Main when, without provocation of any sort on my part, I was suddenly assaulted by two hoodla."

☆ 258

The curator of one zoo was shipping several animals to another zoo, and wrote an accompanying letter which said in part, "Included are the two mongeese you asked for."

The curator paused. "Mongeese" looked funny.

He tore up the letter and tried again, saying, "Included are the two mongooses you asked for."

That looked funny, too.

After long thought, the curator began a third time and now completed it without trouble. He wrote in part, "Included is the mongoose which you requested. Included is also the other mongoose which you also requested."

It's only fair for a jokester to be able to settle the questions he raises. Anyone accustomed to telling Joke 258 is bound to strike on someone, sooner or later, who will say, "What *is* the plural of mongoose?" The jokester should be fortified with the answer. It is mongooses.

In fact, if he's the type, he can go on to other peculiar plurals. For instance a Mussulman is a person of the Moslem faith. And two of them are Mussulmans, not Mussulmen. You might even win bets on that one. (Use discretion, though. If you go too far, you become a pedant — a trap I am forever on the verge of stumbling into — and it is awfully hard to like a pedant.)

And talking about pedantry —

❋ 259

There were not many who could match Winston Churchill when it came to sounding the proper notes on the instrument we call the English language, and it infuriated him to have pedantic mediocrities squeeze his words into a grammatical strait jacket. When some nameless critic corrected a Churchillian sentence on the basis of the old bromide that a preposition was not something we ought to end a sentence with, Churchill countered with a furious note of his own on the page.

It read: "This is the kind of nonsense up with which I will not put."

A preacher is a public speaker, and knowing the profession, I sympathize with him, for there must be a terrible strain in having to deliver a sermon every week with a comparatively narrow choice of topics. It must have been particularly so in the last century, when sermons were expected to be interminably long and hysterically dramatic. The temptation to dip into sermon collections of the past and do a little judicious borrowing must have been enormous.

❋ 260

Mark Twain sat through an exceedingly dramatic sermon one time, one of which the preacher seemed obviously proud.

Afterward Mark drawled, "Well, yes, it was a ripsnorter all right, Reverend Carter, but you know, I have a book at home that has every word of it."

The preacher fired up at once. "Quite impossible. I would certainly like to see that book, if it exists."

"So you shall. I will mail it to you first thing in the morning."

Eventually, a bulky package arrived from Mark Twain with an enormous postage-due attached. The preacher paid the charges and ripped open the wrappings.

Inside was an unabridged dictionary.

✻ 261

My friend Willy Ley (to whom I have referred earlier in the book) had a large and impressive paunch. On one occasion, as Willy sat sprawled at his ease on a couch, a fellow writer (not me, for I am in no position to criticize) tapped that paunch and said, "Willy, Willy, you ought to diet."

Willy looked down at his abdomen, took the cigar out of his mouth, and said, "All right. What color?"

But let me end this section with word play that makes use of punctuation, and with an implication that would be a heart-warming one for any writer, anywhere, any time.

✻ 262

Victor Hugo, the French writer, published his masterpiece *Les Misérables* in 1862 (in ten volumes). Critical acclaim and public interest were his at once, but he well knew that what actually counted, for himself if not for posterity, were sales.

Unable to bear the suspense, he sent a card to his publishers. On it, was simply "?"

The reply was thoroughly satisfactory. It was "!"

ONE OF THE CATEGORIES suggested to me for this book was Tables Turned. This phrase refers specifically to jokes in which there is a sudden sharp alteration in point of view — but it is my contention that all jokes have this in one way or another. It seemed to me, therefore, that we would merely be placing in this category jokes which didn't seem to fit in any of the other sections.

I thought about this for a considerable length of time since I felt that the obvious thing to do was to label the category Miscellaneous and place it at the end — and I didn't want to. For one thing, I dislike any section labeled Miscellaneous, and I had my own idea as to which category I intended to place last.

So in the end, I have decided to make Tables Turned the middle category of the book. And, as a matter of fact, it is convenient to have a section of miscellany (whatever I call it), for where else can I discuss cartoons?

During the last few decades, the cartoon has become a new and very subtle joke form, and one can't help but wonder why it took so long for the cartoon to enter the field in its present form. I suspect this may have been because it was long confused with the illustrated joke.

Suppose, for instance, you had the following He-She joke, which, in its time, was exceedingly popular.

✻ 263

He: How do you like Kipling?
She: I don't know, you naughty boy. I've never kippled.

The combination of the girl's ignorance of Rudyard Kipling (at the height of his fame as a poet at the time the joke was in its heyday) and the lascivious pleasure in guessing what the lady thought one did when one kippled (and to make sure the pleasure is lascivious, you must include the phrase "you naughty boy") raised a sure laugh.

If, now, you placed above that short exchange a cartoon drawing of a young man and woman talking, the result seems to be a funny cartoon, but it isn't; it is just an illustrated joke. The caption itself is just as funny without the drawing. The illustrated joke was a mainstay of the old humor magazines of the twenties, *Judge, Life,* and *College Humor.*

What was needed, and what was developed to a high art in the thirties (thanks chiefly to *The New Yorker*) was a cartoon with a one-line caption, where cartoon and caption were only funny together. The cartoon set up the background that gave the caption meaning, and the caption translated the drawing into whimsy.

The advantage of such a one-liner over the ordinary joke was that it was possible to absorb the background delineated in the cartoon at a glance whereas even the most economical word picture would take several seconds and still be less dramatic. The caption breaks on you almost as soon as you grasp the cartooned background, and the change in point of view is almost instantaneous, so that the laughter can be enormously intense and satisfying. The one-liner is a kind of pure punch line.

The disadvantage of the cartoon is that it can be shown to someone else, but it can't be conveniently told — and almost

never, even by a skilled jokester, without considerable loss in
translation.

To try to include cartoons translated into words in this book
is foolish, considering that there are any number of cartoon collections; but I must try just a couple, simply because they are
among my all-time favorites.

✱ 264

Four people are pictured sitting around a bridge table with cards in
their hands. Behind one of them is a full set of perfectly enormous
railroad signals. Let us call the player in front of those signals Fotheringay.

The player to Fotheringay's right, and therefore one of the opposing partners, is leaning toward him, face suffused with fury.

The caption reads: "You know very well what signals, Fotheringay!"

✱ 265

A young lady is pictured staggering into a ship's stateroom, her
hairdo a mess and her clothing in disarray. She is speaking to her
surprised roommate, another young lady.

The caption reads: "He said a storm was coming up, and like a
fool, I let him tie me to the mast."

I suppose I wouldn't be me if I didn't try to make up cartoons
of my own. I have to do these in my head, unfortunately, for I
cannot draw — not even badly enough to be a cartoonist.

It's possible to send punch lines to magazines that feature
cartoons and sometimes sell them, for the magazine will have
an artist draw what is needed. It is even possible to find someone who can draw and team up with him. Sometimes I consider attempting one or the other, but invariably laziness wins
out. It is enough to compose them in my head. For instance —

✻ 266

It is a Manhattan scene that is pictured. On either side are two enormously tall skyscrapers, with other skyscrapers endlessly fading off into the distance. Between the two skyscrapers in the foreground is a little Cape Cod cottage, with a picket fence, a line of flat rocks leading to the front door, a flower patch in the front lawn, and so on.

The owner, sitting on the front lawn, is in the typical informal costume of the suburbanite at home. He is talking to a visitor.

The caption reads: "Of course, it's a little more expensive in this location."

✻ 267

An astronaut is pictured outside a space capsule at the end of a long curved lifeline. He is at the entrance hatch, knocking, and obviously speaking furiously.

The caption reads: "What do you mean, 'Who's there?'?"

Little can be done, however, even with the best will in the world, with cartoons minus a cartoonist. Let us go on, then, with jokes that require words only.

✻ 268

Professor Williams, an expert on zoological nomenclature, was leading an expedition into the wilds of the upper Nile. One day an underling ran to him in a state of great excitement.

"Professor Williams," he cried, "something dreadful has just happened. Your wife has been swallowed by an alligator."

A deep look of concern came over Williams' face. "Surely, Jackson," he said, "you mean a crocodile."

Actually, this joke is part of a comic poem which is infinitely superior to the version I have given here — provided, of course, you can quote it correctly. Thus, the last two lines go something like:

> The professor could not help but smile,
> "You mean, of course, a crocodile."

If the joke is funny in itself, as in this case, and does not depend entirely on the verse, then tell it in prose. Although the verse, correctly quoted, is much better, the same verse, incorrectly quoted, involving deep thought in the middle, or enforcing a backtracking correction, is ruinous.

Not only can a poem be funny, but to add another dimension, so can a song. For instance, there is a sickly sweet song that asks four questions:

> Tell me why the stars do shine;
> Tell me why the ivy twines;
> Tell me why the skies are blue;
> And I will tell you why I love you.

Well, some nameless student at M.I.T. imbued with a rationalistic view of the universe rejected the second verse, which explains that God arranges each of the four matters (presumably in accordance with His own inscrutable Will). I heard the rationalistic second verse at one of the annual picnics of the M.I.T. science fiction club (to which I was invited as a guest). It went:

❋ 269

> Nuclear fusion makes stars to shine;
> Tropisms make the ivy twine;
> Rayleigh scattering makes skies so blue;
> Testicular hormones is why I love you.

❋ 270

The commencement speaker at the Yale graduation exercises was a gentleman of powerful voice and remarkable wind.

"There isn't a letter in Yale," he said, "that does not tell its tale of wonderment and glory. Y, for instance, stands for Youth . . ." and for half an hour, he told of all the joys of youth in tones of ecstasy.

With scarcely a pause for breath, he went on, "A is for Ambition, and when I think of the importance of ambition joined with youth, words fail me . . ." except that they did not for another half-hour of strenuous exposition.

It was when he was well into the third half-hour portion of his speech, devoting it to L for Labor, that one writhing graduate whispered to his neighbor, "Thank God, this isn't the Massachusetts Institute of Technology!"

⁂ 271

A private, lounging outside the PX on a dark night, observed the dim form of another soldier approaching.

"Hey, bud," he called out. "Got a match?"

"Certainly," said the other. The newcomer struck a match and lit the private's cigarette. And in the flare of the match, the private noted the single star of a brigadier general on the other's shoulder.

Stiffening to attention, the private said in despair, "I beg your pardon, sir."

The general said, "At ease, private; it's all right. Just be glad I'm not a second lieutenant."

⁂ 272

A sergeant was surprised to find one of his new soldiers up at dawn and banging away furiously at a tree.

"Hold on, soldier," he cried. "What are you doing?"

The soldier turned a flushed face to the sergeant and said, "If your damn bugler wakes me in the middle of the night, no damn bird is going to sleep."

⁂ 273

Private Jones sat moodily over his beer when his friend, Sergeant Smith, entered the bar and said, "Hey, Jonesy, I hear you were busted."

"Yes," said Jones. "They took away my sergeant's stripes."

"How come?"

"Oh, I met that chicken Lieutenant Gordon, and I gave him a snappy salute."

"So?"

"So while I was saluting, my nose itched, and I scratched it with my thumb."

Don't underestimate the value of gesturing in connection with jokes. It is a good general rule not to gesture except when necessary, since gestures are usually distracting, can't always be seen properly by everyone in the audience, and in any case, are disapproved of in the Anglo-American culture.

But all rules are made to be broken at the proper moment, and to some jokes, the proper gesture is essential. Thus Joke 273 is doubtfully funny at best, on paper. If, however, as you tell the joke you are capable of bringing up your arm in a perfect soldierly salute at Jones' second speech, and if you can then scratch your nose slowly with your thumb while maintaining a frozen expression at the conclusion of the punch line, you'll fracture every veteran in the audience.

❋ 274

Oliver Wendell Holmes, Jr., one of the most distinguished lawyers ever to grace the Supreme Court bench, served as an associate justice for thirty years, not retiring till he was ninety-one. In his last years, he was walking up Pennsylvania Avenue with a friend, when a pretty girl passed by.

Holmes stopped short, watched her approach, turned, and watched her recede. Then, walking on, he said sadly to his friend, "What wouldn't I give, now, to be seventy-five again!"

❋ 275

Two sardines were startled, in the depths of the ocean, when a submarine glided by.

Said one, "Heavens, what's that?"

"Nothing," said the other. "Just a can of people."

See the trouble one has categorizing? I wasted so much time trying to decide whether Joke 275 was a shaggy dog or a word play, that I ended up putting it into the miscellaneous category of Tables Turned.

❋ 276

Two hunters, unexpectedly encountering a larger bear than they were ready to tackle, dropped their rifles and ran. One managed to get into a tree, the other into a cave. The bear sat down to wait between tree and cave.

Suddenly, the hunter in the cave emerged, nearly ran into the waiting bear, hesitated, and scurried back. He came out a second time, and ran back. When he showed up a third time, the hunter in the tree yelled, "For heaven's sake, why don't you stay in the cave?"

"Can't," cried the hunter on the ground, panting, "there's another bear in there!"

❋ 277

Mr. Johnson and his young son Willy were visiting the zoo. Willy, an inquisitive child, noted that the lock on the lion's cage was not quite snapped, and when his father turned his back, the boy seized the opportunity to open the cage door and pop inside.

A stifled cry sounded in Johnson's ear, but by the time he had whirled around, Willy was gone and the lion was licking his chops in satisfaction. Even as Johnson watched in horror, the lion coughed up poor Willy's shoes.

Beside himself with rage, Johnson raced to the zoo's curator. The curator listened to the tale calmly and said, "My dear sir, it is strictly forbidden for children to annoy the animals and had your Willy not been eaten, he would now be in serious trouble on that score. As for yourself, you seem young and vigorous. I'm sure you will soon have another child."

"What!" shouted Johnson. "Are you suggesting that I wear myself out making love just to feed your lion?"

✻ 278

Mr. Stebbins, a native of Kansas, was at the seashore — partly for a novel vacation since he had never seen the ocean before, and partly because numerous relatives had assured him that for sore feet there was nothing like bathing in salt water. Stebbins was not a swimmer, but he saw no reason why he could not bring a large bucket of salt water to his cabin room and soak his feet there.

He took a bucket to the water's edge, therefore, and began to fill it as best he could without getting his feet wet. A beach guard, detecting the man's inexperience, said, "What are you doing there, mister?"

Humbly, Stebbins said, "I'm getting some salt water to soak my feet in."

"Fine, fine," said the beach guard. "Best thing in the world for aching feet. But there's a small charge, you know. Fifty cents!"

Rather embarrassed, Stebbins passed over the coin, which the guard pocketed with a suppressed smile.

As it happened, the soaking did indeed seem to do Stebbins' feet good, and later in the day, he decided he could well afford another half dollar's worth.

This time he approached the shore at low tide. Pausing in astonishment at the sight, Stebbins cried out, "Good heavens, what a business they did!"

I have an unrequited love for music. I sing just well enough to love the sound of my own voice and just poorly enough to make everyone else miserable with it. I have just enough talent to teach myself to read music and play the piano with one finger, and not enough to learn how to play chords. Naturally, then, I have a longing to tell musical jokes — and can't.

Let me try one, though, just to soothe my longing, even though it can't be transcribed on paper very well.

✻ 279

The trombonist in the orchestra took a much needed vacation, and during that interval he returned to the scene of his labors — but in the audience for once.

When he came back to work his fellow trombonists asked how things had gone.

"The best part," said the returned vacationer, "was the opera."

"Really?" said his friends. "Why?"

"Because I found it so astonishing. You know that part where we go: pah — pah — *pah* — pah-pah? Well, do you know what the rest of the orchestra is doing? They're doing [and here you give a spirited rendition of the Toreador Song or any other operatic selection that strikes your fancy].

❋ 280

The aging naval officer, a veteran of thirty years at sea with many a combat ribbon and citation to his credit, found himself, to his own disgust, condemned to spend the last few years before retirement behind a desk at the Pentagon. It seemed a dreadful fate for an old sea dog, but he bit the bullet and tackled the dull routine of administrative duties with the same rigid discipline with which he had faced the dangers of the angry sea and the sullen enemy.

There was only one catch. Try as he might, the flood of paperwork overwhelmed him. Conscientiously, he read all the items that came his way, dictated his comments, made suggestions, affixed his initials, and rerouted them appropriately — but each day he had to work far into the evening to clear his desk.

And as the weeks passed, things grew worse rather than better. What bothered him most was that, in the course of his duties, he often passed an office in which a young lieutenant sat with a desk that was always sparklingly clear of papers by 5 P.M., however loaded it might have been earlier in the day.

Finally, the old officer could stand it no more. He felt keenly the disgrace of having to ask a junior for advice, but needs must.

He said, "Lieutenant, I am conducting a survey of administrative efficiency among our junior officers and I can't help but notice that you seem to be keeping remarkably abreast of your work. Do you have a particular system?"

The lieutenant said cautiously, "Is this an official survey, sir?"

"No, not at all. Strictly unofficial and confidential. Nothing you say to me will go any farther, on my word."

One does not doubt the word of an aging naval officer. The lieutenant relaxed and said, "Well, then, I'll explain. Actually, most of the papers one deals with here aren't really important. They're just useless red tape so that it doesn't matter what one does with them. I reason this way, therefore: in an organization the size of the Pentagon, there's got to be one Commander Smith somewhere. So I take everything out of my in-box, write *Refer to Commander Smith* on each item, and place them all in my out-box. That's the whole secret."

The naval officer considered that and slowly nodded his head. "Yes, I see. I guess that would work. And now, you young pup, put up your dukes, because I am about to kill you. *I* am Commander Smith."

❊ 281

Jones, although ordinarily eloquent, had the misfortune of stuttering badly when emotionally moved. Once, when walking with his friend Smith down a crowded city street, he said with great excitement, "L-l-l-look at that d-d-d-dame. Wh-wh-wh-what a f-f-f-f-f-f-figure."

"Where? Where?" demanded Smith, equally excited, once Jones had managed to get his message across.

"Too late," said Jones, quite calm. "She walked into a building."

A moment later, he said, "L-l-l-l-look at that c-c-c-car. N-n-n-n-never saw s-s-s-s-s-s-s ——"

"Where? Where?" demanded Smith again.

"Turned the corner," said Jones briefly.

A few minutes passed, and Jones began again, "L-l-l-l-l-look ——"

Smith, weary of having everything over before Jones could finish, said, "It's all right. I see, I see . . ."

There was a brief pause and then Jones said, "But if you saw it, why did you step in it?"

❊ 282

During World War II, there was a period during which cigarettes grew scarce, and stores would only sell a limited quantity to a customer. Panic buying struck among the tobacco addicts, and for a period of time there were lines at every tobacco store.

It was amazing, therefore, when one small store put up a big sign in its window: UNLIMITED CIGARETTES! FIRST COME, FIRST SERVED!

Naturally by 6 A.M. the next morning, a long line had already formed at the door of the closed shop with everyone more or less impatiently waiting for it to open for business. One small man well toward the end of the line was slowly inching his way forward, quietly edging past one man here, writhing through an opening there, tiptoeing against the wall in the other place. Gradually, he worked his way toward the head of the line.

And just as he made it to the very front and quietly oozed ahead of the large-muscled son of toil who had been first in line since the evening before, that same muscular individual seized him by the collar, picked him up, and said, "Listen, bud, get back in line where you belong."

Back went the little fellow, shoved ever farther backward by the laughing, jeering men in line. Finding himself at the end, he heaved a big sigh and once again began his sly effort, patiently weaving, oozing, wiggling, and edging forward. Again, after a long interval, he found himself nearly at the head of the line and again the large fellow in front seized him. This time, short of temper, his nemesis yelled, "Get the devil out of here!" and with one heave, threw him into the middle of the road.

The little fellow lay there stunned for a moment, then gathering his wits, he yelled out, "All right, wise guy, just for that I have half a mind not to open the store altogether!"

As I mentioned earlier, my father owned one candy store or another through the major part of his adult life, and the situation had few virtues. One of them was that it kept us from missing meals, and another was that it taught everyone in my family to regard cigarettes as something to sell and not to smoke. I have stayed a nonsmoker all my life.

It is difficult for me to sympathize with smokers. They smell bad and make their surroundings smell bad. They puff their fetid breath in your face. By smoking in bed, they burn down houses, hotels, themselves, and innocent victims; and they burn down forests by smoking in the wild. And yet —

❋ 283

Did you hear about the woman who grew so disturbed with everything she read about the connection between smoking and cancer that she finally simply forced herself to give up reading?

It was in 1963, when the matter of smoking and cancer was quite new, that I heard Joke 283. I told it endlessly, and so must have many others, for I soon stopped getting laughs. It seemed to me that in a very short time everyone with eyes to read and ears to hear must have read or heard it.

Nevertheless, on November 20, 1963,* facing an audience of eight hundred, I decided that the joke would be appropriate, and chanced telling it, more or less on the spur of the moment. It was a short joke after all, quickly said, and if there were no laughs I could sweep right on, deadpan, and there would be no harm done.

To my considerable surprise, it got a large laugh.

I thought about it afterward, and I decided that the larger the audience the greater the risk one can take. Suppose three quarters of an audience have heard a joke and only one quarter laughs. Had the audience consisted of eight people, with two laughs, the joke would have been an embarrassing failure. But with eight hundred people and two hundred laughs — well, two hundred laughs make a lot of noise, and even the six hundred nonlaughers are impressed.

But though many jokes grow old, even in a matter of weeks, some jokes are much older than most jokesters think.

The strange Islamic sect of the Assassins in the twelfth century placed its adherents under the absolute rule of the Old Man of the Mountains, who dispensed hashish and assured his followers that the drug-induced hallucinations were glimpses

---

* No, my memory is not quite that photographic. It's just that I faced that particular audience two days before the assassination of President Kennedy, and it would be hard to forget such an association.

of heaven to which they would rise instantly if they died for the cause.

The Old Man of the Mountains impressed visitors mightily (and greatly lowered their self-confidence in their ability to fight him) when he ordered soldiers to leap over a cliff to their death and was instantly obeyed. I suspect that among his enemies there then circulated a grim joke which in the thirties was told concerning another subculture just as horrifying — the Nazi.

❊ 284

A British diplomat was visiting the Berchtesgaden mountain hideout where Adolf Hitler, in those terrifying days of the late nineteen thirties, was deliberately attempting to break Western will by displaying how hopeless resistance was.

"What can the British do," he demanded, "against an army so devoted to me that they will go to their death at my nod? Do you see that soldier there? Soldier! Jump out that window!"

Without a moment's hesitation, the soldier leaped out of the window to his death, leaving the British diplomat frozen in horror.

Hitler smiled grimly. "I'll show you once more. Soldier! Jump out that window!"

A second soldier jumped.

A third time Hitler ordered suicide but this time the British diplomat could not sit there idly. He seized the third German soldier by the arm even as he headed for the window, and cried, "How can you abandon life so lightly?"

The soldier replied, "You call this a life?" Then he broke away and jumped.

Humor is where you find it, and there is no predicting what a particular person will find ridiculous. I imagine everyone has had the experience of breaking up over what seems to be an entirely private joke with no one else even smiling.

It happened to me once on board ship — the only time I was ever on a ship in my adult life. That was in 1946, when I was moved from San Francisco to Honolulu. (I didn't actually want to go, but I was a private in the U.S. Army at the time and I feared that if I didn't go I would hurt my sergeant's feelings terribly.)

I was a complete landlubber, and everything on board ship was utterly strange to me. Then, on the third day out, it began to rain and, standing on the deck, I found myself staring at raindrops falling on the Pacific Ocean as far as the eye could see. It was the first time I really grasped the fact that it rained on the ocean!

The sudden idea of the utter futility, waste, and illogic of rain on the ocean caught me, and I fell to the deck in helpless laughter.

But how could I explain to the other soldiers? The laugh alone had raised serious doubts as to my sanity. The explanation would have changed those doubts to certainty.

Then, at other times, the whole world seems to laugh while you maintain a sullen silence. A few years ago the "hippie jokes" spread like wildfire. These were short, and the sharp alteration in point of view was from the world of reality to the world of the drug-ridden. The only one I ever heard that made me laugh was —

❈ 285

A fire truck went racing down the avenue at ninety miles an hour, its siren at an agonized shriek. It passed two hippies standing on the curb. Their heads turned sharply in unison as they followed the whizz of the truck, and while their long hair was still being whipped by the breeze, one said, "Man, I thought he'd *never* leave."

A less stylized form of such a joke is —

❈ 286

Jack and Frank were high on marijuana, and Jack, as was usual for him under such conditions, was in a state of manic exaltation. Whipping out his flashlight, he shone the beam through the fifth floor window and up toward the heavens.

"Climb that light beam, Frank. Reach the clouds."

"Not on your life," said Frank.

"Why not?" asked Jack, honestly puzzled.

"Because," said Frank, "you're such a wise guy that I wouldn't climb more than ten feet up the beam before you would turn off the flashlight."

❈ 287

Bill and Joe, neither noted for vast erudition, had found the perfect fishing spot, had done well, and now found it was time to turn their rented motorboat back to shore.

Bill said, "Gee, if we could only find this place tomorrow."

Joe said, "Mark it. Let's carve a notch right here on the side of the boat, right where we've been casting the line."

Bill said, "Oh, you jerk, that won't work. Suppose they hand us a different boat tomorrow?"

❈ 288

Young Willy, aged eight, came to his father one morning and said, "Daddy, where did I come from?"

Willy's father felt a sinking sensation in his stomach, for he knew he was now up against it. He was a modern parent and realized that a question like that deserved a full and frank answer.

He found a quiet spot, and for the next half-hour, he carefully indoctrinated Willy into what are euphemistically called the facts of life, managing to be quite explicit.

Willy listened with fascinated absorption, and when it was over, the father said, "Well, Willy, does that answer your question?"

"No," said Willy, "it doesn't. Johnny Brown came from Cincinnati. Where did I come from?"

It seems hard to believe now, but as I look back over my life, I realize I have been a public speaker for twenty years. And oddly enough, it seems to me that the hardest part of the speaker's profession consists of living through the preliminaries.

✸ 289

I was once given a plaque for my contributions to communications, and in return, I was asked to give a talk.

As it happens, I have often given a talk (though never twice in exactly the same way) that centers on the difficulties of communications in science. In my mind, I call it my Mendel speech because it is about Gregor Mendel, who discovered the fundamental laws of genetics and published them in a reputable journal, only to have them utterly ignored for thirty-three years.

With that in mind, I ate my dinner in carefree fashion. Over the dessert, the gentleman at my right said to me, "I'm looking forward to your speech, doctor."

I tried hard to be modest. I smirked and said, "You can never tell. I might be rotten."

"Not a chance," he said. "I've heard you before."

"You have? When?"

"About eight years ago," he said, "when you spoke to a large group of the people here in New Hampshire. You gave us a terrific talk about Mendel."

I believe I turned white. I had about ten minutes to reorder my thinking and arrange another speech.

✸ 290

I was scheduled to talk at two colleges on two successive days. On the first day my talk on ecology (a new one I had never given before) went over so well, I decided to get more mileage out of it by giving it the second day as well.

My teen-aged son was with me on both occasions and during the dinner prior to the second talk, I suddenly became aware that my son (to whom I hadn't confided my plans) was regaling the head table with an exact account of the speech I had given the night before and was about to give again.

✻ 291

Just before I was to rise to give a talk once, the gentleman who was to introduce me asked if he might read from the correspondence that had been exchanged prior to agreement on the terms under which I would speak.

Without remembering the details of the correspondence, I said genially, "Sure!"

It turned out that he read the letter in which the committee offered me their usual honorarium which was just half my minimum. He then read my answer in which I had responded, with cheerful conceit (never dreaming it would be made public): "Since I am at least twice as good as the average speaker you will get, I want twice the fee you offer. You will see that I'm worth the extra money when I talk to your group."

Having read this, he sat down, and I was compelled to stand up and face an audience that had just found out it had paid over twice as much as usual and looked as though I had *better* be twice as good as other speakers or else!

By all odds, though, the most astonishing introduction I ever received, with the most astonishing consequences, came about as follows —

✻ 292

At Penn State University once, a friend of mine (also a writer) rose to introduce me. He had painstakingly prepared a fifteen-minute speech that was extremely witty and delivered with professional aplomb. The audience was delighted and howled with laughter, and a kind of grim melancholy settled about my soul. After all, I would never be able to follow him. By contrast, my talk was bound to stink!

And then at the last minute, my friend, who had been loading me with humorous praise, saved me with his final peroration, for it went: "But don't let me give you the idea that Asimov is a Renaissance Man. He has never, after all, sung *Rigoletto* with the Metropolitan Opera."

He sat down; I rose and waited for the polite opening applause to die down; then, without preliminary of any kind, I launched my resonant voice into *"Bella figlia dell'amore,"* the opening of the famous quartet from *Rigoletto*.

An enormous laugh rose from the audience, and the fat was out of the fire.

I attribute bon mots to myself so indefatigably and with such an absence of modesty that in science fiction circles (where I am best known) witticisms I am utterly unresponsible for get attributed to me. On a much larger and worthier scale, the same sort of thing happened to Dorothy Parker, the mordant satirist She must have been the source of any number of rapier thrusts and the alleged source of any additional number. Heaven only knows which of the many stories told about her were true and which apocryphal, but who cares? I'll bet she didn't.

❋ 293

It was said that when Dorothy Parker first came to work at *The New Yorker,* she found herself isolated and lonely in her small office there. Never at a loss, she simply had the word MEN painted on the door of her office.

After that, she said, she had many visitors, and all of them male, too. "Only one thing," she added, "they all seemed to be in a hurry."

❋ 294

Dorothy Parker, it is said, once arrived at the door of an apartment in which a glittering party was taking place. At precisely the same moment, a beautiful but vacuous showgirl arrived at the door.

For a moment, there was hesitation on both sides, and then the showgirl stepped back to make way, saying, "Age before beauty."

"Not at all!" said Dorothy Parker, sailing through. "Pearls before swine!"

I usually tell this last joke to polite smiles and no more, but I
don't care. It isn't my fault if this benighted generation doesn't
know its Bible and has no knowledge of Jesus' statement in the
Sermon on the Mount, "Give not that which is holy unto the
dogs, neither cast ye your pearls before swine . . ." (Matthew
7:6).

May I point out once again to those who wonder about the
value of learning a lot of "dull stuff," that it increases the joy of
life, if only because it enlarges the possibilities of wit and
laughter.

❋ 295

The funniest joke I ever heard on radio consisted of nothing but
silence. On one of his radio shows, Mr. Jack Benny, notoriously the
cheapest man in the world (at least in the image he has built up for
himself), was stopped by a thief who said, "Your money or your
life."

There followed a lengthening silence, and in due course the audience, catching on, began to laugh louder and louder and louder.

Finally, just in case there were a few people who didn't get the
point, the thief said (once the laughter had died down), "Come on,
your money or your life."

To which Mr. Benny replied querulously, "I'm *thinking!* I'm
thinking!"

❋ 296

Stella was describing the events of the evening before to her girl-
friend.

"After the movies," she said, "he wanted me to take him to my
apartment, but I refused. I said, 'I can't. My mother would worry if
I did anything like that.' "

"You were very right," said her friend approvingly. "So what did
he say?"

"Well, he kept after me and after me, and I just kept saying, 'No,
my mother would worry.' "

"You didn't weaken, did you?"

"You bet I didn't," said Stella warmly. "In the end, I just went to his apartment. I figured, what the heck, let *his* mother worry."

* 297

The platoon was going into action, and Private Jones said to his buddy, "Listen, Bill, just in case you return and I don't, here's a letter to give Mary when you get back to the old neighborhood. Tell her my last thought was of her and her name was the last word I spoke. And here's a letter for Helen. Tell her the same thing."

* 298

In the old days when everyone traveled by rail, an irascible old gentleman barked at the porter, "Now see here, George, I'm getting off at Cleveland. We're getting there at 4 A.M. if I can trust the timetable and I don't want to miss it. You wake me up in plenty of time, get my clothes on me, and see that I'm off the train before it leaves. And I'm a hard man to wake, so don't just tell me we're in Cleveland; you stay right with me and make sure I get off."

When our traveler woke, however, it was 8 A.M. and broad daylight, and the train was well on its way toward Chicago. He called for the porter in an agony of indignation and, through a flood of invective, demanded to know why he hadn't been awakened at Cleveland.

All the poor porter could do was shake his head and say, "I'm sorry, sir. Guess I forgot."

When the storm had finally passed and the porter was left to himself, shaken but alive, he muttered throughtfully, "Well, then, I wonder who the gentleman was I *did* put off at Cleveland."

Psychiatrists seem to place a great deal of stress on the importance of slips of the tongue, feeling that people often say accidentally what they try to hide. If so, the world of jokedom has long agreed with them.

❊ 299

John Pierpont Morgan, the great American financier of the early part of this century, was noted, among other things, for a bulbous red nose of surpassing ugliness. He was to be entertained at the home of the American lawyer Dwight Morrow, and Mrs. Morrow was nervous over the possible behavior of her daughter Anne (who was then very young, but who was to grow up to marry the aviator, Charles A. Lindbergh).

"Remember, Anne," Mrs. Morrow kept saying, "you must not say one word about Mr. Morgan's nose. You must not even look at it very much."

Anne promised, but when Mr. Morgan arrived, her mother watched and waited tensely. Anne was as good as gold but Mrs. Morrow dared not relax. Turning to the financier with a gracious smile, she prepared to pour tea and said, "Will you have one or two lumps in your nose, Mr. Morgan?"

❊ 300

In the old days, when young couples went off on their honeymoons by train, the bridegroom said, "Wait here, dear, and I'll get the tickets."

So he did, but long habit would not be denied and he had not yet gotten used to the fact that he was traveling by twos. He had bought one round-trip ticket.

He came rushing back to the bride, who looked at the single ticket in his hand, and whose bright blue eyes promptly filled with tears. The bridegroom looked at her with astonishment, then with horror at his ticket, and in the blink of an eye set all straight by saying, "Oh, darling, in all the excitement I completely forgot to buy a ticket for myself."

❊ 301

The first mate of a certain vessel, having spent an entirely too active leave on shore, staggered on board utterly incapable of assuming his duties. It was not till the second day out to sea that, rather the worse for wear, he managed to stand watch.

Imagine his horror, however, when he noted that in the ship's log there stood the damning statement: "Unfortunately, First Mate Johnson was drunk all day."

He sought out the captain at the first opportunity. "Captain," he said, "this is the first time in my years of service that I have ever been too drunk to serve. Please remove the notation."

The captain scowled. "You know the log can't be changed."

The first mate said, "But with that on my record, I may have trouble ever getting a captain's berth of my own."

"I can't help that," said the captain remorselessly. "The statement is perfectly true, and that is the only thing we should be concerned with."

Whereupon the first mate returned to his duties and entered a notation of his own in the log: "Fortunately, Captain Simpson was sober all day."

✲ 302

Otto von Bismarck, the chancellor of the German Empire in the eighteen seventies and eighteen eighties, the story goes, was once offended beyond endurance by the opposition of the physician-turned-politician, Rudolf Virchow. Bismarck challenged Virchow to a duel, and Virchow, as the challenged party, had the choice of weapons.

Virchow was quite matter-of-fact about it. He produced two sausages. "One of these," he said, "has been inoculated with deadly cholora germs. The other is perfectly wholesome. Do you choose one of these, Prince, and I will take the other, and we will each eat our sausage."

Bismarck called off the duel at once.

✲ 303

There was a time when every small town seemed to have its village idiot, and Jones, who lived in such a town, wanted to display the local dullard to a visitor. "Watch this," he said. "Hey, Elmer."

Elmer shambled toward them, a foolish grin on his face. "Hello, Mr. Jones," he said.

"Hey, Elmer," said Jones, "I've got something for you." Jones held out his hand, and on the outstretched palm were a nickel and a dime. "You can have one of these, Elmer. Which one do you want?"

Elmer fumbled at the nickel. "I'll take the big one, Mr. Jones."

Jones put the dime away and grinned at his visitor. He whispered. "Isn't he a nut?"

But the visitor's sympathies were aroused. He made his excuses to Jones and hastened after Elmer.

"Listen, Elmer," he said, earnestly, "don't you know that the small coin is worth twice as much as the large one?"

"Oh sure, mister. I know that."

"Well, then, why do you let them fool you like that?"

The smile vanished from Elmer's face. "Because," he said, "the very first time I pick up the dime, mister, they stop playing the game."

❀ 304

Old Mrs. Tompkins loved to hear a fiery sermon. She would ensconce her comfortable bulk in the pew, rock back and forth in time to the minister's cadences, take a dip of snuff, and cry, "A-a-a-amen," at every piece of ministerial denunciation.

When the minister spoke harshly of sex, drinking, smoking, drug-taking, dancing, and gum-chewing, she approved heartily, taking snuff at each item and emitting her rolling "A-a-a-amen."

Finally the minister began, "And now let me talk about another vicious habit that, fortunately, is going increasingly out of fashion. I refer to the deplorable practice of snuff-dipping —"

Whereupon Mrs. Tompkins sat bolt upright and muttered under her breath, "Wouldn't you know? He's stopped preaching and begun meddling."

This propensity for judging matters with a variable measure shows up in the game of Conjugation, which expresses the differing manner in which we treat ourselves, present company, and absent unfortunates. It's fun to play the game at first but it quickly wears out, so a few examples will suffice:

✳ 305

I am firm; you are stubborn; he's an obstinate mule.
I am liberal; you are radical; he's a Communist.
I am far-seeing; you are a visionary; he's a fuzzy-minded dreamer.

✳ 306

The young hopeful of the family, Edward, had spent considerable time in the big city, apprenticed to one of the largest undertaking establishments to be found there, and now he was back home on a week's vacation. The family gathered around, delighted to see him, and yet there was some embarrassment too. There was considerable wonder as to how young Edward could possibly find contentment in so gruesome a profession, and many were the halting attempts to put that question into words.

Edward eventually realized what was bothering his loved ones and said, "You think, I imagine, that undertaking is a dismal profession with only depression and the companionship of the dead for one's rewards, but this is not so. Mr. DePinna, the head of our establishment, is the living embodiment of the grace and courtesy inseparable from our work. To see him, dressed in his sober but tasteful and well-fitting garb — his severely cut jacket, his dove-gray gloves, his neat Homburg, and above all, his jet-black walking stick with its ivory ferrule — is to take in a splendid sight.

"Nor must you think that undertaking does not have its numerous problems of great delicacy. Why only recently, Mr. DePinna had to take on a case in which the reputations of two important families and a great hotel were on the line. A young man and woman, each of a family of the greatest social importance, had been forbidden to marry and had therefore entered into a suicide pact. They were lying dead in a room on the top floor of the city's most elegant hotel, and it was up to Mr. DePinna to remove the bodies in such a way that each could be quietly buried in its respective family crypt without reference to love and suicide and, of course, without identifying the hotel.

"Mr. DePinna put on his finest suit, drew on his dove-gray gloves, adjusted his Homburg, took his jet-black walking stick with its ivory ferrule, and made ready to depart on this delicate mission. He asked me to join him, and I agreed eagerly for I was overwhelmed at this display of confidence in me, a mere journeyman.

"Together we went to the hotel and were whisked up to the top floor in an elevator that had been kept carefully empty. We made our way through deserted corridors to the room whose number we had been given. When we entered — but how can I describe it?

"There were the two lovelorn creatures in bed, quite nude, and glorious in their youthful beauty. The young man was an Apollo, the young lady, a Venus, and so gentle had their death been that their cheeks seemed still flushed with life, their mouths were parted as though each were ready to speak. The tears came to my eyes at the sight, and even Mr. DePinna's stern countenance softened and I thought I could detect a trace of moisture about his eyelids. There was only one trouble —"

Young Edward paused, and the assembled audience, leaning closer, cried out as one, "Yes? Yes?"

Edward said, "Well, they were in each other's arms and held so tightly together that I could see no way of separating them without the kind of violence I was loath to apply. Naturally, it would be extremely difficult to handle them as a double load, and I could see that Mr. DePinna's vast mind was struggling with the problem. Suddenly, his eyes sparkled and I knew he had the answer. His ingenuity was never at a loss for long.

"Leaning forward, he inserted his walking stick between the two young bodies. Carefully, he calculated the angle and depth to which he had delicately inserted the stick. When he had adjusted it to a nicety, he levered that stick in a sudden wrench and the two bodies fell apart with a moist, slapping sound."

Edward paused, and his father cried out, "And that solved the problem neatly, didn't it?"

"Well . . . not quite," said Edward. "As it turned out, we were in the wrong room."

This is one of the longest jokes I tell and it has to be told with almost mawkish sentiment. I don't dare even try unless the session has been going long enough to loosen the audience (and myself) and not so long as to have worn them (and myself) out.

Alas for my supposed expertise! I can well remember one time when I told Joke 306 on the lawn of a summer resort and, after working my way all through it, was rewarded with not one laugh, not one snicker — nothing. It was an absolutely humiliating moment, and I haven't the faintest idea what went wrong.

My most successful attempt to tell it seemed, for a moment, to be even more humiliating. It was during lunch hour at the medical school; a half-dozen male graduate students were gathered around; hilarity was in the saddle; and, since I have never really learned how to assume the proper professorial dignity, I somehow got started on the joke.

The students began to react at once, and that sort of feedback encouraged me to add involvements and ornamentation, making the joke longer and longer. With an all-male medical-school atmosphere, I also made it considerably more ribald than the version I have given in this book.

The final consequence was that when I snapped out the punch line, there was a general shattering hysteria and I laughed heartily too, out of the sheer glee of success.

But they kept on laughing, and kept on, and it suddenly occurred to me that they couldn't be laughing only at the joke. Something else was going on. I looked over my shoulder and there, in a disregarded corner of the room, was one more graduate student whose presence I had never noticed. A female graduate student. (Of course, the others had known she was there and deliberately encouraged me to elaborate the joke — the rats.)

Now, while my professorial dignity is nil and while I have always felt myself to be one of the boys as far as the students were concerned (and have been accepted as such, I am glad to say), even I recognize that there is such a thing as going too far. It was not at all my intention to tell a very ribald joke in clinical detail before a girl who might choose to be offended, and I was already thinking of the tiresome complications that might arise with the dean, when the swivel chair upon which the girl was sitting slowly began to turn.

Everyone else stopped laughing at once. We all watched. Slowly, the chair continued to turn, with the girl dreadfully silent. And then it was facing us full, and down the girl's cheeks were running helpless tears of suppressed laughter.

I was saved.

What the graduate students had done was, by the way, a practical joke. A practical joke is generally something you *do*, rather than say, which is what makes it "practical." By tradition, it is intended to embarrass, humiliate, pain, and even endanger the individual on whom it is inflicted. There is no limit here. Men have been killed to the chorus of "But I was only *joking*."

Practical jokes, if mild enough (like not telling a genial but unobservant professor that there is a girl in the room) can be endured, I suppose, especially since any resentment is met with the petulant cry, "Oh, come on, be a sport," and who wants to be a nonsport?

Then, too, practical jokes in which authority figures are snubbed rouse the snickering beast in all of us, since we all have been victimized by petty officials in some mild way or other and want our own back. As an example, who could have the heart not to laugh when two gentlemen buy a park bench, then laboriously carry it through the park, one holding each end, so that each time they are stopped by an indignant policeman, they can present the bill of sale and watch the poor fellow wilt.

Unfortunately, the general approval that meets such jokes allows for easy escalation to altogether unacceptable levels. The simple hotfoot, for instance, can surely be funny only to a dolt.

I could wish then that a word other than joke were used in connection with these atrocities. Though some practical jokes are so ingenious as to compel admiration in the abstract (the television program "Mission Impossible" can be described as dealing with the construction of superelaborate practical jokes at the expense of the villain), there is always an element of sadism in them that spoils them for any humane individual.

True, there is pain and even sadism in ordinary jokes sometimes, particularly in the put-down. But there is a difference: the put-down is often a riposte, a counterattack; it is delivered on the spur of the moment, in hot blood. The practical joke, on the other hand, must be carefully and sometimes elaborately planned, so that it is perpetrated in cold blood, and very often on an innocent victim.

My disapproval of the practical joke does not mean, however, that I have never committed one. In this respect, as in so many others, I cannot lay claim to true purity and innocence. As an example —

When I worked in the chemistry laboratory at the Philadelphia navy yard during World War II, each chemist had his own wash bottle with which, for a variety of legitimate chemical reasons, he could manipulate a fine stream of water by use of a rubber bulb. It was more than we could resist, however, to use the stream (on occasion) to catch some friend by surprise — behind the ear, if possible.

One of us, with an ingenuity worthy of a better cause, so modified his wash bottle as to be able to produce a stream of water far stronger and longer in range, far more accurate in aim, than anyone else, and he overpowered us all.

Once, however, when he was away from his desk for a period of time, I dismantled his wash bottle and plugged it with wax in three different places, and then put it back together so that it looked untouched. When he returned, I walked over to him quietly, and with no attempt at hurrying drew a bead on him and let him have it. Outraged at my effrontery (especially since I made no effort to get out of range) he seized his own wash bottle and, raising it like an artillery piece — got nothing.

We all laughed, of course, and went on laughing, I more than anyone. But think of it. It was cowardly, really. What it amounted to was that I had deliberately attacked a man I knew to be unarmed. (He didn't talk to any of us for days.)

My wash-bottle artillerist suffered no real harm, except to his self-esteem, but actually not all the self-discipline in the world can keep one from laughing at very real misfortunes under certain circumstances. Suppose, for instance, there is a sudden incongruity that seems to place the misfortune into a kind of it-serves-him-right category.

One of the navy yard chemists, for instance, had been promoted to an administrative position, and it gave him some not-so-innocent pleasure to walk into the chem lab on some minor errand, glittering in his business suit while the rest of us wore our messy, smelly, acid-damaged lab coats. (Privately, I was proud of every stain and hole in the coat, but I knew that it was Tom's intention to one-up us and I didn't love him for it.)

One time he came in to get a small sample of carbon-cleaning compound. This substance was vile-smelling and corrosive — unpleasant in every way. Tom picked up a half-full aluminum container of the stuff and prepared to give it a few swirls (to make sure it was well mixed) and then take a small sample.

"Tom," I said, "if I were you, I wouldn't take chances pouring that stuff while wearing a good suit."

"Isaac," he said, with a significance I couldn't miss, "a *good* laboratory technician can work in a tuxedo if he wants to."

What neither he nor (I swear!) I knew, was that the cap of the container was loose. So as he made his haughty remark and gave the container a mighty swirl, the cap flew off and a rainbow of carbon-cleaning compound emerged and drenched him.

He was dragged off at once by a bunch of the others and shoved under a powerful shower, clothes and all. Everything he wore was ruined, down to and including his shoes, and the laboratory smelled of the stuff for weeks.

I was greatly relieved, later, to find he had escaped all personal harm, for I was the only chemist in the place who hadn't pitched in and helped rescue him. I am ashamed to say I was helpless with laughter — but then I was the only one who witnessed the enormous incongruity between his remark and the almost immediate comeuppance.

The ability to add an incongruity to tragedy in order to make
it funny, without the result being either grotesque or unpleas-
antly insensitive, is not easy. Charlie Chaplin was able to do
the tragic and comic at the same time and force us to laugh
with tears in our eyes, but then Chaplin was a handsome man
with the grace of a dancer, and with a legitimate dignity when
he wanted to exercise it.

To my mind, the comedy team of Stan Laurel and Oliver
Hardy had the harder task. They were funny-looking, grace-
less, stupid, and everything, apparently, that was bad. Yet they
made themselves enormously loved and could wring laughter
out of the most unlikely situations.

My own favorite moment of tragedy instantaneously converted into comedy by an eccentric alteration in point of view
brought on by a gigantically inappropriate comment, came in
their picture *Fra Diavolo,* and it is with this that I wish to end
the section.

✵ 307

Laurel and Hardy first appear on screen as men of low estate who
have now retired.

"Well, Stanley," says plump Hardy to his dim-witted partner,
'we've made it!" From an inner pocket, he takes out a small moneybag, presumably filled with gold coins.

"For years," he says, "we've labored, we've scrimped, we've saved,
we've gone without food, done without comforts, slowly accumu-
lated our little nest egg, coin by coin, and here it is" — shaking it
triumphantly in the air — "to take care of us for the rest of our
years."

And as he says that, the picture on the screen widens and we become aware of a bandit standing next to Hardy. A pistol is leisurely
placed in contact with his temple and the brigand says, "I'll take
that, if you please," and walks off with the moneybag.

One can almost feel the moment of horrified sympathy in the audience as a look of utter loss crosses Hardy's face, and then all is shattered into laughter.

For Laurel shrugs and says, "Oh, well. Easy come, easy go!"

THE WORLD OF JOKES IS, as I have implied on several earlier occasions, a world of stereotypes, for it is these stereotypes — conventions understood by jokester and listener alike — which offer shortcuts to laughter.

Because the laugh is quicker and surer, the stereotype is only reluctantly abandoned even when it is completely outmoded. The rolling pin remains the symbol of the angry wife waiting for the belated husband, even when few kitchens boast one and few wives know which end to plug into the electric socket.*

The stoical Indian says "How!" and "Ugh," the Chinaman wears a pigtail, and all the English wear monocles. You can think of many other examples.

And although Jews have long since invaded every field and are included even among golf players, drug addicts, nuclear physicists, and gangsters — in the world of the joke, they are almost invariably inhabitants of the garment district, owners of candy stores, and careful guardians of each nickel.

Does it offend the Jew to be pictured in jokes as a crass materialist, of dubious ethical standards, reluctant to engage in sports or fisticuffs? Well, if the joke were told in hostile fashion by someone clearly non-Jewish, in an accent such as no Jew ever spoke, it well might.

I, however, though Jewish, as you may by now have guessed, tell such jokes with relish. The groups who join me in jokester

* Or do I have it wrong myself?

sessions are usually (though by no means always) largely Jewish. They all tell such jokes, and they all laugh at them.

And why not? There is usually at least a little germ of truth to any stereotype; and if all groups are to live together in this world (and we must if there is to be one world) let us know each other's weaknesses and laugh at them, instead of hating them. And let us know our own weaknesses, too, and then maybe we won't expect too much of the other guy.

But enough moralizing; let's get on with the stereotype.

❋ 308

Moskowitz and Finkelstein met in the garment district one day and Moskowitz, voice heavy with woe, said, "Did you hear about Lieberman?"

Finkelstein, startled, said, "No. What about Lieberman?"

"He dropped dead with a heart attack yesterday."

"What! In the middle of the season?"

Why Jewish? The failing of being so wrapped up in the minutiae of the moment as to be unable to see the universal is to be found everywhere. The joke might easily have been told of two Swedish farmers shocked at the sudden death of a colleague in the middle of harvest time; or of two college students (ancestry unspecified) amazed that a third student should have the poor judgment to choose the week of final examinations to drop dead in.

Suit yourself, of course, but it is the Jewish stereotype that most clearly implies the necessary absorption in business to the exclusion of all else, and I think it is funniest in that version. Besides, as I said, I am most at home in it.

As another example —

❋ 309

Moskowitz, in a fury, finally cornered Finkelstein in the garment district, seized him by the lapel, and said in a between-the-teeth snarl:

"Listen, you dirty rat, I am telling you for the last time to stay away from my wife. If I catch you once more fooling around, I'll break every bone . . . Say," — suddenly peering closely at the lapel he was grasping — "you call this a buttonhole?"

Notice, by the way, that Joke 309 contains what might almost be considered a sight gag. It is rather ineffective in the *telling* of the joke to do as I have done here in the *writing* of it — to make the parenthetical comment, "suddenly peering closely at the lapel he was grasping."

It is necessary, rather, for the jokester to put himself into the furious attitude of the cuckolded husband, shake the lapel (yes, pick some victim and actually hold his lapel), grit his teeth, turn red (if he can), then stop short, stare with decreasing anger and increasing contempt at the lapel he is holding, and deliver the final line with an utter and ludicrous change of emphasis.

The addition of a sight-gag quality makes it harder to tell a joke, since there is that much more that can go wrong. You may have every word and expression right and yet act it inadequately. Still, if you *can* do it, there is that much more gratification to be had out of succeeding. I suspect that every jokester is a frustrated actor at heart (just as every comedian, we are told, wants to play Hamlet in his secret dreams), and a little bit of pantomime is a pleasure.

Jokes 308 and 309 can, by the way, be told in a Jewish accent, and be the funnier for it, if the accent is a good one. I myself would automatically drop into the accent while telling them, without even being aware of it. An accent is rarely absolutely necessary, however, and it is better to tell a joke without an accent than with a bad one. (I have said this before, but this is one piece of advice that bears repetition.)

In writing a joke, it is my opinion that an accent should almost always be avoided. It is a very tricky thing to spell out an accent (the Jewish "goil" for "girl," the Irish "foine" for "fine," the Scots "wurruld" for "world," and so on). It is hard to do, especially if your knowledge of the accent is limited, and somehow the accent in print is more offensive to those whose group is being satirized than the accent in sound. Don't ask me why, but it's so.

And besides, you don't need misspellings and distortions in order to get across an accent. An occasional trick in the idiom or the word order does all that is necessary. If you say, "If I catch you once more fooling around," instead of "If I catch you fooling around once more," you have established all the Jewishness you need.

Agatha Christie gets across the French accent of her detective Hercule Poirot* to perfection with almost nothing more than word order.

This is not to say that an accent isn't sometimes just about essential. For instance —

✳ 310

During World War II, Private Goldstein was anxious to get married before going overseas, but he was stationed in a small town in South Carolina and couldn't get a furlough. His fiancée, Sadie, was perfectly willing to come to South Carolina, and did so; but once there, a difficult problem arose. Sadie was a pious girl and insisted on being married by an Orthodox Jewish rabbi. In the small town where Goldstein was stationed, however, there were no Jews, let alone Orthodox rabbis.

Nothing would do, then, but that they must send for Rabbi Cohen from the Bronx. The good old man agreed to help them in their dilemma; he took a plane to Charleston, and a bus from there to the small town.

When he got off the bus, several youngsters in the vicinity were struck speechless at the sight of an aged man with a long, gray beard, curling earlocks, ankle-length black coat, and conservative black fedora. They had never in their lives seen such an apparition, and they followed after him, running forward once in a while to stare curiously at his face. More and more children joined the pro-

---

* Yes, I know he's a Belgian.

cession until poor Rabbi Cohen found himself leading a full parade.

Losing his temper at last, he whirled at them, shook his fist, and cried out, "What's the matter with you kids! Haven't you ever seen a Yankee before?"

You can see, can't you, that it would break my heart to have to tell Joke 310 with that last line in conventional English. The incongruity between the picture of Rabbi Cohen and the picture of a Yankee can be heightened to mountainous levels if the good rabbi is allowed to make his remark in a quavering falsetto of a Jewish accent.

Oh well, I could have written that last sentence, "You maybe never saw before a Yankee?" and gotten halfway there.

Here is one joke in what sounds like strict accent, without one misspelled word —

✽ 311

Moskowitz came home from a hard day's work, sat down at the kitchen table, and said to his equally harried wife, "Becky, for once in your life don't start with your troubles. Ask, instead, what happened to me at business. Ask, already, what kind of day I had. Go ahead, ask. Just ask."

Whereupon Becky said apprehensively, "So what happened, Jake?"

And Jake buried his head in his hands, groaned, and said, "What happened? Oh, Becky, better you shouldn't ask."

And then, of course, sometimes not only is a Jewish accent almost essential, but actual Yiddish is. It is indeed possible to have a joke that must be bilingual and that can only be truly appreciated by those who thoroughly understand each of the two languages.

Naturally, these are highly specialized jokes, requiring highly specialized audiences, but to know one or two and to be able to appreciate one or two is to feel almost like a gourmet of jokes.

I will have to try to tell you the best bilingual joke I know —

telling it naturally entirely in English, but italicizing the words which you will have to imagine are spoken in Yiddish. (Imagine them spoken in Yiddish even if you don't know a word of the language.)

✱ 312

Moskowitz was very proud of his knowledge of Yiddish and would boast that he could give the Yiddish word for any conceivable English one. He came a cropper, though, when asked to give the Yiddish word for disappointed. He went into a virtual decline because he did not know how to say disappointed in Yiddish.

Finally, his friend Finkelstein said, "Listen, I have an old aunt who speaks only Yiddish. Why not ask her?"

Moskowitz said, "Dolt! If she knows only Yiddish how can I get her to understand the English word I want her to translate?"

"Well," said Finkelstein, "why not speak to her in Yiddish and maneuver her into using the Yiddish word for disappointed?"

Moskowitz snapped his fingers and said in great glee, "The very thing!"

He, Finkelstein, and a crowd of curious friends therefore invaded the old lady's room. Sitting there, white haired and wrinkled, she looked up in surprise and some alarm at the mass intrusion.

Moskowitz said soothingly, "*Grandmother, be not afraid. We wish to ask a few questions. Nothing more. Grandmother, tell me. Suppose an old friend of yours, whom you had not seen for years, came to town. You are sure she will come to visit, but she doesn't. Tell me, grandmother, how would you feel?*"

The old lady bridled and said, "*If she doesn't come, she can go to the devil.*"

Moskowitz took a deep breath and tried again, "*Tell me, grandmother, suppose you had a sweepstake ticket which won first prize — thousands of dollars — and at the last moment you discovered that the ticket had accidentally been thrown out with the trash. Tell me, how would you feel?*"

The old lady shook her feeble fist and said, "*I would be furious, and if I could find out who had done so stupid a thing —*"

But by now, Moskowitz was himself furious. He turned on Finkelstein and said, "For heaven's sake, can't you think of something that would really disappoint her? What does she want more than anything else in the world?"

Finkelstein said, "I have it! Listen, she has eleven grandchildren and every single one of them is a girl. More than anything else, she wants a grandson."

"Aha," said Moskowitz. "Perfect!"

He turned to the old lady and began confidently, *"Grandmother, suppose you discovered your youngest daughter was pregnant. You wait eagerly for her to give birth and then find out it is once again a girl and that you had a twelfth granddaughter! Tell me, how would you feel?"*

This time there was no mistaking the old lady's feeling. She covered her face with her withered hands and rocked back and forth in distress. *"Oh, oh, oh,"* she moaned in anguish, *"I would be so* disappointed."

Because Joke 312 is told monolingually, it is to a certain extent weakened, but I hope not altogether killed. Note that the very last word of the joke is not underlined and is, therefore, English.

Please let me assure Gentiles among the readership, that if the old lady's replies are given in a querulous, cracked, toothless, idiomatic falsetto Yiddish, with the last word coming out in unexpected Jewish-accented English, the result to the jokester can be extremely gratifying.

In telling jokes, incidentally, you must be prepared for all kinds of occasional unpleasantnesses. More than once, when I have told Joke 312, someone in the audience, proud of his own Yiddish, will interrupt the joke to tell you, with great self-importance, that the Yiddish word for disappointed is *entoisht* (or in German, *enttäuscht*).

This is bad manners on the part of the listener (there are rules for listening to jokes as well as for telling them, as I have explained before), and if the pedant is smaller than you are you might feel tempted to knock him down — but don't. Just raise your voice, run him over vocally, and hope the interruption hasn't too seriously damaged the audience's mood.

And now, just to show you that rules are made to be broken, I will tell you a joke where not only is a Jewish accent essential at one point, but where it must even be included in *writing* the joke, distorted spelling and all.

❋ 313

Jake and Becky were traveling cross-country in the bad old days when it was difficult for Jews to get accommodations at decent hotels.

Finally, Jake said, "Listen, with our accents, we could never fake being Gentile. This one we're coming to is a fancy one with a swimming pool and it charges an arm and a leg. I *know* we won't be welcome, but I intend to try to get a room without saying anything. Maybe I'll get away with it. The main thing is for *you* not to say anything, because your accent is ten times worse than mine."

Jake managed. He pointed regally at the rate schedule, nodded decisively at the room offered, signed a false name, and all without saying a word.

He was jubilant, but Becky had studied the swimming pool on the way in and she wanted a dip. "It is so hot," she said, "and I would enjoy a little swim."

"No," said Jake, "there are women all around and you'll strike up a conversation, and in ten seconds they'll know we're Jewish and go out of their way to embarrass us."

"Jake," said Becky, "I promise not to say a word; not one word."

Reluctantly, Jake agreed, whereupon Becky whipped into her bathing suit and bathing cap, ran daintily out to the pool, smiled at all the others there (but said not a word), and jumped in.

The water, unfortunately, was considerably colder than Becky had expected, and completely involuntarily, she yelled out, "*Oy, gevalt!*"

Coming up for air, she smiled sweetly at the thoroughly astonished women who rimmed the pool and added, "Votever *dot* minnz."

Oh, well, telling complicated Jewish jokes with an authentic accent and perfect intonation is a privilege few Gentiles can experience — but don't begrudge it. There aren't all that many privileges that come with being Jewish. In fact, there have been many times in my life when, reading the news of the day, I strongly sympathized with the following story —

❊ 314

At the height of the Hitlerian persecutions an old Jew prayed fervently in the synagog: "Lord, four thousand years ago, on the slopes of Mount Sinai, You chose the Jews as a people peculiar unto You, a holy people, a nation of priests, to bear the yoke of Your holy Law and to serve as witness to all the world. Lord, I am deeply sensible of the honor, but Lord, enough is enough. Surely it is time you chose somebody else."

But never mind, we all have our own troubles; so let's get on with the jokes.

❊ 315

Moskowitz, having grown wealthy, decided to buy a good oil painting for his living room. Entering an art gallery, he asked for guidance. The dealer took him at once to a painting which was entirely black except for one white dot in the lower left-hand corner.

"What is that?" asked Moskowitz in astonishment. "It is simply solid black."

"Ah," said the dealer, "but you must understand the symbolism involved. The black is not merely black; it represents the illimitable vastness of space — the cold, the emptiness, the horror, the inexpressible depths — and here in the lower left is one white dot representing the soul of man facing, naked and alone, the frightful chasm without."

Impressed, Moskowitz bought the painting for a huge sum, displayed it prominently, explained its significance to every visitor, and quickly became known as a profoundly perceptive art critic, a reputation he himself valued greatly.

Deeply satisfied with himself, Moskowitz returned to the gallery a year later for another painting. This time the dealer showed him an oil which was completely white except for two black dots in the lower right-hand corner.

"And the significance?" asked Moskowitz at once.

"The white," said the dealer, "represents the ineffable brilliance of the Lord, His supernal light, His all-encircling knowledge and goodness. And here in the lower right are the two black dots which represent man and woman — sinful man and woman — humbly facing their Maker."

Moskowitz surveyed the picture critically from various distances, approached, studied it at close quarters, and finally shook his head in a decided negative. "With *two* dots," he said, "it becomes too busy."

Alas, Joke 315 is another example of intranslatability. The lordly dismissal of the painting as given by Moskowitz in the original Yiddish is "*tsoo feel ungepyatschket,*" which is, literally, "too much besmeared," carrying the connotation of a kind of unbearably overdone ornamentation. The English "too busy" is a terribly pallid parallel. If the audience were, in my opinion, suitable, I would try, "too rococo," instead.

Here, by the way, is a chance for creative adaptability. The effect of the joke depends, to a great extent, on the pretentious nonsense uttered by the dealer, and this must be delivered with eloquence and a straight face. If you can't feel at home with the kind of religiosity I used, try something else. The one white dot can well be the soul of the home batter facing the visitor's baseball team; the two dots, a pitcher and a catcher in the glare of the bleacher audience.

However you adapt it, though, it is important to get through the turgid eloquence without pause or hesitation. It is worth practicing this sort of thing a little if you are a serious jokester, as you will often have to use it.

❋ 316

Moskowitz, meeting Finkelstein in the garment district, said, "Finkelstein, I'm terribly sorry to hear about the fire in your shop yesterday."

Whereupon Finkelstein, looking about nervously, whispered, "for heaven's sake, not yesterday. *Tomorrow!*"

❋ 317

During a Yiddish play being given on Second Avenue (the old center of the Yiddish theater district), the curtain fell suddenly and the manager of the theater stepped out before the audience in the last degree of agitation.

"Ladies and gentlemen," he said, "I am distressed to have to tell you that the great and beloved actor, Mendel Kalb, has just had a fatal heart attack in his dressing room and we cannot continue."

Whereupon a formidable middle-aged woman in the balcony rose and cried out, "Quick! Give him some chicken soup."

The manager, surprised, said, "Madam, I said it was a fatal heart attack. The great Mendel Kalb is dead."

The woman repeated, "So quick! Give him some chicken soup."

The manager screeched in desperation, "Madam! The man is *dead!* What good will chicken soup do?"

And the woman shouted back, "What harm?"

The Jewish joke is more widespread than ever before in history, thanks to movies, television, and the heavy representation of Jews among the scriptwriters who work for these visual media. What was once understood in New York alone, is now national property. Everyone knows that chicken soup, for instance, is considered particularly nourishing by Jewish mothers of a not-too-assimilated bent, and is commonly fed to ailing children. You will hear of chicken soup being called Jewish penicillin, and you will hear the tale of the Jewish woman who had two chickens and when one began to ail, killed the healthy one, made chicken soup out of it, and fed it to the ailing one.

And this brings up the matter of the Jewish mother. Philip Roth sang her a dubious paean in *Portnoy's Complaint,* but long before that the Jewish joke had marked her for its special target — with her oversolicitousness, her interfering ways, her selfish demands hidden under a strident appearance of sacrifice. Feh!

I must say, though, that the stereotype, like all stereotypes, is greatly exaggerated, and that Jewish ladies do not take kindly to it. If I didn't know it before, I found it out one time —

❋ 318

A whole gaggle of Jewish ladies at a party were discussing the problem of one of their daughters, who looked very much as though she were planning to marry a Gentile boy. Everyone was disturbed about it, and I could not help interrupting.

"Why not?" said I. "Let her marry a Gentile boy. I'm all in favor of Jewish girls marrying Gentile boys."

"Why?" chorused the women.

And I said, "Because why should the Jewish boys have all the bad luck?"

I am accustomed, usually, to being forgiven the outrageous things I say, but this time I was utterly ostracized for the rest of the evening, and one of the women (I swear) still bridles when she sees me.

And yet —

❋ 319

Once at a dinner party, I listened to an Indian (from India, not from Arizona) telling funny stories about his mother. I listened with interest for he looked thoroughly Indian, and finally I could no longer resist. I asked in mock amazement, "Is your mother Jewish?"

He looked at me quite calmly and said, "My friend, *all* mothers are Jewish."

❊ 320

In the bad old days of Cossack pogroms in Tsarist Russia, a band of
Cossacks came sweeping through a small Jewish town. Bursting into
one two-room hovel, two Cossacks drew a chalk circle on the floor,
stood the miserable man of the house at its midpoint, and said,
"Leave that circle and we kill you."

With that, they dragged his shrieking wife into the next room. An
hour later they left.

The woman dragged herself out of the next room and said to her
husband bitterly, "You miserable coward. Don't you know what
they were doing to me in there?"

Whereupon the husband replied indignantly, "You call *me* a coward? Do you know what I did while they were in there with you?
On three separate occasions I stepped outside the circle."

❊ 321

A band of Cossacks burst into a house full of frightened Jews. The
Cossack leader cried, "Every man out. The women must stay for we
intend to rape them all."

One of the young women present threw herself in front of an older
woman and said, "Do as you will with me, you villains, but spare my
aged aunt."

Whereupon the aged aunt thrust her protectress roughly to one
side and said indignantly, "Don't interfere, busybody. A pogrom is a
pogrom."

It seems odd to be telling jokes about a pogrom, but they are
told by Jews and laughed at by Jews, too. There is no event so
tragic that a laugh (albeit perhaps a wry one) cannot be raised.
The laugh is even useful in that, to a certain extent, it relieves
apprehension, deadens fear, and makes it possible to live with
the otherwise unbearable.

To take it to an utter extreme, there is an occasional joke
even about Hitler. Witness —

❊ 322

Hitler, while walking alone along the shores of a lake, somehow managed to fall in, was seized with a cramp, floundered into deeper water, and was soon thrashing about helplessly. Fortunately for him, a teen-ager who happened to be in the vicinity came running, threw himself into the water, and pulled out the dictator.

Once Hitler recovered, he said, "What is your name, young man? You will be rewarded."

The young man, aware now of who it was he had rescued and finding men in Nazi uniforms all around him, said through chattering teeth, "My name is Abraham Mendelssohn, sir."

"A Jew!" said Hitler with astonishment. "Well, no matter. You saved my life. What can I do for you?"

"Just one thing," said the teen-ager. "For God's sake, don't tell my father."

The Hitler jokes, those few that exist, are not a dead loss, of course. They can easily be transferred to Nasser of Egypt — and with greater effect. Against Nasser the Jews have at least been able to defend themselves.

❊ 323

Moskowitz had placed his young son with a rabbi in order that he might gain a smattering of a Hebrew education. His son was not a particularly bright boy, and Moskowitz watched anxiously for progress. After a month or so, the boy was able to say a faltering word or two which Moskowitz recognized as the opening syllables of Kaddish, the prayer which every pious son is expected to intone on every possible occasion to honor the soul of his dead father.

Furious, Moskowitz visited the rabbi. He said, "I want you to teach him some Hebrew, yes, but why instantly the prayer for the dead? Do I look feeble to you? Aged? Do you expect me to die at any moment?"

The rabbi raised a placating hand. "No need for anger, sir. You should only live so long as it will take your son to learn Kaddish."

As it happens, I attended Hebrew school for a few months when I was eight years old. It was enough to teach me to know the Hebrew alphabet, printed and written, so that I can still to this day read and write Yiddish or Hebrew (though I understand only the Yiddish).

I was even able to get a bit of the flavor of the old rabbi engaged in teaching the young. He stood for no nonsense, the old rabbi. Not for him any modern theories of education. To him the best cure for stupidity (or anything else, for that matter) was a clunk on the side of the head. Thus —

* 324

Young Irving was explaining, under the eyes of the dour rabbi, what he had gathered from the Hebrew verses he had been reading out of the book of Leviticus.

He said, "It forbids various abnormal sexual practices. The only thing is, Rabbi, I don't think I understand about those abnormal sexual practices."

Smack! went the rabbi's gnarled hand upon the boy's head as he said, "And about normal sexual practices you understand?"

I have already mentioned that my father was too dignified to have a sense of humor and that I told him funny stories in vain. Well, not always. Once and only once did I crack the veneer and make him laugh, and it was with the following:

* 325

In the little Jewish towns of eastern Europe before World War I, it was quite customary to make marriage arrangements without consulting the young folks most intimately concerned. The marriages so arranged had many material advantages, but love (if the old folks thought of it at all) was irrelevant.

In any case, young Samuel had been told to dress up because he and his father, together with a few other male relatives, were to travel to a neighboring town to sign a marriage contract, and this

would afford Samuel a chance to meet the family of his future wife
for the very first time.

Dressed in their finest and most formal clothes, the party of the
groom made its way over the snow to the village in question and
reached the home of the future in-laws. There a group of some
twenty grave men, relatives of the bride, was gathered for the sign-
ing.

Once inside the house, Samuel's father whispered to him on impulse, "Tell me, Sammy, can you guess who, of all these fine-looking
men, is going to be your father-in-law?"

"Of course I can," said Samuel, and he pointed.

His father was astounded. "You are quite right," he said, "but how
did you know?"

"Easy," said Samuel. "One look at all of them and that one in
particular I already can't stand."

Why did my father laugh? I don't know. My mother's father
was already dead at the time of their marriage so he could have
had no personal father-in-law trouble, but he laughed anyway.
And I didn't ask questions. It was my victory.

✳ 326

The beloved rabbi was on his deathbed, and life was slowly ebbing
away. Around the bed was a group of sorrowing disciples who felt
the coming loss keenly and who talked in whispers among themselves of the manifold virtues of the old man now leaving them.

One said, "So pious, so pious! Which of the many commandments
of the Law did he fail to keep? Where at any point did he deviate in
the slightest from the commandments of God?"

And another mourned, "And so learned. The vast commentaries
of the rabbis of the past were, so to speak, imprinted on his brain. At
any moment, he could call to mind some saying which would illuminate any possible theological question."

Still a third said, "And so charitable, so generous. Where was the
poor man whom he did not help? Who in town is ignorant of his
kindness? Why he kept for himself only enough to hold body and
soul together."

But as this litany of praise continued, a faint tremor appeared on the rabbi's face. It became obvious that he was trying to say some-thing. All the disciples leaned forward, with pent breath, to hear those last words.

Faintly, from the rabbinical lips, there came the words: "Piety, learning, charity! And of my great modesty you say nothing?"

✣ 327

The beloved rabbi on his deathbed, surrounded by his crowd of dis-ciples, managed to say with great difficulty, "Life is like a cup of tea."

The words were repeated, with reverent whispers, from one to another of the disciples, until this final bit of wisdom had reached those farthest removed from the bedside. And at the very back of the crowd, a young disciple dared question the remark. Hesitantly, he whispered, "But *why* is life like a cup of tea?"

Back through the crowd came the shocked comment, "He asks why life is like a cup of tea." "He asks why life is like a cup of tea."

Finally, the murmur reached the very bedside, and at a question-ing glance from the dying rabbi, the foremost disciple leaned for-ward and said, "Someone has asked *why* life is like a cup of tea."

And the rabbi whispered, "All right, then. Life is *not* like a cup of tea."

It can never be too often repeated that jokes can be varied endlessly. Take Joke 326, remove both the rabbi and the punch line, and you still have left the same joke with the same flavor. Thus —

✣ 328

Moskowitz and Finkelstein were in a cafeteria, drinking tea. Mosko-witz studied his cup and said with a sigh, "Ah, my friend, life is like a cup of tea."

Finkelstein considered that for a moment and then said, "But *why* is life like a cup of tea?"

And Moskowitz replied, "How should I know? Am I a philoso-pher?"

Considering the subtle variations one can ring on jokes, can we work out a few basic jokes (or *one* perhaps) of which all others are modifications? And if we do that well enough and then work from those basics through organized modifications, can we design a computer to make up jokes?

I wouldn't be surprised, but I hope not in my time.

✳ 329

Two eager young disciples were disputing the comparative piety of their respective rabbinical teachers.

"My rabbi," said the first, "is so holy that he receives the special attention of the good Lord. One time last spring when it was raining all over the city, there was a little circle around my rabbi's head where no rain fell and where, instead, beams of sunlight shone down to illuminate him."

"Just the same," said the second, "my rabbi is much more pious."

"How can you say that?" said the first in shocked tones. "Your rabbi lacks the very basic elements of piety. Why on last Yom Kippur — the holiest day of the year, when fasting is obligatory — I saw your rabbi eating a chicken sandwich."

"Exactly," said the second in triumph. "While all over the city it was Yom Kippur, in a little circle around my rabbi's head, it was the day *after* Yom Kippur."

In telling a Jewish joke, what does one do if reference is made to some cultural point unfamiliar to non-Jews, and both Jews and non-Jews are in the audience? (Analogous dilemmas would exist in other varieties of ethnic and generally subcultural jokes.)

Obviously, the two disciples in Joke 329 know what Yom Kippur is and don't have to explain it to each other, or to any Jew in the audience. If you try an explanation, you kill the plausibility of the joke and irritate the Jewish portion of the audience.

There are no set rules to follow here and I can only appeal to

ingenuity. Sometimes there are ways of introducing an explanation in such a way that it sounds like part of the joke.

When I tell Joke 329 to an audience that is part (or entirely)
Gentile, I would recite the first disciple's accusation in shocked
tones, introducing explanation under the guise of an intensifier.
I would shake my finger high in the air, place a look of holy
disapproval on my face and say, "On last Yom Kippur — *the
holiest day of the year — when fasting is obligatory —*" and
go on.

❄ 330

The desirable seats at the posh suburban temple had long since been
distributed for the high holidays, and the sexton stopped a stranger
from entering on the New Year, saying suspiciously, "Do you have a
seat?"

"No, no," said the stranger. "I just want to see Rosenbloom."

"You can't go in," said the sexton firmly.

"You don't understand. I have an important message. It won't
take but a minute. Please!"

The sexton hesitated. "All right," he said at last, "but hurry. And
listen," he called after him, "don't let me catch you praying."

❄ 331

An elderly Jew, with every white hair in his head and beard bespeak-
ing piety, carefully studied the display counter in the delicatessen.
Finally, he pointed and said, "A quarter pound of the corned beef,
please."

The delicatessen owner said gently, "I'm sorry, sir, but that's ham."

Whereupon the customer said, "And who asked you?"

❄ 332

The small synagog was rocked by scandal. On Yom Kippur, not
only did the rabbi not show up, but word reached the congregation
that he was in a neighboring seafood place eating oysters. To eat on

Yom Kippur was bad enough, but to eat shellfish — which even on ordinary days was not kosher and therefore unfit for Jews to eat — seemed to pass all bounds.

It was decided to send a delegation of the most respected and dignified men of the congregation to the restaurant where they might confront the erring rabbi.

No sooner said than done; and the rabbi, even while he was lifting an oyster to his mouth, found himself staring with surprise at four stern faces looking down on him.

One of the delegation, in holy sorrow, said, "Rabbi, how can you sit here on Yom Kippur, eating oysters?"

And the rabbi said, "And why not? There's an *R* in Yom Kippur."

It is wise to realize that in telling jokes you are *never* safe. I once told this joke to a particular individual and drew a complete blank. Believe it or not, he had never heard about the tradition that one must not eat oysters in months not containing the letter *R* (May, June, July and August).

✻ 333

The story goes that the Israeli government, concerned over the fact that the public image of Israel in many parts of the world left something to be desired, decided to hire a public relations firm to study the situation and make recommendations for methods of increasing the world popularity of the nation.

The best and most expensive Madison Avenue firm was put on the job, and for six months its representatives considered the situation from every angle.

At last the final report was ready, and the first paragraph read: "To begin with, it is the considered judgment of the firm that nothing can be done unless the name of the nation is forthwith changed from Israel to Irving."

Joke 333 means a great deal to me, because my name is Isaac, and because my immigrant parents, back in the nineteen twenties, were under great pressure from their more Americanized friends to change my name. Isaac, they explained, would advertise my Jewishness too blatantly and introduce all kinds of difficulties in later life, so that my name ought to be changed to the aristocratic English name of Irving. After all, it kept the same initial, so it wasn't a complete betrayal of the heritage. (Irving *is* aristocratic English in origin, but once enough Jewish boys received the name it began to sound Jewish so nothing was gained.)

In any case, young though I was, I strenuously resisted any notion of a change. I liked the name Isaac and still do.

A few years ago, by the way, a fellow guest at a summer resort, upon hearing my name, seized my hand and gave it a congratulatory shake. I naturally assumed he had read my books and wished to tell me how much he liked them, but not so. He didn't know me from a hole in the wall. He said, "I want to congratulate you for your courage in keeping the name Isaac. You are very much to be admired."

And after saying that, you can imagine my disgust when he consistently addressed me as Zack, a name I find repellent.

✴ 334

Two Jews were sitting in a Tel Aviv café in the precarious days after Israel first had won its independence, and one said to the other, "I only see one way out."

"What's that?"

"Israel must declare war on the United States."

"What are you talking about? How could that possibly help us?"

"Well, we'd lose at once and the Americans would send an occupying force. They would form an alliance with a new pro-American government, guarantee our boundaries, flood us with American capital, establish our industries, and make us prosperous."

"Hmmn! I see your point, but it won't work."

"Why not?"

"Because with Jewish luck, we'd win the war and spoil everything."

Most of the jokes with an Israeli setting and told by an American would not, I suspect, get much of a laugh in Israel. In fact, were I ever to visit Israel, I would be careful not to tell an American-type Israel joke, lest some strapping young fellow with a submachine gun slung over his shoulder pound me into the ground.

The Israel jokes I hear and tell generally assume that Israelis have the social and cultural background of the first- and second-generation Jews living in New York City in the first third of the twentieth century (my parents and myself, for instance). I am certain there is no resemblance there at all, and that the modern Israelis are much more akin to the grim fighters who followed Judas Maccabeus.

Still a joke's a joke, and as long as there are no Israelis in the audience, how about this one —

✵ 335

>Question: What is the motto of the Israeli Navy?
>Answer: Don't give up the ship. Sell it!

Would I tell that to an Israeli sailor? Would I want to be badly damaged?

And, talking about Israel, I heard the following tale *before* the Six-Day War of 1967, and it was told me by a Gentile —

✵ 336

The Syrian government had finally decided to end the tension and wage a preventive war against Israel. On the night before H-hour at dawn, three divisions had lined up at the border, ready for the signal to advance. As they waited, fidgety and tense, a single Israeli soldier walked up to the border, submachine gun over his shoulder. He looked at the line of tanks, artillery, and soldiers with surprise.

"Hey," he said, "you men better be careful. You'll get into trouble."

"Get that man," snapped a Syrian officer.

At the command, two men dashed forward after the Israeli soldier, who retreated hastily behind a nearby ridge. After a few moments, the Israeli appeared once more, came forward, and said, "I'm warning you. If you're still here by dawn, you'll all be in a heap of trouble."

The Syrian officer swore and gestured quickly. This time a dozen soldiers and a tank pursued the Israeli soldier behind the ridge. There was the sound of shouting and screaming, and then silence fell. The officer smiled, but the smile vanished when the Israeli soldier once again appeared and said, "That does it, you dumbbells. Now you're going to get it."

The Syrian officer's head swam in a red haze of fury. He could wait for H-hour no longer. "Forward," he screamed.

As the entire Syrian fighting front moved into Israeli territory, there emerged from behind the ridge a battered Syrian soldier from the previous pursuing force.

He waved desperately and screamed, "Go back! Go back! It's a trap! There's a second Israeli soldier hiding here!"

Joke 336 seemed a little less ridiculously funny after the Six-Day War. That war, in fact, brought on a whole flurry of wit based (to my way of thinking) on *hubris*, a Greek word that means overweening pride, the pride that proverbially comes before a fall. Example —

✳ 337

A shrewd travel agency, in the course of the Six-Day War, stole a march on its competitors by putting up a huge sign reading VISIT ISRAEL AND SEE THE PYRAMIDS.

✳ 338

An Egyptian felt the need of a brain transplant and walking into a surgical supply store asked what they had in the way of brains. He was shown the brain of an excellent mathematician who had died the year before at the age of sixty. In view of its age, he could have it for five hundred dollars.

The Egyptian felt the age was a disadvantage. "Do you have anything younger?"

A peasant's brain was shown him. He had died at the age of twenty-five.

The Egyptian shook his head. He was a little too high-class for a peasant's brain. "What is this one?" he said suddenly, for one brain was encased in a beautiful glass-walled refrigerator with a spotlight on it.

"That," said the dealer, "is our prize possession. It is the brain of an Egyptian general who died fighting gallantly against Israel, and it costs a hundred thousand dollars."

"A hundred thousand dollars!" said the would-be customer, shocked. "Why so much?"

And the dealer said, "Because it's never been used."

There is no question, by the way, that the Six-Day War and, indeed, the entire history of Israel since 1948 and independence, have given Jews a new way of looking at the world. During the course of the war, I got into a taxicab and the driver (Jewish) spoke gleefully of the latest headlines. Being a disbeliever in gloating (when I am strong enough to refrain), I said, "Well now, it's not over, you know, and there are a great many Arabs."

But the driver said loftily, "Don't worry. We Jews will take care of them no matter how many there are."

Deplorable though this is from the standpoint of my antinationalist feelings, I couldn't help thinking it was a rather refreshing change from the attitude that made Jews view themselves as fit bait for pogroms and gas chambers — a view expressed in many jokes, some of which I quote in this book.

Consider, for instance, the viewpoint-of-self expressed in the following joke which I have heard Jews tell:

❉ 339

Two Jews were up against the wall, hands tied behind their backs, waiting to be shot.

The officer in charge of the firing squad came to them and asked curtly, "Do you want a final cigarette?"

The first Jew replied, "Keep your cigarette, you murdering bum!"

Whereupon the second Jew whispered anxiously, "Quiet, Jake. Don't make trouble."

And even the Six-Day War could be made into material for the older stereotype:

❋ 340

Question: Why did the Six-Day War last only six days?
Answer: Because Israel's weapons were rented by the week.

Though there is also a megalomaniac answer to that question: Because on the seventh day they rested!

Well, perhaps both kinds of jokes have their uses. Both self-abasement and megalomania are invariable components of men's thinking. By exhaling them both in the form of sardonic stories, what is left behind may more closely approach the golden (but unwhimsical) mean.

❋ 341

Moskowitz and Finkelstein, partners in the garment district, found they had made a deplorable error. They had sunk all their capital and all their borrowings into a line of men's suits which wasn't moving at all. Everything they owned and hoped to own was down the drain and suicide seemed the only way out.

At the last minute, though, a buyer from Texas entered, cast an approving eye at the stock, and offered to buy everything, but everything, at the asking price. It was the difference between bankruptcy and affluence, and the partners could hardly control their ecstasy.

"Only one thing," said the Texan. "I've got to get approval from the home office. I'm sure that's just a formality, so unless you get a telegram from me by next Thursday at five, calling it off, you can consider it a deal."

He left and for a while all was delirium. But then that Thursday deadline began to obtrude itself upon them. With each day they watched the mail more uneasily, waited for the telephone to ring with a more quaking heart.

By Thursday, they were half-dead with anxiety. They sent the office staff home early, sat through a miserable lunch hour without being able to eat, and now sat watching the clock dully.

Three o'clock came, then four o'clock. Would he really not call? Would it really be a deal? And at four-thirty came the dreaded sound outside of a voice crying, "Telegram!"

Moskowitz looked at Finkelstein; Finkelstein looked at Moskowitz. After a fifteen-second eternity, Moskowitz dragged himself out of his seat, opened the door, accepted the telegram, tore it open with shaking fingers, and unfolded the message.

Then with a great shout, he called out, "Finkelstein! Good news! Your brother died!"

❋ 342

The firm of Moskowitz and Finkelstein was in deep trouble, and Moskowitz could stand it no more. Suicide seemed logical and it was on suicide he decided. He took the elevator from the tenth floor on which the offices were housed, to the seventieth floor which was the observation tower. With one last prayer, he jumped.

As he passed the sixtieth floor, he recognized through the window the representatives of the most important department store chain in the world. He caught just a snatch of phone conversation, which went, "All right, then, we're going to push velvet garments next year —"

Down, down, fell Moskowitz, and passing the tenth floor, through the window he saw Finkelstein, sitting depressed at his desk.

"Finklestein," he cried, "cut velvet! Cut velve-e-e-e —"

I have heard Joke 342 uncounted times from uncounted sources. People who know no other Jewish joke seem to know that one. It is, to my way of thinking, an old chestnut. But if they're good I don't hesitate to tell old chestnuts, and so I don't hesitate to include them in this book.

✻ 343

Mr. Liebowitz, having grown fabulously wealthy, was set to retire and, for the purpose, had had built a huge mansion in exurbia. Proudly, he displayed this house and all its glories to a party of old friends.

Finally, they arrived at the dining room, a chamber so large that from one end, the other end appeared a hazy blue with distance. Liebowitz pointed to the lovely mahogany table that ran the full length of the room and said, "And in this one room, we can entertain, at one time, as many as a hundred and twenty people — God forbid."

✻ 344

To celebrate a grand business coup, Moskowitz and Finkelstein decided to treat themselves to dinner in a fancy restaurant which they had frequently seen from the sidewalk but within whose august doorway they had never previously dared step.

They marveled at the menu and at the many utterly strange dishes, chose those which they felt they could conceivably eat, and all things considered, had a wonderful meal.

Or they did have until just at the end, when the waiter placed a finger bowl before each.

They stared, and Moskowitz said cautiously, "And what's this?"

"Not soup," said Finkelstein, after a judicious examination. "And not tea either."

Moskowitz said, "Finkelstein, call back the waiter and ask him."

Finkelstein was outraged. "What! Expose my ignorance! Make myself a laughingstock!"

Moskowitz said, "I myself would ask, but your English is better than mine. Go ahead. It is no disgrace to ask for information."

Finkelstein, not proof against the compliment to his English, but embarrassed in the extreme, signaled the waiter and said, "Pardon me, but could you tell me the purpose of these dishes — of — of liquid?"

The waiter said in cultured tones, "These, gentlemen, are finger bowls. You dip your fingers into the perfumed waters and then dry them on your napkins."

With that he left, and Finkelstein, turning furiously on Moskowitz, said, "See! You ask a foolish question; you get a foolish answer."

✻ 345

Jake and Becky had been invited to a dinner party at which, Jake suspected, the general level of intellect and education would be greater than that to which he was accustomed. He was pretty sure that he would be able to carry it off reasonably well, but he was just as sure that Becky wouldn't.

He therefore said firmly, "Listen, Becky, at this party, if anyone asks you if you want a second helping, answer yes or no. If anyone asks you if you're in a draft, answer yes or no. Otherwise, don't say a word. Do you understand me?"

"I promise, Jake," Becky said humbly and submissively.

For a while, all went well at the party. The conversation veered all over the fields of science, literature, and culture generally, with Jake putting in only an occasional careful word and Becky saying nothing at all.

The hostess, noticing that Becky had not said a word, and feeling it her duty to draw her out, said suddenly, apropos of the current topic of conversation, "Tell me, Mrs. Moskowitz, are you acquainted with Beethoven?"

Becky, caught unawares, floundered and then managed to say, "Oh, yes, I met him the other day on the D bus to Coney Island."

A pall of silence descended on the entire group and all eyes turned on poor Becky. It was a solid two minutes before the conversation managed to get started again.

When they left, the brooding Jake managed to restrain himself until they got home. Then he broke out in fury. "I thought I told you to keep quiet. You made a fine jackass of yourself; I hope you know that. There wasn't a single person present at that party who didn't know that the D bus does *not* go to Coney Island."

❋ 346

A gentleman from the charity drive had come to visit Mr. Goldberg at his office.

He said, "Mr. Goldberg, we have frequently tried to solicit funds for our worthy charity from you and you have never responded. This has seemed odd to us and we have checked up on you. We find you not only have an elaborate townhouse here in New York, but you also have a summer place in Miami. You have three Cadillacs, two expensive country-club memberships, and of course a thriving chain of clothing stores in a dozen of the largest cities. How can you refuse a contribution to a cause as useful as ours in view of your great prosperity?"

Mr. Goldberg considered, then said, "Actually, I also have a place in Long Island you seem to have overlooked, and my chain of stores extends to twenty cities. However, have you any idea of the situation in my family? Did you, by any chance, find out that my mother has a heart condition that keeps her under continual hospital care — with hospital prices what they are now? Do you know I have three sisters with three sons apiece, all of whom are at fancy colleges with tuitions out of this world? Do you know how much of a fortune it takes to educate them? And if I don't give any of them one red cent, why should I give anything to you?"

I heard this joke told on stage before an entirely Jewish audience which collapsed in delight at the punch line. The effect was achieved precisely because it was so entirely antistereotypical. A rich Jew who would hesitate to give to charity could be accepted, but a rich Jew (or even a poor one) who failed to contribute to the support of his family, and even of a sick mother, is unthinkable — so no one thought of it, and the alteration in point of view enforced by the last line was radical indeed.

And yet I heard a famous standup comic tell the following joke and get no laugh at all, not a snicker —

✳ 347

The rich Mr. Goldberg was brooding one day. Finally, he muttered to himself: "What good are my steamship lines to me; my oil stock; my department-store chain; all my hundreds of millions of dollars — when my poor mother is starving in an attic?"

Why didn't he get a laugh? I've heard him get laughs any number of times, why not then? Perhaps it was because he preceded this joke with some indignant words about its not having gotten a laugh on another occasion — so that he put the audience on notice that if they did not laugh they would annoy him, and what audience could resist?

In other words, don't dare audiences not to laugh at your jokes.

✳ 348

Buddy Hackett told of the time he had moved to a suburb and was besieged with suggestions that he join the local temple.

"Why?" he demanded.

"So that your children will realize they're Jewish."

"But they already realize they're Jewish," said Buddy. "They have heartburn."

To anyone who has experienced the heavy, fatty, spicy cuisine of the first- and second-generation Jew (as I have) and the quantities one was expected to stow away as a tribute to the proud, motherly cook, Buddy Hackett's remark is luminously clear.

But I must add this. Natural selection can produce stomach linings of remarkable toughness. Having survived years of Jewish food, my digestion is steel strong. Others may gasp and faint away when I place a full teaspoon of hot Chinese mustard in my shrimp fried rice, but I merely smile — and eat.

* 349

Mrs. Moskowitz found herself at a resort far above her social status and was trapped with two high-toned ladies at the pool.

The first said, "I have found the most marvelous place for cleaning my diamonds. It is done rapidly and well, and the diamonds are returned when promised. Really, it is so comforting to know that when you must wear your diamonds, they will have the proper fire."

The second looked at her own jewel (she was wearing only one, for they were at the pool and the accent was on informality) and said, "You are indeed fortunate. I have had the largest jewelry firm in New York handling mine but I must admit I am not entirely satisfied. Of course, in the circles in which I move, standards are enormously high and it isn't easy to find work done just so."

After a short pause, during which Mrs. Moskowitz said nothing, one of the other women turned on her just a shade wolfishly and said, "And you, Mrs. Moskowitz? How do you arrange to have your diamonds cleaned?"

To which Mrs. Moskowitz responded, "It's not a problem that affects me. When my diamonds get dirty, I just throw them away."

Poor Mrs. Moskowitz must frequently labor to keep her end up at these resorts (similar to the one in which this book was, thank goodness, started). At one time —

* 350

The ladies sitting around the dining table at the resort were discussing, in turn, their respective marvelous trips to Europe. And finally one turned to Mrs. Moskowitz, who had said nothing, and asked, "And you, Mrs. Moskowitz? Have you visited Europe lately?"

And Mrs. Moskowitz replied, "Who wants to? I was only too glad to come from there."

Though it may be the same Mrs. Moskowitz who is reported to have said once, "Last year I went around the world. This year I think I'll go somewhere different." But one more —

❋ 351

Under the stress of the necessity of a fourth, Mrs. Moskowitz was invited to join a bridge game in which the other three players obviously considered themselves a social cut or two above her.

As Mrs. Moskowitz seated herself, one of the others said in austere tones, "Mrs. Moskowitz, you must observe the conversational rules at this table. There are some subjects we never discuss. We never discuss husbands. They are all miserable. We never discuss fur coats. All our coats are gorgeous. We never discuss grandchildren. All our grandchildren are geniuses. And we never discuss sex. What was, was!"

❋ 352

A Texan, having at the last minute tried to buy fifteen tickets to a Carnegie Hall concert for himself and a party of friends was most annoyed when told that no more tickets were available. He hastened out of his hotel, intending to storm into the Carnegie Hall lobby and buy the whole thing outright, when he was brought up short by the fact that he didn't know where Carnegie Hall was located.

Looking about, he espied a small hot-chestnut vendor of Jewish persuasion at the curb, and called to him, "You there!"

The small vendor looked up. "Yes?"

"Listen. How do you get to Carnegie Hall?"

The vendor thought, then lifted an admonishing forefinger, and said, "Morning, noon, and night, mister — practice — practice — practice."

Practice! The roads to fame and fortune were few to the ghetto Jew, but one was to be a musical prodigy. The number of Jewish children condemned to the purgatory of practice — practice — practice for that reason is incalculable. I was prevented from being one of them (and oh, how I wish I had not been prevented) only by the fact that my family couldn't afford a violin string, let alone a violin. But —

❋ 353

A friend, whose family was slightly more affluent than my own in its time, had been condemned to endless piano practice despite the fact that she was virtually tone deaf. Painstakingly, she memorized enough piano compositions of one sort or another to complete the course and then never ceased to bewail the fact that she had not been allowed to have dancing lessons, for it was dancing that she had *really* wanted to learn.

I said, "At least you won't make your mother's mistake with your own daughter."

"Certainly not," she said fiercely. "Whether she likes it or not, my daughter is going to *dance*."

❋ 354

Ginsberg was off on a trans-Atlantic cruise for the first time in his life, and all was strange to him. He was assigned a table in the dining room at which the only other diner was a Frenchman who spoke no English. Ginsberg, needless to say, spoke no French.

Ginsberg and the Frenchman reached the table at the same time. Ginsberg sat down at once, but the Frenchman first bowed in most elegant fashion and said, "Bon appétit."

Ginsberg, terribly abashed at not having introduced himself, struggled out of his chair, attempted a bow of his own, and said, "Ginsberg!"

This went on for several meals. The Frenchman would bow and say, "Bon appétit," and Ginsberg would bow and say, "Ginsberg!"

One lunch, the Frenchman was not present and Ginsberg casually asked the steward where Mr. Bone-apatee might be.

"Who?" asked the steward, naturally. Finally, as Ginsberg continued to explain, the light dawned. The steward said, "Oh, you mean Monsieur Dupin. He is at the captain's table now; he will be with you for dinner."

"But," said Ginsberg, "if Bone-apatee isn't his name, why does he always announce himself that way to me at every meal?"

"Ah," said the steward, suppressing a smile. "He is saying 'Good appetite.' He is wishing you an enjoyable meal."

Ginsberg was utterly humiliated. He could hardly wait for dinner.
He arrived late to make sure the Frenchman would already be
seated. He then hastened over, bowed elaborately from the waist,
and said, "Bone-apatee."

And the Frenchman rose from his seat with a dazzling smile,
bowed, and said, "Ginz-bairg!"

✿ 355

Jake and his wife Becky were on their way to a masquerade party,
and Jake, who was being compelled to wear a devil's suit and mask
that were to cover him completely, was very woebegone about it.

"Becky," he said, "I will feel like such a jackass."

"Shut up," she replied, for she was very perturbed over the fact
that her own costume had not arrived. "You leave now," she said.
"I'll come along when my costume arrives."

Muttering to himself, Jake left, and Becky resumed her agitated
pacing. Suddenly an idea occurred to her. Why worry about the
costume? In the attic there was her grandmother's wedding gown.
She could wear it with some minor alterations, include a mask, and
go as a fairy princess.

With great excitement she readied the dress and then, with even
greater excitement, realized that Jake, expecting to see her as a pi-
rate lass, would not recognize her. She would be able to observe
how he behaved when he thought she was absent. What wife could
resist that?

At the masquerade, she had no trouble locating him. The bright
red of his devil's costume made him stand out. And, having located
him, she became grimly aware of the fact that he was surrounded by
half the women in the place, all of them giggling and one of them
saying, "Oh boy, you're a *real* devil."

Feeling quite furious, Becky approached and without a word (for
she did not wish her voice to give her away) she sidled up and,
through her mask, gave her erring husband a smolderingly flirtatious
glance over one shoulder. It merely enraged her further when he
responded at once.

She gestured him into the garden and he followed without hesitation. Grinding her teeth, she determined to see how far her husband

would go with this person he believed to be a strange, but willing, woman. And, as it turned out, he went as far as one could. What made it the worse was that it seemed to Becky that Jake put into the entire procedure a vim and an enthusiasm that was entirely lacking in their marital bed.

She broke away at length, adjusted herself as well as she might, and dashed for home. There was nothing now left to do but wait for Jake and let him have it.

Eventually, Jake came home, looking weary and with his red devil's suit slung over his arm. He said to Becky, "And where were you?"

"Never mind me," said Becky. "And what did *you* do, while you were there?"

"Me?" said Jake. "Nothing. I played pinochle with some of the boys all evening. That's all."

"Pinochle! So!" said Becky, scarcely able to speak for fury. "And you didn't maybe have a rather good time in other ways?"

"Me? No. But I tell you — The fellow I lent my suit to — Boy, did *he* have a terrific time!"

I think it was George Bernard Shaw who described Great Britain and the United States as two nations divided by a common language. The division can even strike father and son, as witness —

❋ 356

My father, aware of my growing interest in science fiction when I was in my teens, asked me if I had ever read any books by Zhoolvehrn.

I stared at him blankly. "*Who?*"

"Zhoolvehrn," he repeated.

"Never heard of him," I said emphatically.

"He wrote science fiction," said my father in annoyance. "He wrote about going to the moon and to the center of the earth and, oh yes, about a man going around the world in eighty days."

That gave it away. My father had never heard the name pro-

nounced in anything but the French fashion (as used in Russia). So
I gave it to him English fashion, as modified by Brooklyn.

I said, "Oh, the author you mean is *Joolz Voin.*"

And my father said, "*Who?*"

❋ 357

Dave Levine looked terribly depressed and a friend stopped to ask
him what was wrong.

Dave shook his head dolefully. "Applied f-f-f-for a j-job," he said
through his usual stutter. "D-d-d-d-didn't get it."

"What kind of a job?"

"T-t-television announcer. Th-th-they asked my n-n-n-nuh-name
and all I ever s-s-said was 'D-d-d-david Luh-luh-levine,' and they
turned me d-d-d-down at once. L-l-l-lousy anti-Semites."

The telling of Jewish jokes has become so common in the
United States that some Yiddish words have almost entered the
language. We all know that a *yenta* is a scolding, garrulous
woman; a *shikseh,* a young Gentile girl; a *goy,* a Gentile male;
and so on. I just mention this, and now let's proceed —

❋ 358

Moskowitz, having grown wealthy, felt the need to get up in the
world. He therefore tried to join the town's fanciest country club
and was turned down. It was quite plain that he had been black-
balled only because he was Jewish, and in his fury at that, he found
himself with a new and all-devouring ambition in life.

Somehow he was going to manage to get into that country club,
then reveal that he was Jewish and resign in scorn.

He liquidated his business and for three years underwent an intensive course of education. He learned how to speak English with the
most beautiful accent, learned the best manners, and how to wear
the best clothes. In great detail he learned what one did and didn't
do. He even had his nose operated on.

Finally, he presented himself at the country club once again, prepared to answer any question.

"Your name?" he was asked.

"Archibald Manly-Smythe," said Moskowitz unabashedly, presenting the necessary (forged) identification.

"Place of abode?"

"I live in the mansion on the hill. You can see it from here. I bought it last week."

"Education?"

"Groton! Harvard! Oxford!"

"Occupation?"

"My family," said the Gentilized Moskowitz loftily, "has for four generations not had to work for a living. I myself, however, collect stamps and engage in antiquarian research."

The official of the country club said, "Really, I see no reason why we can't accept you. But there is one question — purely routine — that I must ask you. Your religion, please."

Archibald Manly-Smythe, née Moskowitz, drew himself to his full height and said in cultured tones, "I, sir, am of the goyish faith."

✲ 359

Danny Thomas, that excellent comedian of Lebanese extraction and the proud possessor of a majestic hooked nose, told his audience once of having been honorary member at a country club reserved for Jews only. It was because of his own Christianity that he could not become a real member, and he remained a guest only.

He argued with the membership committee, pointing out that by restricting membership on religious grounds they were every bit as bigoted as were those country clubs who would not admit Jews. To set an example they ought to nonrestrict membership.

Finally, and reluctantly, the members of the country club agreed, and such artificial restrictions as race and religion were lifted.

Rejoicing, Danny Thomas rushed down to be the first Gentile to join as a member under the new dispensation — and was refused!

Astounded, he said, "But why?"

And he was told. "Because we're going to a lot of trouble to let in Gentiles, and if we're going to let in Gentiles, we want them at least to *look* like Gentiles."

❊ 360

Moskowitz, applying for a job, had no hesitation in laying claim to any characteristic which would serve to qualify him. Time enough after the job was clinched to worry about coming through.

Finally, the prospective employer said, "In selling our encyclopedia, it is particularly important that you have a thorough grasp of American history. Do you understand that?"

Moskowitz said with a broad smile, "I know our country's history in all its details from beginning to end."

And while the employer paused to make a notation on the form before him, Moskowitz pointed to the pictures of Washington and Lincoln on the wall and said, "Fine-looking men. Your partners?"

❊ 361

Moskowitz and Finkelstein were attending an evening function one day and both partners were in a carefree mood indeed, when suddenly a spasm crossed the former's face.

"Finkelstein!" he gasped. "I just remembered! I forgot to shut the office safe when we left this afternoon."

"So what," said Finkelstein, unperturbed, "we're both here!"

❊ 362

Moskowitz's young hopeful, Sammy, asked one day, "Papa, what do they mean when they say 'business ethics'?"

Moskowitz beamed. "Very good, my son. It is delightful to see you take a spontaneous interest in such things. Let me explain this rather subtle concept to you by means of an example. Let us assume a woman comes into the store, orders a small item, and places a twenty-dollar bill on the counter. You make the change, which comes to $18.12, and turn to take care of your other customers. A few minutes later you become aware that she has left the store but has forgotten to take her $18.12 in change, which remains on the counter. Do you see the picture, my son?"

"Yes, Papa."

"Now comes the question of business ethics. Do I, or do I not, tell my partner?"

* 363

Mrs. Moskowitz met Mrs. Finkelstein for the first time in many years, and after the initial greetings and tears of joy were done with, they settled down to the important task of asking after family.

"Tell me, Mrs. Finkelstein," said Mrs. Moskowitz, "and how is your daughter Rosie?"

"My daughter Rosie," said Mrs. Finkelstein, "is the most fortunate girl you can imagine. She has married an absolute perfect person, a professional man, a professor. How he loves her! How well he treats her! Every morning he brings her breakfast in bed. He has hired a maid for her and won't as much as allow her to lift a finger around the house. He happens to like to cook and he fixes her the finest meals. And on top of that, he takes her out to the theater every week. It is such a happy marriage, you can't imagine."

Mrs. Moskowitz made all the suitable clucking sounds of gratification and said, "And your son Joey? How is he?"

Now all happiness faded out of Mrs. Finkelstein's face. Her eyes flashed fire.

"My son Joey," she said somberly, "is a professional man, a professor, but he is as miserable as Rosie is happy. He married a perfectly terrible woman. How disgracefully she treats him. She sleeps to all hours and demands breakfast in bed. She is too fancy to lift a finger around the house and insists on having a maid. She is too helpless to do the cooking and makes my Joey fix the meals. And on top of that, she insists on going out to the theater every week. It is such an unhappy marriage, you can't imagine."

* 364

Mr. Levene was dying, and his sorrowing family was gathered around his bed.

Mr. Levene, eyes closed, murmured weakly, "Are you there, Becky?"

"I'm here, Jake," said Mrs. Levene, weeping.

"And Sammy, you're there?"

"I'm here, Papa," said the oldest son.

"And Toby?"

"I'm here, Papa," said the oldest daughter.

One by one, Mr. Levene went through the list of children down to the youngest, and each assured him of his or her presence.

Whereupon Mr. Levene's eyes opened wide. He raised himself to his elbows and cried, "So who's minding the store?"

The question "Who's minding the store?" is a poignant one to me since for sixteen years of my boyhood and youth, *I* minded my father's candy store a good part of the time. The question always strikes me (perhaps purely out of personal experience) as a particularly Jewish one — and after all, a version of it even occurs in the Old Testament.

You don't believe me? Here is the story, and you can check it for yourself:

✻ 365

David was the youngest son of Jesse. His older brothers were fighting in Saul's army against the Philistines, but David remained behind in charge of the family flock of sheep.

Once Jesse sent him to the army to bring back news of his brothers. When he got there, however, he made himself a little too conspicuous and his oldest brother Eliab was annoyed. But let the Bible tell it (1 Samuel 17:28):

". . . Eliab's anger was kindled against David, and he said, Why camest thou down hither? and with whom hast thou left those few sheep in the wilderness? . . ."

In other words, Who's minding the store? Right?

It's not often that a Jewish joke will make a Jewish *girl* laugh, for Jewish jokes are particularly hard on Jewish girls, as you already may have noted. Once many years ago, though, I walked into a business office where the girl behind the desk (she was Jewish) looked particularly woebegone.

She was having her troubles, poor thing, and I sympathized and racked my brain for something that might make her laugh. It took bigotry to do it, but it worked, and here it is —

❋ 366

Young Sammy Moskowitz approached his father one day and said, "Pop, I'm getting married."

Mr. Moskowitz looked up in surprise from his newspaper and said, "To whom, Sammy?"

"To Rosie O'Grady, down the street."

"To a shikseh?" cried out Mr. Moskowitz, highly scandalized. "And why not to a nice Jewish girl?"

"Because," said Sammy, "all my friends have married your so-called nice Jewish girls and I don't want any part of it. All these nice Jewish girls do is complain. They have headaches and their feet hurt them. Or their back hurts them. Or they have stomach trouble, or eye trouble, or tooth trouble. Who needs it?"

"And what do you think?" expostulated Mr. Moskowitz. "A shikseh doesn't have aches and pains?"

"Sure," said Sammy, "but with a shikseh — who cares?"

Bigotry, alas, is a two-way street, and being on the receiving end of prejudice does not seem to preclude its possession. However, although I like to tell the story and although the young lady I mentioned as having troubles laughed heartily and said it was the first good laugh she'd had in a week (poor girl, she has since died in an automobile accident), I disapprove of the attitude portrayed in the joke. In fact, I wish to offer a personal assurance to any shikseh who may be reading this book that I myself *do* care.

❋ 367

Mrs. Moskowitz urged the hors d'oeuvres on one of her guests, who shook his head with an embarrassed smile.

"Really, Mrs. Moskowitz," he said, "they're delicious, but I've had six of them already."

Mrs. Moskowitz said, "Why worry? Actually, you had eight, but who's counting?"

This is another one of those punch lines that is so familiar, it has almost become a part of the language. Yet despite its familiarity it always, in my experience, gets a laugh. In fact, so confident am I of that laugh that I use it frequently to soften up an audience whom I plan to address. It goes this way —

I turn out books so rapidly (well, we all have our failings) that when introduced prior to one of my addresses, the total given is almost invariably too small. Then I get up, look embarrassed, and say, "Our kind chairman reported that I've published a hundred and three books. Actually —" I pause and look very flustered, "I've published a hundred and six." Then, in a burst of friendliness, "But who's counting?"

And the laugh never fails.

✳ 368

Three men at a resort, who knew each other only by what they had told each other over the last two or three days, were smoking peacefully on the lawn one evening, when one of them, Cohen, said, in a reminiscent mood, "Talking about Vietnam, I once told Johnson —"

"President Johnson?" asked Moskowitz.

"Of course! There's another Johnson? This was back in 1967 when he was still President. I had lunch with him and he asked me to stay for the afternoon and we talked about Vietnam. Unfortunately, he didn't take my advice —"

Moskowitz, unable to endure more of this, interrupted. "I wonder if what you had to say was anything like what Sharl told me."

"Sharl?" said Cohen.

"Charles de Gaulle, before he resigned. The French call the name Sharl. I spent a weekend with him in 1967. We knew each other during the war and he thinks highly of me. Now what he said about Vietnam —"

But now Finkelstein, the third man, interrupted. "When I was in Rome with Paul in 1967 —"

"Paul who?" chorused the other two.

"His Holiness, Paul the Sixth, the Pope," said Finkelstein calmly. "He's an old friend of mine. Different religion of course, but friends are friends. I was with him in 1967, at the time of a big holiday in the course of which the Pope sits on a big throne and is carried through the streets of the city on the shoulders of a dozen men. Naturally, there's usually immense cheering and enthusiasm, and so I was a little embarrassed when His Holiness suggested that I come with him on this occasion. I said I didn't really belong, but he said he got lonely up there on the throne by himself, so I agreed, as a favor to a friend.

"Actually," continued Finkelstein, with both the others far too stunned to interrupt, "it was a nice occasion. From the throne I had a good view and it was very impressive. But of course the crowd was puzzled because there were two men on the throne. Everywhere we went we could see people nudging each other and whispering, 'Who is that fine-looking man up there on the throne with Finkelstein?'"

✻ 369

Private Cohen made life miserable for every commanding officer he ever had during the days of World War II. A superlatively ingenious goof-off, he could never be called to account. Yet by his example he would corrupt entire companies. His commanders could merely pull strings to have him transferred.

From place to place he was shunted, until he finally ended up in New Guinea. Then, suddenly, from that primitive island, came a series of headlines: PRIVATE COHEN CAPTURES ENEMY DIVISION SINGLE-HANDED; PRIVATE COHEN SURROUNDS AND DESTROYS TWENTY ENEMY TANKS; PRIVATE COHEN SHOOTS DOWN HIS FIFTY-NINTH AND SIXTIETH ENEMY PLANES.

A dozen American officers, utterly astounded, separately sent wires of inquiry to Cohen's commanding officer in New Guinea. Each received a mimeographed reply which went: "Gentlemen: This is Colonel Ginsberg writing to you. As it happens, I understand

Private Cohen. I know what makes him tick. On his first day here, I took him out on the base, placed my arm around his shoulders, and said, 'Cohen, my boy, see those tanks? They're yours! See those planes? They're yours! See those supplies, weapons, men? They're all yours! Cohen, my boy, from now on, you're in business for yourself.' "

✲ 370

In eastern Europe half a century ago, when marriages were still arranged by marriage brokers, young Samuel had been introduced to the young woman of whom the marriage broker had sung a gorgeous hymn of praise.

After a short interview, Samuel motioned the marriage broker into a corner and said to him in a furious whisper, "What is this woman you have brought me? She is ugly; she has a cast in one eye; she limps; she is unintelligent; and she has bad breath."

The marriage broker said, "But why are you whispering? She is deaf, also."

✲ 371

Finkelstein, who had been out of town for a long, long time, was in New York on a visit and met his old friend Moskowitz. The two greeted each other enthusiastically and it was not long before they were asking after each other's business affairs.

"Alas," said Moskowitz, raising a mournful eye to heaven, "not two weeks ago, a vicious fire swept my establishment and reduced it to ashes. Were it not for the heavy insurance I carried, I would, today, be an utterly ruined man. And you, Finkelstein?"

"How odd, but my own situation is rather similar. I had a fine establishment in Miami Beach, and last autumn a hurricane coming in off the sea destroyed it utterly. It is with the insurance money only that I am now able to come to New York to re-establish myself."

"Is that so?" said Moskowitz thoughtfully. "But tell me, Finkelstein, how does one go about arranging a hurricane?"

I happen to have a true story about hurricanes. When I was first married, I lived in Philadelphia, as I have explained several times already. World War II was on, I had only one day off a week, and travel was difficult. Holidays were therefore hard to arrange, but my wife and I decided to go to Atlantic City early the following Sunday and spend the day there.

Sunday approached, and it was clear I was going to be confined to bed with some mild gastro-intestinal ailment. I offered to go anyway rather than spoil the plans, but my wife would have none of it.

She said, "We can just as well go next Sunday. After all, the boardwalk won't blow away."

You guessed it. Before the next Sunday, there came a hurricane and the boardwalk, honestly and literally, blew away.

It wasn't till 1965 that I finally got to Atlantic City and when I did — you guessed it — I was caught in the tail end of a hurricane. The boardwalk didn't blow away that time, but I got soaked. That, however, is a different story.

❋ 372

An Arab, lost in the desert, was in the last extremes of the agony of thirst. His camel was dead; his possessions were strewn behind him; and he himself was crawling feebly forward. His eyesight was dimming and his brain was whirling, when his fingers touched a stoppered flask in the sand.

Thinking it might contain water, he unstoppered it. A swirl of smoke issued forth, coalescing into a giant turbaned figure.

"My deliverer!" boomed the figure. "I am a long-imprisoned genie, and as a reward for freeing me, I will give you three wishes."

"Water!" gasped the Arab.

At once a huge flagon of sparkling clear, cold water was in his hand. He drank thirstily.

"Your second wish, my deliverer," said the genie.

"A palace," said the Arab, "of a hundred rooms in a fruitful oasis, with palm trees all about, herds of camels, and bevies of beautiful dancing girls."

And as he wished, so it was.

"And your third wish, my deliverer?" asked the genie.

"Well," said the Arab, "I have saved my life with my first wish, insured my future with my second, and for the third wish, it is time to consider my people. Oh, genie, for my third and last wish — destroy the nation of Israel."

And at once the palace was gone and the Arab was back on the desert dying of thirst.

Moral: Be careful of what you wish. The genie you rescue may be Jewish.

✻ 373

A half-century ago, before the quota system had drastically reduced the rate of emigration to the United States, a vessel plowed across the Atlantic toward the Land of Liberty, loaded to the gunwales (whatever they are) with hopefuls from eastern Europe.

Unfortunately, about halfway across, a storm struck the vessel. It grew rapidly worse, and the cry to abandon ship was given.

There followed a scene of unbelievable confusion. Children screamed, women wailed, men shouted and rushed wildly to and fro, while the crew struggled to impose order and place as many as possible in the lifeboats. The sheets of rain and the heavy seas added the last touch of nightmare to the situation.

And through it all, watching everything with interest, was Yankele, a tailor from Warsaw. He sat on a coil of rope, utterly calm, and hummed to himself.

A friend rushed to him, crying, "Yankele, Yankele, how can you sit there so calmly? The ship is sinking. It is being completely destroyed!"

"So?" said Yankele. "The ship isn't *my* property."

✻ 374

Mr. Moskowitz was giving his oldest son, the pride and joy of his life, the bar mitzvah, or confirmation, which all Jewish boys receive when they attain their thirteenth year. The bar mitzvahs given by the more affluent Jews, it seems, have assumed many of the characteristics of parties given by the wilder Roman emperors, but even on such a scale, the Moskowitz bar mitzvah was noteworthy.

The guests were stunned by the magnificence and utter lavishness of everything, from the fountain that yielded champagne to the three large bands that played three different selections simultaneously.

But most magnificent of all was a gigantic bust of the young bar mitzvah boy, true in every detail and molded out of gefilte fish. It was so beautiful the guests hesitated to attack it with knife and fork, as they were obviously intended to do.

Mr. Finkelstein was particularly impressed. Turning to Moskowitz (who was observing the proceedings with a smug smile that hid an aching wallet), Finkelstein said, "You are sparing no expense, I see, Moskowitz. It happens that I am a connoisseur of bar mitzvah art, and I can see at a glance that you have commissioned the great Louis Shmelewitz to carve that bust of your boy."

"That the bust is a great work of art, I realize," said Moskowitz, "but that you are a great connoisseur of bar mitzvah art, I deny. If you were really a connoisseur you would know that Shmelewitz couldn't possibly have carved that bust. Shmelewitz, as every child should know, works only in chopped liver."

❋ 375

Mrs. Garfinkel drove up in her chauffeured car to the fanciest resort hotel in the East. She was a resplendent symphony in jewels and furs.

"Boy," she called out. "No, not just you. All of you. Everyone."

The bellboys flocked, and Mrs. Garfinkel gave her orders with rapid-fire precision. "You, take that suitcase. You, take the other. The tall one can take my hatbox and the little one, my wig box."

She went on and on, apportioning the tasks, until finally she said to the last remaining bellboy, "And you can carry my son Harold."

She pointed to the plump teen-ager sitting beside her. The bellboy cast a horrified look at the size of the boy and said, "But, madam, surely the young man can walk."

"Of course he can walk," said Mrs. Garfinkel indignantly. "But, thank God, he'll never have to."

❋ 376

Bernie Shapiro, intensely musical himself, was cursed with a brother-in-law who had the virtue of being wealthy, but who was undeniably

the least cultured person for miles around. Bernie found this very
humiliating and labored to introduce the miserable creature to the
finer things in life.

At last, through incredibly strained machinations, Bernie persuaded his brother-in-law to accompany him to a presentation of the
opera *Carmen.* He held his breath, fearing that some last-minute
event would spoil everything, but the day and the moment came and
Bernie and his brother-in-law actually entered the opera house and
took their places in an excellent box.

To Bernie's relief, the opera seemed to catch his brother-in-law's
fancy at once. The brother-in-law listened open mouthed and round
eyed, following every move, absorbing every note.

Bernie was absolutely triumphant when, as they were leaving after
the final curtain, he heard his brother-in-law intoning, under his
breath, "To-ray-a-dor-uh-to-oh-ray-a-dor —"

Bernie said, beaming, "You like the Toreador Song, do you?"

His brother-in-law turned to him with excitement. "Of *course,* I
like it, and as a practical business man, I'm not afraid of making a
prediction. That song is going to be a *hit!*"

✳ 377

Young Abie Levinson said, "Papa, was Adam Jewish?"

Mr. Levinson put down his newspaper and thought for a moment.
He was an expert at Talmudic reasoning and the art of making a
point by an unanswerable question.

He said, "If we can determine that Eve was Jewish, my son, we
would at once see that Adam was Jewish, for who but a Jew could
bring himself to marry a Jewish girl?" (Here he turned his head a bit
nervously to make sure Mrs. Levinson wasn't listening.) "Therefore
we drop the Adam problem and ask ourselves instead: 'Was Eve
Jewish?'

"To answer that we have only to ask the question: Would anyone
but a Jewish girl say, 'Here, have a piece of fruit'?"

Of course, if the audience isn't familiar with Jewish ladies of
the old school and their habit of diligently pressing fruit on
guests, the joke won't work. So remember never to give up a
joke merely because you told it once to no response at all. The

joke may still be a good one and you may merely have mis-
gauged your audience. Try again!

And incidentally, while it is habitual for Jewish males to
make derogatory remarks about Jewish females, there is nothing to it, you may be sure. I say this because Jewish girls may
be among the readers of this book, and each year they seem to
find all these jokes less humorous. (I'm just kidding, girls, honest!)

A new editor of mine at a particular publishing house which
shall here remain nameless,* since it isn't Houghton Mifflin, is
absolutely gorgeous — and Jewish, too. And when I look at her
with affected astonishment and say, "Listen, are you *sure* you're
Jewish?" her glorious dark eyes flash, and she shakes a lovely
finger at me and says, "Now get it straight. Jewish is *better.*"
(But she went ahead and married a Gentile.)

❄ 378

Question: What is the favorite nine-letter word used by a Jewish
grandmother to her grandchild?
Answer: Eateateat!

Only today I told this joke and then instantly said, in all honesty, "Oh, my God, I forgot to call my mother!" That got a
bigger laugh than the joke.

❄ 379

Mr. Gottlieb, now a wealthy investment counselor, had for many
years been away from the ghetto in which he had been brought up,
and suddenly a longing to see the old neighborhood overcame him.
Dressing in one of his older suits and abandoning his limousine for
the subway, he made his way down to the well-known area and
found himself in the dingy tenement district that had once been
home.

He had never particularly admired it when he had lived there, but

* But I'll name it in the footnote. It's Doubleday & Co.

now nostalgia held him in its grip. He looked about at the small stores scattered along the row of dilapidated buildings — the candy store, the tailor shop, the grocery. He looked at the plump, middle-aged ladies leaning out their windows in the warm afternoon sun, the men playing checkers on the stoops, the distant shrillness of mothers seeking errant sons, the clothes hanging from the lines in row over row in the backyards.

Tears came to his eyes, and he said to himself, "Here is the true source of ambition, drive, and creativity; here is the strength and tradition of my people."

He had hardly thought this when he noticed on one corner an old man in earnest conversation with a young boy. The aged man, with a flowing white beard, was wearing a long coat, old cracked shoes, and a black hat from under which white locks escaped. He was the epitome of the east European patriarch. The young boy, perhaps twelve, with his face eager and his eyes bright, listened attentively.

"There," said Mr. Gottlieb, "is the essence of it all. This is age imparting its wisdom to youth. This is tradition being handed down the generations. I must listen; I *must* catch the flavor of this precious conversation."

Unobtrusively, he drifted closer and finally caught the quavering voice of the old man as he said to the boy, "So is that how you speak to a grandfather? You say 'drop dead'?"

Depending on the permissiveness of the audience, you can substitute a more pungent phrase for drop dead. I leave that up to you.

❊ 380

Mr. Moskowitz had married off four of his children but the fifth was a problem. Young Jake had no visible virtues that would make him a desirable husband. He had neither good looks, charm, intelligence, manners, nor conversation. Yet it was unthinkable that he remain single. Moskowitz stooped to the last resort and called in a marriage broker.

The marriage broker listened and said, "I have just the girl for the young man — Princess Anne."

"Who?"

"Princess Anne. The daughter of Queen Elizabeth II of Great Britain."

"A *shikseh?*"

The marriage broker sighed. "Why the prejudice? In these enlightened times, what's wrong with a Gentile girl? She comes from a good family, with very little anti-Semitism in it. They fought Hitler, if you'll remember. They have the very best social connections. They're wealthy and the princess is a real beauty. See. I'll write the names down together."

Suiting action to words, he painstakingly wrote Jacob Moskowitz in his little book and right below it, Princess Anne Mountbatten.

Moskowitz had to admit the names went well together, but he said, "You don't understand. I have to consider my old aunt. She is extremely pious. If she found out Jake was marrying a shikseh, she's go out of her mind."

The marriage broker put away his little book. "Let me talk to her."

An appointment was arranged, and for hours, quite literally for hours, the marriage broker pleaded, stormed, raged, cajoled, and slowly broke down the old lady.

Her faded eyes awash with tears and her little chin trembling, the aunt said at last, "Well, maybe you're right and I shouldn't be so old-fashioned. If, as you say, the girl is a fine girl, and if she will make Jake happy, and if the children will be brought up Jewish, all right. For myself, I can always move out of town and change my name so no one will know my shame. Go ahead; I will make no objection."

The marriage broker nodded gleefully and staggered out of the room. The session had worn him out and left him but a shell of his normal self. Emerging into the street, he opened his little book to the page on which both names had been written. He put a firm checkmark after the name Jacob Moskowitz and said, with a huge and tremulous sigh of relief, "Half done!"

❋ 381

A liner, cruising down the Caribbean, noted an island in the distance from which a thin line of smoke was curling upward. This was not in itself surprising, but it was clearly marked on the charts as an uninhabited island. Use of the spyglass made it clear that some sort of habitation existed there, so the liner heaved to and sent out a small boat to investigate.

As the boat approached the island, the officer on board couldn't help but note a small but very neat pier. On it was an elderly man, dressed in faultless yachting costume.

The elderly man greeted the officer enthusiastically when he landed. "Sir," he said, "my name is Abramowitz, and I have been here ten years, ever since I was marooned here — the only survivor of a ship sunk in a storm."

"The only survivor?" said the officer. "But I see numerous houses here."

"I built them myself," said Abramowitz, "so I could have the feeling of living in a community. I also built this pier, and an electric generating plant run by water power. I have a small textile factory where I produce my clothes, including these which I am wearing. I have everything I need here."

"But this is remarkable," said the officer. "Unbelievable!"

Abramowitz shrugged. "If you really want to see something, come with me." He led the officer to one corner of the island and there they came upon a miniature synagog. "In this temple," said Abramowitz, "I pray every Sabbath and every holy day. I don't have the necessary ten men to make it official, but it gives me great comfort nevertheless."

The men from the ship were more astonished than ever. The temple was small but it had pews, a balcony, a seven-branched candlestick, a recess for the Torah, and seemed in every way to be neat and tasteful.

Drinking in the obvious stupefaction of the officer, Abramowitz said, "Let me show you something else."

The officer followed him to another corner of the island, and there they found another synagog, larger and considerably more elaborate than the first.

The officer said, "But if you are the only one on the island, and you use the first temple you showed me, what is this?"

"This," said Abramowitz, with a gesture of contempt, "is the temple I wouldn't go to for anything."

The reference to the tendency of Jews to find it difficult to be suited as far as temples are concerned is not a trait necessarily confined to them. I've heard it said that when three Frenchmen get together, they promptly found four political parties.

❊ 382

Moskowitz did not bother to conceal his jubilation. "Guess, Finkel-stein," said he, "how much I cleared in that deal I closed this morning?"

"Half!" said Finkelstein.

❊ 383

The neighborhood grocer was weary to death of Mrs. Goldfarb and her habit of stretching her credit as far as it could possibly be stretched. Finally, he decided to have it out with her.

"Mrs. Goldfarb," he said, when she arrived on her next shopping expedition, "I am sorry, but before you make another purchase, I would like to have you settle your bill. All of it. Let's start fresh."

Mrs. Goldfarb drew herself up and allowed a haughty expression to cross her face. She said, distinctly, "Go halfway to hell," turned on her heel, and began to stalk out.

The grocer called out, "One moment, Mrs. Goldfarb. Just out of curiosity — why just halfway to hell? Why not all the way?"

Mrs. Goldfarb sighed. "The trouble is," she said, "I have an equally large bill with the baker."

Actually, "go to hell" is a very pale version of the phrase which is actually used in the Yiddish form of this joke. Yiddish is very rich in colorful bad wishes of all kinds, but as it happened my father never used them. When driven past all endurance, he would deliver himself of an "Oh, nuts!"

My mother, on the other hand, was a far more earthy character, and had a tremendous vocabulary of invective. What's more, she had no hesitation whatever in using it upon her family when moved. I was the target of many a ripe phrase, and naturally, I picked them up and on occasion made use of them.

This would shock my father, who would say, "Where did you learn such vile language?"

And, being an honest little boy, I would say, "From Mama!"

And my father would say, "Never! Mama never uses such language!"

Nor could I ever persuade him otherwise. He was an odd character, my father.

* 384

The cult of the elaborate bar mitzvah has reached the stage where affluent families, determined to make of the occasion something that will be a lifelong memory, are almost at a loss to find a sufficiently ostentatious device.

Mr. Levy, therefore, was brimming over with delight at the wholly unique fashion in which he planned to celebrate the thirteenth birthday of his oldest son.

"A safari!" he explained. "I have arranged for an air flight to Africa. The bearers are hired, the jungle trails chosen, the guide obtained. It will be completely novel. We will go there, listen to native chants, shoot at some wild game. Standing on the body of a dead lion, my son will recite his prayer in Hebrew, there will be services, and we'll return here for the champagne. How's that?"

The invited guests were ecstatic over the sheer enormity of the bad taste involved. On the appointed day, all were flown to Africa. The bearers were lined up and the guide led the way. The guests, all in appropriate costumes down to pith helmets and mosquito nets, threaded their thrilling way along the trails through the rain forest.

Suddenly, the column came to a halt and the guide called out, "There will be a delay of one hour."

"Why?" demanded Levy indignantly.

And the guide said, "What can I do? There's another bar mitzvah safari ahead of us on the trail."

* 385

The Moskowitz family was planning a daughter's wedding and the guest list was being made out. There was no use in being foolishly extravagant, so only the minimum number of invitations was sent out. That is, one to: every member of the family to the tenth cousins, and all their relations by marriage; all the bride's friends back to kindergarten, and their relatives; all the neighbors, and their relatives; and, of course, such strangers as happened to be in the vicinity.

When that was done, Mrs. Moskowitz looked at the list ruefully and said, "There are still the guests on the groom's side to consider."

Mr. Moskowitz nodded. "Well," he said, "it has to be. And it will only be fair to give him free choice. Whichever he wants — either his mother or his father."

✳ 386

Mrs. Goldfarb entered the delicatessen and announced that she was in the market for some sliced corned beef.

"How much would you want?" asked the man behind the counter.

Mrs. Goldfarb pointed to a huge slab of corned beef and said, "Put that on the cutter and cut. I'll tell you when to stop."

The counter man did as he was told. The cutter hummed its cheery song as slice after slice peeled off and piled up. When the pile had grown unusually high, and the customer had said not a word, the counter man asked, "Enough, lady?"

Imperiously, she said, "Cut, cut. I'll tell you when to stop."

Twice more, as the pile grew increasingly mountainous, the counter man asked if she had enough. Twice more came the cry, "Cut! Cut!"

Finally, when the man had disappeared behind the avalanche of corned-beef slices, Mrs. Goldfarb called out, "Have you reached the middle of the piece?"

"Just about," said the counter man.

"Good!" said Mrs. Goldfarb. "Now from that middle, please cut me a quarter-pound of corned beef."

Talking about delicatessens, the father of Shelley Berman, the comedian, had a delicatessen, I think.

At least I once heard Shelley Berman on television give what in my opinion was his very best routine — a monolog representing his father, on the occasion when Shelley was asking for a largish sum of money with which to go to New York to attend acting school, a monolog in which the humor, little by little, turned into touching pathos.

The details don't matter, but his father's accent as rendered by Shelley, his intonations, his idioms, his whole personality, were so close to my father's in the well-remembered candy store of my childhood, that I felt a little queer.

Well, there was no use trying to be sentimental with my dignified father, but I had to make a long-distance call as soon as the routine was over.

My father answered and I said, "Hello, Papa. It's Isaac. Did you hear Shelley Berman on the TV just now?"

"Yes," said my father, and nothing more.

Rather at a loss for words, I finally said, "I heard him, too, so — so — so I thought I'd call and ask how you are."

And my mother said, "He's fine."

I was astonished. "Mama!" I said. "What are you doing on the phone? Where's Papa?"

My mother said, "He's in the corner, crying."

My father and his unemotional dignity! What a fake he was! And how I miss him!

❋ 387

Mrs. Moskowitz was bursting with pride.

"Did you hear about my son Louie?" she asked Mrs. Finkelstein.

"No. What's with your son Louie?"

"He's going to a psychiatrist. Twice each week he's going to a psychiatrist."

"Is that good?"

"Of course, it's good. Forty dollars an hour he pays, forty dollars! And all he talks about is me."

❋ 388

The aged rabbi, who was undertaking to teach the young hopeful all the intricacies of the Hebrew language, explained to the boy's father that payment for the entire course of lessons would have to be handed over in advance.

"Why is that?" asked Mr. Moskowitz, frowning.

"You see," said the rabbi, "it has happened in the past that a student has died before the course was over. In that case, the father generally forgets to pay me for the lessons given, and I haven't the heart to press him in his sorrow. So I prefer payment in advance."

Mr. Moskowitz said, "But excuse me. You are much older than my son. In the course of nature, it is much more likely you would die in the midst of the course, and if so, you would have received payment for all, while having only taught part."

Said the rabbi, reprovingly, "And would you begrudge an old man his chance at a lucky break?"

� 389

Mrs. Moskowitz was trying to describe to the interior decorator exactly how she wanted her house done.

She said, "I leave the art and design entirely to you. I ask only that whatever you do, it be spectacular. I want it done in such a way that when my dear best friend, Mrs. Finkelstein, should come in for the first time, she should instantly have a stroke with jealousy and drop dead."

✲ 390

Moskowitz met Finkelstein on Seventh Avenue one day and said, "Finkelstein, have I got a bargain for you! An elephant! A whole, living elephant! For just one hundred dollars."

Finkelstein said, "Are you crazy? What do I want with an elephant?"

"It's a beautiful elephant. All gray. Ten feet tall with a complete trunk."

"But I have nothing to feed it. I have no place to put it; I live in a three-room apartment."

"Two beautiful tusks, maybe two feet long each. It's a magnificent beast. They don't make them like that anymore."

"Moskowitz," said Finkelstein, almost screaming, "I have a three-room walkup apartment on the fifth floor. Where will I keep an elephant?"

"You're a hard man, Finkelstein," said Moskowitz. "I'll tell you what. I'll throw in a second whole elephant for only fifty dollars extra."

And Finkelstein said, "*Now* you're talking."

❊ 391

Becky nudged her husband late one night.

"Jake," she said, "get out of bed and close the window. It's cold outside."

Jake mumbled and tried to shake her off, but she was insistent. "Get out of bed, Jake, and close the window. It's cold outside."

Jake pleaded, "Becky, let me sleep."

But Becky grew firmer and louder. "Jake," she ordered. "Get out of bed this minute and close the window. It's cold outside."

Shaking with fury, Jake climbed out of bed, slammed the window shut, and cried, "Are you satisfied? Is it now warm outside?"

It is almost every man's experience, I think, that women are hard to suit where temperature is concerned. I once saw a cartoon which showed nothing but a wall bearing two thermostats, marked His and Hers. The one marked His had the usual indicator markings, showing degrees from sixty to ninety. The one marked Hers had only two notations: Too Hot and Too Cold.

❊ 392

Jones had ordered a suit from a neighborhood tailor who had been highly recommended to him, but considerable time had passed and the suit had not yet been delivered.

In rather a passion, Jones stepped into the tailor's shop to have it out. He said, "See here, Mr. Levy, you promised to let me have the suit in two weeks, and four weeks have already passed."

"I'm working. I'm working," said Mr. Levy. "The suit is hanging right there. It's almost finished."

"*Almost* finished? But why does it take you so long, Mr. Levy? The good Lord made the whole world in only six days."

Mr. Levy put down his needle, stood up, and said, "Come here, mister. I want you should feel the material on this suit I am making for you. Okay? Now I want you should come to the window and take a look at this phooey world."

✻ 393

One time, young Sadie Moskowitz took her grandmother to the movies to see one of the chariot spectaculars involving the usual distortions of Roman history. The grandmother watched with peaceful lack of comprehension until the inevitable scene in the amphitheater, where unarmed prisoners are thrown to the lions.

At the sight of helpless men and women facing the ferocious beasts, the old grandmother broke into loud wails, crying out, "Oh, the poor people; oh, the poor people."

Sadie, terribly embarrassed, whispered fiercely, "Don't scream like that, grandma. Those are Christians who are being punished by the Roman government, and it's only a movie."

"Christians!" said the grandmother. "I see." She quieted down at once. But only a few minutes passed and then she began wailing louder than before.

"Grandmother!" demanded Sadie. "What is it *now?*"

"In the corner," said the grandmother, pointing. "That poor little lion there. He's not getting anything."

✻ 394

Becky was on her deathbed, with her husband Jake at her side. He held her cold hand and tears silently streamed down his face.

Her pale lips moved. "Jake," she said.

"Shush," said Jake. "Don't try to talk."

But she insisted. "Jake," she said in her tired voice. "I have to talk. I must confess."

"There is nothing to confess," said the weeping Jake. "It's all right."

"No, no. I must die in peace. I must confess, Jake, that I have been unfaithful to you."

Jake stroked her hand. "Now, Becky, don't be concerned. I know about it. I know about it. Why else did I poison you?"

Somehow one doesn't think of the Beckys of the world as being unfaithful. Managing a house, caring for a husband and children, and for all I know, running a Hadassah too, leaves precious little time for frills and fripperies. What's more, I suspect the quiet, heavy-laden Jakes have no time for sexual luxuries either. But in the world of jokes, sexual mores are those of the barnyard.

❊ 395

The firm of Goldberg and Finkelstein had hired a new secretary, a knockout, and finally Goldberg managed to get a date with her. He was at work the next morning, brim full of triumph.

He said to Finkelstein, "She's a real honey. I took her to dinner and a show, and then we went up to her apartment, and got just as friendly as we could get — know what I mean?" He chuckled lecherously and added, "And you know what, Finkelstein, she's a million times better than my wife Becky."

Finkelstein said, "That sounds very intriguing. Would you object to my taking her out?"

"Of course not. Partners are partners."

Finkelstein found an occasion, took her out, and the next morning said, "You've got poor taste, Goldberg. She was a lot of fun, I admit, but all in all, not a patch on your wife Becky."

Individual jokes have all kinds of connotations to jokesters. It is possible for a joke to be disliked not for any inherent badness, but because it may once have been told under distressing circumstances or by a particularly inept narrator.

I remember once, a good number of years ago, when I was asked under particularly public circumstances whether I was a jokester. With my usual passion for truth at all costs, I promptly said, "Yes, and a good one."

Naturally he said, "All right. Tell me a joke."

And suddenly, for some fool reason, I was aware of many people staring at me and froze. The only joke I could think of, after a painful half-minute, was the following, and I proceeded to tell it lamely indeed. I have hated the joke ever since.

❀ 396

Moskowitz, anxious to buy an exotic present for his aged mother, came across a very accomplished parrot and decided it was just the thing. He had it delivered.

Some weeks later, he had occasion to visit his mother. "Tell me," he said, "did you receive the bird I sent you?"

"Yes, indeed," said his mother. "You are a thoughtful son."

"Were you pleased?"

"Absolutely. It seemed to me at first he would be small and stringy, but the soup was delicious."

Moskowitz leaped from his seat. "You *ate* it? But that bird could speak seven languages!"

His mother, equally startled, said, "But in that case, when he saw me pulling out the pot, why didn't he say something?"

❀ 397

Mr. Finkelstein, a long-time widower, had astonished his entire family by announcing, at the age of seventy-seven, that he was going to marry a young lady of twenty. The sons and daughters of the old gentleman, themselves in their fifties, and his grandchildren, some of them over twenty, were horrified at the utterly unfitting alliance thus being suggested and pleaded with him not to do this thing — but to no avail.

In desperation, they consulted the rabbi of their temple. He was a young man of advanced notions whom they did not entirely trust, but necessity drove them.

The rabbi was rather reluctant to interfere. He said, "I am going to Europe tomorrow for an extended trip, but I will talk to your father briefly and I will see what I can do."

He drove out at once to see old Mr. Finkelstein and talked at length concerning the lack of fitness in the projected marriage, the unhappiness it would cause not only to his family, but to the girl and to himself. Mr. Finkelstein was oblivious to all reason, however.

"I love the girl," he repeated over and over, "and she is willing to marry me."

The rabbi said, "In that case, let me suggest something that perhaps is not the most appropriate course of action, but one that strikes me as highly practical. You are an elderly man; you are in no position to go to parties, dances, and such like affairs. She, on the other hand, is a young lady, no doubt as frivolous and pleasure-bent as most young ladies are. She will grow tired of your inability to join her, or you will get tired of trying to keep up with her. It would be a wise thing then if you were to take in a boarder."

The rabbi paused impressively, then went on. "A *young* boarder, you understand, who could keep her company. She would still be your wife; she would take care of you and see that you were comfortable. She would also have a companion who would see to it that she had a good time. It is irregular, but these are times of a broadened view on morality so I'm sure you understand what I mean."

Slowly, Mr. Finkelstein nodded. "Sure, I get it. My family won't like it, but what business is it of theirs? If I am satisfied, why should they object; and the young lady, as you say, would be taken care of in the way of companionship and so on."

The rabbi, deciding he had made the best of a bad situation, and had done so in a way suiting the atmosphere of the new age, went off to Europe. It was many months before he returned and one of his first acts was to pay a visit to old Mr. Finkelstein.

"Well, Mr. Finkelstein," said the rabbi, "did you get married?"

"Oh yes," said Mr. Finkelstein, "and I want you to know we are both very happy. What's more, to the surprise of my family, my wife is pregnant."

The rabbi suppressed a smile. "I suppose, then," he said, "you took in a young boarder as I suggested."

"Yes, indeed," said Mr. Finkelstein, "and to the surprise of my family, the young boarder is also pregnant."

I happen to like a long joke better than a short one and, if conditions are right, tell a long joke with particular gusto. My feeling is that a good long story is much better than a good brief story for the same reason that a good novel is much better than a good novelette.

On the other hand, you may not like long jokes. You may not have the patience for them, or you may just feel that the risk is too great and that if anything goes wrong, a long joke is bound to be worse than a brief one, just as a bad novel is much worse than a bad novelette.

This does not necessarily mean that the long jokes are barred from your repertoire. There are few long jokes that can't be cut drastically; and sometimes if you feel it is a shame to cut a long joke (like putting ketchup on prime steak) there are short-joke cousins. For instance, if you are in a hurry or for any other reason don't want to tell Joke 397, how about —

❄ 398

Finkelstein, at seventy-seven, had decided to marry a young girl of twenty and his friends were scandalized (and perhaps more than a little jealous).

One of them said, "Finkelstein, do you realize that sex with a young girl at your age could be very dangerous — even fatal?"

Finkelstein considered that for a while, then shrugged and said, "Oh well, if she dies, I'll just get myself another one."

❄ 399

The little man got onto the subway car which was clearly marked TIMES SQUARE in various places, and said apologetically to the large man next to him, "Pardon me, does this train go to Times Square?"

Intent on his newspaper, the large man said rather shortly, "Yes, it does."

A moment later, the little man said, "Are you *sure* it goes to Times Square?"

Irritated, the large man said, "Of course, I'm sure."

The little fellow said argumentatively, "But how can you be sure?"

At this the large man exploded. He said, "Can't you see the signs in this car? Read them. Don't they say Times Square? What more do you want?"

The little fellow shrank within himself and sat motionless thereafter. At the next stop, however, another anxious-looking individual stepped onto the train. He approached the little man and asked apologetically, "Does this train go to Times Square?"

At which our small friend jumped to his feet in agitation, shook his fist at the newcomer, and said, "Now look what you did! You made me uncertain again."

Notice that I told Joke 399 without any names (and, of course, without any indication of accent). Yet I've put it in the section of Jewish jokes. Why? Because I always tell it with a Jewish accent. Tell it with an Irish accent, and it might go just as well. So don't be too inhibited by what I say is a Jewish joke. Unless there is the direct mention of a temple, a bar mitzvah, Israel, or a few other things, almost any so-called Jewish joke can be Gentilized. And I suspect that the reason I have so many Jewish jokes in my repertoire is that I Judaize many a Gentile joke.

❊ 400

Mrs. Moskowitz kept eyeing the very distinguished man who sat next to her in the subway.

Finally, unable to control her curiosity, she nudged him and said, "Pardon me, sir, but are you Jewish?"

The gentleman looked up from his *Wall Street Journal* and said, in cultured tones, "No, madam, as it happens, I am not."

Several moments passed, and Mrs. Moskowitz asked again, "Are you *sure* you're not Jewish?"

The gentleman, heaving a patient sigh, said, "Madam, I have nothing against the Jews and if I happened to be Jewish, I would be glad to admit it. It just happens that my ancestors are not Jewish. Please forgive me for that."

Mrs. Moskowitz shifted uneasily in her seat for another few moments, then nudged him again. "Listen," she said loudly, "are you absolutely *positive* you're not Jewish?"

Despairing of any chance of reading his paper while the inquisition continued, the gentleman lowered his paper and said calmly, "Well, madam, you have found me out. I *am* Jewish."

Whereupon Mrs. Moskowitz surveyed him critically and said, "Funny! You don't *look* Jewish."

Joke 400 is one of the few where I know two punch lines of which I don't find one immeasurably superior to the other. As a consequence, I am usually uncertain as to which to use. I wouldn't use both in one joke session, but this book is not really a joke session, so here is the other —

❈ 401

The man on the subway had been badgered by Mrs. Moskowitz into admitting he was Jewish even though he plainly wasn't.

At which, Mrs. Moskowitz sighed with satisfaction and said, "What a relief! In that case, could you tell me the time please?"

❈ 402

Moskowitz was describing the funeral of a lodge brother.

"No expense," he said, "was spared. The casket alone came to over seven thousand dollars."

"Seven thousand dollars?" marveled Finkelstein. "Why so much?"

"It was titanium, with a stainless steel lining, and a nitrogen atmosphere sealed inside. He will never decay."

"But he just lies there," said Finkelstein.

"Of course, what else?"

"For that kind of money, he could have been buried in a Cadillac — seated at the wheel."

❈ 403

A century ago, a certain rabbi in eastern Europe was renowned for his facility at telling stories that were to the point of any discussion and enlightened any problem.

One of his disciples asked him about this. "How do you manage, Rabbi, to find a story to illustrate every point?"

"Let me explain," said the rabbi, "with a story. Once a certain landowner was riding through a small town, when he noticed that on a certain wooden fence, there were painted a dozen targets, and in the bull's-eye of every single one was a bullet hole. He had never seen such shooting and at once he stopped his conveyance and ordered his retainers to find the marksman, for he badly needed people with that kind of talent to patrol his lands.

"A quivering tailor was brought before him. This, he was told, was the man who had shot at the targets.

"The landowner stared. 'Did you shoot the bullets?'

" 'Yes, sir,' said the tailor, 'but I meant no harm.'

" 'But you are an expert marksman then?'

" 'No, sir, it was the first time I ever held a gun in my hands.'

" 'Why then, how did you hit the bull's-eye every time?'

" 'I didn't, sir,' said the tailor. 'I merely shot the gun a dozen times at the fence, and then painted targets around every bullet hole.'

"And so," concluded the rabbi, "I have a fund of stories ready at hand, and whenever I happen to think of one, I wait until something is said to which I can apply it."

I use very much the same system, frankly, and it is frightening to think that if I had been born a century before I was, I might have been a parable-telling rabbi in some little town in western Russia.

But my favorite Jewish stories are almost invariably those that somehow or other involve a rabbi (even though I know hardly any in private life), and of all the rabbi stories I know, the following is the one I tell with the most relish, and so I will end the Jewish section with it —

❊ 404

Young Leah, in the old days of eastern Europe, was the sole support of her mother, and had been fortunate enough to marry a substantial young man, despite the miserable state of her dowry. Leah was happy and her mother was ecstatic.

Imagine her mother's shock then, when, on the morning after the wedding, Leah returned in misery and announced she would not return to her husband. "I love him madly," she said, "but I had to leave him."

Stubbornly, she refused to give the reason, but from what she said, it was apparent that the young man had made some rather sophisticated sexual demands on her.

As the days passed, both mother and daughter grew more and more miserable, the former out of frustrated finances, the latter out of frustrated love. Finally, the mother suggested that they visit the town rabbi, the beloved Rabbi Joshua of Khaslavich. After all, in such matters one needed guidance.

They were granted an audience and when the rabbi demanded the details and Leah hung back, Rabbi Joshua said kindly, "Whisper it into my ear, my daughter. No one will know but we ourselves and God."

She did so, and as she whispered, the rabbi's kindly brow furrowed, and lightning flashed from his mild eyes.

"My daughter," he thundered, "it is not fitting for a Jewish girl to submit to such vile indignities. It would be a deadly sin, and because of it a curse would be laid on our whole town."

Back went mother and daughter, disconsolate, and after a week of continued privation, the mother said, "You know, our rabbi is a wonderful man, but it is sometimes wise to get a second opinion. Why not consult Rabbi Samuel of Krichev? He is very highly spoken of as a man of learning."

Why not, indeed? They got into the wagon and bumped their way to the next town. As Leah whispered the tale into Rabbi Samuel's ear, the old man's earlocks uncurled and turned distinctly grayer. He said in strangled tones, "My daughter, it was for sins such as this that the Holy One, blessed be He, sent down upon the earth a flood in days of yore. You must not agree to his demands."

Again mother and daughter returned, and now, for a long time, the dreary round of day-to-day living continued, until the mother said, "Let us make one final attempt to obtain guidance. Let us go to the Grand Rabbi of Vilna. There is no one in the whole world as wise as he and as learned. And whatever he says we may accept as the final word."

They bought their railway tickets to the tune of a serious depletion of their meager savings and rode to Vilna. Once again, for the third

time, Leah whispered her story into a rabbinical ear. The Grand
Rabbi listened with equanimity and then said, "My daughter, be
guided by your husband. He is a young and vigorous man, and it is
fitting that you both enjoy yourselves. Have no qualms concerning
this thing."

Leah was thunderstruck. She said, "But, Grand Rabbi, how can
you say this? Rabbi Joshua of Khaslavich said it would bring a curse
upon our town. Rabbi Samuel of Krichev said such sins caused the
flood."

But the Grand Rabbi merely stroked his white beard and smiled.
"My daughter," he said, "what do those small-town rabbis know
about big-city sex?"

<PART VIII>
PART VIII *Ethnic*

THE JEWISH STORY is but one subdivision of a larger group sometimes called dialect stories, in which the dialect itself is funny (if well done), and in which the stereotype of the group represented by the dialect guides the listener in certain directions that intensify the eventual laughter.

Since in this book I am not telling my stories in dialect, and since I don't want to encourage anyone to use dialect, I will not use the term. Instead, I will make use of a word that has been introduced to replace the unpopular word race and call them ethnic jokes.

By calling *this* section Ethnic, I don't mean to imply that Jewish jokes are not ethnic. They are. It's just that I have so many Jewish ones that I put them in a special section. This part of the book I ought perhaps to call Other Ethnic, but that is clumsy and we'll leave the Other understood.

Needless to say, ethnic jokes are risky ones. The line between funny satire and outright offense is almost vanishingly small, and it exists in different places for the person who is of the ethnic group being satirized and the person who is not; for the person of an ethnic group who feels secure because he is surrounded by others of his group, and for the same person who feels alone because he is not; for the person of an ethnic group who is feeling good that day, and for the same person who has been unsettled by the morning headlines.

The jokester must judge these things carefully and must allow himself leeway. He should err on the side of caution. It is better to give up what he may consider a good joke rather than take even a moderate chance at giving offense — for his own sake as a jokester, as well as out of common decency.

Once I was invited to attend a banquet given by a certain group at which a high official of that group was to give an address. A good proportion of the large group sitting in the banquet hall was Jewish; the high official who was speaking was not. A good proportion of the large group was stone sober; the high official who was speaking was not.

It turned out that the high official knew a great many Jewish jokes and decided to tell them all, in a rather indifferent accent. The laughter that greeted the first few faded away after a while into frigid silence, and the speaker was just too drunk to know that anything was wrong. He kept on to the bitter end while the audience studied their water glasses in growing embarrassment and resentment. I listened in disbelief, for never before had I witnessed so persistent a patter of jokes in the face of absolutely no response.

For years after, whenever I met anyone who had been at that disaster with me, it was inevitable that he or she would say, "Do you remember that jackass who . . ." Whether it hurt him in a business way I don't know, but I for one would go to considerable pains to avoid being present at any function where he was expected to speak.

In this book, I can't very well follow my own advice, since I can't judge the nature of the emotions and sensitivity of every reader at the time he is reading. I can only say that I mean no harm; that I try to include no joke that seems to me to be gratuitously offensive; and that if I misjudge, I am sorry.

And just to show you the complications that any scheme of classification gets one into, there is the multi-ethnic joke where several targets are aimed at —

❊ 405

It is said that when you tell an Englishman a joke, he will laugh
three times. He will laugh the first time — when you tell it — to be
polite. He will laugh a second time — when you explain it — to be
polite. Finally, he will laugh a third time in the middle of the night
when he wakes from a sound sleep and suddenly gets it.

When you tell a German the same joke, he will laugh twice. He
will laugh first — when you tell it — to be polite. He will laugh a
second time — when you explain it — to be polite. He will never
laugh a third time, because he will never get it.

When you tell an American the same joke, he will laugh once —
when you tell it — for he will get it.

And when you tell a Jew the same joke, he won't laugh at all.
Instead, he will say, "It's an old joke, and besides, you tell it all
wrong."

❊ 406

It is reported that several men of various nationalities were engaged
in writing books on the elephant.

A German put out a three-volume tome replete with footnotes,
entitled *A Short Introduction to the Study of the Elephant*.

A Frenchman put out a slim and graceful book entitled *The Elephant and His Love Life*.

An Englishman put out a heavily illustrated travel guide, entitled
Hunting Elephant in Deepest Africa.

An American put out an advertising brochure, *How to Raise Elephants in Your Backyard for Fun and Profit*.

And a Jew published a fiery pamphlet entitled *The Elephant and
Anti-Semitism*.

It is easy to switch, add, or subtract ethnic groups in such
jokes, to suit time and place. Before World War I, the final
item could have been a Pole writing on *The Elephant and the
Polish Question*, but that has lost meaning. Sometimes I exper-

iment with having a Russian write a vituperative book entitled
The Elephant as an Imperialist Swine.

As a matter of fact, the nationalities can be changed to members of other subdivisions, sometimes exceedingly specialized
ones. I was at a scholarly conference once, at which there were
a number of college deans. In the social mingling afterward, I
discovered, rather to my astonishment, that there were dean
jokes. Actually these were ordinary jokes which were suitably
modified.

Of course, one had to have some special knowledge.   A
school of general studies, for instance, is usually a school devoted to adult education and utterly unspecialized in nature.
So, presumably, is the dean of such a school, who must be a
jack of all trades and capable of improvising anything. With
that in mind, consider the following joke, which I heard then as
a dean joke but had heard in slightly modified form on other
occasions as a multi-ethnic joke —

✲ 407

A dean of a school of comparative theology, a dean of a school of
law, and a dean of a school of general studies were engaged in scholarly studies on a low-lying coral island far off in the South Pacific. A
radio message reached them to the effect that a tidal wave was advancing on the island and would sweep it completely in six hours.
Because of storms at sea, moreover, it was doubtful if rescue could
reach them in time.

At once, the dean of the school of comparative theology began a
series of prayers, in appropriate form, to the gods of all the major
religions on earth, and to those of such minor religions as he had
time for.

At the same time, the dean of the school of law began to write an
elaborate will hedged in with all the clauses that lawyers had ever
dreamed up.

And at the same time, the dean of the school of general studies
began an intensive six-hour rehearsal of the art of breathing under
water.

There are few national stereotypes as firmly fixed and as well-known as that of the Scotsman's penchant for thrift. *Webster's New International Dictionary*, second edition unabridged even lists one meaning of "Scotch" as "parsimonious" and categorizes the definition as "humorous."

There are few national stereotypes that don't have any basis (however tenuous) in reality. After all, Scotland is a poor nation — much poorer than England, which has the larger and more fertile portion of their common island and which has been developed, commercially and industrially, to a far greater extent. A poor person is compelled to be economical, and one who is better off, if callous, can sneer at that economy and call it parsimony. Then once the stereotype is established, it feeds on itself, for it becomes easy to say "A certain Scotsman —" and have the audience at once get in the mood for a "cheapness joke." Thus —

❋ 408

Young Sandy MacTavish came home in great excitement, saying, "Father! Father! On returning from school, I ran home behind the streetcar all the way and saved sixpence carfare."

Whereupon the exasperated father slapped his son's cheek resoundingly and said, "Spendthrift! Why did you not run home behind a taxicab and save three shillings?"

❋ 409

Jamie MacDougall was back in Aberdeen after a week's vacation south of the border, and he was asked how he had enjoyed himself.

"Well enough," he said broodingly, "but London is a fearfully expensive place. I had not been there a day and a half, when bang! went sixpence."

Nor need you consider cheapness the only notable component of the Scots stereotype. There is also the well-known Scottish respect for the invigorating qualities of strong drink.

☆ 410

Sandy MacTavish was cycling home one dark stormy night, after a gay evening at the pub. He was singing heartily and had the comfortable feel of an unopened pint of whiskey in his hip pocket. Neither the darkness nor the rain disturbed him, and he was just drunk enough not to care whether he was actually on the road or not.

The to-be-expected happened. The bicycle struck a rock, and Sandy went flying through the air. He hit with a thud and was knocked senseless for a minute or two. He came back to consciousness, rather sobered, and almost the first thing he felt was a trickle of something warm and sticky making its way down his thigh.

Remembering the contents of his hip pocket, he raised his voice in anguished prayer, "Oh, God, I hope that's blood."

That's two jokes out of three for Sandy MacTavish. I would have made it three out of three, but I did want you to see I know another Scottish name.

Just as I use Moskowitz and Finkelstein so often in Jewish jokes, I have pet names for other ethnic groups. There's Sandy MacTavish for Scots jokes; there's Pat and Mike for Irish jokes (something made almost obligatory by the great flood of Irish jokes a century ago, when the Irish were so new an element in our country and therefore so natural a target for mockery — and not always good-natured mockery, either; Pierre and Jacques for French ones; Reuben and Silas for farm jokes, and so on. Pick your own combinations and stick to them.

One warning, though: if you are not certain of authentic-sounding names, do without. If you are certain, but are pretty sure the audience isn't, do without. If you are telling a Hungarian joke for instance, you might speak of Janos and Bela, and their sister Ilona, but the chances are the names will carry no particular atmosphere of a particular kind of humor. The audience will merely judge you a pedant and grow hostile, losing you your laugh. If you're anxious to show erudition to an audience not as erudite as yourself, for heaven's sake don't do it while you're telling jokes.

Of course, it would be nice not to be confined merely to such things as names to establish background. Oh, to be able to handle a number of different accents — but I can't.

Still I am only human, and sometimes I am so taken with a joke that *demands* an accent I can't handle, I try it anyway. And occasionally there is a joke that is foolproof enough to withstand a clumsy accent —

❋ 411

An American was hunting in the north woods, along with his guest, a Scotsman in America for the first time. At one point, a large animal thrashed across their field of vision. The American, caught by surprise, had no time to take aim and fire, and the Scotsman, startled, said, "What was that?"

"A moose," said the disappointed American.

"A moose!" cried the Scotsman. "Are you serious! If that was a moose, then I dinna care to see one o' your r-r-rots."

❋ 412

Sandy MacTavish was sinking fast, but managed to whisper one last wish to his doctor.

"Before I die," he said, "let me hear for one last time the skirl of the pipes. Let me mount to heaven on the wings of the wild cry of the bagpipes which, on so many occasions, has lifted the hearts of Scotsmen at feast and in battle."

To a wish so earnestly expressed, the doctor felt he had to accede. A piper was brought in, and for an hour the drone of the pipes resounded through the corridors of the hospital.

The doctor recounted the consequences afterward. He said, "It was a medical miracle. Sandy, who was near death, perked up at once at the sound and now seems well on the road to recovery. That isn't all there is to the miracle, either. Six Englishmen in the same ward, who were only mildly ill, are now dying."

Some ethnic jokes can be shifted from one classification to another. A cheapness joke can be shifted from Scots to Jewish, though in the latter case the cheapness component of the stereotype is less well-defined. At other times, the shift is difficult, as when the punch line depends on a specific piece of Scots dialect.

There are times, however, when a joke told ethnically is quite universal and can be told in connection with any ethnic group or, indeed, without reference to anything narrower than the general human condition. Nevertheless, to the jokester himself the feel or flavor of the joke may demand a particular ethnic group and, all things being equal, the jokester's mood is to be respected. Thus —

✻ 413

It was not so long ago that the social organization of Scotland was a matter of clans, with the head of each clan — *The* MacGregor, for instance — supreme in his territory.

There was an occasion once when the MacGregors wished to consult a man of law concerning a knotty problem of litigation in the king's courts. For the purpose, a learned lawyer was brought in from Edinburgh and, very ill at ease, he was surrounded by the rough, large clansmen.

But it was time for dinner, and as a gesture of courtesy, the stranger was taken to the long table and directed to the huge armchair that loomed at one end of the table.

The lawyer shrank back, "Oh, sir, I could not sit in the chair of The MacGregor himself."

"You may sit," said The MacGregor, "since it is he himself who invites you to do so."

"But it would be wrong," protested the lawyer, "only The MacGregor should sit at the head of the table."

"Sit where you are told, you foolish little man," roared The MacGregor, "for wherever The MacGregor sits, *there* is the head of the table."

The joke stereotype of the Irishman includes such things as a liking for liquor and a propensity for brawling, but in addition, the Irishman is supposed to be particularly apt to make self-contradictory or incongruous statements. This part of the stereotype has been so well-established that such statements are called Irish bulls, and you will find the phrase in the dictionary.

I am not aware that the Irish are more prone to commit Irish bulls than are people of any other nationality, and actually you will find a number of them in my Jewish section. However, there is no way of wiping out the stereotype.

❋ 414

Pat had fallen headlong down a steep incline and lay motionless at the bottom.

Mike, fearful of the consequence, leaned over the lip of the incline and called out, "Pat, are you dead?"

Pat groaned and called back, "I'm badly bruised, but quite alive."

Mike shook his head dolefully and said, "I hope you are, but you're such a liar, I don't know whether to believe you."

❋ 415

Pat and Mike, bricklayers both, were the greatest of rivals. They were forever disputing as to who could lay a straighter line of bricks, who could lay them faster, who could handle the mortar with the greater grace and skill. No conclusion was ever reached.

Then, one day, Pat said, "I will bet you ten dollars that I can put you in my hod, and climb up the scaffolding *with* the hod and with you *in* the hod, all thirty stories to the roof of this structure we are building, and do it in less than fifteen minutes."

"Done!" said Mike, and climbed into the hod.

Mike was rather a lightweight, but even so, Pat, who began climbing with all the speed made possible by his powerful frame, found that he had undertaken a formidable task. The perspiration poured down his cheeks and at the twentieth floor, a misstep nearly precipitated him and his load to destruction below. Regaining his balance with the greatest of difficulty, he finally made it to the thirtieth floor with only seconds remaining of the fifteen minutes he had demanded.

Panting strenuously and unable to speak, Pat held out his hand for the ten dollars.

Shaking his head, Mike located a bill in the recesses of his pocket and passed it over in chagrin, saying, "Well, you did it; I'll have to give you that. But on the twentieth floor there, for one minute I had high hopes."

❋ 416

Father Mulcahey had just checked into the hotel. The bellboy had taken up his suitcase, then showed him how to turn on the television set and operate the thermostat. He indicated the bathroom with a grand sweep of his hand, turned over the key, and delicately kept his hand outstretched.

Father Mulcahey shook it.

Disconcerted, the bellboy coughed and said, "It is customary, Father, to give a small gratuity on an occasion like this."

With a sad smile, Father Mulcahey said, "My son, I'm afraid I have no money, but tell me, are you a drinking man, now?"

The bellboy's eyes glistened. "Yes indeed, Father."

"In that case, my boy, kneel down and, as a gratuity, I will have you take the temperance pledge."

❋ 417

A brigade of Irish soldiers was being sent out to keep the peace in some obscure corner of the world at the behest of the United Nations, and a grizzled sergeant was briefing them.

"Now, men," he said, "in that place where you are going, there are poisonous snakes, and it may well be that one or more of you will be bitten. Let me tell you that the old story about the internal application of whiskey in such a case is nonsense. I'm not opposed to a drop of whiskey at odd times, but it will do no good for snakebite.

"If you are bitten by a snake, men, the very first thing you must do is cut the place where you have been bitten so that it bleeds freely;

then apply your mouth to the cut and suck out as much blood as you can."

At this one soldier said nervously, "But, Sergeant, suppose you are bitten on the backside."

The sergeant stared at the questioner coldly and said, "In that case, my bucko, it will be then you'll know who your friends are."

❋ 418

The scene is Ireland, about half a century ago. Bridget was getting married and said, "Pat, I'll tell you the truth so you won't have the shock of finding out after marriage, and so I won't have to live with the fear that you will. A few years ago, during the troubles, our family was so poor we almost starved, and for a short while, I had to turn prostitute just to make enough to live."

Pat stared at her in horror. "Bridget," he said, "what have you done? There is no excuse for that. None! Not even the prospect of starvation would permit such a thing even temporarily. We can never marry."

Bridget was crushed and the tears began to flow. "Oh, Pat, dear," she moaned. "Surely you won't turn away from me because, for a little while, I was a bit of a whore?"

Pat looked puzzled for a moment and then his face suddenly cleared. "Oh, you said *prostitute*," he cried. "In that case, all is well. We can get married. I thought you said *Protestant*."

It is possible to tell Irish jokes set in the United States, if you place the locale in Boston. I lived in that metropolitan area for twenty years and liked it, and —

❋ 419

Shortly after moving to that area, someone said to me, "Now that you're in Boston, do you know the quickest way to get to City Hospital?"

Naturally, I said, "No."

And the answer was, "Just walk up to the nearest crowd and say, 'To hell with the Pope!'"

The stereotype of the Englishman — with his insularity, his self-assurance, even his lack of humor (derived, as in the case of my father, from an assumption of dignity) — is the result of an observation of the English aristocrat. The Englishman was the nineteenth-century version of the twentieth-century American in a world that was more willing to accept the calm assurance of superiority, and the English aristocrat had no reason therefore to doubt himself as God's favored child.

But then, long before the days of Waterloo, or even of the defeat of the Spanish Armada, there was the assumption of calm dignity even under the most trying conditions. If one can joke at the moment of death, it is least surprising that an Englishman would do so.

❋ 420

Sir Thomas More, the English scholar and lawyer, was condemned to execution by the headsman in 1535 for the dreadful crime of disagreeing with King Henry VIII.

As he approached the steps leading up to the execution block, he paused. He was rather weak from the strain of long imprisonment and he said to the executioner with typical courtesy, "I pray you, sir, help me up the stairs. As for coming down, I can shift for myself."

He is also reported to have arranged his beard so that it would not be in the way of the headsman's axe. He wanted it left intact, for as he said, "My beard, at least, has not offended His Majesty."

❋ 421

An Englishman was registering in an Argentinian hotel. The hotel clerk, reading the name, shifted to English himself and said in friendly fashion, "Ah yes! Foreigner, I see."

The Englishman, turning purple, said, "Certainly not! *English!*"

❉ 422

An American approached a pink-faced man with a large mustache and haughty appearance, and said to him, "Pardon me, sir, I heard you speak just now and I wondered if you were English."

The other started and, in the thickest possible gargle of an accent, said, "English? Good God, man, if I were any more English I couldn't speak at all."

❉ 423

An American soldier in wartime England was holding forth in a London bar. Rather hilarious with drink, he said, "I've got to hand it to you limeys. You've got one swinging country here. Everything's wide open and you can get anything for money."

Two properly staid English brothers were listening, but one was hard of hearing. The deaf one turned to his brother and said, "What's he saying?"

The one with hearing said calmly, "He says he likes England."

The American went on, "Mostly, though, I like the dames you've got here. What a bunch of broads! What a bunch of gin-swilling, lovemaking babes! All you've got to do is wave a pack of cigarettes in front of them and they're ready for you."

"What's he saying?" asked the deaf one.

Said his brother, "He says he likes Englishwomen."

And now the American grew lyrical indeed. "But if you really want something," he said, "there was this old broad I met last night that took the cake. She drank a quart of Scotch, danced on the table, ripped off her clothes, tackled me, threw me onto the bed, and kept me busy for three hours. And when I was all worn out she still kept yelling for more."

"What's he saying?" asked the deaf one.

Said his brother, "He says he's met Mother."

Really offensive ethnic jokes have generally been driven underground in recent decades, and yet, oddly enough, there is an exception. A recent fad for what are called Italian jokes or Polish jokes, told in question-and-answer form, has defaced the landscape. The humor rests in displaying in comically extreme form how stupid and dirty Italians or Poles are.

As a matter of principle, I find jokes of this sort offensive and refuse to laugh at them. But alas for human ideals, every once in a while someone insists on telling me one that is sufficiently successful in its play on words or its presentation of an incongruity to force a laugh out of me.

It then becomes difficult for me to refrain from repeating them. Here are two examples of what I mean, in which I substitute "Ruritanian" for the nationality to avoid contaminating the page with direct ethnic insult.

❋ 424

Question: How do you define gross vulgarity?
Answer: One hundred and forty-four Ruritanians.

❋ 425

Question: How do Ruritanian dogs get bumps on their heads?
Answer: From chasing parked cars.

The final word on the matter was given me by a very good friend of mine, who happens to be of Italian extraction. I said to him once, as I was bubbling over, "Listen, I must tell you an Italian joke I've heard, but I can't unless you give me permission."

"First," said my friend in the most amiable possible manner, "listen to this one."

❋ 426

Question: What is black and blue and floats down the river?
Answer: A Jew who tells Italian jokes.

So I didn't tell him.

Yet insults, as is true of everything else, are curiously relative sometimes. For instance —

❊ 427

During the Six-Day War between Israel and the Arab nations, some-one came to me excitedly and said, "Did you hear the news from Rome?"

"No," I said. "What?"

"The Italian government heard there was a war going on some-where, so just to be on the safe side, it surrendered."

Clearly, this is meant to poke fun at the Italians for having done poorly in recent wars, and any Italian or any American of Italian extraction could scarcely be blamed for feeling a little irritated. And yet, think a bit — is the Italian reluctance to fight an efficient war a mark of cowardice or a mark of civiliza-tion? Do we admire the modern Germans for their efficiency in warfare? I certainly hope not.

Which reminds me —

❊ 428

Mr. Fenwick had led a sinful life but not a *very* sinful one. There-fore, when he was consigned to hell by the recording angel, he was at least allowed the privilege of a choice — either the German hell or the Italian hell.

"But what is the difference?" asked the downcast Mr. Fenwick.

"In the German hell," explained the recording angel, "you spend half your time eating all the food you want, listening to music, and disporting yourself with girls. In the other half of the time, you are pinioned to the wall and beaten mercilessly, your nails and teeth are pulled out, and boiling oil is poured over you."

"And in the Italian hell?"

"In the Italian hell, you spend half your time eating all the food you want, listening to music, and disporting yourself with girls. In the other half of the time, you are pinioned to the wall and beaten mercilessly, your nails and teeth are pulled out, and boiling oil is poured over you."

"But there's no difference."

"There is, in some of the details. In the German hell, you have German food, German music, and German girls, whereas in the Italian hell you have Italian food, Italian music, and Italian girls."

"But both nationalities are first-class in this respect."

"Certainly. As for the more painful part, the tortures in the German hell are conducted in the usual German fashion, whereas —"

"I'll take the Italian," said Mr. Fenwick hastily.

Alas, I can't do an Italian accent, but I have a special fondness for a joke that *imposes* one, and therefore can't miss:

✳ 429

Tony and Angelo were on the dock watching the fleet coming into port. Floating past, high in the water, was a submarine.

Tony pointed to it and said, "Is that a U-boat?"

And Angelo replied, "No, that's-a not-a my boat."

Here's a true story that requires a German accent, which I can *almost* do.

✳ 430

My friend, Willy Ley, though he had been in the United States for thirty years and more, had a thick German accent. There were not wanting among his friends those who theorized that he valued that accent (what else for a rocket expert?) and practiced it every morning. And, indeed, it seemed to grow thicker with the years.

At a social gathering once, a young man said deferentially to Willy, "Is it all right to call you Willy, sir, or is it better to use the German pronunciation and say Veelee?"

And Willy Ley replied, "Veelee oder Veelee, id mages no divverence."

✻ 431

During World War I, a German soldier on the eastern front expressed his absolute certainty of victory. "Franz," he said, "we Germans are pious people who pray to God on the eve of each battle. How can we lose?"

Franz said, "I know that, Dietrich, but the Russians are pious, too. They pray to God before each battle also."

Dietrich said, "Of course. But who understands Russian?"

It is a measure of America's sad success in handling the Indian problem that Americans have managed, until very recently, to be so oblivious of the very existence of that problem. By killing off most and pushing the remainder into out-of-the-way reservations, we have been able to put them out of our minds. I once read a letter to the *New York Times* in which a reputable liberal American historian contrasted American continental expansion with the Russian by saying that the Americans, at least, had expanded over an empty land.

Not so, of course, and as Indians move into our consciousness, jokes about them will too.

✻ 432

One of the legendary friendships of all time, to anyone who lived during the golden age of radio, was that between the Lone Ranger and his loyal Indian companion, Tonto. Together, they fought off outlaws and wicked men.

In later years, however, when minority groups in the United States grew increasingly self-assertive, matters altered, and the story went around that the Lone Ranger, looking across the prairie, once said to his faithful Indian friend, Tonto: "Good heavens, Tonto, there are two thousand wild and maddened Indian warriors swooping over the prairie and only we are here to stop them."

And Tonto replied, "What do you mean *we*, paleface?"

※ 433

A Navajo Indian, who had come East to attend college, was fascinated with Manhattan. His frank astonishment at all he saw at-
tracted the attention of a New Yorker who asked with amusement,
"How do you like our city?"

The Indian shook his head in wonder and said, "It is marvelous,
marvelous. But tell me, sir, how do you like our country?"

※ 434

Back in the nineteen-twenties, Americans were not yet accustomed
to strangers of particularly exotic appearance, and when Wellington
Koo served as Chinese representative at the Washington Conference in 1921, he was much more a curiosity than he would have
been a generation later.

At one social function, a Washington lady found herself next to
Koo and was utterly unable to think of a thing to say. Finally, after
the soup, she nerved herself to ask, in very clear tones so as to be
understood, "Likee soupee?"

Koo smiled and nodded. Worn out with the effort, the Washing-
tonian attempted nothing more.

After dinner, Koo rose to deliver the speech of the evening which,
of course, he did in impeccable English. When he sat down again,
he turned to the red-faced lady and asked blandly, "Likee speechee?"

Of all ethnic stereotypes, that of the black is least tolerable
under present conditions. There are few collections of jokes
antedating the nineteen-fifties that don't have Negro-dialect
stories in which the black is routinely pictured as lazy, cowardly, dirty, and impenetrably stupid. Such jokes can, of
course, no longer be told (would that they never were!) except
in circles that are insensitive or apathetic toward the black
plight.

What's more, it is difficult to avoid the stereotype, since it has
been ground so deeply into the American consciousness. Here

is a joke, for instance, which apparently avoids the stereotype
— but only apparently:

❄ 435

During World War II, Mrs. Anderson decided to celebrate Thanks-
giving by having several soldiers in as guests. She called the neighboring army base, was connected with one of the first sergeants, and
asked that three soldiers be sent to her house the following
Thursday.

"And Sergeant," she added, "I do not wish any of them to be Jewish."

"I understand, ma'am," said the sergeant.

Came Thursday and on Mrs. Anderson's doorstep stood three fine-
looking black soldiers in spotless uniforms. "We're here for Thanks-
giving, ma'am," said one of the soldiers politely.

Mrs. Anderson, eyes wide, sputtered, "But — but — but — your
sergeant must have made a mistake."

"No, ma'am," said the black, positively. "Sergeant Cohen doesn't
make mistakes."

Even if you tell this joke without describing the blacks as
though they were shambling, grinning gorillas, and even if you
don't have them talk in an illiterate patois, and even, in fact, if
you go out of your way to present them favorably — the fact
remains that the point of the joke is that blacks are even worse
than Jews.

You might sometimes feel impatient that blacks should be so
sensitive to unfavorable stereotypes. After all, I as the author
of this book and a Jew, have included dozens of jokes that
present Jews according to some unfavorable stereotype.

Well, it depends on the level of security one feels. I would
not have written this book in this way thirty years ago during
Hitler's oppression, and perhaps I would not write it this way
thirty years from now — but at the moment American Jews are
secure enough to be able to laugh at themselves a little.

And "laugh at themselves" is an important phrase. Were I not Jewish, I don't know that I'd feel comfortable about including some of the jokes I did include.

As it happens, there are a number of black comedians who find it possible to get a good deal of mordant humor out of the situation in which the blacks find themselves today — but they can do what the nonblack cannot.

Does this mean that the humane jokester ought to take into account the present delicate situation and tell no jokes about blacks at all? That would certainly be a pity, for it is quite possible to tell jokes which trenchantly illuminate a social situation that needs the barb of satire. Consider the following joke, which I heard when the question of school integration first arose down South in the late nineteen-fifties.

✻ 436

Two blacks found themselves in a small hotel in Mississippi with a long evening ahead and nothing to do.

Said one, "Why don't we call the desk and have them send up a couple of white girls?"

Said the second, "Are you crazy? Ask for white girls in Mississippi?"

"Why not?" said the first. "I'm just figuring on making love to them. I don't plan to go to school with them."

I suppose the only solution is to use one's good sense and exercise particular care in selecting jokes on subjects sufficiently sensitive to strain the sense of humor of those involved. And to make it more complicated, the situation changes from day to day. There is a current tendency, as I write, toward greater self-awareness among the white ethnic groups (Americans of Italian, Polish, Hungarian — and so on — extraction), partly as a reaction to growing black consciousness and partly out of resentment at having been underrated by the intellectual and social Establishment. It may be then that ethnic jokes, which have gained popularity in the gradual relaxation that followed World War II, may lose popularity again as tempers exacerbate and the urge to laugh evaporates.

If so, too bad — but it is not the jokester who decides this. He can only follow the fluctuating standards of good taste, which, after all, is just a shorthand phrase for considering the other fellow's feelings.

Or perhaps I am too pessimistic. Perhaps I ought to take the view that every change in social conditions brings with it a new target for the shafts of humor to find. As black self-consciousness increases, the following becomes possible —

❊ 437

Massachusetts Senator Edward W. Brooke is the only black in the Upper House. He is a cultured and capable Senator who makes no attempt to obscure the fact that he is black, though he is not prominent in any of the black causes.

This gives point, perhaps, to the black youngster who was complaining that American society gave him no black heroes to look up to, except for musicians and athletes.

He was asked, "What about Senator Brooke?"

"Brooke!" said the young man, his lip curling. "Why, he's five-fourths white!"

The target may even be the attempt to *avoid* intolerance.

❊ 438

A jokester, stifling a laugh, said, "Listen to this: One day, Moskowitz and Finkelstein were going to —"

At this, Mr. Cohen, who happened to be in the audience, said, "Moskowitz and Finkelstein; Moskowitz and Finkelstein; always two Jews. Why do they have to be Jewish? Can't you tell the joke with other nationalities involved? Why don't you make them Chinese for a change?"

The jokester, sobered and rather embarrassed, said, "I'm sorry. I didn't mean to offend. Here's the joke: One day, Hong-lee Yang and Mao-chen Foo were going to the synagog to attend the bar mitzvah of Hong-lee Yang's nephew —"

* 439

A teacher in a rural area, attempting to broaden the outlook of her narrow-horizoned class, asked each student to write an essay on his views of foreigners. All turned in more or less acceptable pieces except for hard-bitten young Billy, whose essay, in full, was "All foreigners are bastards."

The shocked teacher made no direct comment but devoted her next lecture to a description of Greek architecture, Roman law, English drama, German music, Italian poetry, Russian novels, Chinese philosophy, and African sculpture. She then asked the class to write another essay on foreigners.

With beating heart, she reached Billy's paper. It said, in full, "All foreigners are bastards. Some are cunning bastards."

It is important to remember that an ethnic group does not have to be distinguished by the background of a distinct nationality. Any subculture can give rise to jokes with the ethnic flavor. In the days when the United States was pretty sharply divided into country rubes and city slickers, there were many jokes holding up each to ridicule.

Now with the number of farmers reduced to a small minority of the population and with cultural differences smoothed out by the mass media, such jokes tend to have a slightly old-fashioned flavor to them — but perhaps we can stand a few:

* 440

A car with two city men in it worked its way down the country road and passed a tumbledown shack with a stubble-faced farmer on the front porch.

It had been a dull day and the driver felt he could use just a little fun, so he stopped the car and said, "Hey, mister, can you change an eighteen-dollar bill?"

The farmer nodded. "Sure thing, but I have to go inside to get the money." With that, he disappeared inside.

The driver's companion said, "What are you planning to do?"

"I'm giving him a ten," snickered the driver. "I'll mark up the zeros to look like eights. He'll never know the difference."

The farmer reappeared with a battered wallet. He took the bill offered him with the barest glance and put it into his pocket. Then he looked up at the driver and said, "How do you want the change? Two nines or three sixes?"

✻ 441

A hard-bitten Maine farmer, attending a fair with his wife Bessie, was much taken with the open-cockpit airplane in which fairgoers were being given rides for a fee. He had never been in an airplane and he powerfully yearned to see what it was like. The five-dollar fee was, however, rather steep for him, and he began a course of hard bargaining to reduce it to two-fifty.

The pilot, in desperation, finally said, "I'll make a deal with you. I'll take you up for *nothing*, if you promise to keep your mouth shut. If you make a single sound, you'll have to pay the full five dollars."

"Done," said the farmer. "That includes Bessie, doesn't it?"

"Okay," said the pilot. "Your wife, too."

The farmer and his wife climbed into the plane and wedged themselves into the cockpit well behind the pilot's seat, and the pilot took off. For a period of time, there was dead silence behind, which surprised the pilot who had counted on the splendid view eliciting cries of admiration and, therefore, his full fee.

Annoyed, the pilot banked suddenly and went into a series of loops and spins designed to force cries of dismay out of the stoutest heart. Yet still there was absolute silence from the farmer and his wife.

Defeated, the pilot came back to earth. Helping the farmer out of the plane, he said, "I have to hand it to you. You sure kept your mouth shut."

"Yes," said the farmer, "and so did Bessie. Though for a minute there I thought she'd give a little scream when she fell out."

✻ 442

Farmer Johnson was visiting relatives in the city and one of them asked, "Is there any good scenery out your way, Uncle?"

Johnson thought carefully. "Well," he said, "from my kitchen window, I can see Ed Simpson's barn, which is painted really nicely. Beyond that, though, there's nothing but a lot of mountains."

✻ 443

Jones stopped his large and expensive car on the country road and gazed about in confusion. He noticed a young farm hand leaning on a fence nearby and called out, "Hey, you, how far to Schuylerville?"

The farm hand thought about it and said, "Don't know."

"Well, then, what's the best way to get there?"

Again the farm hand thought and said, "Don't know."

"Well look, where's the nearest gas station where I can pick up a map?"

The farm hand thought a little longer but said yet again, "Don't know."

The man in the car said with contempt, "You don't know much, do you?"

And the farm hand said, "I'm not lost."

✻ 444

The Texan visiting Vermont asked a farmer how large an acreage he cultivated. The Vermonter said meditatively, "Oh, it's quite large. My farm extends for about a hundred yards in that direction and for nearly a hundred-twenty yards in that. And how large an acreage do you handle?"

The Texan could not help but smile. "Back home," he said, "I have a ranch with my house at one end. I can get into my car at the house, turn the ignition key, step on the gas, and at the end of the day, still not have reached the other end."

The Vermont farmer nodded sympathetically. "Tough! I once had a car like that, too."

❋ 445

The Yankee farmer kept looking curiously at the man sitting next to him in the railway train.

Finally he spoke. "Hey," he said, "you're Jewish, aren't you?"

"Yes," said the other.

"I thought so," said the farmer. "Well, I'm proud to say that in the little village in Maine where I come from, there isn't a single Jew."

"That's why it's just a village," said the other.

❋ 446

The New Yorker was building himself a summer house in Maine, and for the purpose hired a local carpenter.

The New Yorker explained, "I've got the plans, and if you can follow a blueprint you'll have no trouble."

"Oh, I can follow one," said the carpenter. He unfurled the blueprint and studied it closely. "In fact," he said, "I can follow one well enough to see that you can't build this house as shown here."

"I certainly can," said the New Yorker. "That was prepared by one of the best architectural firms in New York and they assured me —"

"I don't care what they assured you," said the carpenter. "Anyone can see at a glance that what they have here is ridiculous —"

The New Yorker said, "Listen! There's the blueprint and you build it exactly like that, or I get another carpenter!"

The carpenter shrugged and folded the blueprint again. "Okay, mister, have it your way; it's your funeral. But I warn you — you're going to end up with two bathrooms."

There's also the regional variety of ethnic humor — the rich Texan, the insular Bostonian, the perennial rivalry between neighboring cities (*any* neighboring cities, you name them).

❋ 447

Two Texans returning from lunch stopped before the window of a Cadillac automobile agency. The first said, "You know, I need a new Cadillac. As I recall, I haven't bought one this year."

The second Texan said, "Guess I'll join you."

They walked in, and the first Texan pointed and said, "Sign me up for two of those," and reached for his wallet.

The second stopped him at once and said, "Now wait, Jim, the cars are on me. You paid for the lunch."

⁂ 448

Two reasonably friendly rivals for state office in California, one from Los Angeles and one from San Francisco, found themselves speaking from the same platform. The gentleman from the south, first at the podium, said: "My worthy opponent is from San Francisco. There is nothing wrong in that, for he was born there at an age when he was too young to object. Still, I am reminded of a friend of mine who had to move from Los Angeles to San Francisco. My friend had a five-year-old daughter who was heartbroken at the news, and as they drove out of the city limits, she sobbed in anguish and murmured, 'Good-bye, God, we're going to San Francisco.' "

The gentleman from San Francisco smiled politely through the titter that welled up from the audience. When he rose to take his turn, he said: "My worthy opponent from Los Angeles tells the story with great accuracy except for the fact that, like all Angelenos, he is uncertain in his punctuation. What the dear little girl said was, '*Good*, by God! We're going to San Francisco.' "

A joke such as 448 can be transferred to any two neighboring cities in the world, including Tokyo and Yokohama, but it is also possible to have nontransferable jokes.

⁂ 449

A little girl from Minneapolis came home from Sunday school with a frown on her face.

"I'm not going back there anymore," she announced with finality. "I don't like the Bible they keep teaching us."

"Why not?" asked the astonished mother.

"Because," said the little girl, "the Bible is always talking about St. Paul, and it never once mentions Minneapolis."

✻ 450

The two elderly ladies from Boston found themselves in Los Angeles one day in late September when the warm season was at its very warmest and the temperature had reached above the hundred-degree mark.

"Heavens, Louise," said one. "It is certainly very hot."

"Ah yes," said the other. "But then, we must remember that we are fully three thousand miles from the ocean."

The Boston stereotype is a source of puzzlement and awe to those of us who have lived in Boston. Presumably there are Boston Brahmins somewhere, but few of us ordinary mortals are ever vouchsafed a sight of one. The schoolmarms who invade the cattle ranches in the movie Westerns invariably come from Boston, too, but they're gone now.

As in so many other cases, however, the world of jokes preserves, as in amber, a city and a condition that no longer exist; and that perhaps may never have existed, really.

✻ 451

A Boston matron who had long been a fixture on Beacon Hill had returned from a trip to California and was rather complacent about it.

A friend asked her, with some awe, "And what route did you take?"

"The southerly," she said. "We went by way of Dedham." *

✻ 452

A fresh-faced young lady from the West, visiting Boston, kept interlarding her conversations with "Back home in Iowa —"

* For aliens and non-Bostonians it might be necessary to explain that Dedham is a suburb adjoining Boston on the south. The good folk at Houghton Mifflin, that staunch Bostonian firm, wondered if this joke might be deleted. I'm not sure why. I think it's because they think the northerly route, through Cambridge, is more scenic and don't want to mislead the reader.

Finally, one Boston matron could stand it no longer. Leaning forward, she placed a warm and friendly hand on the girl's arm and said, "My dear, here in the East, we pronounce the name of your state as Ohio."

One of the less-known stereotypes (in the United States, at least, which is blessed with the lack of a titled aristocracy) is the one which states aristocrats are stupid — and this, too, involves an ethnic division, after a fashion. The stereotype undoubtedly consoles jokesters, who are so often members of the middle and lower classes (and the cultural descendants of the medieval jesters).

The stereotype has this justification, however — if social position depends on ancestry alone, why bother being intelligent as well?

Naturally, where aristocrats are (or were) most privileged, they are (or were) considered most stupid — so that the fallout strikes Hungarian, Polish, and Russian aristocrats most often.

When, during the Nazi invasion of Poland, the under-equipped Poles were forced to pit horse cavalry against tanks, the bravery of the Polish aristocracy (who filled the cavalry) was admitted, but an element of stupidity was assumed, too. (This feeling tended to vanish in 1940 when the French did even more poorly than the Poles had in 1939 — for a number of reasons, undoubtedly, but no one dared accuse the French of being stupid.) Even so —

❋ 453

In the play, *Jacobowsky and the Colonel*, set in the days of the French debacle, the colonel was a Polish aristocrat who had survived the Polish defeat. He was so vain and rigid in his thinking, that Jacobowsky, the sad and supple Jew, was prompted to say, "He is one of the finest minds of the fifteenth century."

❆ 454

Two Hungarian noblemen fell into a deadly quarrel, but since neither was anxious to risk his life with either sword or pistol, a blood-
less duel was decided upon. Each was to speak a number, and the
one presenting the higher number would be adjudged the winner.

The seconds were of course at hand, and the excitement and suspense were extreme as the two noblemen, seated at opposite ends of
a long table, bent to the task of thinking of a high number.

The challenged party, who had the privilege of going first, thought
long and hard. The veins in his temples swelled and the perspiration
stood out on his forehead.

"Three," he said finally.

The other duelist said at once, "Well, that beats me."

When I first told Joke 454, by the way, I fell prey to the natural temptation of dramatizing the ending. After the first duelist
had said three, I went on to describe the Homeric struggles of
the second in his turn. "His lips clenched, his eyes narrowed,
his forehead furrowed —" and so on.

No good! By indicating the second one is having trouble
also, you telegraph the punch.

A joke may be dragged out as long as you wish, but when the
punch line approaches, you *must* shift to full speed ahead. The
change in the point of view must be as sudden as possible, and
all else must be sacrificed to that.

❆ 455

The lack of intellect in the aristocrat is by no means a modern
theory. Early in the third century B.C., the great geometer Euclid
was reported to have been employed to tutor the heir to the Egyptian throne of the Ptolemies.

Patiently, Euclid went over some of the steps in proving the first
few geometric theorems, until the young Ptolemy, who was having
the greatest trouble following, finally burst out, "Is there no simpler

way you can get to the point? Surely the crown prince need not be
expected to concern himself with such minutiae."

And Euclid put a phrase imperishably into the language when he
said, "Sire, there is no royal road to learning."

* 456

In the eighteenth century, France had its effete and privileged aristocracy, and a poor scholar was hired to teach geometry to the scion
of one of the nation's dukedoms.

Painstakingly, the scholar put the young nobleman through one of
the very early theorems of Euclid, but at every pause, the young man
smiled amiably and said, "My good man, I do not follow you."

Sighing, the scholar made the matter simpler, went more slowly,
used more basic words, but still the young nobleman said, "My good
man, I do not follow you."

In despair, the scholar finally moaned, "Oh, monseigneur, I give
you my word what I say is so."

Whereupon the nobleman rose to his feet, bowed politely, and
answered, "But why, then, did you not say so at once so that we
might pass on to the next theorem? If it is a matter of your word, I
would not dream of doubting you."

I have not mentioned my brother Stanley anywhere in this
book so far. He is my only brother, and nine years younger
than myself. He is, at present, a most successful newspaper-
man, and assistant publisher of the Long Island *Newsday.*

We get along marvelously well, he and I, largely because he
is the picture of gentleness and serenity, unlike myself. In fact,
I am a self-centered person (writers *have* to be) and am given
to making the calm but irritating assumption that I am the important member of the family.

My brother sighs at this but shrugs it off amiably, even
though he is perpetually harassed by people who, on meeting
him, want to know if he is related to me. The first words addressed to him by the very charming girl who later became his
wife (he tells me) were "Are you a relative of Isaac Asimov?"

Only once, as far as I can remember, did my brother ever bring himself to say anything wounding to me.

He said to me one time, "You know, Isaac, I am very fond of you, despite your character."

"What's wrong with my character?" I demanded (naturally).

"Well," said my brother judiciously. "You're intelligent, industrious, responsible, dependable, efficient, punctual. In short, you have every one of the unlovable virtues."

I intend to work up a retort to that but so far all I've been able to think of is "Oh, yeah?"

Anyway, there is some consolation in the thought that a whole national group is stereotyped in that same fashion. Aren't the Germans considered intelligent, industrious, responsible, dependable, efficient, punctual — and unlovable?

In honor of my brother, then, I would like to end the ethnic section with a joke which his remark always reminds me of.

✻ 457

Among the Germans, Berlin is considered the very epitome of Prussian brusqueness and efficiency, while Vienna is the essence of Austrian charm and slipshoddery.

The tale is told of a Berliner visiting Vienna, who was lost and in need of directions. What would such a Berliner do? He grabbed at the lapel of the first passing Viennese, and barked out, "The post office? Where is it?"

The startled Viennese carefully detached the other's fist, smoothed his lapel, and said in a gentle manner, "Sir, would it not have been more delicate of you to have approached me politely and to have said, 'Sir, if you have a moment and happen to know, could you please direct me to the post office?'"

The Berliner stared in astonishment for a moment, then growled, "I'd rather be lost!" and stamped away.

That very same Viennese was visiting Berlin later that year, and it turned out that now it was he who had to search for the post office. Approaching a Berliner, he said politely, "Sir, if you have a moment and happen to know, could you please direct me to the post office?"

With machinelike rapidity, the Berliner replied, "About face, two blocks forward, sharp turn right, one block forward, cross street, half-right under arch, sharp left over railroad tracks, past newsstand, into post office lobby."

The Viennese, more bewildered than enlightened, nevertheless murmured, "A thousand thanks, kind sir —"

Whereupon the Berliner snatched furiously at the other's lapel, and shouted, "Never mind the thanks! *Repeat the instructions!*"

ONE OF THE FUNCTIONS of the joke is to speak the unspeakable.

In the world of jokes, nothing is sacred — disease, death, misfortune, tragedy, disappointment, frustration, grief — least of all, heaven or hell.

And so much the better.

The human spirit cannot be stretched on the rack forever without finding refuge in numbness. A religion that is never anything but solemn becomes, most certainly, never anything but mechanical.

So I proceed, without embarrassment, to take sacred names in vain. For instance —

✣ 458

Moses and Saint Peter took a day off from heaven in order to indulge themselves with an invigorating game of golf.

Moses, stepping up to the first tee, surveyed the course with a practiced eye and, addressing the ball, sent it screaming down the fairway. He watched it roll onto the green with a certain smugness.

Wordlessly, he made way for Saint Peter who, a bit chagrined, hit the ball forcefully, too, but, alas, hooking it in his haste. From the curved nature of the trajectory, it appeared certain to disappear into the woods. Moses was smiling even more smugly, but at the last moment, an eagle made its appearance from nowhere.

The great bird snatched the ball just as it was about to disappear into the foliage forever and then, with powerful beatings of its pinions, made its way to the green. It circled downward in a tight spiral and, five feet from the ground, let go of the ball, which dropped neatly into the hole.

And Moses said, "Look, Pete, you want to play golf, or you want to fool around?"

Here is another one of those cases in which I cannot decide between punch lines. The alternate is —

❊ 459

The eagle having deposited Saint Peter's ball in the hole, Moses turned to his opponent and said, "Aw, come on, Pete, not when we're playing for money."

I can't advise you which to use. I've had successes with both, and failures with both too.

One thing you should *not* do, however, is try to rescue a fall-flat situation by saying, "Of course, there's another version of the punch line which goes —" If one version gets nowhere, the pall that follows will absolutely prevent the second from getting anything more than a polite snicker. Don't waste the alternative punch line. Cut your losses and tell a completely different joke.

Another point to remember about any joke which you know to be good and which, nevertheless, falls flat, is that it may signal the end of the session. No joke-telling session can last forever. Participants become laughed out, and you reach the point where you are throwing away excellent stories on tired smiles. In every fall-flat situation you should seriously consider saying, "Incidentally, what did you think of the President's speech last night?" or maybe, "Well look what time it is. We're going to have to get home or the baby sitter will kill us."

❊ 460

A preacher of the old school was describing, in most graphic language, the events on Judgment Day, and, of course, he used Biblical phraseology whenever he could.

"Oh, my friends," he intoned, "imagine the sufferings of the sinners as they find themselves damned at last and cast into the outer darkness, removed from the gracious presence of the Lord, and given over to the eternal flames. Oh, my friends, at such a time there will be weeping, wailing, and gnashing of teeth among them."

At this point, one of the elders of the congregation interrupted to say in words that whistled through his ancient toothless gums, "But, Reverend Jones, what if one of the damned has no teeth?"

The preacher broke off, stared at the questioner, then cried out with a crash of his fist on the pulpit, "My friends, is anything too hard for the Lord? When a soul is sent to perdition, rest assured that teeth will be supplied!"

As a non-Christian, I find myself rather inhibited when it comes to telling jokes in which Jesus is one of the characters. I don't mind God the Father — I have equal rights there — but God the Son is another matter. Thus, I first heard Joke 458 as a golf game between Moses and Jesus, but automatically change it to Saint Peter so as to keep the essence of the joke and lessen my own uneasiness.

This is not cowardice; this is good sense. The fact that I am uneasy about the very word Jesus is a matter of childhood conditioning and many years of hearing it only in the context of swearing. That the uneasiness still persists into adulthood may be too bad, but while it is there, it is reasonable to avoid telling jokes that needlessly activate that uneasiness. A joke told uneasily is a joke told poorly.

Some jokes, however, absolutely require Jesus to be a character. And if so — well — the duties of a jokester are paramount. So I tell them.

❊ 461

One of the many legends that have grown up around the Crucifixion involves the two Roman centurions who guarded the Cross.

One of them, worried and ill at ease, turned to the other and said, "Marcus, I cannot help but feel that this day we have witnessed an atrocious deed."

"How so, Caius?" asked the other.

"This man on the cross should not have been executed in this fashion. I believe he was a great, great teacher."

"Oh come on, Caius," said Marcus, shrugging, "after all — how much has he published?"

It is important, by the way, to be perfectly clear as to what the point of a joke is, and who or what is its butt. I can imagine perfectly well that many people, hearing Joke 461, would feel, indignantly, that the Crucifixion is no laughing matter and therefore find it impossible to laugh.

If that is your suspicion, however, a little thought will show that it is not the Crucifixion that is being derided here — or Jesus either — but those college administrators who make the quantity of one's publications (never the quality) the sole criterion for advancement.

Naturally, if after the joke you are going to have to explain this in order to lift the heavy pall of disapproval, don't tell the joke. Pick an audience sufficiently well acquainted with the academic world to know what the phrase "publish or perish" means.

But then almost any joke requires you to pick your audience to some extent, as I have emphasized several times before.

* 462

Mrs. Ginsberg, having arrived in heaven, addressed the recording angel bashfully. "Tell me," she said, "would it be possible to have an interview with someone who is here in heaven?"

The recording angel said, "Certainly, assuming the person you have in mind *is* here in heaven."

"Oh, she is. I'm sure of that," said Mrs. Ginsberg. "Actually, I want to see the Virgin Mary."

The recording angel cleared his throat. "Ah, yes. As it happens, she is in a different section, but if you insist I will forward the request. She is a gracious lady and she may wish to visit the old neighborhood."

The request was duly forwarded, and the Virgin was gracious indeed. It was not long at all before Mrs. Ginsberg was favored with the Virgin's presence.

Mrs. Ginsberg looked long at the radiant figure before her and finally said, "Please forgive my curiosity, but I have always wanted to ask you — Tell me, how does it feel to have a son who is so wonderful that ever since his time hundreds of millions of people have worshiped him as a god?"

And the Virgin replied, "Frankly, Mrs. Ginsberg, we were hoping he would be a doctor."

❊ 463

Back in the days before World War I, two suffragettes had been placed in jail for willfully interfering with the police in the performance of their duty.

One of the two, a young girl who was involved in her very first fracas, was terribly frightened and only with difficulty restraining her tears.

The other, a toughened veteran of dozens of street demonstrations in favor of the great cause of votes for women, said, "Don't be afraid, Smithers. Have faith in God. She will protect us."

❊ 464

Old Simpson was a constant thorn in the side of the Parent-Teachers Association, with his steadfast opposition to innovation. For one thing, he was vociferously against the introduction of foreign languages in the town's junior high school curriculum.

Waving his Bible high in the air, he shouted, "If English was good enough for the prophets and the apostles, it's plenty good enough for me."

❊ 465

A Jewish seminary student died, went to heaven, and found himself before God's great judgment seat.

The ineffable voice of the Lord made itself heard beautifully to the student's ears. "My son, what was it you did on earth?"

"Oh, Holy One," said the student, "I studied the Law."

"Well done, my son. Expound, then, a point of the Law to Me for My pleasure."

Thus confronted with the request of the Lord, the student felt his mind go blank. For an agitated moment or two, he could find no point he could make.

And then he cried out, "At the moment, oh Holy One, I can think of nothing adequate for Your hearing, but I tell You what. If *You* expound a point of the Law, I will show You how to refute it."

In connection with Joke 465, let me point out that a good joke can make a sardonic point which can burst into flower long after the immediate grotesquerie has been laughed at and forgotten.

Thus, the immediate fun in the joke here is the cheerful gall of the student thinking he can refute God.

The more subtle delayed point is that every segment of the Law can be subjected to many interpretations, each of which can be refuted, and that a clever student stands ready to support or refute at will. You can talk about the matter of sophistry for hours without making it as clear as this joke does.

Another example is —

❋ 466

A few years ago, when Catholic church reform began to be much in the news, Mrs. Moskowitz said to Mrs. Finkelstein, "Tell me, Becky, have you by any chance heard what's going on in Rome?"

"No," said Mrs. Finkelstein. "I haven't. What's going on in Rome?"

"A meeting of high Catholic churchmen has, among other things, decided that the Jews are not responsible for the crucifixion of Jesus."

Mrs. Finkelstein raised her eyebrows. "Indeed? And who *is* responsible, then?"

"I'm not sure," said Mrs. Moskowitz. "I think they suspect the Puerto Ricans."

Does Mrs. Moskowitz miss the entire point? Sure she does. But isn't there also a point about the connection between religion and unreasoning prejudice?

In telling Joke 466, one runs a distinct risk that after a short laugh, someone will say argumentatively, "Well, if you look at the Puerto Rican problem —" and suddenly everyone is off and running on the matter of racism in America.

If joking is *all* you're interested in, then you may not wish to tell this joke. On the other hand, jokes offer a way of supplying serious commentary in a matter, which is made more incisive by its seeming triviality. Abraham Lincoln used jokes in this fashion constantly, and it is possible to argue that Jesus allowed his parables to perform a similar function.

I suspect, actually, that few dedicated jokesters would be annoyed at having a joke turn into a subject for serious social discussion, for I think most dedicated jokesters recognize their hobby (profession?) as a kind of social commentary at one end of its spectrum. And what's wrong with that?

✤ 467

The Austrian-born physicist Wolfgang Pauli had one of the keenest minds in scientific history. He was well-known for his quick penetration into the very essence of the theoretical analyses presented by his colleagues, and for his sure nose for error. It was consequently not at all surprising (the story goes) that God awaited his arrival, after his death in 1958, with anticipation.

"I presume," said God, "that there is much in the world of physics that puzzled you during your lifetime and that you would be glad to have the opportunity of understanding now."

"Yes, Lord," said Pauli, "for to tell you the truth I am weary of watching my colleagues go wrong. For instance, I have always been disturbed over the fact that the proton has exactly 1836.11 times the mass of the electron though the electric charges are the same. Why so odd a multiple? Yet there must be a reason. It is just that all the theories I have seen which were designed to explain the matter were so ludicrously wrong."

"Ah," said God. "Here then, in the language of twentieth-century quantum mechanics, is the explanation of the proton/electron mass-ratio." And he handed a sheaf of papers to Pauli.

Pauli looked through the sheets eagerly and rapidly, turned back to the first page, took a quick look at the fourth, and handed them all back to God.

"Still wrong!" he said with a sigh.

God is, at least in part, the butt of Joke 467. In fact, I have never heard a joke involving God where He wasn't — at least in part. This may sound sacrilegious, but it is the reverse. To have God get the worst of it, makes Him more human and therefore more lovable; and who can quarrel with that?

Besides, where would the fun be in having God get the best of it? The odds are so heavily in His favor that there would be no sporting flavor to such a joke.

✳ 468

The greatest computer that had ever been designed and built up to that moment was finally to be put into action, and from all over the world scientists had gathered to be present at its unveiling. Far more complex than anything that had gone before, it was capable of solving intricate problems that would previously have defied analysis.

But those present were at loggerheads as to the question with which to initiate its operations.

While they argued over Lagrangian functions, stress analysis, and the price of wheat, the janitor suddenly pushed himself forward. Still holding his broom, he called out, "Is there a God?"

A deathly silence fell over the room, as all waited for the result. Slowly, the vast machine began to go into action. Lights flashed and a solemn clicking whirr sounded.

And then a deep voice from the vitals of the computer said, *"Now* there is."

Even the funniest joke in the world can't be counted upon necessarily to raise a universal laugh. There may always be private reasons for a joke eliciting other responses. Thus, when I first heard Joke 468, the laughter in the audience was quite general, but all that was elicited from me was a howl of outrage.

It wasn't that the joke was not inherently funny; it is. Or that it wasn't told well; it was. It was just that in June 1956, I wrote a story called "The Last Question," which appeared in the November 1956 issue of *Science Fiction Quarterly*. It was, in my own opinion, one of the best stories I ever wrote, and its very nub involved the gradual development of computers until one eventually became God.

Perhaps the joke was older than my story, but I had never heard it before I wrote the story, and it bothered me that people might think the joke inspired the story.

But that was some years ago, and I have recovered.

❋ 469

Jones was playing golf with Father Callahan and was badly off his game, monstrously off. Each time he missed a drive or foozled a putt, he muttered in anguish, "Holy Virgin, I missed."

The good father grew nettled at last and said, "Now, my son, there is no need to swear at small matters. You merely face divine anger. I would not be surprised if a lightning stroke awaited your next offense in this respect."

Jones tried hard to control himself but at the very next blooper, he began, "Holy Virg —" and at once a gigantic lightning stroke ripped through the atmosphere.

When the debris settled, Jones was still there but where Father Callahan had stood, there was nothing but a charred pit.

And from the heavens came a distant voice, "Holy Virgin, I missed!"

The following is a cartoon I have invented, but which exists, so far, only in my imagination:

* 470

Imagine, please, a small globe which is obviously the earth immediately after the week of creation, for you can make out upon it a small tree with the little nude figures of a man and woman underneath, and (of course) a snake curled about a branch of that tree.

Above the new earth is a benign figure with the appearance of a man in white drapery with a flowing white beard — obviously God.

And above God is a still more benign figure with longer white drapery and a longer white beard.

The upper figure, pointing to the earth, and addressing God, says, "And for this you expect a Ph.D.?"

Of all the jokes I know, Joke 470 most successfully divides the audience accurately into two parts. All academic people who have struggled through the attainment of graduate degrees laugh heartily, while nonacademicians, who know nothing of the struggle for a doctorate, don't laugh.

So sure am I of this and so confident that the academicians can't help but laugh out of the bitter experience they remember so well, that I break one of the cardinal rules I always preach and dare them not to laugh. I tell them that if they are academicians they will have to laugh, though I know that means they will try not to — and they laugh just the same.

It's very satisfying.

And while I'm at it, here is another religious cartoon I have made up, with either of two possible captions:

* 471

The earth is pictured as having just blown up in thermonuclear warfare. Only half the sphere is left and over the jagged remnant is a huge mushroom cloud. Over the ruins hovers the robed and bearded figure of God.

The caption reads "Well, there's six days' work shot."

❋ 472

Same picture as in Joke 471.

The caption reads: "It just shows you. Take your eye off them for a *minute!*"

Other religions have their jokes too, of course. Humor is not restricted to Judeo-Christianity.

❋ 473

In the pagan period of the Roman Empire, emperors were granted divine honors after death. In A.D. 79, Vespasian, who had spent most of his life as an energetic general and his final ten years as an energetic emperor, felt death approaching.

He ordered his servants to help him to his feet, for he felt that an emperor ought to die standing. Then, as the world darkened about him, he said sardonically, "I feel myself becoming a god." And with that, he died.

But back to Judeo-Christianity.

❋ 474

Pious old Levine was praying with mountain-moving fervor. Tears streamed down his cheeks as he swayed back and forth, beating his chest and mumbling his thoughts to God.

"Oh Holy One," he said, "I come to You again in my trouble, for surely my life is nothing but trouble. All my life long I have known nothing but poverty, illness, and misery. I have been unable to support my family, unable to bring them happiness. And yet I have prayed to You constantly; I have turned to You morning, noon, and night; I have never forgotten You.

"Why, then, oh Holy One, am I so visited by misfortune while that atheist Bloom has nothing but wealth and happiness? I know for a fact, oh Holy One, that Bloom never prays, never as much as enters a synagog, yet his every move coins gold. Why does he prosper; why do these good things befall him?"

And in the silence that followed, a deep voice suddenly sounded in old Levine's ear. "Because Bloom isn't always *bugging* Me, that's why!"

Notice, by the way, that Joke 474 is an attempt to answer the great problem posed in the book of Job in a manner that (as far as I know) no theologian has ever considered.

As I said earlier, when God appears in jokes, the joke is usually on Him. What's more, the voice of God is, in itself, rather automatically a cause for laughter. There was a sequence on one "Smothers Brothers Show" on television, for instance, which was censored out for a time, simply because the voice of God was played for a laugh, though it was eventually shown and proved harmless enough. (It's a general rule, I think, that censors are essentially humorless. Or, to put it in reverse, no one with a sense of humor could possibly be jackass enough to want to be a censor.)

<h2>❋ 475</h2>

The scene is laid in the garden of Eden. Eve is being tempted by the serpent and is reaching for the apple.

As she does so, lightning flashes, thunder rumbles, and the deep, overwhelming voice of God fills the scene with a solemn, "That's a *no-no!*"

<h2>❋ 476</h2>

Sister Mary and Sister Theresa sat in the small restaurant and studied the menu, while a waiter hovered respectfully, ready to take the nuns' orders.

Finally Sister Mary said, "I will have a ham sandwich, waiter."

The waiter said, "But this is Friday, Sister."

Sister Mary sighed. "I forgot! Bring me a cottage cheese salad, then."

Sister Theresa looked up from her menu and said to the waiter, "Is it still Friday?"

The jokester is constantly plagued by obsolescence. Catholics are now permitted to eat meat on Friday, and someone is sure to be so crass as to point that out if you tell a meatless-Friday joke. You might react with hatred and violence; but if you are an experienced jokester, you need use it merely as an opportunity to say "You're right," and go on to tell a nonmeatless-Friday joke. You might describe the following cartoon —

※ 477

The scene is Satan's office in hell, with Satan himself at his desk. Through the open door is thrust the head of a junior imp.

The caption reads "Chief, what do we do with all the people who are here for eating meat on Friday?"

As it happens, my own subculture has its dietary laws as all well know, and its share of consequent nonsense. Here, for instance, is a true story —

※ 478

As it happens, I don't practice the formal rites of religion and generally pay little attention to even the most sacred days. I once tried to make a luncheon date with a friend for a particular day and horrified him, for I had unwittingly chosen Yom Kippur. (This holiday, the Day of Atonement on which all Jews must fast, is located by a lunar calendar and hops about from one day to another in different years by our own solar calendar.)

Abashed, I explained I hadn't realized it would be Yom Kippur and changed it to a dinner date after sundown, when the fasting restriction was over.

At supper, my friend saw fit to lecture me on my laxness, while I squirmed half in embarrassment and half in exasperation. Finally, he ran down, and since the waiter was approaching, he quickly consulted the menu and said, "Ham steak, please!"

You can bet it was my turn then, and I had a few choice comments to make concerning what I thought God would do if forced to choose between honest disbelief and hypocritical piety.

❊ 479

Mrs. Clare Boothe Luce, well-known playwright and wife of the late publisher of *Time*, became a Catholic in middle life and had, of course, all the enthusiasm of the convert. Under President Eisenhower, she was appointed ambassador to Italy, and while she was there (an apocryphal story goes), a reporter once spied her in earnest conversation with the Pope.

It occurred to him that a conversation between Pope and ambassador might have enormous news value, and he drifted closer in an attempt to overhear.

He finally made it, and the first words he heard were those of His Holiness, saying in accented English, "But you don't understand, Mrs. Luce. I already *am* a Catholic."

❊ 480

Rabbi Joshua, having lived an exemplary life that had been admired by all, died in the fullness of time and went to heaven. There he was greeted with hosannas of delight. Inexplicably, he shrank back, covered his face with his trembling old hands, and refused to participate in the festivities held in his honor.

All persuasion having failed, he was ushered respectfully before the high judgment seat of God Himself.

The tender presence of God bathed the noble rabbi, and the divine voice filled his ears. "My child," said God, "it is on record that you have lived entirely in accord with My wishes, and yet you refuse the honors that have, most fittingly, been prepared for you. Why is this?"

Rabbi Joshua, head bent low and voice meek, said, "Oh Holy One,

I am not deserving. Somehow my life must have taken a wrong turning, for my son, heedless of my example and my precepts, turned Christian."

"Alas," came the still voice, sweet with infinite sympathy, "I understand entirely and forgive. After all, My Son did the same."

I have heard this joke told in stages. A Jew, while still alive, mourns that his son has turned Christian, comes to his rabbi for help, and finds that the rabbi's son has done the same. They go to a more important rabbi and find that his son has done the same. They then decide to pray to God for help and find —

But that's exactly how not to do it. Unless you tell it with the kind of skill I can't envisage, you will telegraph your punch. The listeners will see what is coming even if they have never heard the joke, and are liable to anticipate you out loud and cut short the boredom. No greater humiliation than that could befall a jokester.

You see, stories *are* told in stages sometimes — stories for children. Children enjoy the cumulative effect, and they *like* to know what is coming. Jokes must never be told in that fashion. The only time you want stages is when the last one doesn't follow and you have your change in point of view. Let me explain what I mean by an example —

✻ 481

Three individuals, all strangers, met at the summer resort golf course, and decided to play through together.

Said one of the men, "Well, we might as well introduce ourselves. My name is Ben Ezra, but I'm not a rabbi."

The second man said, "My name is Peter Paul, but I'm no saint, you can bet."

The two men turned to the third person, who was a sweet young lady. She blushed prettily and said, "My n-n-name is M-m-mary, but I'm afraid I'm not a v-v-v-very good golf player."

As in all categories of jokes, the religious joke can tumble into bad taste; and here, too, the boundary is vague. I offer the following as an example of a joke that, at best, is near the boundary.

❋ 482

The cares of the universe had been resting more heavily than usual on God's shoulders, and He frankly confessed the need for a rest.

"Why don't you take a short vacation, Boss?" suggested the archangel Gabriel.

"Yes, but where?"

"How about that little place, Earth? You haven't been there for a good while."

God shuddered. "No, no. It's a world of busybodies. I was there two thousand years ago and that's enough, thank you. I had an affair with a little Jewish girl and they're still talking about it down there."

❋ 483

A thoroughly apocryphal story tells of Joseph and Mary on their way to Bethlehem to be taxed. Mary, being great with child, was on the donkey, of course. Joseph walked patiently at her side.

It happened that Joseph turned his ankle on an unexpected stone in the road and nearly fell. Caught by surprise, he muttered under his breath *"Jesus!"*

Mary turned to him, eyes sparkling, and said, *"Just* the name for the child."

I like the subtle joke, the kind that is caviar to the general. It flatters the jokester to sound intellectual and have a joke rest, for instance, on a tolerably obscure literary allusion; it also flatters the audience to laugh at something of the sort and thus show their own erudition. But remember that subtlety can go too far. If it takes *too* long to catch the point, the listener grows embarrassed, feels he has failed, and the whole thing is a small disaster. Consider the following version of Joke 483 —

❊ 484

Joseph the carpenter was hammering away in old Galilee when he hit his thumb a good one.

He swore loudly, and his boy came in from the next room and said, "Did you call me, Dad?"

I never get a laugh with that one. The connection between swearing and the boy's name doesn't come fast enough, and I doubt that you would see it if I hadn't told Joke 483 first.

Jokes 483 and 484 offer an interesting method for studying a fallacy in logic, that of placing the effect before the cause in a tempting way. (Like the old bromide about the man who found a Roman coin dated 100 B.C. How many people, do you suppose, told this in a straight-faced fashion, would see at once that this was impossible and be able to explain why?)

❊ 485

Israeli soldiers, under conditions of tension in the Middle East, are understandably nervous over the possibility of the infiltration of their lines by Arab guerrillas. Almost anything is under suspicion.

Thus it came about recently that one Israeli sentry stopped two individuals toiling up a rocky road. One was a woman, obviously pregnant, seated on a donkey. By her side was an elderly man, trudging along on foot.

"Hold it! Where are you going?" demanded the sentry.

"To Bethlehem!" said the elderly man wearily.

"Your name?" said the sentry.

"Joseph!"

At this point the sentry paused. "Is this woman your wife?"

"Yes, she is."

"Is her name Mary?"

The elderly man looked surprised. "Why, yes. How did you know?"

The sentry paused a long time now. He said, "Listen, are you planning to name your child Jesus?"

The elderly man said, in even greater surprise, "Why, yes. How did you know?"

Nervously, the sentry stepped back and in a deeply troubled whisper said, "Well, move on! Go on to Bethlehem!"

The man and his pregnant wife proceeded along the road for several hundred yards and then the man turned to the woman and said, softly, "It seems to have worked, Fatima. For some reason, that Israeli thought we were Puerto Ricans."

If you'll consider this a moment, you will see that this is effect-before-cause also.

But let's move on to a couple about Moses —

✻ 486

Moses was leading the children of Israel out of Egypt and had come up hard against the Red Sea. Back there on the horizon were the chariots of the Egyptian army in hot pursuit. All around him were Israelites in despair.

So Moses called over Hymie Epstein, his publicity man.

"What is it, Moses, baby?" asked Hymie.

"Things look bad, Hymie," said Moses, "but I have an idea. Suppose I hold my rod out over the waters and make them part. After they part, all our own people can cross without trouble, but when the Egyptians try to follow — whoosh, the waters come back and drown them. What do you think of that?"

"Moses, baby," said Hymie, "you do that and not only will you get rid of the Egyptians, but I guarantee you at least three extra pages in the Bible!"

✻ 487

During the period when the Israelites were suffering in Egyptian bondage, God traveled over the earth seeking those who might follow His mild Law. He came across an Arab and said to him, "Would you like to follow My commandments?"

The Arab frowned suspiciously. "Like what, for instance?"

"One is: Thou shalt not kill!"

The Arab said, "You must be mad. Follow that commandment,

indeed! My profession consists of lying in wait for camel trains, slaughtering the merchants when they arrive, and confiscating all their goods. A commandment like that would just about ruin the whole system of private enterprise."

God turned away and traveled to Babylonia. There He accosted a merchant and said, "Would you like to follow My commandments?"

The Babylonian said, "For example?"

"Thou shalt not steal!"

"Friend," said the Babylonian, "I am sorry. My entire living is made up of buying cheap and selling dear, of misrepresentations and dishonesty. If I cannot steal, I cannot live."

Rather discouraged, God turned westward, and in Egypt, He found a bearded old man haranguing the ruler of the land in an attempt to get him to free certain slaves.

God called to him. "Moses," he said, "would you like to follow My commandments?"

And Moses said, "How much do they cost?"

"Why, nothing," said God. "I'm giving them away free."

"In that case," said Moses, "I'll take ten."

❋ 488

Reverend Brown stopped during his walk to view with gentle concern the actions of a man bending over the wheel of his car. The rear had been jacked up, and the man was tugging at the wheel futilely, muttering wild imprecations. Now he stood up, kicked at the wheel, and expressed his feelings at the top of his voice.

"My good man," expostulated the kindly minister, "surely there is no need for such blasphemous heat. Why do you not compose yourself and try the power of prayer?"

The man turned savagely. "You mean pray over this miserable thing? How do I do that?"

"Why, I'll show you. It is the simplest thing in the world." Reverend Brown raised his eyes to heaven and said, "Our Heavenly Father, if it be Thy pleasure, help guide this man to faith and make him aware that all in the universe, from the mightiest star to the tiniest fly, is in Thy hands at all times. Let this man in true contrition of soul find that the removal of this wheel is not a hard task for one with faith."

And as the final sonorous syllable trembled into silence, the tire quivered and, of its own accord, plopped off the wheel, made a short spinning clatter on one side, and lay still.

The good Reverend Brown stared at it for a moment, then muttered, "Well, I'll be darned."

It is sometimes difficult for convinced freethinkers to understand that men of the cloth really believe what they say they believe. But that is by no means a new phenomenon —

✻ 489

Marcus Porcius Cato was a curmudgeonly Roman statesman of the second century B.C. Possessed of all the unlovable virtues, he was hardworking, honest, and rigidly moral. He was a rationalist, too, and had only the profoundest contempt for those who sought knowledge of the future by consulting the augurs who studied the stars, the entrails of dead beasts, and so on.

Grimly, Cato once said, "I wonder how one augur can pass another without laughing."

To be truthful, matters work the other way as well, and those with faith find it difficult to believe that there can really be convinced atheists. There is the feeling that you don't find atheists in foxholes, or that, faced with death, every atheist will recant in terror. I wonder if that's so, and I suspect it isn't.

✻ 490

Armstrong played a twosome on the golf course with the minister of his church one or two times a month. Reverend Brown was a good golfer and the competition between them was keen, but Armstrong had to admit that the matches offered a special strain on his internal workings.

Armstrong had, as so many of us do, a gift for rich invective, and on foozling a shot he had a habit of voicing his feelings by addressing the ball, the green, and the general surroundings with a wealth of purple passion. Yet in the presence of Reverend Brown, he found himself restrained from indulging himself, and by the end of the round he would be pale with repressed verbiage.

The minister, on the other hand, though he also foozled shots now and then, would on such occasions observe a patient silence that irritated Armstrong.

Finally, Armstrong said, "Reverend Brown, I must ask — Tell me, how is it you manage to keep your temper when you slice the ball into the rough, or when you miss your putt because there's a twig on the green you didn't see?"

Reverend Brown replied, "My good friend, it is a matter of sublimation. I need not shout or use vile language. Surely that will not alter the situation and will, on the other hand, imperil my soul. Yet since I must do something, I sublimate. I spit!"

"You spit?"

"That's right." Here, Reverend Brown's eyes darkened. "But let me tell you this! Where I spit, the grass never grows again!"

❊ 491

Smith had died and gone to hell and the imp-receptionist, entering his name in the books, said, "Where do you want to go?"

"Do I have a choice?" said the surprised Smith.

"Certainly," said the imp. "This anteroom is surrounded by closed doors. Just listen at each one and decide which you want."

Smith approached the first door and placed his ear to it. From the other side, he could hear, faintly but clearly, horrible shrieks of agony. Shuddering, he went to the second, then the third. Always he heard screams, cries, yells.

Finally, at the seventh door, he heard nothing but a gentle murmuring — oh, so gentle.

He said quickly, "I'll take this one."

Instantly, the door was flung open, and he was propelled inside. He found himself up to the lower lip in a vast sea of overwhelmingly putrid sewage.

With him were uncounted millions of others, and now the murmur he had heard from outside the door resolved itself into words as everyone, standing strainedly on tiptoe, kept muttering, without quite daring to open his mouth, "Don't make waves! Don't make waves!"

The expression "don't make waves" is a well-known way of advising someone not to stir up trouble. I suspect it comes from this joke, and I hope that lexicographers of the future will take note of that fact.

❉ 492

The word had gone about the little east European town several generations ago that one of its most respected citizens, Abram the cobbler, had become an out-and-out atheist. The whole town was shaken by the news. It was the sole topic of conversation. Nevertheless all admitted to a dearth of hard information, for no one had spoken to Abram the cobbler about it, and so far it was still only rumor.

On the following Saturday, however, it became clear to everyone that for the first time in thirty years, Abram the cobbler did not occupy his customary place in the synagog. Could he be sick? No, for when services were over, they found that Abram the cobbler was walking quietly in the street, the picture of health.

All stared, and finally Yussel the tailor, with a sudden burst of bravery, pushed forward and accosted the cobbler. "Abram," he said, "there is a rumor that you have become an atheist. And you were not at the synagog just now. Is it true? Are you indeed an atheist?"

Abram looked quietly at Yussel and turned away without a word.

Everyone looked after him in consternation, and by the next day it was clear that no work would be done in the town unless the matter were cleared up. A delegation was appointed, with Yussel the tailor at its head, and it was understood they were to face Abram in his shop and insist on an answer once and for all.

In they went, and Yussel said, "Abram, we must have an answer. You cannot leave matters as they are. Are you now an atheist?"

Abram looked up from the shoe he was mending and said quietly, "Yes, I am!"

Astonished at the quick and unequivocal answer, Yussel said, "Then why didn't you say so when I asked you yesterday?"

Abram's eyes grew wide with horror. "You wanted me to say I was an atheist on the *Sabbath?*"

It is difficult, you see, to be a pure atheist. Within the Judeo-Christian culture, a man who denies the existence of God is denying the existence of the specific God of the Bible. It wouldn't even occur to him to deny the existence of Brahma.

To show you what I mean from a different angle altogether —

❊ 493

Once when I was quite young, one of my editors asked, "What do you see with your eyes closed?"

"Nothing," I said at once.

"Don't you see blackness and little flashes of light?"

"That's nothing," I insisted.

"Is it?" he said. "What do you see with your ear?"

Very analogous to this, if you think about it, is the following —

❊ 494

A Catholic lost his faith once and became a hard-bitten atheist. His new credo was "There is no God, and Mary is his mother."

Or, my candidate for the shortest joke with meaningful philosophy —

❊ 495

"I'm an atheist, thank God," said Jones.

But if atheism finds clinging to it the stigmata of religion, it is also possible for religion to become so libertarian as to be rather indistinguishable from atheism.

※ **496**

Young Sammy Moskowitz had just bought himself a motor scooter, but he had been brought up in orthodox fashion and wasn't the least bit sure whether it was fitting for an orthodox Jew to ride one. He thought that the best way out would be to get his revered rabbi to teach him a *barucha* (a traditional prayer of blessing) to intone over the motor scooter before he drove it. Surely that would make it proper for him to use it.

He therefore approached his rabbi and said, "Rabbi, I have bought a motor scooter and I wish to know if you could teach me a *barucha* to say over it each morning?"

The rabbi said, "What is a motor scooter?"

Sammy explained, and the rabbi shook his head. "As far as I know, there is no appropriate *barucha* for the occasion and I strongly suspect that riding a motor scooter is a sin. I forbid you to use it."

Sammy was very downhearted, for from his very soul he longed to drive his motor scooter, which had set him back a considerable sum. A thought occurred to him. Why not seek a second and perhaps more liberal opinion — from a rabbi who was not orthodox, but merely conservative?

He found a conservative rabbi, who, unlike the orthodox rabbi earlier consulted, was not in the traditional long coat at all, but wore a dark business suit. The conservative rabbi said, "What is a motor scooter?"

Sammy explained.

The rabbi thought for a while, then said, "I suppose there's nothing wrong about riding a motor scooter, but still I don't know of any appropriate *barucha* and if your conscience hurts you without one, then don't drive it."

Sammy was on the point of giving up, but then a rather wild thought occurred to him. Off in the suburbs there was a reformed temple where Judaism was very liberal. How about that?

He journeyed out to the suburbs and met Rabbi Richmond Ellis, in his knickerbockers, about to leave for the golf links on his motor scooter.

Sammy grew terribly excited. "It's all right for a Jew to ride a motor scooter?" he said. "I've got one, but I didn't know."

"Sure, kid," said the rabbi. "Nothing wrong with the motor scooter at all. Ride it in good health."

"Then give me a *barucha* for it."

The reformed rabbi thought, then said, "What's a *barucha?*"

❊ 497

The fires of hell are occasionally banked for individual sinners for a longer or shorter period of time, depending on the egregiousness of their particular sins. At one time, three inmates of the hot place, their brief vacations happening to coincide, met and engaged in conversation.

One said, "I was Jewish when I was on earth, but my weakness, frankly, was ham sandwiches. So you see what happened."

"We could eat ham freely," said the second, "because I was Catholic. Unfortunately, I was too free with the ladies. Adultery was my chief sin and that's the reason I'm here."

The third remained silent and the other two turned to him. "Well," they asked, "why are you in the hot place?"

And the third said, firmly, "I am a Christian Scientist; this place is not hot; and I am not here."

To be perfectly honest, I am not particularly in sympathy with Christian Science and find its attitude toward modern medicine both mystical and medieval. Still, I would not want to give offense to any sincere believer of any sect, so I'll mention that Joke 497 was told me by a Christian Scientist.

❊ 498

Jones had died and gone to heaven and, as a reward for a most exemplary life, was given the grand tour. To his amazement he found that heaven was made up of many sectors, each utterly different.

He passed through the Jewish heaven where millions of people in prayer shawls sang exultantly before the Ark of the Covenant. Then there was the Catholic heaven filled with organ music and incense, where an eternal mass was celebrated in a star-high, skywide cathedral.

"Oh," said the archangelic guide, "we're ecumenical here; we have something for every taste. After all, a good man is a good man and deserves his reward whatever little difference in ritual may exist. Over there is the Moslem heaven with its houris; yonder the Buddhist heaven of contemplation and nirvana. And here — here is rather a little curiosity."

They crossed a bridge of the firmament and entered into a scene of whitewashed simplicity in which a relatively small number of men and women were singing hymns.

The guide tiptoed past and whispered, "This is a small sect of Christians called Sandemanians. There were only a few thousand altogether. The great scientist Michael Faraday was one. You can see him there."

"Fascinating," whispered Jones. "But tell me, why are we whispering?"

"Because they mustn't hear us. They think they're the only ones in heaven."

I'm not kidding. There really was a small sect called the Sandemanians, and Michael Faraday really was a member, and they really did think that they alone had the key to truth — but then so do most sects.

✻ 499

Robinson's favorite dog had died. They had been together for many years, and Robinson had loved him like a son. Now, in his brokenheartedness, he felt the only comfort he could get would be to see that the dog had a burial ceremony as elaborate and as solemn as a human being would get.

He was not a churchgoer, but there was a Baptist church on his street and it was there he applied. The Baptist minister heard him out politely, but could offer no hope. He said, "I am sorry, sir, but it would be blasphemous to bestow upon a dog, lacking a soul, the solemn ritual we offer a human being made in the image of God. This, however, may not be the view that all men take. There is a synagog two blocks down. Their attitude may be different."

The rabbi listened but was even more discouraging. "You must understand," he said, "that a dog is ritually unclean. While many Jews these days keep dogs as pets, I am afraid I could not lend this temple to such a ceremony. It may be different elsewhere, however. There is a Catholic church a few blocks from here, and perhaps they can help you."

Father Sweeney listened and shook his head. "I appreciate the tenderness of your feeling and sympathize with you in your sorrow. A dog can be a wonderful companion. Still, it cannot be done, I'm afraid."

By now, poor Robinson was in despair. He said, "Well, Father, if it can't be, it can't be; but it grieves me. Why, to show you how much this meant to me, I was prepared to donate a thousand dollars to any house of worship that would have taken care of my little dog for me."

And as he rose to go, Father Sweeney lifted a hand and said, "One moment, my son, perhaps I was hasty and did not understand all the facts of the case. Did I understand you to say that the dog was a Catholic?"

When I was a young boy, I lived right across the street from a Catholic church, and I had a vague fear of it and its priests, though I delivered papers to them and they went out of their way to be pleasant to me. The fear has long since disappeared, I am glad to say. A certain diffidence in the presence of nuns lingered longer, but that too is now gone, thanks to certain pleasant experiences such as the following —

❊ 500

Once I gave a talk at a Catholic girls' college, and when someone behind me asked a question during the social period afterward, I turned and found it was a young and beautiful nun who was speaking. After I answered the question, I looked at her admiringly and said, "You're exactly the kind of nun I always see in the movies."

She said, "Oh, don't say that. You have no idea how we suffer when we go to see nun pictures. And the things we say to each other!"

"What!" said I, in mock horror. "Surely, you don't use bad language?"

The nun hesitated. "Well, no," she said, "but we use very harsh good language."

✻ 501

Sadie took her aged grandmother to the art museum one day, for she felt that even though the old lady was completely unsophisticated and had lived a life entirely and utterly restricted to her family, she could still be delighted by great paintings.

And indeed so it seemed, for her grandmother moved from painting to painting in a state of great joy. She had never seen anything like it in the old country nor, for that matter, in America.

But then, to Sadie's intense embarrassment, her grandmother stopped in awe before a remarkable rendition of the Nativity. She prayed inwardly that her grandmother would ask no questions, for she did not know how to explain matters to one of so narrow and parochial a Jewish background.

Inevitably, the grandmother *did* ask questions. She said wonderingly, "The woman just had a baby, but there are animals around. Why animals?"

"It's a stable, grandma," said Sadie cautiously.

"And she's barefoot."

"She's very poor, grandma."

The grandmother considered this, then said, "And where's the father?"

"Well, grandma," faltered poor Sadie, "there isn't a regular father, sort of."

The grandmother looked at the painting again and shook her head. "I can't understand it," she said. "She's so poor she can't afford shoes and has to live in a stable. She has a baby that doesn't have a regular father. What put it into her head to have pictures taken?"

✻ 502

Pierre Laplace was a mathematician and astronomer who, in Napoleon's time, wrote a ponderous five-volume work on celestial mechanics. In it, using Newton's law of gravity, he painstakingly worked out the motions of the solar system in finest detail.

Napoleon, who fancied himself (with only partial justification) an intellectual, leafed through the early volumes and said to Laplace, "I see no mention of God in your explanation of the motions of the planets."

"I had no need of that hypothesis, Sire," said Laplace politely.

Another astronomer, Lagrange, hearing of the remark, is reported to have said, "But it is a beautiful hypothesis, just the same. It can be used to explain so many things."

✻ 503

The great fifth-century theologian Saint Augustine was once approached by a curious person who asked, "What was God doing through all the eternity of time before He created heaven and earth?"

And Saint Augustine thundered, "Creating hell, for those who ask questions like that."

I much prefer the viewpoint of a certain archbishop who said that since he believed the Bible, he was sure there was a hell, but that since he believed in God's mercy, he was also sure it was empty.

✻ 504

The ecumenical spirit which pervades the various religious establishments these days does not always entirely prevail.

A minister of one of the more liberal Protestant sects, glowing with interdenominational charity, said once to the minister of a more conservative sect, who was sharing a speaker's platform with him, "After all, we are both serving God."

"Yes, indeed," said the other austerely. "You in your way; I in His."

To continue the nonecumenical bickering in not too harsh a
way —

☀ 505

Father Shaughnessy found himself next to Rabbi Ginsberg at a charity function and could not help but notice that the rabbi was picking
at his food as though he suspected it of being less than kosher.

Smiling slyly, the good priest whispered, "Come, Rabbi, when are
you going to break down and eat a nice slice of ham?"

"At your wedding, Father," said Rabbi Ginsberg at once.

Of course, with the modern drive within the Church to
modify the celibacy rule, the rabbi's bluff may be called someday. Nevertheless —

☀ 506

Over a friendly game of chess, Father Shaughnessy said to Rabbi
Ginsberg, "Tell me, Rabbi, have you ever tasted ham? Be truthful,
now."

"Once," said the rabbi, reddening slightly, "when I was in college,
I must admit curiosity overcame me and I had a ham sandwich. But
tell me, Father, be truthful, now, did you ever, perhaps, with a
girl —"

It was Father Shaughnessy's turn to blush. He said, "I must confess that once in college, before I was ordained, I did have — a
little —"

Silence fell, and then the rabbi said, with a small smile, "It's better
than ham, isn't it?"

☀ 507

Two little Irish boys passed an Episcopalian minister. At the sight of
the reversed collar, one of them said automatically, "Hello, Father."

For his reward, he got a sharp elbow in the ribs from the other
boy. "He's no father, you dope," said the second boy. "He's married
and got three kids."

❈ 508

Poor Johnson had spent his life making wrong decisions. If he bet on a horse, it would lose; if he chose one elevator rather than another, it was the one he chose that stalled between floors; the line he picked before the bank teller's cage never moved; the lane he chose in traffic crawled; the day he picked for a picnic was the day of a cloudburst; and so it went, day after day, year after year.

Then, once, it became necessary for Johnson to travel to some city a thousand miles away and do it quickly. A plane was the only possible conveyance that would get him there in time, and it turned out that only one company supplied only one flight that would do. His heart bounded. There was no choice to make; and if he made no choice, surely he could come to no grief.

He took the plane.

Imagine his horror when, midway in the flight, the plane's engines caught fire and it became obvious the plane would crash in moments.

Johnson broke into fervent prayer to his favorite saint, Saint Francis. He pleaded, "I have never in my life made the right choice. Why this should be, I don't know, but I have borne my cross and have not complained. On this occasion, however, I did not make a choice; this was the only plane I could take and I *had* to take it. Why, then, am I being punished?"

He had no sooner finished when a giant hand swooped down out of the clouds and somehow snatched him from the plane. There he was, miraculously suspended two miles above the earth's surface, while the plane spiraled downward far below.

A heavenly voice came down from the clouds. "My son, I can save you, if you have in truth called upon me."

"Yes, I called on you," cried Johnson. "I called on you, Saint Francis."

"Ah," said the heavenly voice, "Saint Francis Xavier or Saint Francis of Assisi. Which?"

* 509

During the hours before D-day, three chaplains sat together and solemnly discussed the possible imminence of death.

"It makes one feel the necessity of unburdening one's soul," said the Catholic chaplain. "I must own up to a terrible impulse to drink. Oh, I fight it, I fight it; but it is my besetting sin and often I take a little too much."

"Well," said the Protestant chaplain, "I don't have too much trouble with liquor, but I must own up to a terrible impulse toward women. I fight it desperately, but every once in a while, I am tempted and I fall."

After that, there was a pause, and finally both turned to the Jewish chaplain and one said, "And you, Chaplain Cohen, are you troubled with a besetting sin, too?"

The Jewish chaplain sighed and said, "I'm afraid so. I have this terrible, irresistible impulse to gossip."

In the many jokes about men of the cloth, it rarely matters to which one you give the final word. I tend to give it to the rabbi, for obvious reasons, but just change the labels on the speeches to suit your own preference and the joke stands.

Not always, though, not always. Here's one that can't be switched.

* 510

An Episcopalian minister, in a puckish mood, said to his friend, Rabbi Levy, "You know, Rabbi Levy, I dreamed of a Jewish heaven the other night. It was very lifelike, and it seemed to me to just suit the Jewish ideal. It was a crowded tenement district with Jewish people everywhere. There were clothes on lines from every window, women on every stoop, pushcart peddlers on every corner, children playing ball on every street. The noise and confusion was so great that I woke up."

The rabbi said, "By a strange coincidence, Reverend Thompson, I dreamed the other night of an Episcopalian heaven. It was very lifelike, and it seemed to me to just suit the ideal of Episcopalians. It was a neat suburb, with well-spaced houses in excellent condition, with beautiful lawns, each with its flower bed, with clean, wide, tree-lined streets, and all was immersed in mild sunshine."

Reverend Thompson smiled. "And the people?"

"Oh," murmured Rabbi Levy, "there were no people."

I suppose we are all entitled to a favorite joke, and I will use mine to end this section with. I really mean it is the favorite joke of all those I know, and I often think of it lovingly. And it's not an old acquaintance of mine, either. I came across it in Leo Rosten's excellent *The Joys of Yiddish*, and I was too delighted even to laugh. Here it is in the version I usually use.

❋ 511

Mr. Ginsberg died and went to heaven, and was greeted by the recording angel with great jubilation.

"We have all been waiting for you, Ginsberg, for you have been a good man. Look at your record here" — and the recording angel opened a gigantic ledger and ran his finger down one page after another. "Look at that — good deed — good deed — good deed — good deed. Ginsberg, you are loaded with good deeds —"

But as he turned the pages, the recording angel grew solemn and his face took on a look of anxiety. Finally, he closed the ledger and said, "Ginsberg, we're in trouble."

"Why?" asked Ginsberg in alarm.

"I hadn't realized it, but you have nothing but good deeds. You have no sins at all."

"But isn't that the whole idea?" asked Ginsberg.

"In a manner of speaking, it is," said the recording angel. "But in actual practice, we always get a few sins. That fellow there — a good man — committed two sins in his life; that other fellow committed three; that tall man committed only one, but it was a real whopper. Now if you come in with no sins at all, it will create envy and hard feelings, there will be murmurings and backbitings. In short, you will bring dissension and evil into heaven."

"So what do I do?" said poor Ginsberg.

"I tell you what," said the recording angel. "This is irregular, but maybe I can get away with it. I'll erase the last page of your record and you will have six more hours of life. You will have another chance. Please, Ginsberg, commit a sin and then come back."

No sooner said than done. Ginsberg suddenly found himself back in his hometown. He had a few hours in which to commit a sin and get away from his perpetual good deeds, and he was desperately eager to do so for he wanted to go to heaven. But what kind of sin could he commit? He had been so virtuous, he scarcely knew what sin was.

After much thinking, he recalled that if one had sexual relations with a woman not one's wife, that was a sin. It also seemed to him that a certain unmarried woman past her first youth had often cast meaningful glances at him which, being virtuous, he had ignored.

He would ignore them no longer. With a determined step, he walked to the house of the young lady — a Miss Levine — and knocked. She opened the door, saw him standing there, and said in surprise, "Why, Mr. Ginsberg. I had heard you were sick, and feared you were dying, but you look completely yourself."

"I am perfectly well," said Ginsberg. "May I come in?"

"Of course," said Miss Levine eagerly, and locked the door behind him.

What happened afterward was inevitable. In almost no time, they were clearly sinning, and Mr. Ginsberg, with the vision of a waiting heaven, made up in enthusiasm for what he lacked in experience.

Anxious to make the sin a good one, and something that would thoroughly satisfy the recording angel, Ginsberg took pains not to hasten. He kept matters going till an inner feeling told him his time was nearly up.

Anticipating heaven with lyrical joy, Ginsberg rose and excused himself. "Miss Levine," he said, "I must leave now. I have an important engagement."

And Miss Levine, smiling up at him from bed, murmured softly, "Oh, Mr. Ginsberg, darling, what a good deed you have done for me this day."

As I HAVE SAID BEFORE in this book, joke sessions are largely a male preserve. Women rarely take part, and if they do, they are almost always passive and never venture telling a joke themselves. (There are occasional exceptions, of course.)

We can speculate as to the reasons. Telling a joke is aggressive, and girls are taught from childhood not to be aggressive. Their role is to laugh at jokes told by men, not to compete by telling them. Then, too, any joke-telling session is apt to grow coarse and (until recently, at least) women might fear compromising their respectability if they took part.

Often they feel defensive when they listen without contributing. Uncounted times I have heard women say, "I've heard a million jokes but for the life of me, I can never remember any."

That in itself is a feminine stereotype. Girls are taught early in life that to be flighty and forgetful is cute. That they are not really flighty and forgetful is demonstrated by the fact that the typical woman seems to remember, without trouble, the exact color, price, and place of purchase of every item she, or any of her friends, has ever worn; the furniture in every house she has ever visited; and the detailed scandal in the lives of all her friends, associates, enemies, and assorted movie stars. But she can't remember a joke.

The result is that jokes are left to men, and in consequence, a large percentage of jokes are a libel on womanhood and a prolonged sneer at the married state.

And I am no better than any other male in this respect. Here, for instance, is the most successful of all the jokes which (as far as I know) I have personally constructed. It is short, biting, speaks volumes, and most important of all, has never failed to get me my laugh under all circumstances.

❉ 512

> Jack: Did you hear about my wife?
> Jim: No! What about your wife?
> Jack: She ran off with my best friend.
> Jim: What are you talking about? *I'm* your best friend.
> Jack: Not anymore.

We might argue that jokes like this do useful work; that they work off private frustrations; that they allow a group of men, laughing heartily at the thought that anyone who would run off with a wife automatically becomes the husband's best friend, to feel a lessened tension over their own marriages. Perhaps this is the equivalent of the relief from tension women get by gossiping about their friends.

Maybe, but I mistrust such arguments. They serve too clearly the cause of male chauvinism. I am strongly sympathetic to the principles of Women's Liberation and reject any arguments that stem from the assumption that men and women have different natures, so that one sex must relieve social tensions in one way and the other sex in another way. I *know* that men can gossip as copiously and as viciously as women, and I see no reason why women can't tell jokes as well as men.

Of course, to the jokester, nothing comes ahead of a joke. I may be a fiery Women's Lib-er, but comes my opportunity, and neither idealism nor wild horses can stop me. Here's something that happened to me quite recently:

❉ 513

I was going down an elevator with three or four women, all of whom were strangers to me. At the first floor, I automatically stepped to one side to let them all off. As the last one preceded me, she turned and said, "When Women's Lib takes over, *you'll* get off first."

"Listen, lady," I said, smiling, "I'm a Women's Lib-er myself. I want all women to be free."

"You *do?*" she said, rather astonished.

"Yes," I said. "I hate it when they charge."

She laughed rather hollowly, I'm afraid.

✣ 514

Mrs. Jones, reduced to tears in the course of a family argument, said to her husband, "You brute! How can you treat me so cruelly after I have given you the best years of my life?"

And Mr. Jones replied, "Good heavens! Were *those* your best years?"

Here, too, jokes can speak the unspeakable. Few husbands, in my experience, ever complain about their wives' sexual shortcomings. There is something particularly ungentlemanly about making such a complaint, and what is perhaps more important, it would give rise to more than a suspicion that it was the husband's abilities in that line that were at fault.

Can it be, though, that husbands *don't* have such fault to find? Yes? Then why is it that there are so many successful jokes about wifely lack of interest? The man who is too gentlemanly (or perhaps too fearful of his own image) to complain will laugh heartily in the comparative anonymity of an audience. Thus —

✣ 515

A brief television skit I once saw dealt with a caveman and cavewoman who were kissing wildly and hysterically. They broke apart only to say, "Gee, this is great!" Then they returned to kissing.

Finally, the cavewoman pulled away to say, "Listen, do you suppose this wonderful thing we've discovered means we're married?"

The caveman bent his small mind to the matter and finally said, "Yes, I guess we're married. Now let's kiss some more."

Whereupon the cavewoman put her hand to her head and said in sudden anguish, "Oh, I have such a headache."

It may have been my imagination, but it seemed to me that the sound of laughter that followed was unusually baritone in character, as though only the men were laughing (each one in relief, perhaps, at the thought that his own problem was not, after all, unique).

Perhaps it might pay marriage counselors to make a closer study of the jokes men tell. The use of sex by wives as a system of reward and punishment may go far toward explaining the prevalence of mistresses. This got a brief but telling exposition on the stage once —

* 516

In the play *Born Yesterday,* a successful self-made man with more drive than culture explained why he didn't marry his mistress. "Now," he said, "when I get her a mink coat, I'm a great guy. Once we're married, it's *coming to her.*"

For some reason or other, Jewish jokesters seem to think there's something particularly cold about Jewish women, at least judging from the jokes they tell. Is it a matter of personal investigation, I wonder? Is it ethnic pride, the we've-got-it-worse-than-anybody syndrome? Is it the kind of anti-Semitism in which Jews tend to wallow? (Someone has defined anti-Semitism as the process of hating Jews more than you have to — and that someone was Jewish, I'm sure.)

I'm sure that this stereotype, like all stereotypes, is not really valid, and yet such is the sizable fraction of Jewish comedy writers in the media that the coldness of the "nice Jewish girl" has become nationally known. Thus the following little squibs are passed around:

✻ 517

Have you heard of the Jewish nymphomaniac?
No matter what, she has to have a man at least once a month.

✻ 518

How do you keep a nice Jewish girl from wanting to have sex?
You marry her.

✻ 519

Why does a Jewish wife close her eyes when having sex?
Heaven forbid she should see her husband having a good time.

I suspect that many Gentiles may find it irritating to see Jews arrogate these miseries to themselves as though they had them patented. A friend swears that the following little episode really happened to him.

✻ 520

He was in a cab once and made some mild comment concerning the size of the fare.

"So what?" said the driver offhandedly. "You can afford it."

"I know," said my friend, trying to evade the connotation of being cheap, "but my wife will make me feel guilty about it. You know what Jewish wives are like."

There was a short silence, and then from between clenched teeth, the taxi driver said, "Italian wives, too."

Obviously, there is such a thing as a counterattack. Husbands of any variety who suffer (or who imagine they suffer) from the coldness of their wives can find solace in implying their ladies' charms are resistible.

❋ 521

Louis, having been away on a business trip, returned home unexpectedly a day in advance and, as is usual in tales of this sort, found his wife in the arms of his best friend.

He staggered back and said, "Max! I'm married to the lady, so I've *got* to. But you?"

❋ 522

Johnson was recounting to a friend the events of the previous day, which had been his wife's birthday.

"I gave her a diamond-studded wrist watch as a present, then took her to a show, front row center, with a fancy dinner in between."

The friend leered. "After that," he said, "I'll bet there was lots of loving."

"Not on your life," said Johnson. "I did more than enough for her as it was."

There *are* a few jokes in which the women are awarded the last word. Undoubtedly, there would be many more of them if women participated in joke-telling sessions more fully. Then they might think better of themselves and relinquish some ways of getting back that hurt a great deal more than a joke does. (There are no limits to my own views on the therapeutic qualities of good jokes.)

❋ 523

Having come home unexpectedly, Louis found his wife in the arms of his best friend.

His wife scowled at him over the friend's shoulder and said, "Uh-oh! Here comes Mr. Big Mouth! Now the whole neighborhood will know."

❋ 524

Louis, having come home to find his wife in the arms of another man, was stricken to the heart.

"Darling," he said, more in sorrow than in anger, "how can you treat me so? Have I ever deprived you of anything? Have I ever begrudged you your slightest wish? Have I ever in any way mistreated you? Have I not in everything thought of you, bent all my efforts . . . And you, you dirty bum, at least leave her alone while I'm talking to her."

❋ 525

Louis, having come home to find his wife in the arms of another man, rushed out of the room, crying, "I'm getting my shotgun."

His wife dashed after him despite her unclothed state. She seized him and shouted, "You fool! What are you getting excited about? It was my lover who paid for the new furniture we recently got. My new clothes, the extra money you thought I earned sewing, all the little luxuries we've been able to buy — all came from him."

But Louis wrenched away and continued up the stairs.

"No shotgun, Louis," wailed his wife.

"What shotgun?" called back Louis. "I'm getting a blanket. That poor fellow will catch cold lying there like that."

In-laws are a cross every married person has to bear, and I'm sure it's miserable at times for everyone involved. And yet in the world of jokes it's mothers-in-law ten to one over all other in-laws combined who are the butts. And it's much more often the husband's mother-in-law than the wife's. Why this should be I will not risk speculating on. I will leave the problem to each reader.

❋ 526

Wife (bitterly): My mother always told me not to marry you.
Husband: Did she? God, how I have wronged the woman!

* **527**

> Question: What's the penalty for bigamy?
> Answer: Two mothers-in-law.

* **528**

A cavewoman came running to her husband in the greatest possible agitation.

"Wog," she called out. "Something terrible has just happened. A saber-toothed tiger has gone into my mother's cave and she's in there. Do something! Do something!"

Wog looked up from the mastodon drumstick at which he was gnawing and said, "Why should I do something? What the devil do I care what happens to a saber-toothed tiger?"

I have observed that men laugh more nervously over mother-in-law jokes than over wife jokes. It is as though they feel that wives can manage to be good sports about themselves (maybe) but not about their mothers.

I remember one New Year's Eve party about 1 A.M., when everyone was good and sloshing (except me, for I don't drink, although I can act pretty sloshing on plain ginger ale). A friend and I were swapping jokes and the laughter came easily from all spectators. But then I told Joke 528, and rather to my surprise, it broke up the party. All the men present went into hysterics and no more jokes were possible.

The joke is funny, of course, but not *that* funny. My theory is that everyone was just drunk enough to laugh the way he wanted to laugh at a mother-in-law joke. Had they been a bit more sober, they would have held back in the fear that their wives might be within earshot.

* **529**

Over a glass of beer, Johnson said to Smith, "My psychiatrist keeps talking about something he calls ambivalence, and I'm darned if I understand it."

"No problem," said Smith. "To be ambivalent is to feel contradictory emotions; to be both pleased and displeased with something; to both love and hate someone."

"That's what he says, too," said Johnson, "but I just don't see how you can experience two contradictory emotions simultaneously."

"Here's an example, then. Suppose you had just bought a brand-new Cadillac for ten thousand dollars and suppose the very first day you owned it, its brakes failed and it went over a cliff a mile high. How would you feel?"

"I'd feel *terrible*."

"But suppose your mother-in-law was the only one in the car at the time?"

✤ 530

Mr. Smith had killed his wife, and his entire defense was based on temporary insanity. He was a witness on his own behalf and was asked by his lawyer to describe the crime in his own words.

"Your Honor," he began, "I am a quiet, peaceful man of systematic habits, who virtually never bothers anybody. I get up at seven every morning, have breakfast at half-past seven, punch in at work at nine, leave work at five, come home at six, find supper on the table, eat it, read my newspaper, watch television, and go to bed.

"Day after day — up at seven, breakfast at seven-thirty, work at nine, leave at five, come home at six, find supper on the table, eat it, read, watch, bed. Until the day in question —" Here he paused to breathe passionately.

His lawyer said gently, "Go on. What happened on the day in question?"

"On the day in question," said Smith, "I woke at seven, had breakfast at seven-thirty, began work at nine, left at five and came home at six. There was no supper on the table and no sign of my wife. I searched through the house and found her in the bedroom in bed with a strange man. So I killed her."

"What were your emotions at the time you killed her?" asked the lawyer, anxious to get the point on the record.

"I was in a white-hot fury," said the defendant, "mad with rage, simply out of my mind, and unable to control myself." He turned to the jury and, pounding the arm of the witness chair, cried out, "Gentlemen, when I come home at six o'clock, *supper has to be on the table.*"

Here's an example where a good accent can be a great help. Joke 530 can easily get a laugh if told in impeccable English, but change Mr. Smith to Mr. Angelo and give it a beautiful Italian accent, and coming to your aid is the well-known stereotype of the Italian husband as a monster of jealousy. With the audience well-conditioned in that direction, the sudden change in point of view from adultery to kitchen mismanagement becomes particularly unexpected — and therefore particularly funny.

❋ 531

Joe, having spent too many hours at the poker table the night before, showed up at the office in a haggard state. Frank, a fellow poker player, who nevertheless appeared spruce and sharp, asked in concern, "What's the matter, Joe?"

Said Joe, "Listen! Coming home so late last night was bad enough, but my wife woke up and spent the rest of the night blatting and yelping at me."

"Oh, you jerk. Why did you wake her?"

"What do you mean, wake her?" screamed Joe. "I parked the car three blocks from the house and walked home. I took off my shoes at the corner and walked up the drive in my stocking feet. I opened the front door with an oiled key, undressed in the front hall, went up the stairs on all fours, spent ten minutes easing into the bedroom. Then I breathed, and she heard me."

"Nuts," said Frank contemptuously. "Why don't you use my method? I come into the drive with my brakes squealing. I throw open the front door, shut it with a bang, turn on all the lights and go stamping up the stairs singing an old sea chantey. I whistle coming into the bedroom, slap my wife on the rump, and say, 'Let's make love, baby!' And for *spite,* she pretends to be asleep."

❋ 532

At the twelfth hole of a hotly contested match, the grounds overlooked the highway, and as Smith and Jones approached the green,
they saw a funeral procession making its way along the road.

At this, Smith stopped, took off his hat, placed it over his heart,
and bent his head till the procession disappeared around a bend.

Jones was astonished and, after Smith had replaced his hat and
returned to his game, said, "That was delicate and respectful of you,
Smith."

"Oh, well," said Smith, "I couldn't do less. I'd been married to the
woman for twenty years, after all."

The bitterness in the marital relationship, as expressed in
jokes and the laughter that greets them, is surprising. Some
years ago, the psychotic Boston Strangler was running amok in
Beantown, and half the women in the city were locking themselves in at night in a state of great nervousness.

It was at this time that I found a number of men, presumably
happily married enough, laughing loudly at the following:

❋ 533

Mild-mannered John Smithers answered the knock at the door and
there, facing him across the threshold, was a wild-eyed slack-jawed
individual who said in a high-pitched, breathless tone, "I'm the Boston Strangler!"

Smithers eyed him for a moment, then called out, "Mary! It's for
you!"

But the marital relationship can also be portrayed as rather
sweet —

❋ 534

Jake said to Becky one day, "Becky, I'm getting on in years and I can
no longer live a lie. I must tell you that I have had a girl friend for
quite some time now. What are you going to do about that?"

Becky considered carefully. The children were grown and married. She had a trust fund in her own name that gave her absolute security. Jake had been a good husband, and their marriage had been a comfortable one. She was no longer captivated by sex, and it was rather a relief to have someone else take over the responsibility.

So she said, "Jake, if that's how it is, let it be. I won't interfere. As long as you keep up appearances and don't shame me before the neighbors and before my relatives, I will not object."

Jake found this delightful, and life went on swimmingly. Several weeks later, he and Becky were in a restaurant and Jake waved at someone before sitting down.

Becky said, "Whom are you waving at, Jake?"

Jake said, "Do you see the blond girl in the corner? That's my mistress. And the brunette girl next to her happens to be the mistress of my partner, Max."

Becky looked, sank back in her chair, and said, "You know, Jake, of the two, ours is much prettier."

It seems to me that a joke such as 534 could be of great use to psychiatrists in a manner analogous to the Rorschach test. Suppose the joke is passed to a patient, printed on a card as I have it here, and he is asked to interpret Becky's character. Is she:

1) A warm, generous woman, willing to let Jake have his pleasure and even willing to share in it vicariously, or

2) A grasping, cold woman, who will not let her husband have anything he can call his own, not even a mistress.

Both interpretations are possible, of course, but which the patient selects and the reasons he gives for selecting it, might tell volumes about him. (I'm advancing this jokingly but the funny part is that I'm serious.)

The henpecked husband is a copious source of humor to men, perhaps because misery loves company —

❋ 535

Mrs. Jones pursued her small husband through the crowds at the zoo, brandishing her umbrella and emitting cries of menace. The frightened Mr. Jones, noticing the lock on the lion's cage had not quite caught, wrenched it off, flew into the cage, slammed the door shut again, pushed the astonished lion hard against the door, and peered over its shoulder.

His frustrated wife shook her umbrella at him and yelled furiously, "Come out of there, you coward!"

❋ 536

On another occasion, Mr. Jones had managed to make his way into a closet, just one step ahead of the pursuing Mrs. Jones. He locked the door and stood there panting.

Mrs. Jones banged peremptorily on the door. "Come out of there, you worm!"

"I will not," shouted Mr. Jones from within.

"Do as I say," thundered Mrs. Jones.

"I *won't*," yelled her husband. "I'll show you who's master of the house."

❋ 537

Saint Peter was dividing the crop of newly arrived souls for easier processing. "All right, you men, come up here. Just the men, please. We'll take care of the women later. How many of you are married men here with your wives? Good. All those of you who are boss in your family form a line here. The henpecked ones in that other line there."

The line of the henpecked formed immediately and grew longer. The other line was nonexistent until one lone person appeared in it — a little fellow with a weak chin and a frightened look on his face.

Saint Peter paused to look at him. "Are you aware that this is the line for those men who are boss in their family?"

"Yes, sir," muttered the little fellow.

"Are you sure you belong here?"

"I have to be," he said. "My wife insists."

The converse — the frightened and browbeaten wife — is much more rarely met with. Do joke-telling husbands prefer to dismiss the matter out of guilt? Or because they don't believe it is possible?

* 538

A hard-bitten farmer had wooed and won a wife by correspondence. Now, with the ceremony completed, the married couple was driving home in the mule-drawn wagon.

The farmer said not a word till the mule stumbled. At that the farmer pointed at the mule and said, "That's one!" Some time later the mule stumbled again. The farmer pointed and said, "That's two!"

Again the mule stumbled, and the farmer said, "That's three!" Then he took his rifle, got out of the wagon, and shot the mule dead.

The new bride was scandalized. "Why did you do that, Zeke?" she protested. "Now how do we get back to the farm, with you doing such a cruel and stupid thing?"

The farmer pointed somberly at the woman and said, "That's one!"

* 539

Tony's wife had died, and the poor man was beside himself with grief and distraction. His loud weeping as the coffin was lowered into the grave impressed the bystanders, and one of them was moved to make an attempt at consolation.

"Tony, Tony," he said, patting the widower's shoulder in gentle commiseration, "it seems terrible now, but time is a great healer, and in six months I am sure you will have another wife."

Tony pushed aside the other's arm roughly. "Six months!" he said furiously. "What am I going to do *tonight?*"

It would only be fair to tell a joke in which the death of a husband is treated with less than respect, though in the male-chauvinistic world of the jokester, it is not easy to find one. However —

❋ 540

Murphy had died in a tragic accident on a construction job, and it fell to the foreman to carry the sad news to Mrs. Murphy. He knocked at the door of Murphy's house and inside found Mrs. Murphy engaged in demolishing a large platter of pigs' feet.

As delicately as he could, the foreman discharged his duty.

Mrs. Murphy listened stolidly, then swallowed the mouthful she was chewing, cleared her throat, and said, "I thank you. And if you'll care to wait till I've finished my pigs' feet, you will have the pleasure of hearing some hollering as is hollering."

❋ 541

The funeral cortege was being set up for the wife of the dour Sandy MacTavish, who was dressed somberly in the appropriate black.

The funeral director said to him in a respectful whisper, "And you will be sitting in the lead car with your mother-in-law."

Sandy frowned. "With my mother-in-law?"

"Yes, of course."

"Is that necessary?"

"It is essential. The bereaved husband and the bereaved mother — the two closest survivors together."

Sandy turned to look at the large and sobbing figure of his mother-in-law and said, "Well, all right then, but I tell you right now that it's going to spoil the pleasure of the occasion."

I can't pretend to explain the intensity of this feeling against mothers-in-law. But it's a matter of historical fact that in old-fashioned cars, the rumble seat (does anyone remember it?), which was exceedingly uncomfortable, both from the point of view of the breeze and the vibration, was called by the Germans, the *schwiegermuttersitze* or the mother-in-law seat. And worse yet —

* 542

When rayon was first invented, and placed on the market as a silk substitute, it had one enormous disadvantage. It was made out of modified cellulose in such a way that it was extremely inflammable.* Rayon garments would sometimes catch fire at the touch of a candle, and before anything could be done the wearer was a mass of flames.

So rayon gained the name of mother-in-law silk for, as people explained, the ideal present for a mother-in-law was a rayon dress — and a lighted match.

I guess, as a Women's Lib-er, I must insist that women learn to invent and tell jokes. Then, perhaps, we can redress the balance somewhat by hearing some home truths about sons-in-law who, in my opinion, are probably every bit as hard to endure as mothers-in-law.

* 543

It is said that a hostile voter once accosted Churchill immediately after an election in which the latter had retained his seat in Parliament. The voter said with a sneer, "I presume we may expect you to continue to be humbly subservient to the powerful interests that control your vote."

To which Churchill replied with a growl, "I'll thank you to keep my wife's name out of this."

* 544

It is difficult (especially in popular legend) to tell a cataleptic trance from death on some occasions, and when the former was mistaken for the latter, Mrs. Armstrong was laid out reverently in her bed, while family and friends came to the house to pay their last respects.

Mr. Armstrong received the many expressions of sympathy with a sorrowful expression, and all were in ecstasies over the bravery with which he bore up under his sad bereavement.

* The process has been altered since and rayon is now much safer.

There was a gasp of horror, then, when Joe Smith, Mr. Armstrong's next-door neighbor tripped over the throw rug and fell heavily upon the bed. Horror turned to amazement, however, and then to delight, when the shock snapped Mrs. Armstrong out of her trance. Her lips fluttered, her arm moved, and she sat up. What had been a sad occasion became a celebration of rebirth.

For nearly ten more years, Mrs. Armstrong lived and fulfilled her functions as wife and mother, but then came the inevitable day when she really died. The same scene was now repeated, though all concerned were ten years older.

Again Mr. Armstrong bore up nobly, and again family and friends filed past. Once again, Joe Smith approached.

And Mr. Armstrong said savagely, "Now this time, you clumsy jackass, don't trip."

⁂ 545

Clancy was brooding over his beer at the barroom and said to his friend, "I tell you, Mulligan, I don't know what I'm going to do about my wife."

"What is it now?"

"The same old thing — money. She's always asking for money! Only last Thursday, she wanted ten dollars! Yesterday, she was around asking for twenty. And this morning, if you please, she demanded fifty dollars."

"What does she do with all the money, for heaven's sake?"

"There's no way of finding out. I never give her any."

⁂ 546

Jones, who had been away on an extended trip, had very romantic plans for his first night home. He broached them to his wife, who promptly said, "Oh, I'm sorry, dear, but I've got to get through with these clothes you brought home. There's a great deal of mending and washing to do. Another time, please."

The next night Jones tried again, and his wife said, "Oh my, I would like to, dear, but it wouldn't be any good. What with all the work yesterday, and cleaning house today, I have this terrible headache. Please let me have a rain check."

By the third night, Jones was rather impatient. "How about it?" he said urgently.

Whereupon, Mrs. Jones snapped out. "This is the third night in a row you've asked. What are you? Some kind of sex maniac?"

There is a popular assumption (based on heaven knows what evidence) that while a woman's sexual appetite may be less than that of a man, her capacity is far superior. Thus:

❊ 547

Jones had made up his mind to kill his wife, but needed a foolproof plan. In desperation, he confided his problem to his best friend, Smith, who was about to set off on a long business trip.

Smith said, "But there *is* a foolproof method. Kill her with kindness. Make love to her every night."

"Every night?" said Jones, doubtfully.

"Every single night. You do that, and in a year she'll be dead of too much sex and no law in the land can touch you. You will merely have been fulfilling your husbandly duty."

It was nearly a year before Smith returned and one of the first things he did was visit his old friend, Jones.

Smith was shocked when he did so, for he found Jones in a rocking chair with a blanket tucked round him. Jones had lost weight, his face was gaunt, his cheeks sunken, his hair sparse and gray, and his hands trembling.

Smith said, "Jones, old boy, what happened?"

Jones said, "I'm a little tired, that's all. Been making love to my wife every night, the way you said, and it takes it out of a man. Tomorrow rounds out the year."

"And where is your wife?"

"Oh, in town giving a weightlifting exhibition. Poor thing! She little knows that tomorrow she'll be dead."

❊ 548

It was a terrible night. The rain was cold, and coming down in torrents. The wind was nearly a gale. The streets were deserted, and

Jones the baker was about to close his shop when a little man managed to make his way through the door.

He carried an umbrella, which had been blown inside out, and wore two coats over a thick sweater. He was soaked to the skin and looked utterly bedraggled and miserable as he unwound his scarf so that he could speak.

"Give me two bagels to go, please," he said faintly.

The baker said in astonishment, "Two bagels. Nothing more?"

"That's all."

"You came here in this weather for just two bagels?"

"That's all. One for me and one for Bernice."

"Bernice is your wife?"

And the little man, exasperated past the last shred of endurance, shrieked, "What do you think? Would my *mother* send me out on a night like this?"

❊ 549

Two longshoremen were having lunch together, and one said thoughtfully to the other, "Joe, do you go for fat women with long greasy hair?"

"Not on your life."

"Well, do you like them with flat faces, snub noses, and cross-eyes?"

"Of course not!"

"Maybe you go for women with crooked teeth and bad breath?"

"Never!"

Silence fell between them, and then the first one said reflectively, "In that case, Joe, how come you made love to my wife?"

The institution of mistresses is probably not as prevalent as the lascivious imaginings of settled married men would have it. It may not be as prevalent as supposed even in France. However —

❊ 550

Jacques and Pierre, strolling down the boulevard, spied two attractive women in the distance, walking together and approaching them.

Jacques said, "Good heavens, Pierre, what an unusual coincidence! Walking there toward us, arm in arm, are none other than my wife and my mistress!"

"Odd," said Pierre, thoughtfully. "Perhaps we should learn to know one another better, for I was on the point of saying precisely the same thing."

Which always reminds me of the toast that goes "To our wives and sweethearts! May they never meet!"

⁂ 551

Mary Jane, the very good friend of a wealthy broker, opened the door cheerfully one day and then quickly attempted to close it when she discovered the person on the threshold to be her lover's wife.

The wife leaned against the door and said, "Oh, let me in, dear. I don't intend to make a scene — just have a small, friendly discussion."

With considerable nervousness, Mary Jane let her enter, then said cautiously, "What do you want?"

"Nothing much," said the wife, looking about. "I just want the answer to one question. Tell me, dear, just between us, what do you *see* in the dumb jerk?"

⁂ 552

An eccentric millionaire once sent a henchman around the countryside. He was to interview the householders, and to every man who was boss in his house, he was to give a horse. To every man who was henpecked, he would give a chicken.

Everywhere the henchman went, he handed out chickens with never an occasion to give anyone a horse.

At last, though, he arrived at the house of a burly farmer, with a bristly, unshaven face, a deep bass voice, and muscles like an ox. In the background was his thin and wizened wife.

The henchman said, "Are you boss in your family, sir?"

The farmer leaned his head back and bellowed with laughter. "You bet, little man," he said. "What I say around here goes." And he opened and closed fists the size of hams.

The henchman was convinced. "You get a horse," he said. "Do you want a brown horse or a gray horse?"

The farmer leaned his head back and shouted, "Tilda, do we get a brown horse or a gray horse?"

Tilda called back, "You get a brown horse."

And the henchman said, "You get a chicken."

❋ 553

The Rosenthals had an outstandingly happy and successful marriage, and Mr. Rosenthal was once asked to what he attributed this remarkable situation.

"It's simple," he said. "Division of labor. My wife makes all the small, routine decisions. She decides what house we buy, where we go on vacation, whether the kids go to private schools, if I should change my job, and so on."

"And you?"

"I make the big, fundamental decisions. I decide if the United States should declare war on China, if Congress should appropriate money for a manned expedition to Mars, and so on."

Here is another case in which I must mention a variation —

❋ 554

The husband has explained the division of decisions, small ones to his wife and large ones to himself, as the method for making marriage happy. He describes his wife's small decisions and the questioner says, "And what kind of big decisions do you make?"

The husband answers, "I don't know. Big decisions haven't come up yet."

❋ 555

A gentleman at a social function remarked to the stranger at his side, "Heavens, what an ugly woman that one is."

"That woman," said the other, "is my wife."

The first man flushed painfully and could only stammer, "I'm sorry."

"Not as sorry as I am," said the other.

There is no question but that in many jokes one detects an actual male fear of women and, particularly, of marriage. In the course of his TV monologue, I once heard a standup comedian say, concerning a bachelor friend, "I can't understand how come he never married. At school he wasn't so smart."

A friend of mine who also was listening, doubled up over that one, and from the look he got from his wife (who did not as much as snicker), I suspect he found his reaction to have been a most injudicious one before the night was over.

And then —

＊ 556

George Johnson, a hard-bitten man of early middle age, had evaded many a marital trap, but was now helplessly in love with pretty young Nancy. Finally he said, "Will you marry me, Nancy?"

She smiled and said, "Oh yes, George."

There followed a long silence, till Nancy said, "Well, say something more, George."

And Johnson said hollowly, "I think I've said too much as it is."

Lest this section of the book seem tiresome and even anger-provoking to any women who may be reading it, let me say (rather apologetically) that nothing personal is intended. The tendency of men to malign their mates seems irrepressible and universal.

Thus, a century ago, William Schwenk Gilbert (the words man of the Gilbert and Sullivan combination) wrote a poem called "Etiquette," which dealt with two survivors of a shipwreck on a desert island who couldn't speak to each other because they hadn't been introduced while on board ship. They eventually did strike up a friendship through the discovered existence of a common acquaintance, and gradually became very close. As an instance of this closeness, wrote Gilbert, "They told each other anecdotes disparaging their wives."

Why this should be, I leave to psychiatrists, but I doubt that any wife, however soft and tender, however loving and dutiful, however perfect in all respects, can expect to be utterly free of disparagement by her gross and bumbling mate.

With that in mind, let me close this section with a joke which in my own opinion expresses, with ultimate bitterness, the joke-ster's version of a husband's feeling toward his wife.

✵ 557

Pierre was celebrating his silver wedding, and while all were unre-strainedly merry over the ample liquor provided by the host, Pierre himself remained in the corner, nursing a drink and following one of the guests with baleful eyes.

A friend noticed this strange action, all the more strange on so happy an occasion, and said, "At whom are you glaring, Pierre my friend?"

"At my lawyer, may his soul rot."

"But why are you so angry with him?"

"It is a sad tale. After I had been married ten years, I decided I had had enough and that the cleanest solution would be to kill my wife. Painlessly, of course, for I am no monster. Being a methodical man, I approached my lawyer — that one there — and asked him of the possible consequences. He told me that whereas killing a hus-band is, here in France, a mere misdemeanor, killing a wife is a felony, and that even with a most skillful defense, I would have to count on fifteen years in jail. He urged me not to do it and I let myself be guided by his advice."

"Well, then, why are you angry?"

"Because," said Pierre, "if I had not listened to his idiotic advice, on this very day I would have been a free man at last."

SINCE IN JOKES we can speak the unspeakable, we have what is often called the dirty joke, dirty because the bathroom and the bedroom are brought out into the light of day.

But we've got to ask whether a dirty joke is also a good joke, for it is so easy in the dirty joke to confuse the merely shocking with the funny. There is undoubted pleasure in defying convention, a certain thrill in using forbidden words, detailing forbidden acts, admitting that what we pretend doesn't exist actually does. The pleasure of all this may induce laughter.

But is this the real thing?

Suppose our society accepted, with some degree of sanity, the existence of the so-deplorable acts our body finds necessary and even pleasurable. Suppose we indifferently admitted the necessity of defecation or the pleasure of intercourse, and never gave either a second thought? Would a joke involving such matters be laughed at then if it offered nothing more than the mention of such things in more or less bald detail?

Obviously not. In addition to such matters, there must be the requirements that make jokes, in general, successful. Before all, there must be that element of incongruity, that unexpected change of view.

If this exists, then the dirty joke is good, rather than merely dirty. Why not, then, if you are a jokester worth your salt, leave in the element that is essential and omit that which is not? If you do not use dirty words except where absolutely essential; if you do not describe any excretory or reproductive

function in any greater detail than is absolutely necessary —
then you have lost absolutely nothing.

In fact, you have gained a good deal. I am not so virtuous
that I advocate the omission of "dirt" simply in order to be
clean and pure. I am enough of a jokester to advocate it for
what is to me a much better reason — you will get bigger
laughs, and it is in that way that you will have gained a good
deal.

This is so, for two reasons —

1) By being as clean as possible, you avoid arousing feelings
of embarrassment or revulsion in any audience with pretensions
to some standard of refinement. After all, no matter how liber-
ated and nonhypocritical a group of people may be, they may
not actually wish to wallow in such matters. They *do* wash
their hands after visiting the bathroom and they *do* pull down
the blinds before making love. By eliminating any unnecessar-
ily unpleasant emotions, you are eliminating something that
weakens the impulse to laugh.

2) By specifying as little as possible, you leave as much as
possible to the imagination of the listener, and that is good
strategy. Everyone has a dirty mind in the sense that he knows
more about the forbidden functions and thinks more about
them than he is usually willing to say openly. Furthermore,
everyone has his own individual way of thinking about them.
By not imposing your own notions on your audience, you allow
everyone to exercise his own dirty mind in his own particular
way, and the results he achieves will please him better than
would those you prepare for him.

An an example, consider Joke 404. As told, it seemed so
inoffensive and so undirty (at least to me) that I didn't at any
time consider placing it in this final section. It involved sex, of
course, since the heroine of the joke had left her husband because he had made unacceptable sexual demands on her.

The joke could easily have been turned into a dirty jc'e by
describing the nature of those demands. You could go .to all
the details without in any way altering the point of .ie joke.

You would only (whatever details you chose) direct attention away from the point of the joke, making it more shaggy-dog and less funny, or might actually embarrass or disgust the audience. By leaving it as I told it, with no indication whatever of what the young husband wanted, each listener will surely supply the details for himself. Each will probably supply different details, choosing those which, in the privacy of his mind, will neither embarrass nor disgust him; and in the end, he will laugh all the more joyously.

So I don't call this final section a collection of dirty jokes, for I am going to considerable pains to keep them from being merely dirty. Instead, I am calling them bawdy jokes. The word bawdy means indecent, to be sure, but it also carries the connotation of a certain rollicking good nature about it that I consider fitting.

✽ 558

A young lady was eating lunch alone at a restaurant and couldn't help overhearing a discussion among the four men at a neighboring table.

Said the first man, "Just spell it the simplest possible way — W-O-O-M."

"There's a B in it, you dope," said the second. "It's spelled W-O-O-M-B."

"You don't have enough letters," objected the third. "I think it ought to be spelled W-O-O-O-M-M-B."

"Nonsense," said the fourth. "It's ridiculous to put in all those letters. Besides, there's a final R. It's W-O-M-B-R-R."

The young lady could stand it no more. Having finished her meal, she approached the other table and said, "Gentlemen, if you'll consult the dictionary, you'll find that the word is spelled W-O-M-B. That's all." And she walked away.

The men gazed after her with astonishment.

"Do you suppose she's right?" asked one.

"How can she be?" said a second. "A slip of a girl like that! I'm sure that never in her whole life has she heard an elephant fart!"

Am I breaking my own rule by using that final word? Could I have cleaned the joke somewhat without losing the point by saying "breaking wind" instead?

No! "Breaking wind" is the kind of genteelism that is hardly ever used. If a person cannot or will not say "fart," he says nothing at all. To suppose that four men in an earnest discussion of such a matter will have said "breaking wind" is to introduce a note of utter implausibility. Not only that, but the listener will find it so unfamiliar an expression that by the time he has puzzled it out the laugh will be gone.

This, then, is an example where the impolite word is essential.

✳ 559

A certain well-established author found, to his horror, that he was having trouble selling his most recent novels. He consulted his agent, who said, "Joey baby, I'll level with you. You're not up with the times. Novels these days are sexy, you know what I mean? You've got to have lots of explicit sex, or you're dead. And let's face it, Joey baby, your novels aren't cruddy enough."

The novelist returned home and got to work at once. If sex was needed, sex they would get.

Eventually, he brought a manuscript to his agent and said, "Well, how do you think this will do?"

The agent shifted the cigar in his mouth from one corner to the other as he leafed through the pages. Then he shook his head, "Sorry, Joey baby, I'll do my best to place this, but I don't think it will make it. It's not sexy enough."

"Not sexy enough?" shouted the author. "What are you talking about? Look, right here on the first page the heroine dashes out of the room stark naked and runs out into the street with the hero following her just as naked and in an explicitly described state of sexual arousal."

"Yes, yes," said the agent, "but look how far down the first page."

One of the more unlikely places where sex might be found is on the stage of the Yiddish theater which, when I was a young boy, was still flourishing on Manhattan's Second Avenue —

❊ 560

The Yiddish theater was in a state of decline, and one producer decided that the trouble was that it was not keeping up with modern trends in stage sex. He said to one of his most reliable playwrights, "Max, we've got to put sex in the plays."

Horrified, Max said, "I don't know how."

The producer said, "Well, not the dialog, maybe; but let's figure out some sexy business."

When the new play opened, with a great deal of ballyhoo concerning new departures, there was a packed house. The first act closed with the heroine preparing for bed. For twenty minutes, no detail was overlooked, and while the audience sat in a frozen hush, what amounted to an elaborate striptease took place on the stage.

Finally, the last garment fell and the heroine was, for a bare second, in a state of total nudity. She leaped into bed and the lights went out.

And from the still silent and thoroughly shocked audience came one voice from the balcony, "Well, and to the bathroom she doesn't have to go?"

❊ 561

Anderson's business had been collapsing during the depression, and his family faced utter destitution. Anderson's loyal wife therefore decided to take the ultimate step of walking the streets in order to earn enough to keep things going till matters improved.

Reluctantly, she left the house; reluctantly, Anderson bade her farewell.

Three days later she was back, haggard, bone tired, but with an air of triumph.

"Here!" she gasped, and placed eighteen dollar bills and one dime into Anderson's hands.

Anderson looked at the one coin with astonishment. "Who gave you a dime?" he asked.

And his wife said, "Every single one."

✲ 562

Jones was having difficulties in business. "If I had as little as a thousand dollars in actual cash right now, this minute," he said to his wife sadly, "it might make all the difference."

"If that is all," said Mrs. Jones, "then all is well."

She ran upstairs and came down with a large jar filled with bills. "I've kept this as a secret nest egg. You see, ever since we got married, I put a ten-dollar bill into the jar every time we made love. You can have it now. There's almost three thousand dollars there."

Jones looked at the jar with stupefaction. Finally he said, "Oh, if I had only given you *all* my business."

✲ 563

Joe Smith was a far-out nut on golf, and it had come to be his only topic of conversation. Mrs. Smith bore it with increasing impatience and felt herself being slowly driven to the brink of distraction by the constant discussion of birdies, drivers, and sandtraps; of his golf clubs, his caddies, and his scores.

Finally, at dinner one day, her patience snapped. "Listen," she said, "I'm tired of golf, golf, golf, day in and day out. For once, I don't want any discussion of golf at this meal."

Joe raised a pair of hurt eyes and said plaintively, "But what do I talk about, then?"

"About anything," said Mrs. Smith angrily. "Talk about sex, for goodness' sake."

"Okay," said Joe sullenly. He fell silent for a moment, then brightened up and said, "Say, I wonder who my caddie is screwing these days?"

❅ 564

Jones and Smith, walking home from a late session at the neighborhood bar, paused at City Hall Park to watch a pair of dogs copulating.

"Did you ever try it that way with your wife?" asked Jones.

"No," said Smith, "I can't say I ever have."

"Nor I. But I think I will. It might be interesting."

"I will, too. Tell you what. When we get together at next Tuesday's bowling game, let's compare notes."

Next Tuesday they met again.

Jones said, "How'd it go?"

Smith said, "Okay. Nothing special."

Jones said in astonishment, "Your wife didn't object?"

"Of course not."

Jones shook his head. "I can't understand it. I even promised my wife a mink coat and she *still* wouldn't come out to City Hall Park."

The presence of a psychiatrist or a gynecologist seems to legitimize bawdy jokes. In fact, it is possible that the hostility toward these professions one easily detects in jokes, is at least partly owing to the average man's envy of these gentlemen for being able to involve themselves in sex without having to feel prurient or ashamed. After all, sex is their business.

❅ 565

The psychiatrist polished his glasses and said to his patient, "It will help me understand your problems better if I may set up some free associations. Please answer the following questions with the first thought that comes into your mind. First, what is it that a man does standing up, a lady sitting down, and a dog on three legs?"

The patient replied, without hesitation, "Shakes hands."

"And what is it that a dog does in the back yard that produces something you would not care to step into unexpectedly?"

The patient said, "Digs a hole."

"And what part of you emerges stiffly out of an opening in your pajamas when you wake up in the morning?"

"My head, of course."

"Well," said the psychiatrist, "your responses are perfectly normal, but you wouldn't believe some of the weird answers I get."

✻ 566

Old Mrs. Lefkowitz, who was ailing, was persuaded to visit a gynecologist for the first time in her life.

The efficient young doctor soothed her, helped her onto the table, and began a thorough gynecological examination.

Mrs. Lefkowitz, looking down at him with deep disapproval, said, "Young man, does your mother know how you make your living?"

✻ 567

A woman of advanced years was anxiously consulting a psychiatrist.

"Doctor," she said, "I have a problem. My husband is losing his potency and I am anxious to discover if the condition is psychogenic or if the cause is physical."

The psychiatrist was thunderstruck. Cautiously, he asked, "How old are you, madam?"

"Eighty."

The psychiatrist pondered and a thought struck him. "Ah! But how old is your husband?"

"Eighty-three!"

Now the psychiatrist seemed stumped. He brooded a bit and tried again. "Well, when did you first notice he was losing his potency?"

"Oh, I first noticed it last night, doctor; but what troubles me is that I noticed it again this morning."

Once when I was in the army, I was assigned to be a typist for the psychiatrist tending the soldiers. I told him a mild anti-psychiatrist joke, expecting a sportsmanlike laugh. Instead, there was a dreadful pause, after which the psychiatrist placed the tips of his fingers together and said thoughtfully, "Tell me,

Asimov, just why did you feel it necessary to tell me that joke?"

I have brooded about that for years and have often wanted to meet him again so that I could tell him the most viciously anti-psychiatrist joke I have ever heard —

❋ 568

The young lady nodded her head at what the psychiatrist was telling her, and said, "Yes, I see, Dr. Schmidt. At least, I see everything but one point. The one thing I'm hazy about is this phallic symbol you mentioned. What's a phallic symbol?"

"A phallic symbol," said the psychiatrist, "is anything that can be used to represent or symbolize a phallus."

"But what is a phallus, doctor?"

The psychiatrist said, "I think I can explain that most clearly by a demonstration." He stood up, unzipped, and said, "This, my dear young lady, is a phallus."

"Oh," said the girl, suddenly comprehending. "I see. You mean it's like a prick, only smaller."

Oh well, he would just put the tips of his fingers together and say, "Tell me, Asimov —" With a psychiatrist, you can't win.

In the Ethnic section, there were few jokes about Frenchmen. This was no accident. The French stereotype involves, most prominently, the assumption that the French are particularly interested and involved in sex. This means that almost any joke involving Frenchmen (at least when told by Americans) automatically belongs in the Bawdy section.

And, of course, as is true of all stereotypes, there is a kernel of truth behind it. The uptight Anglo-Saxon, on either side of the ocean, is apt to be startled by the easy French acceptance of the sexual side of life. Or as Eamon de Valera, the grand old man of Ireland, is reported to have said when he returned from a visit to France in his youth, "Gentlemen, all I can say is that sex in Ireland is as yet in its infancy."

❋ 569

"Tell me," asked an American of three Frenchmen, "what is *sang froid*? I know it means cold blood literally, but what are its connotations?"

"That," said André, "is best answered with an example. Imagine, my friend, that you are away on a business trip, but have come back unexpectedly soon, and find your wife in bed with your best friend. You do not wish to get emotional, to heat your blood. Instead you stay cool. If, like a true Parisian, you can smile, wave cheerily, and say, 'Pardon the intrusion,' you, my friend, have *sang froid*."

"Nonsense," scoffed Jacques, "that is merely tact. To explain *sang froid* let us imagine the same situation. If, on finding your wife in bed with your best friend, you say, 'Pardon the intrusion; please continue,' *then*, my friend, you have *sang froid*."

"Bah," sneered Pierre, "that is ordinary politeness. Let *me* explain *sang froid*. Let us return to the same situation. If, after you have said, 'Pardon the intrusion; please continue,' the gentleman in bed can indeed continue, then *he* has *sang froid*."

To do a French accent is most tempting. It is easy to suppose that all one need do is come down hard on the final syllable of every word and throw in a few Gallic expletives like *mon dieu* and *parbleu*. Don't be fooled. It may seem easy, but a French accent is just as hard as any other. Avoid it unless you can really do it.

Incidentally, just because certain physiological functions may not be directly mentioned in polite society, this doesn't mean they can't be indirectly mentioned. In fact, while reproduction can be altogether banished under most circumstances, we remain stuck with excretion no matter what we do.

Which means we must have euphemisms (pretty words that replace unpretty ones) and must watch each euphemism become dirty as it is used, and therefore come to need a new replacement.

What is so innocuous as a water closet — a small room in which water is available with which to wash one's hands? Unfortunately, it isn't the only facility there that is available, and water closet becomes an improper phrase to use. A washroom means the same thing; a toilet is a place where a person can comb his hair, brush his teeth, and so on. (It comes from a French word for dressing table.)

The attempt is made to cover the place and the action with the most innocuous terms. One speaks of the men's room or ladies' room — just a place where men or women are. There is the rest room or lounge — you just rest there; you just lounge around.

But in the end no word at all quite suits, and you say to your hostess, "Could you tell me where — uh —" with a vague motion of the hand. In such a case, all possible motions mean, "I have to perform a bodily function that you and I must pretend never takes place. Where can I go to do it?"

I imagine that a member of a sane society would find this funnier than any joke on the subject, but I'll have to offer the joke —

❋ 570

Johnson, a hardworking farmer invited as a guest to one of the better homes of the district, was graciously asked if he would care to wash his hands.

"No thank you, ma'am," said Johnson, with laborious courtesy, "I just washed my hands against the fence outside before I came in."

And can we have bawdy jokes with never a mention of a bawdyhouse? Of course not.

❋ 571

A rather diffident young man presented himself at one of the better brothels and said to the proprietress, "I would like to be accommodated, but I have a rather special requirement —"

The madam drew herself up proudly and said, "Pray, sir, you need not specify. Our girls here are of the finest, and can give complete satisfaction."

"But you don't understand. I am asking for special treatment. In my case, it is necessary —"

"I don't care *what* is necessary. You will have Theresa who, I assure you, is equal to any emergency."

Theresa appeared, and the young man followed her up the stairs. In three minutes, he was down again.

"What? Finished?" said the madam.

"Well, no," said the young man. "Actually, the lady wouldn't agree to do it —"

A look of astonishment crossed the madam's face. "Wouldn't agree? In *my* house? I shall have something to say to Theresa, you may be sure. But first we have still to give you satisfaction, young man, and prove to you that we consider you a valued client. I myself was, in my time, renowned for the excellence of my performance. I am now older than I once was, and my joints lack the suppleness of youth, but I shall not flinch. Tell me how you want it, young man, and I shall personally see that you get it."

"Well," said the young man, blushing, "I want it on credit."

There is a tendency, once jokes begin to get bawdy, for the bawdiness to deepen steadily. The joke-telling session is then all too likely to become a contest to see how offensive a joke can be. An experienced jokester realizes this should be avoided.

Nevertheless, it is surprising how bawdy a joke can be told without unreasonable offense if it is told in a respectable manner. No matter how deplorable the subject matter, if the characters speak a literary, rather than a colloquial, English, then the audience is far less apt to be offended.

But I never recommend virtue for virtue's sake alone. It is my experience that the incongruity of a madam saying, "I myself was, in my time, renowned for the excellence of my performance," is itself a source of laughter and readies the audience for the final explosion.

* 572

Robinson came home in great excitement and said to his wife, "You'll never believe it, dear, but I've discovered an entirely new position for lovemaking."

"Really," said Mrs. Robinson, interested at once. "What is that?"

"Back to back."

"But that's crazy. We can't do anything back to back."

"Yes we can. I've persuaded another couple to help out."

* 573

Neil Smythe, Professor of Sexual Physiology at Oxford, was lecturing his class: "And so, gentlemen, as you can see through a consideration of the anatomical possibilities, there are precisely seventy-six distinct positions possible in the sex act. If we classify these positions —"

At this point, however, a deferential French student rose in the back of the classroom and said, "Monsieur le Professeur, I am sorry to be forced to interrupt you, but there are, actually, seventy-seven distinct positions possible."

Professor Smythe regarded the French student with a frown. "My dear young man," he said, "my statement reflects long and serious research in the field by many of the most highly respected authorities, men of age and experience. We are ignoring mirror images and trivial variations, of course —"

"Of course, Monsieur le Professeur. But I, too, speak with knowledge. The fact is that I, myself — I who am speaking to you at this moment — can personally, of my own experience, vouch for the existence of seventy-seven."

"Well," said Professor Smythe, "in a dispute such as this there is an easy way of settling the matter. I will carefully describe the seventy-six distinct positions, and when I am done I will ask you to describe a seventy-seventh, different from all the rest. The remaining students in the class will, I trust, keep careful count and judge between us."

"Begin, monsieur," said the Frenchman.

"I will," said the professor. "We will start with the prime-basic, or common, position: woman horizontal-dorsal, man horizontal-ventral,

parallel in line and direction through a vertical axis of symmetry —"
"*Sacrebleu*," cried the Frenchman, "seventy-*eight!*"

It is part of the hypocrisy of the times that children are supposed to know nothing at all about sexual matters until they are
informed about the subject by perspiring and embarrassed parents.

How this can be, I don't know. We can assume that parents
are not amnesiacs — that they remember how young they were
when *they* learned, and just what part of the gutter *they*
learned it in. Barring a program of intelligent sex education in
the schools from the earliest grades on, what more do they expect of their children?

The truth, as usual, is to be found in jokes involving the
worldly-wise children. Concerning French children, given the
French stereotype, there is, of course, no argument —

❊ 574

Three French youngsters, respectively six, seven, and eight years of
age, were skipping along the street.

The six-year-old, who was in front, looked into an open street-level
window he was passing, stopped, and waved excitedly to the others.
"Come quickly," he said. "A man and a woman are fighting in
there."

The seven-year-old, coming up, looked in and said, "Oh, you little
fool, they are making love."

The eight-year-old came up, looked in, and said, "Yes, and badly."

❊ 575

It seemed to Mr. Smith that, now that his son had turned thirteen, it
was important to discuss those matters which an adolescent ought to
know about life.

So he called the boy into the study one evening, shut the door
carefully, and said with impressive dignity, "Son, I would like to
discuss the facts of life with you."

"Sure thing, Dad," said the boy. "What do you want to know?"

❊ 576

Mr. Jones, having determined to have it out with his older boy, now a pronounced adolescent, spent several hours painstakingly explaining sexual physiology to him. At the conclusion, feeling utterly wrung-out, and knowing that he did not want to go through it again with his younger son, he said, "And, Johnny, now that I've explained it to you, can I count on you passing it on to Jimmy?"

"Okay, Dad," said young John.

Mr. Jones' stalwart elder son went out in search of his younger brother at once.

"Jimmy," he said, when he found him, "I just had a long lecture from Dad, and he wants me to pass on what he told me to you."

"Go ahead," said Jimmy.

"Well, you know what you and I were doing with those girls behind the barn last month? Dad wants me to tell you that the birds and the bees do it, too."

I was on a talk show once, scheduled for midnight, a time when a fair amount of latitude is permitted, and the conversation led me to make what I hoped would be a sensible remark.

I said that I saw no point in freezing dying or recently dead people in the hope of bringing them back to life some far time in the future when whatever was wrong with them (including old age) could be cured. The technical problem of revivifying frozen organisms as complex as man might well prove insuperable, and even if not, there was an alternative device that was much more practical. Every complete cell had enough genetic information to produce an entire organism, in theory, and biologists were already succeeding in producing fairly complex organisms from specialized cells (a process known as cloning).

Why not, then, amputate the little toe of individuals while still young and healthy? This would represent a great saving of space, and from the little toe, much easier to revive, an organism genetically identical with the original could be cloned.

So far, so good, but the host interrupted to say, jokingly, "But what if you only grew a giant little toe?"

I made a quick decision and continued exactly as I was going to, ignored the interruption, and said, "Or better yet, for males, at least, you could have every baby circumcised and freeze the —" Then I turned to the host and said, with an attempt at innocence, "You were saying?"

✲ 577

Mr. and Mrs. Jones were consulting a marriage counselor, and the one fact that had become abundantly clear was that there was sexual incompatibility.

Mr. Jones shook his head sadly. "I admit there's something wrong," he said, "and I can't account for it. The first time I tried it, everything was great and I enjoyed it. The second time, however, I broke into a perspiration and everything was clammy and it was hard to breathe. And since then I haven't been enthusiastic about it."

The marriage counselor turned a questioning eye toward the wife, who snorted and said, "Well, of course! The first time was in December and the second time was in July."

✲ 578

O'Houlihan walked into the offices of a talent agent and said, "I have a pianist you must hear."

The agent said, "Sorry! Pianists are a drag on the market."

"Not one like this," said O'Houlihan urgently. "I have a twelve-inch pianist."

The agent's lower jaw dropped. He managed to say, "You mean a foot high?"

"Yes," said O'Houlihan. Reaching into a large attaché case in which the agent now noticed breathing holes, O'Houlihan drew out a perfectly formed little man just one foot high. "Go ahead, Roscoe," he said to the little fellow, "bang those ivories."

The little man leaped onto the piano stool and, with his tiny hands flashing too fast to be anything but a blur, played a variety of tunes with absolute perfection.

The agent said, "This is amazing. Where did you find him?"

"Well," said O'Houlihan, "I was visiting Ireland last month, and while I was tramping through the fields of the old sod, what should I come across but one of the little folk? It was a leprechaun, so old he was half blind and half deaf, so old his voice was almost too weak to hear.

"But I heard the tiny cry for help and bent down. I found him there caught under a small log and pinned to the ground. Carefully, I lifted the log, brushed him off, and set him upright.

" 'Oh, my deliverer,' said the leprechaun. 'For your kind deed, I will grant you a wish. But I can only grant one, so choose wisely.'

"As it happened, I knew exactly what I wanted, and I asked for it at once; and that half-deaf old leprechaun thought I had asked for a twelve-inch *pianist*."

✳ 579

Jones was a contestant on the famous TV show of yesteryear — "The $64,000 Question" — and he had chosen for his category of questioning, "Sexual Techniques."

He had answered all the questions asked, with verve and delicacy, and had finally surmounted the $32,000 hurdle. It was up to him to decide whether to return for the final $64,000 question, and if he decided to do so, he might bring an expert of his own choosing who would be allowed to help him.

Jones *did* decide to try again, and he brought with him none other than Monsieur Pierre, the great and internationally renowned French expert on all phases of sex. The two were placed in the isolation booth (so that they might not hear any hints thrown out by the audience), and the question was asked: "Suppose, Mr. Jones, you had exactly three kisses to bestow on your loved one and wished to do it in such a way as to elicit maximum response. Where would you place the first kiss? Where the second? Where the third?"

A minute was allowed for consideration while rhythmic, suspenseful music played. Then the master of ceremonies said, "Well, Mr. Jones, where would you place the first kiss?"

Without hesitation, Jones said, "On the lips."

"*Correct,* sir, and where the second?"

This time Jones considered for a moment. Then, somewhat hesitantly, he said, "On the back of the neck."

"*Correct,* sir," cried the master of ceremonies, while the audience howled with approval. "Now for the third and last part of the question. For $64,000, where would you place the third kiss?"

This time, Jones was in trouble. The perspiration stood out on his forehead. He seemed on the point of answering but then turned hastily to his companion. "Monsieur Pierre —" he began.

But the Frenchman shook his head violently. "Do not ask me, my friend. In my mind, I have already been wrong twice."

❊ 580

The prim Miss Thompson called the police station to complain of the indecent behavior of her neighbor.

"Exactly what has he been doing?" asked the policeman on the telephone.

"Why, every morning when he passes my house," she said indignantly, "he deliberately whistles dirty songs."

Joke 580 is one of those you can use to test an audience with. If most or all of them look blank, beware of subtleties. And it is no use saying indignantly, "How can *tunes* be dirty?" or "How can she know they're dirty unless —" As I have said before, a joke can be explained, but it can't be brought back to life.

And yet if Joke 580 is seen at once, what a lovely description of the censor's soul.

❊ 581

Miss Thompson also complained to the police that the neighborhood boys swam in the nearby river in the nude. "I can see them from my kitchen window," she said, "and I find it most offensive."

The police spoke to the boys, who grumbled but agreed to move on.

A week later, Miss Thompson was on the phone with the same complaint. The policeman protested, "Madam, the boys have moved a quarter-mile downstream. You can't see them now."

Said the lady firmly, "With my binoculars, I can."

❊ 582

The golf pro came into the clubhouse one evening with a wild look in his eyes and the air of one who had been through purgatory. A friend looked at him in astonishment and said, "What happened?"

The pro said in a low, suffering voice, "I just played a round with old Brown."

"The club duffer?"

"Yes. You see, no one will play with him, and as the club pro, it's my duty to give him a game."

"No wonder you look like the devil. Playing with old Brown would destroy anyone."

"You don't understand," said the pro. "I lost!"

"You lost? What did Brown score?"

"Oh, I don't know. Maybe one hundred thirty, maybe one hundred forty."

"And you *lost?*"

"It's this way," said the pro heavily. "We got to the first tee and he asked, 'Do I get a handicap?' I said, 'Sure. You can have any handicap you want.' Heck, I could give him a handicap of fifty and win. He said, 'Give me two gotchas.' Naturally, I said, 'What's a gotcha?' and he said, 'You'll find out.' Well, I figured, let's get this thing over with so I said, 'Okay, you can have two gotchas.' "

The pro paused to sip at the drink he had ordered, then went on. "Brown addressed the ball at the first tee and hit it about fifty feet. I got up and took a powerful swing, or, rather, the beginning of one, for just as the club was at the very top of its swing, Brown grabbed at my groin, squeezed hard, and said, 'Gotcha!' Naturally, I missed my stroke."

"Naturally," said the friend, horrified, "but that's only one stroke, and he had only one gotcha left."

"Yes," said the pro, "but have you ever tried swinging at a golf ball while waiting for that second gotcha?"

Joke 582 is an example of a double-barreled one. It is one in which a laugh (not a big one, perhaps) is possible *before* the punch line. If told properly, there will be laughter when you suddenly reveal the nature of the gotcha. A few in the audience may even think that's the end of the joke.

You are best advised to disregard the laughter and continue right on, for if you don't, the laughter, light though it may be, will have a chance to unwind the listeners and they won't be able to get back into the joke properly. If you do continue, and move quickly to the real punch line, then the first laugh will serve to intensify the second. The line between a first-laugh-intensification and a first-laugh-unwinding is thin, however, and I can only wish you luck.

Of course, if the first laugh turns out, for any reason, to be a howler, you might seriously consider ending the joke right there, at least on that occasion. This is especially true if the two laughs are adjacent. Thus —

❋ 583

A shipwreck in the far reaches of the Pacific had left only seven survivors who, clinging to assorted flotsam, had managed to make it to an uninhabited island. These consisted of Bill Johnson and six young women.

The island was a paradise with a delightful climate and ample food and water, and the seven made themselves completely comfortable. Bill Johnson found it particularly ideal, in fact, for in their isolated state it seemed the most natural thing in the world for him to supply any necessary affection to each of his six female companions. Indeed, the women came to an amicable agreement among themselves, and he devoted a particular weekday to each one of them.

Much to Bill's own surprise, however, the duties waxed onerous after some months had passed, and he began to value his one day off each week more and more.

Then, on one of his off-days, as he sat wearily on the beach and gazed out to sea, he saw a speck on the horizon. Could it be a ship? Could it be rescue? He sprang to his feet and waved vigorously.

The speck came closer and turned out to be a fragment of raft with a single man on board. Another wreck! Another survivor! Bill swallowed his disappointment. At least another man would take over half the sixfold duties with which Bill had been encumbered.

But as the raft came closer, the man revealed to be a willowy fellow with delicate features who waved with a limp wrist and called out, "Oh, thay, I'm tho glad to thee you."

And Bill said, "Well, there go my Sundays!"

If the joke is told well and if the sissified tones of the man on the raft are delivered properly and with as little warning as possible (in telling the joke rather than writing it you don't need the giveaway adjectives I have been forced to insert), a big laugh is liable to come at the next to the last line. It might then simply not be worthwhile to go on to the final line.

It is the height of amateurism to start yelling, "Wait, that's not the punch line! I'm not through yet." You'll accomplish nothing — unless you call making a fool of yourself something.

Incidentally, a good many years ago, a woman was telling this joke at a gathering and stretched it out just a little too long in my opinion. By the time she approached the end, I could resist no longer and delivered the punch line for her.

She stopped short, turned on me in a rage, and cried out, "You damned punch-line pincher!" And although till then we had been perfectly good friends, it was weeks before she spoke to me again. She was completely in the right and I was completely in the wrong.

It is a horrible breach of etiquette to squelch a joke at the last minute. If you've heard it before and don't care to hear it again, stop the jokester at the beginning. If you don't recognize it until he's well on, then just bite the bullet and listen. And try to laugh.

* 584

The newcomer at the bar had modestly laid claim to an absolute ability to identify the nature and make of any drink placed before him. The others present at once ordered the bartender to mix drinks, and money began to fill the air as bets were laid.

The newcomer took the barest taste of each drink, rolled it about on his tongue, narrowed his eyes, then carefully identified the contents and brand. He was never wrong. The bartender went to imaginative extremes, but the newcomer could even tell the year in which the components were bottled. It was most impressive.

During all this, a man at the end of the bar, somewhat owlish with drink, was observing closely. Finally, he came to life. Sliding a glass with its amber contents down the bar, he shouted, "Identify that, wise guy."

The liquor expert took his usual small sip, then spat it out and said in a strangled voice, "That's piss!"

"Well, of course," said the drunk, "but *whose?*"

* 585

Mr. Perkins, the biology instructor at a posh suburban girls' junior college, said during class, "Miss Smythe, would you please name the organ of the human body which, under appropriate conditions, expands to six times its normal size, and define the conditions."

Miss Smythe gasped, then said freezingly, "Mr. Perkins, I don't think that is a proper question to ask me. I assure you my parents will hear of this." With that, she sat down red-faced.

Unperturbed, Mr. Perkins called on Miss Johnson and asked the same question.

Miss Johnson, with composure, replied, "The pupil of the eye, in dim light."

"Correct," said Mr. Perkins. "And now, Miss Smythe, I have three things to say to you. One, you have not studied your lesson. Two, you have a dirty mind. And three, you will some day be faced with a dreadful disappointment."

❊ 586

An American tourist, on a train which wended its way through the picturesque Scottish ranges, could not help but overhear a loud English voice on the platform when the train stopped at one of the smaller towns.

"George," said the voice, "I had a ripping time. Thanks ever so much for inviting me. The grouse shooting was superb, and the salmon fishing was sensational. As for your wife, she is absolutely super in bed."

Astounded, the American stared at the two men who were shaking hands, and gazed in wonder at the voice's owner, who now came in to share his compartment.

His curiosity overcame his reluctance to invade an Englishman's privacy, and he said hesitantly, "Pardon me, but wasn't that you on the platform just now?"

The Englishman said amiably, "Yes, indeed."

"I must ask you to forgive me for thus intruding myself on a stranger, but I am an American and perhaps don't understand your customs. Did you say the grouse shooting was superb and the salmon fishing sensational?"

"Yes, indeed. And so they were."

"And is it possible that you praised the manner in which your host's wife performed in bed?"

Now the Englishman blushed. "Actually," he said, "she wasn't much at all but George is such a good fellow I just couldn't bring myself to hurt his feelings."

❊ 587

An American and an Arab, somewhere in the less advanced parts of northern Africa, were engaged in a lengthy debate on their respective sexual proficiency. In the normal course of events, such a debate could have no satisfactory conclusion, but the fact that the region was quite backward had its advantages.

The Arab said, "My dear American friend, it is useless to discuss this matter from a merely theoretical viewpoint. I have, praise Allah, an enormous harem. Do you take your pick of those damsels who appeal to you, and I will make free with the rest. Let us each spend the night in the delights of love and let us, on the word of gentlemen, keep honest score. Tomorrow we need only compare."

"Agreed," said the American with deep satisfaction, for it seemed the only fair way out of the dilemma.

Accepting half the harem and retiring to the private quarters assigned him, the American paid all due attention to a lovely black-eyed beauty who cooperated with the respect due a guest. Having completed the task, the American kept score by making a bold mark on the wall with his ball-point pen.

A very short time passed, when a second bold mark appeared by the side of the first. It took considerably longer, but eventually still a third bold mark joined the first two. The three now bore proud witness, side by side.

The American sank into his slumbers thereafter with a feeling of delightful weariness to which was added the warming thought that he had patriotically upheld the honor of the United States of America.

In the morning, the Arab entered after having duly announced himself. The American got out of bed and stretched, and the Arab was about to proceed to the usual amenities of asking how his guest had slept when his eye fell upon the three marks on the wall.

He started and said, "Is that your score?"

"Well and honestly counted," said the American, smiling modestly.

"Now, by Allah," said the Arab, crestfallen, "I find I must concede defeat. I had not thought it possible and yet you have beaten me by two."

"By two!" exclaimed the American, rather astonished.

"I'm afraid so," said the Arab. "Alas for my declining powers, but I managed only 109."

If you think that because I am Jewish I will never let an Arab have the better of it, Joke 587 proves you wrong, you see. There's a variation on this joke that goes as follows:

❋ 588

An Arab appeared before a theatrical agent and asked for help in entering show business.

"Any particular talent?" asked the agent.

"Yes, as a matter of fact. In my native land of Saudi Arabia, I was renowned for my sexual prowess. I can make love to fifty girls, one after the other, without pause."

The agent was goggle eyed. He had never heard of such a thing, but the Arab's credentials, his news clippings and references, seemd unimpeachable. The agent took a chance, therefore, and wangled a limited engagement in a private club for an enormous fee.

When the fifty girls were lined up and waiting, and the curtain was about to rise, the agent said to his client nervously, "Are you sure you can work this thing, Ahmed?"

"Have no fear," said Ahmed, with a broad grin. "It is certain."

And yet, after not more than eleven young ladies had been taken care of, the Arab collapsed. The infuriated audience was loud in its demands for money back, and the Arab and his agent were turned out by an even more infuriated management.

"You said you could do it," wailed the agent.

"But I took every precaution," said Ahmed. "Just before the show started, I took on the fifty girls in rehearsal just to make sure I could do it — and I could."

In ringing variations on jokes, it is quite possible to convert a bawdy one into another that is impeccably clean. If you want to tell Joke 588 and don't think you have the audience for it, you have no real problem. Change the fifty girls to fifty dozen eggs and the lovemaking to eating, and you have a joke that couldn't offend your maiden aunt and is still reasonably funny.

✱ 589

During World War II, a Russian soldier, much decorated, had returned home on furlough from the Finnish front. His small home town was jubilant over the return of the hero, and the reporter from the local newspaper interviewed him.

"Ivan Ivanovich," said the reporter, "our readers would be curious to know what was the first thing you did to greet your wife when you reached home."

Ivan Ivanovich blushed, "Ask me rather, Comrade Reporter, what was the second thing I did."

"Very vell," said the reporter. "What was the second thing you did?"

Said Ivan, "I took off my skis."

Stereotypes in jokes exhibit a social lag, surviving in the telling and retelling long after the foundations have been kicked out from under the reality.

The ministers in jokes remain nineteenth-century, and very frequently the picture of the Protestant minister is one of a grave moralist who frowns on dancing, is shocked by oaths such as "shucks," and considers a three-hour sermon an edifying Sunday-morning amusement. Undoubtedly, he exists somewhere in this country but not where jokesters are likely to meet him — except in the jokes they tell, where he forces an unwonted rigidity on all in his presence —

❋ 590

Farmer Jenkins and his wife were entertaining the local minister and his wife over a genteel cup of tea and some light sandwiches, while making careful conversation.

The farmer was most ill at ease, however, for he had been able to rent a blooded bull to service his two cows for that day only, and it would mean a deal of money out of his pocket if the bull had chosen this moment to indulge in a period of asceticism. Therefore, his hired hand had been given clear instructions to keep Farmer Jenkins discreetly up to date on the bull's performance.

This the hired hand did, but not discreetly, for he came bursting into the living room in a state of high excitement and said, "Boss! Listen! The bull just screwed the hell out of the white cow."

His voice died out on the last word as he observed the nature of the company. The silence hung heavy, and finally Jenkins stood up and said, "Come with me, Zeke."

In the next room, Jenkins, keeping his temper with difficulty, said, "Listen, Zeke, if you ever want to tell me something like that in public, say surprised, not screwed. There's such a thing as polite language."

"Sorry, boss," said Zeke contritely, "I'll try."

Jenkins returned to the parlor where the unpleasant incident had been put aside. Twenty minutes had not passed, however, when the hired hand rushed in again.

"Boss! Boss!" he cried. "The bull — the bull —"

He couldn't make it. He just stood there, frozen.

Jenkins, restraining his fury, managed to say, "Well, Zeke, did the bull surprise the red cow this time?"

The hired hand was at once enthusiastic. "Surprise the red cow? I should say he did. He screwed the hell out of the white one again!"

❉ 591

There is a story of two bulls, father and son, who, having reached the crest of a hill, looked down into the valley below to see a most delectable herd of cows.

Said the younger bull, eagerly pawing the earth, "Pop, let's run down this hill full speed, snorting and bellowing, and have us each a cow."

And the older bull said gravely, "Son, I have a better idea. Let's walk down this hill slowly, breathing quietly, and have us each every cow."

❉ 592

Farmer Jones was amazed to see that his neighbor had hitched his prize possession, his prize-winning bull, to the plow and was guiding it across his fields.

Jones said, "Elmer, have you gone crazy? That bull is worth twenty-five thousand dollars. Why are you letting him pull a plow?"

"That bull," said the other grimly, "has got to learn that life isn't all play."

❉ 593

Young Frank Jones was an absolute nut on physical fitness. Every morning before his early breakfast, unless the weather was unusually cold or foul, he put on his gym suit and jogged around the reservoir in the park. That done, he would indulge in calisthenics of some sort.

One morning, when the sun was peeping over the horizon and the
dew lay refreshingly cool on the grass in the deserted park, Frank,
his jogging done, threw himself down behind a line of hedges and
began a strenuous series of pushups.

That same morning old Lushley was also in the park, wending his
way home; but for him it was still the evening before. His tuxedo
was incredibly rumpled, his hat unimaginably askew; and there
emerged from him in every direction a powerful aroma of some alcoholic beverage. His tottering footsteps somehow brought him behind the row of hedges, and he stopped short as he watched Frank at
his pushups.

After a few moments, he extended his cane uncertainly and managed to tap Frank on the shoulder. "Young man," he said, "I hate to
be a bearer of ill tidings, but if you will take a close look, you will
notice that your girl is no longer here."

❊ 594

Constable Hawkins prodded at a young couple embracing in the
middle of the country road in broad daylight. "Here now," he said.
"What's all this?"

The young man looked up, blinking, and said, "Oh hello, Constable. I have something wrong with the transmission. So I'm trying
to fix it, and my girl friend is helping me."

Constable Hawkins said gruffly, "What transmission are you talking about?"

The young man looked about in astonishment, then cried out,
"Great Scott, Florrie. Someone has stolen our car!"

As a matter of fact, I can tell you a true story of what happened to me once in my salad days. A young lady and myself
were lolling on the sands of a public beach and were more or
less engrossed with each other. It was only with difficulty that
we became aware of a kind of thickening of the crowd about
us.

Looking up, we saw that we were indeed near the center of
an enormous crowd and that not far from us was a police car
which had driven onto the sand and was now driving away.

We had somehow missed it all. Why the police car had come there, what it had done, and indeed, what everything was all about — I never found out.

❋ 595

The preacher in a small town had become very perturbed, and he decided to lay it on the line to the congregation.

"Brothers, sisters," he said solemnly, "it has come to my attention that there are tales to the effect that immorality is rampant in our fair town. To be specific, it is being said that there is not one virgin left here. This vile lie must and shall be refuted. In order to do so, I ask every virgin in the congregation to rise."

Not a woman stirred.

The preacher said, "I understand the modesty that would make a young lady hesitate to announce her condition publicly, but it is necessary to do so. Young women, I conjure those to rise who are truly virgins."

And still not a woman stirred.

Wrath now moved the preacher. "Will you, for the fear of experiencing a small shame, incur a great one? This is an order from the Almighty: Let all virgins stand!"

And as his thunderous tones died away, a young lady, far in the rear, with a baby in her arms, rose bashfully.

The preacher stared with astonishment at the baby, then said, "Young woman, I'm asking *virgins* to stand."

And the young lady answered indignantly, "Well, do you expect this six-month-old girl to stand by herself?"

❋ 596

Young John and Mary, newlyweds, were spending their honeymoon on Mars (for this is a science fiction tale), and the native Martians, who as yet had had an opportunity to see very few Earthlings, went all out to make them feel at home. The couple from Earth had a perfectly wonderful time exploring Martian customs.

At one point, though, they were unable to hide their astonishment.

A Martian couple, inserting a lump of rock in what seemed to be a gigantic slot machine, opened a compartment and walked off with what was obviously a Martian baby.

John asked, "Is that how you get your babies?"

"Why, of course! Is there another way?" said the Martian guide.

"Well," said John in confusion, "on Earth, we do it differently."

The Martian's curiosity was instantly aroused; all the more so since the young Earthling couple had difficulty in explaining. Finally, the Martian said, "Well, could you demonstrate? We Martians know almost nothing about Earth customs and our sociologists would be fascinated."

John and Mary conferred for a long time. They were terribly embarrassed at the thought of the demonstration, but after all — the Martians weren't really human; they had been so hospitable; it was for science in a way; and well, they were on their honeymoon. In the end, they agreed to oblige the Martians.

A huge auditorium was made ready for the purpose; a tremendous audience attended; full planetwide television circuits were arranged; and by the time John and Mary moved into position, the entire planet was watching with absorption.

When it was all over, the Martian guide said, "How disappointing!"

"Why?" demanded John and Mary in unison, more than a little offended.

"Because," said the Martian, "that's just the way we make automobiles."

A bawdier conclusion to Joke 596, and one more in keeping with the tenor of the joke, is —

✳ 597

Once John and Mary had completed their exhibition of the Earth system of making babies, their Martian friend asked them, "Well then, where's the baby?"

"Oh," said John. "We would have to wait nine months for that."

"Indeed?" said the Martian. "In that case, what was the big hurry you displayed right there at the end?"

Oddly enough, I know hardly any science fiction jokes; nor do I hear any at the numerous science fiction conventions I attend.

This is not to say that conventions aren't hilarious for those attending, for they are. But the humor is not particularly science fictional. The funniest thing that ever happened to me at a convention wasn't really funny at all (though I wish I could get such laughs for statements intentionally funny), and for a while I thought it was nothing short of tragic.

At the awards banquet, I was at the head table for some reason (well, I was the guest of honor, actually), and one after another, the award winners were being called up to accept their statuettes. One winner wasn't present, and so the toastmaster called up a young lady who had, until recently, been a good friend of his, and who had also edited certain anthologies.

"Accepting the award for so-and-so," said the toastmaster, "will be Miss so-and-so, by whom he has been so often anthologized."

My eyebrows shot up and I muttered facetiously to my neighbor, "Anthologized? Always euphemisms."

What I didn't know was that there was a live microphone immediately in front of my lips, and to my own horror, I became aware that my words had boomed out over the hall and that the poor young lady was walking up to the podium through gales of laughter.

It took quite a while for me to locate the young lady afterward so that I might offer her an abject apology. She shrugged it off and said, "Listen, I've been carrying the torch for him for months, and I've been miserable. And when I heard everyone laugh, I said to myself, 'No one else takes it seriously. Why should I?' I feel much better now."

Science fiction conventions are particularly hilarious when a certain brilliant young writer attends who has the quickest and sharpest and most dangerously cutting wit of anyone I know. To avoid offending him I shall call him H.E. because that is not his name.*

He and I, on more than one occasion, have had a battle of impromptu badinage before an audience of fans screaming for blood, and it has been rough going indeed, let me tell you. (Fortunately, we are good friends off-stage.) My theory as to how it all started involves a moment when I had the last word, so that the theory arose that I could handle H.E. Here's the story.

At one particular session of a particular convention, the scheduled program event was late in starting, and the audience seated in front of the empty stage was growing restive.

Whereupon my good friend Randall Garrett — also a science fiction writer, also an extrovert, also on the large and stout side — said, "Come on, Isaac, let's entertain them."

Nothing loath, I rose from my seat. Together we walked onto the stage, and with one arm about the other's shoulder, we sang Gilbert and Sullivan songs interspersed with impromptu patter.

Actually, I thought we were doing fine, and so did the audience, when I saw H.E. enter the hall from the back.

My heart sank. H.E., although a giant among men intellectually, is, in point of fact, a little on the short side. He claims he is five feet four inches tall but if so, this means he is wearing two-inch elevator shoes. Anyway, he views with particular disdain elliptical men who give an impression of physical dimension.

And sure enough, his voice rang out from the back of the hall. "There they stand! Tweedledum and Tweedledee!"

I let the laughter die down and called back, "Come up here and stand between us, H.E., and be the hyphen." And the laughter was much louder that time. (Remember, H.E., old pal?)

* Just his initials.

❄ 598

The experienced veteran bellhop was explaining the ropes to the young trainee.

"This thing," he said, "isn't all carrying bags. In a big hotel, you're forever encountering delicate situations and you have to think fast. For instance, I had to deliver some ice to a particular hotel room and walked into the one across the hall by mistake. The door shouldn't have been open, but it was. Inside the room, the bathroom door was open (which it shouldn't have been), and inside the bathroom was a fat lady taking a bath. In a minute, I knew the fat lady was going to scream her head off. Thinking fast, I said, 'Excuse me, sir,' and left. The 'excuse me' was politeness, but the 'sir' was tact, and it saved the day. She figured I hadn't been there long enough to see anything and she calmed down. Get it?"

The trainee got it, but the next day he was in the infirmary with a black eye and assorted bruises. The veteran said, "And what happened to you?"

The trainee said, "I was following your advice. I was delivering ice and I got into the wrong room and there were a man and a woman on the couch with almost all their clothes off. So I said quickly, 'Pardon me, gentlemen,' and the guy got off that couch and nearly killed me."

It's remarkable how many jokes remind me, in one way or another, of perfectly true events in my own life. Maybe I lead a ridiculous life, but listen to this —

❄ 599

I was once attending a chemical convention in Atlantic City and managed to get caught in a sudden squall on the boardwalk. By the time I got back to my room, I was soaked to the skin. Since it was well into the evening, I decided to take off all my clothes and go to bed.

Once in bed, though, I found the reading lamp wouldn't work.

Since it was too early to sleep, I would *have* to read, so I called the desk and they promised to send up a maintenance man.

Then the phone rang and it was an old school friend I had not seen in years. I greeted him gladly, and he came up. Then we talked, as he sat in the chair and I sat cross-legged and almost nude on the bed.

It was not long after that when the maintenance man came and fixed the lamp. When he left, I said to my friend, "I'm glad you're not a girl. I wouldn't have been able to let the maintenance man in, with me sitting here with no clothes on."

"Actually," said my friend, grinning wickedly, "it's much worse for your reputation this way."

❊ 600

Bill was planning an extended trip to Europe, and all problems were solved except for the disposal of his parrot, the creature he loved above all others. Urgently, he made a request of his old chum Jim.

"Listen, Jim," he said. "You have two parrots already. It would be easy to take care of a third. How about it?"

Jim shook his head. "I don't know, Bill. I've heard stories that your parrot makes use of foul and obscene language. She would be a very bad influence on my two dear young boys, who have been brought up with extreme piety."

Said Bill, "I admit Clarabelle does get off a few ripe ones now and then, but you can keep her on the other side of the room. Put a cover on her if she acts up. I'm sure your birds won't be affected."

"Well, all right," said Jim, weakening.

Came the day of Bill's departure and he brought in his parrot. Bill was grateful for the chance, since the room was clearly made to order for parrots — light, airy, and with a delightful odor of crackers. What's more, at the other side of the room, were Jim's two birds in adjoining cages, each holding a rosary, and each mumbling in low tones as they told their beads. Bill could not help being impressed by their piety.

He put down the cage he was carrying, and whipped off its cover. Blinking in the light, Clarabelle promptly called out, "Awr-rk, I want to make love —"and added a few direct details that had even Bill blushing.

At the new parrot's loud, libidinous cries, one of Jim's parrots looked up in surprise and, in cultured tones, said to the other, "Brother Ignatius, put down your beads. Our prayers have been answered."

❊ 601

The severely ascetic Reverend Smith had surprised his entire congregation by marrying a beautiful young lady, after years during which he had seemed utterly indifferent to women, and indeed even ignorant of their existence.

While he was away on his honeymoon, the altar boys could talk of nothing else, and when he returned, as grave-faced as ever, and just as ascetic in his demeanor as before, the altar boys drew straws.

The loser approached him, with more than a touch of fear, and said, "Reverend Smith, about your honeymoon —"

"Yes, my boy?" said Reverend Smith severely.

"Tell me — How did you find it?"

"With difficulty," said Reverend Smith.

❊ 602

Jones had been suffering from enormous tension and finally visited a doctor. The doctor made the usual measurements of blood pressure, temperature, pulse rate, and so on, and said, "Before we go any further, Mr. Jones, tell me about your sex life."

"But I have none."

"In that case, before we go into your problem any further, why don't you have some? The tension, after all, may be nothing more than sexual frustration. There is a pleasant establishment not too far from here. I'll give you the address." He pulled his prescription pad to him and scrawled an address. He then went on, "Tell the proprietress of the establishment that I suggested Lucille." He wrote that name under the address.

With some qualms, Jones did as he was told. The madam looked at the slip of paper which he nervously presented and promptly rang for Lucille.

For much of the night, Lucille kept Jones delightfully busy. By morning, he felt a new man, utterly relaxed. The world seemed a wonderful place to him as he showered, shaved, and dressed.

He walked out through the lobby with a cheerful whistle, when the madam stopped him with an anxious cry of, "Sir, one moment. That will be fifty dollars, please."

Jones turned, waved carelessly, and said, "Don't worry. I've got Blue Cross."

✻ 603

The police precinct captain had been ordered to raid the local bordello, something which was an embarrassment to him and his men, for they patronized it themselves on occasion and were friendly with the madam.

The captain therefore rang up the establishment and found that all the girls, and the madam too, were off on a picnic and that the place was closed. There was only the cleaning lady to answer the phone.

"Listen," said the captain, "pass on this message because it won't be safe to call again. Tell the madam that tomorrow we've got to stage a surprise raid on the place. When we come, however, we'll honk the horn, go round the block, honk the horn, go round the block, honk the horn, then go round the block a third time, and *then* we'll come dashing in. But by that time, we want everyone safely out of the place. You understand?"

The cleaning lady said she did, but of course she didn't, and the madam never received the message. The next day it was business as usual at the establishment.

The police, blissfully unaware of the slip in their plan, arrived, honked, circled, honked, circled, honked, circled, and then charged in. As they dashed up the stairs with the captain at the head, they collided with two nude girls who were hastening down the stairs with a mattress between them.

The police captain roared, "What the devil are you two girls doing?"

"Don't blame us," cried one of the girls indignantly. "Some jerk outside is honking for curb service."

❊ 604

Joe Smith was mounting the steps of the local bordello, anticipating a pleasant interlude, when whom should he meet coming down the stairs, nattily dressed and hat jauntily askew, but his own father.

Joe staggered back in shock. *"Pa!"* he cried. "What are you doing here?"

Old Mr. Smith blanched, but quickly recovered. "Now, son," he said softly, "in order to save a lousy five dollars, would you want me to wear out your poor, hard-working mother?"

❊ 605

The hard-bitten Vermont farmer greeted the news of his wife's pregnancy without the flick of a facial muscle.

"Ain't a bit surprised," he said to the doctor. "I've given her every opportunity."

Unsophisticated humor never dies. If farmers decline in number, rest rooms increase; and in recent years much has been made of graffiti, the writing with which habitués of public toilets decorate the walls. You can't help seeing them, of course, and by far the large majority of these decorations are appallingly dull, uselessly offensive, or both.

On at least two occasions, however, I laughed:

❊ 606

Gravely, someone had written above the urinal in neat handwriting:
>   He either seeks for fame too much,
>   Or his deserts are small,
>   Who puts his talent to the touch
>   Above the urinal.
   (And it was carefully signed, too.)

❧ 607

Once, standing at the urinal, I noticed a message on the wall just at eye level. It said "Look upward," and there was an arrow pointing up. I couldn't resist. I looked up and several feet above on the wall was another upward arrow and the word "Higher."

I looked higher, and near the ceiling was the phrase "Still higher," and an arrow bending onto the ceiling.

I was now staring directly upward, and on the ceiling was written, "Quick! Look down! You're pissing on your shoes!"

❧ 608

In a certain town, there were so few Jews that services had to be held in a private room rented for the purpose by an old woman, and even so it was only with difficulty that the necessary number of wor-shipers (ten) could be gathered to make the services proper. On one occasion only nine showed up, and it appeared that the other more or less regular members were either sick or out of town.

"Perhaps we can get a passerby to join us," said one of the would-be worshipers hopelessly.

"Leave it to me," said the old lady, who was reluctant to lose the day's rent. "I'll find someone."

She bustled to the front window, overlooking the street, and waited. Before long, a patriarchal person, whose beard and dress marked him as clearly Jewish, approached. Excitedly, the old lady tapped on the window with her ring.

Astonished at a sound which he associated with red-light districts, where it was used to attract customers, the white-bearded patriarch looked up.

The old lady threw up the window and called, "Mister, would you like to be the tenth man?"

And the patriarch replied with a grimace, "I wouldn't even want to be the first."

�֍ 609

Miss Smith, who was sufficiently stricken in years to qualify as an old maid, had as her dearest companion a small French poodle, also feminine and also an old maid.

For some time now the poodle had been behaving in an agitated fashion, and poor Miss Smith, alarmed for the health of her pet, took her to the veterinarian.

"Let me know the truth, doctor," she said. "What is wrong with poor little Fifi?"

The veterinarian, having completed the examination, found himself rather embarrassed in the face of Miss Smith's obviously rigid spinsterhood. He said, "Well, Miss Smith, I must explain that there comes a time in the life of a bi —— of a dog who happens to be a young lady, when companionship is required. Fifi ought to make the acquaintance of a nice young gentleman dog."

Miss Smith blushed. "I don't think I could have two dogs in the house."

"No need, Miss Smith, there are places you can go where such companionship can be arranged, and with young male dogs of the finest breeding."

"Well, that will be all right, but will I have to be present?"

"Not at all. The dogs will know exactly what to do. But I must warn you of one thing. You will find the stud fees quite high."

At which Miss Smith rose to her feet with flashing eyes and said, "You mean *Fifi* pays?"

✷ 610

The lady from Boston said, "In Boston we place our emphasis entirely on breeding."

And the lady from Philadelphia said, "In Philadelphia, we think it's a lot of fun, but we do other things, too."

✷ 611

One of the funniest lines I ever heard in the movies came in Woody Allen's motion picture, *Take the Money and Run*.

Woody was being interviewed for a job and the man who was probing his psychic stability said to him, "Do you think sex is dirty?"

And Woody nodded his lugubrious face animatedly and said earnestly, "Yes, I do — if you do it right."

* 612

Mrs. Moskowitz was having her house painted, and between the smell of paint and the inevitable disarray, she found life hard. It seemed the last straw when Mr. Moskowitz came home and managed to prop himself against the wall while removing his rubbers, in such a way as to leave a distinct hand mark on the fresh paint.

Mrs. Moskowitz made her feelings eloquently clear, but her husband said, "What's the problem? The painter is returning tomorrow, so he'll paint it over."

Nevertheless, Mrs. Moskowitz found it difficult to sleep. The thought of that hand mark bothered her. The next morning, the painter had barely stepped over the threshold when she was upon him, saying, "Oh, am I glad you're here! All night long I've been thinking of you and waiting for you. Come with me; I want to show you where my husband put his hand."

The painter started violently. "Please," he said, "I'm an old man. A glass of tea, and maybe a cookie, is all I want."

* 613

Question: What is the difference between a virgin and a light bulb? Answer: You can unscrew a light bulb.

* 614

For a number of years, Smith and Jones and their respective wives had been occupying neighboring cabanas at the beach, and Smith was beginning to feel the monotony of it.

So he said to Jones, "Listen, pal, I have a rather daring suggestion. How about switching? We're all friends, and there's no need for me to be with my wife and you to be with your wife all the time, if you know what I mean."

"Hmmm," said Jones, "I must admit I've thought of it myself. Let's consult the ladies. If they're willing, why not?"

Very diplomatically, each consulted his wife, and to the surprise and delight of both Smith and Jones, they seemed amenable. When cabana time came, therefore, the foursome split up so that each was not with his or her married partner.

On the morning after the first night, Smith said to Jones, "How did you enjoy it?"

Said Jones, "You know, it was fun. I liked it and I think we ought to continue."

Said Smith, "Exactly my feelings. Now shall we go next door and see how the two girls made out?"

❋ 615

New York subway riders are not noted for the ease with which they give up their seats to those who need them. It was Mr. Smith's practice, for instance, once he had a seat, to stare firmly at his newspaper, paying no attention to any woman or elderly person who might be standing in front of him.

On this occasion, however, a woman took the initiative. She leaned over his paper and said, "Pardon me, sir, but I'm pregnant. Could you let me have your seat?"

Shamed, Mr. Smith jumped up. The woman sat down and Mr. Smith seized the strap in his turn, holding his paper with the other hand. It was not very long, however, before it dawned on him that the young lady who had taken his seat had a slim figure, very slim indeed.

Outraged, he leaned over and said, "Young lady, how long have you been pregnant?"

And she said, "Half an hour. And boy, am I *pooped!*"

❋ 616

A lady with nine children boarded a bus and began the complicated business of paying the fares. The driver could not help but be surprised, for the children seemed to be in three groups of three very similar youngsters.

"Pardon me, ma'am," he said, unable to repress his curiosity. "Are these children three sets of identical triplets?"

"Yes, they are."

"And are they all yours?"

"Yes, they are."

The driver was astonished. "Do you have triplets every single time, ma'am?"

"Oh, no," said the lady. "Almost every time I have nothing at all."

❊ 617

Mr. and Mrs. Simpson had tried everything, but had failed to have children. Finally, their doctor said, "Listen, there is absolutely no physiologic reason why you should not have children. It is undoubtedly a matter of tension. You're trying too hard. Go home and forget the whole thing. Don't take temperatures. Don't worry about the time of the month. Just live a normal life as though children were the last thing that concerned you. *However,* if on any occasion you should have the impulse to make love, then don't wait — make love."

Some months later, Mrs. Simpson was back and the tests showed that she was clearly pregnant. The doctor smiled. "Did you follow my advice?"

"Yes, we did, doctor, and it worked. We lived a normal carefree life, and then one evening at dinner, I dropped my napkin. I bent to pick it up and so did my husband. Our fingers touched beneath the table and it was like an electric shock going through the two of us. We remembered what you said, and we just stopped in the middle of dinner and made love under the table. And that's when I got pregnant."

"I'm delighted," said the doctor, "and I can imagine how happy you are."

"Completely happy, doctor, except for one thing."

"Oh, and what's that?"

"Well, they won't let us into Schrafft's anymore."

❊ 618

Father Riley was intent on obtaining a bar of candy from a coin-operated machine which unfortunately only accepted dimes. Father

Riley poked through his coins and looked up in chagrin just as a waitress from the restaurant upstairs came running down to make quick use of one of the pay phones.

As it happened, however, the restaurant was one of those currently popular topless places, and the bare-breasted waitress flushed deeply when she found herself unexpectedly face to face with a priest.

In great embarrassment, the waitress crossed her arms over her chest and said, "I beg your pardon, Father."

Father Riley smiled. "Don't be embarrassed, young lady. We priests may be celibate, but in our work we grow accustomed to a great many things. I assure you your condition does not trouble me in the least. In fact, you can perhaps do me a favor. Would you have a dime for two nipples?"

✽ 619

Mr. Jones and Miss Smith, attending a large convention, found themselves, through an accidental oversight of the hotel, assigned to the same room. Since both were mature individuals and aware of the difficulties attendant on attempting to rectify the situation under the crowded conditions then prevailing, it seemed simpler merely to accept the situation.

Each chose a bed and a dresser and proceeded to ignore the other with a kind of tactful politeness.

But on the second night, it turned out that Miss Smith had neglected to make proper allowances for the temperatures. She was cold.

Hesitantly, she called out, "Mr. Jones, would you be so good as to get me one of the blankets from the chest?"

Mr. Jones, who had been nearly asleep, thought that over and said, "Listen, if you're going to be this friendly and as long as we *are* in the same room, how about acting as though we were man and wife?"

Miss Smith thought that over, giggled, and said, "Well, Mr. Jones, I think — perhaps — I might be willing."

Mr. Jones said, "Good! In that case, as my wife, get your own darned blanket and leave me alone."

✻ 620

Mr. Robinson, in the course of an out of town trip, had met a most accommodating young lady and had spent a satisfactory night with her in the motel at which he had registered.

Or at least it was most satisfactory until about 3 A.M., when the young lady began to weep in heartbroken fashion.

Mr. Robinson, most uneasy lest the noise of the weeping attract unwanted attention, and utterly uncertain as to what might follow, said nervously, "What's wrong, miss?"

The young lady said between sobs, "I teach school back home. I have a third-grade class, and I was just thinking what my dear little pupils would say if they knew I had made love twice in a motel room with an utter stranger."

Mr. Robinson, deeply embarrassed, said, "I'm sorry, miss, to have made you feel so bad, but frankly, if we want to be absolutely accurate about this, we only made love once."

The young lady's sobs stopped instantly. She said sharply, "You mean you're not planning to do it again?"

In some ways, these are hard times for the jokester. The broadened view of sexual morality is such that the shock value (and therefore laugh-provoking value) of certain conditions has greatly diminished. With movie stars calmly having children out of wedlock, and doing so with great publicity but no censure, how are we going to capitalize on the terrific taboo that once enveloped any suggestion of bastardy? Consider the weakened point of the following, for instance:

✻ 621

Three army veterans had met after a long separation, and over a table at the cafeteria were reminiscing in low voices, recalling various unsavory events in their army careers and enjoying themselves hugely. All was ruined, however, when an elderly woman of most proper appearance murmured an apology and took the fourth seat.

The three men found themselves reduced to speechlessness, and glowered at the old lady who, ignoring them, ate slowly, steadily, and calmly.

Clearly, they would have to maneuver her into leaving.

One of the soldiers suddenly had an idea. Winking at the others, he said, "Fellows, I was at a wedding last week. My old man finally married my old lady, and all of us kids were there. It was a great affair. I got looped."

The second man caught on and said, "That's a coincidence. My father is planning a June wedding with my mother next year. I'm the only kid, as it happens, so why don't you two join me and help make it more festive?"

The third man heaved a sigh. "You guys are lucky. I don't think my dad is ever going to marry Mumsy."

With that all three cast sidewise glances at the old lady, who said, "Will one of you three bastards pass the salt, please?"

❊ 622

An American, studying at the Sorbonne, received a telegram, and his face broke out in smiles. Said his French roommate, "Good news, Robert?"

"You bet, Jacques. My grandfather and grandmother just celebrated a golden wedding."

"Golden wedding? What is that?"

"Well, you see, they've been together for fifty years —"

Whereupon Jacques broke in, "And now he's married her? Oh, bravo!"

❊ 623

The waitress at the topless restaurant approached one of the diners and said in great dudgeon, "Sir, this is not my table and I'll thank you to stop staring at me."

❊ 624

"Kiss me," said the young lady urgently. "Please kiss me."

But the young man turned his head away, saying, "Of course not.

How can I? I'm your own brother-in-law. Heck, we shouldn't even
be lying here making love."

❋ 625

The bilingual play on words is a rather subtle art form, and I have
always admired the fellow who translated the French expression
"hors de combat" as "camp followers."

❋ 626

It is reported that Dorothy Parker was once asked to use the word
horticulture in a sentence and promptly said: "You can lead a horticulture but you cannot make her think."

❋ 627

The young husband was waiting for the verdict when the doctor
emerged from his thorough examination of the still new bride who
had been suffering pains in her shoulders.
   The doctor said gravely, "I must tell you that your wife has acute
angina."
   The young husband grinned. "You can sure say that again, doc."

   This is a typical medical student joke, but it is easy to make
the quick jump from angina, which is a serious disorder of a
major artery, to vagina.
   You would think that, having spent considerable time in a
medical school, I would have a rich supply of this specialized
source of humor, but I don't. I was only a Ph.D., and I never
got into the inner councils.
   One funny remark made by a medical student lingers, however.

❋ 628

Having heard that a particular student was getting married on
Christmas Eve (to take advantage of the Christmas vacation for his

honeymoon), I said jovially, "Well, Santa Claus will be coming *that* night."

"I don't know about Santa Claus," said the student, "but *I* intend to."

❊ 629

Question: What do you call people who use the rhythm method of birth control?
Answer: Parents.

For some reason, the pleasant little verse form known as the limerick is at its best when it is bawdy. The trouble with limericks, as with question-answer jokes like 625 and 629 is that their form is constricting. They must be told as given and there is no opportunity for trivial variations and elaboration, which make a joke one's own and add the real fillip to joke-telling. However —

❊ 630

A couple named William and Nellie
Spent their honeymoon belly to belly,
        Because, in their haste,
        They'd used library paste
Instead of petroleum jelly.

❊ 631

A certain young fellow from Ransome
Had a dame seven times in a hansom.
        When she shouted for more,
        Said he from the floor,
"The name, miss, is Simpson, not Samson."

✻ 632

> From a niche in the church of St. Giles
> Came a scream that resounded for miles.
> "My goodness gracious,"
> Said Brother Ignatius.
> "How'd I know the bishop had piles."

✻ 633

> There was a young lady of Exeter,
> So pretty that men craned their necks at her,
> And one daring young knave
> Even ventured to wave
> The distinguishing mark of his sex at her.

✻ 634

> There was a young lady of Chichester
> Whose face would make saints in their niches stir.
> Her elegant style
> And the warmth of her smile
> Made the bishop of Chichester's breeches stir.

But back to prose —

✻ 635

A gentleman, having a quiet dinner alone in a restaurant, could not help overhearing the conversation at an adjoining table, where sat four women.

One of them said, "Poor Sylvia. The doctor has told her that she can't have any babies. It seems she's impregnable."

The second tittered. "That's not the word, dear. The correct term is impenetrable."

The third snorted. "Heavens, what malaprops you two are. The word is inconceivable."

The fourth hoisted her nose. "Not at all, the word is unbearable."

The gentleman could stand no more. Leaning toward them, he said, "Ladies, ladies, the word you're all looking for is inscrutable."

Sophisticated word play can reach a most satisfactory pitch when we consider the medieval habit of using different words to describe particular groups of creatures. We still say a herd of cattle, a school of fish, a band of men, a covey of quail, and a bevy of girls.

In medieval times, it went much farther. There was an exaltation of larks, a pride of lions, a skulk of foxes, an ostentation of peacocks, and so on. Obviously, these terms make sense. Larks singing in the morning seem exalted, lions seem proud, foxes seem to skulk, and peacocks seem to be ostentatious. Well, then, couldn't we invent new terms according to those principles?

❊ 636

Four scholars, on a walk off campus, encountered a group of ladies clearly of that class described as being of easy virtue.

"Ah," said one of the scholars, " a jam of tarts."

"Not at all," said the second, "say, rather, a flourish of strumpets."

"Or," said the third, "an essay of Trollope's."

And the fourth said, "Rather, I think, an anthology of pros."

Thanks to society's insistence on euphemisms, this by no means exhausts the possibilities. So I have made up one right now for this occasion. How about a frost of hoars?

❊ 637

Frank was getting married and was becoming more and more nervous over certain small points in connection with his forthcoming marital duties. He had, after all, a keen sense of the deficiency of his experience in such matters.

Yet he had a friend, Bill, who had no such deficiencies. It was an open secret in their circle of acquaintances that there was no nuance in the subject, however fine, which Bill had not mastered.

Frank approached him with a certain diffidence. "Bill," he said, "I'm getting married tomorrow and I wonder if you'd answer a few delicate questions."

"Of course, Frank," said Bill genially. "Ask away."

"These are silly little things, I guess, but you know that without the proper experience they can be very inhibiting. For instance, is it all right to talk to your wife while you're making love?"

Bill considered that with an expression of some surprise, then said, "I've got to admit that in all my life I've never done that, but I suppose there's nothing to stop you from doing so if you really want to — and if there happens to be a telephone within reach."

❊ 638

Young Miss Anderson was painfully shy. The freedoms of modern life had her in a perpetual burning blush. The words and actions accepted calmly by everyone around her reduced her to quivering embarrassment. In particular, any profanity, even the mildest, was agony to her.

She said to a friend, "I keep trying to say the words myself but I just can't. I can only spell them out in a whisper. I say d-a-m-n, and then I think, Oh, what would my dear mother say if she knew? and I could *die*."

Said her friend, "You had better see a psychiatrist. It's nice to be ladylike, but you go too far."

The two girls did not meet again for a long time, and when they did, the friend asked Miss Anderson, "Did you ever see a psychiatrist?"

"Yes, I did," said Miss Anderson. "Three times a week for six months."

"And did it help?"

"It certainly did. Only the other morning, when I was provoked, I just came right out and screamed 'Bullshit!' at my m-o-t-h-e-r."

In Joke 638 and in a few others scattered through the book, particularly in this last section, I have made use of a word commonly excluded from polite society. Such exclusions are far fewer now than they used to be, and even that four-letter word par excellence, the one used to represent the sex act, is no longer such an outcast.

You can find it in almost any work of fiction these days, any novel, any magazine. I must admit I'm old enough to feel uncomfortable over this, but not because I fear that children will be corrupted by the appearance of such words in print.

People who believe in the innocence of children have surely never lived near a junior high school (as I have) and listened to the joyful shouts back and forth as the children come and go. Many a stevedore would hesitate to use the language those children routinely lay their tongues to.

Still, I would like to make a distinction when a word must be used, when it serves a purpose, and when it is simply thrown in to shock or keep up with the fashion. I am prepared to use any word if it is essential to the laugh, but not otherwise. For instance —

❊ 639

Smith came home from work, bubbling over with suppressed laughter and hardly able to talk.

His wife said, "What's the matter?"

Smith said gaspingly, "I've just heard the dirtiest limerick in the whole world."

"Tell me, tell me," said his wife, intrigued.

"I *can't*. It's too dirty."

"What are you talking about? You tell me dirty jokes all the time."

"Not like this. This one is just too dirty."

Mrs. Smith, in the last extreme of curiosity, said to her husband, "Well then, look. Repeat the limerick and say 'dash' whenever you come to a word you think is too dirty for me. Don't worry; I'll be able to fill it in in my mind."

Smith said, "All right." Carefully and solemnly, he recited:
Dash-dash, dash-dash-dash, dash-dash-dash,
Dash-dash-dash, dash-dash-dash, dash-dash-dash,
Dash-dash, dash-dash-dash,
Dash-dash, dash-dash-dash,
Dash-dash-dash, dash-dash-dash, dash-dash-fuck.

My objection to the use of words like the final one in Joke 639 is by no means a matter of prudery, but one of respect for the English language. A word has a meaning, a function, a purpose. It is a tool of communication. To use it wrongly is to ruin it and make it valueless. And every word that is so ruined helps debase the richness of the language and represents a loss to all who use that language.

In an entirely masculine environment like the army, the use of the common word for the sex act serves to give the soldier the illusion of freedom from feminine or family restraint, thus making up for the existence of other forms of restraint. Soon it becomes nothing more than a general intensifier without meaning.

I remember one of the first nights I spent in the army. I couldn't sleep on the lumpy cot, and dimly I could hear the whispered conversation of two other soldiers some beds away. Through a trick of my semiconsciousness the only word I heard clearly was "fuckin'," and it came two or three times in every sentence with the monotonous beat of a tom-tom.

I told myself then that only utter illiterates could fall into so dreary a habit — and yet the time came when, through sheer force of custom, I too began to use it in every sentence. Fortunately, the habit was easy to break once I got out of the army.

Still, to explain exactly what I mean, let me present the moral in the form of a joke which will be the last one in this section and in the book:

❊ 640

A soldier, filled with obvious triumph, returned from his twenty-four-hour pass and was besieged by his buddies who wanted to know, in detail, how he had made out.

The soldier, nothing loath, said gleefully, "What a piece of fuckin' luck I had. I hadn't been off camp more than half an hour when I met this fuckin' broad and was she *stacked!* We got to talking and I took her out for some fuckin' hamburgers. Then we went to a fuckin' movie where we got friendly. Then she took me to her fuckin' apartment and in less than five minutes I had every fuckin' stitch off her."

He paused for breath and everyone cried out, "So what happened? What happened?"

And the soldier said, "What do you think happened, you fuckin' jerks? We had sexual intercourse."

Index

[*Note:* All index entries are keyed to the number of the joke, *not* the number of the page. Items in my commentary are numbered as either preceding or following a particular joke. Thus, 265p means "preceding Joke 265" while 265f means "following Joke 265." In the unlikely case that you get confused, just re-read the entire book.]

Absent-mindedness, 135, 136
Accents, 10f
   French, 569f
   German, 430
   Italian, 429
   Jewish, 310f, 311f, 312f, 313
   Scottish, 411
   word order and, 309f
Ace, Jane, 54p
Adam and Eve, 377, 471, 475
Adultery, 14, 94, 309, 395, 512, 523, 524, 525, 530, 549, 562, 569, 586, 624
Aesop, 122p
Airplanes, 131
Alexander the Great, 197
Allen, Gracie, 54p
Allen, Woody, 611
Alligators, 268
Ambassadors, 153
Ambiguity, 229

Ambivalence, 529
Americans, 406
Amnesia, 42
Angina, 626
Anniversaries, wedding, 557
Anticlimax, 2f, 46p
Anti-Semitism, 313, 314, 320, 321, 357, 358
Apples, 100
Arabs, 372, 485, 587, 588
Aristides, 126
Aristippus, 180
Aristocrats, 453p, 453, 454, 455, 456
Army life, 26, 26f, 30, 32f, 164, 271, 272, 273, 297, 369, 640p, 640
   Russian, 589
Art, 139, 315
Asimov, Isaac (see Me)
"Asimov's Game," 121f
Assassins, 284p
Astor, Lady Nancy, 183
Astronauts, 267
Astronomy, 79
Atheism, 492, 494, 495
Athens, 126, 199, 199f
Atomic bomb, 471, 472

Bad language, 212
Bagpipes, 412
Barbers, 189

The Author

Isaac Asimov was born in Petrovichi, U.S.S.R., in 1920, came to the United States in 1923, and grew up in Brooklyn, New York. He became an American citizen in 1928. After attending public schools in Brooklyn, he went on to Columbia University from which he received his B.A. in 1939, M.A. in 1941, and Ph.D. in 1948 — all in chemistry. In 1949 he joined the Biochemistry Department of the Boston University School of Medicine, where he became an Assistant Professor in 1951 and Associate Professor in 1955. He began writing in 1938. In addition to being one of the finest science fiction novelists living, he is also the author of a number of textbooks and popular works on scientific subjects, and so many magazine articles and stories he has lost count. A few of his recent books for Houghton Mifflin Company include: *The Human Brain, Fantastic Voyage, The Dark Ages, Words From History, The Near East,* and *Opus 100.*